Crime, HIV and Health: Intersections of Criminal Justice and Public Health Concerns

Bill Sanders • Yonette F. Thomas
Bethany Griffin Deeds
Editors

Crime, HIV and Health: Intersections of Criminal Justice and Public Health Concerns

Springer

Editors
Bill Sanders
School of Criminal Justice and Criminalistics
California State University, Los Angeles
Los Angeles, California, USA

Yonette F. Thomas
Office of Regulatory Research Compliance
Howard University
Washington, DC, USA

Bethany Griffin Deeds
Division of Epidemiology, Services and Prevention Research
National Institutes of Health
National Institute of Drug Abuse
Bethesda, USA

ISBN 978-90-481-8920-5 ISBN 978-90-481-8921-2 (eBook)
DOI 10.1007/978-90-481-8921-2
Springer Dordrecht Heidelberg New York London

Library of Congress Control Number: 2012948421

Printed on acid-free paper

Springer is part of Springer Science+Business Media (www.springer.com)

Dedication from Bill Sanders
For Elliz: It's nice to be nice!

Introduction

Significant overlaps have emerged between the fields of criminal justice and public health. For instance, in 1985 then Surgeon General C. Everett Koop convened a workshop on violence and public health, indicating that violence had reached epidemic proportions, claiming an estimated four million victims each year, particularly children, women, and the elderly (Koop 1986). While violence is a traditional criminal justice concern, violence profoundly affected the public health of Americans, and Koop called for more exchanges and interrelationships between professionals whose work straddles violence: psychiatrics, pediatricians, researchers, the police, and the media.

Years later, Hawkins and Catalano were part of a team that developed the 'Causes and Correlates' study. Here, the authors promoted the use of a 'risk factor' approach towards the study and treatment of substance use (and later delinquency) that was refined from a public health model on reducing the risk of disease (Hawkins et al. 1992). For instance, Hawkins and Catalano indicated that drug use and offending, like health, could be somewhat predicted by the number of risk factors in an individual's life. The more risk factors that are present, the greater the risk. Risk for heart disease included poor diet, smoking, and a lack of exercise, and that by reducing participation in these behaviors individuals were significantly less likely to develop heart disease. In a similar vein, intervening among the risk factors in a youth's life that were related to substance use and delinquency – peer influence, negative parent/child interactions, deprivation – would reduce that youth's involvement in those behaviors. Research from the risk factor approach also led to the development of screening tools used by professionals in the juvenile justice system to offer more objective and comprehensive assessments of youth in custody (Krisberg 2005).

Common ground between criminal justice and public health have been explored in edited collections, including Kawachi and Berkman's (2003) *Neighborhoods and Health*, Levy and Sidel's (2006) *Social Injustice and Public Health*, and Greifinger's (2007) *Public Health Behind Bars*, and in presentations at annual meetings of two national academic associations: the American Public Health Association (APHA) and the American Society of Criminology (ASC) – the largest associations in the world for their respective fields.

The ASC has contained a handful of presentations that investigated public health-related issues. Examining the relationship between health and high crime environments, reviewing public health approach towards understanding youth violence, and evaluating public health strategies for public safety have all been session themes (Block et al. 2006; Loeber 2007; Taxman and Gallagher 2009). Other ASC sessions have also included topics on the health of prison inmates, the role of mental health in criminal justice policy and practice, and crime as a public health problem (DeLone and DeLone 2008; Willison and Debus 2009; Zaitzow and Lanier 2010).

On the other hand, the APHA conferences have had presentations that also examine criminal justice-related concerns. For instance, the APHA annual meetings have had sessions about programs that tackle gun violence as well as those that focus on collaborations between mental health professionals and law enforcement (Broussard and Compton 2010; Webster et al. 2010). Another APHA session entitled 'Must prisons remain dangerous to the public's health?' was co-sponsored by the World Health Organization and offered presentations on the physical and mental health of incarcerated populations, as well as how different countries have different approaches towards incarceration in terms of promoting public safety (Boyington 2007; Gatherer 2007; Moller 2007; Weinstein 2007). The phrase 'co-occurring disorders', which is often used to describe populations who have both public health related concerns (e.g. symptoms of mental health disorders; substance use; sexually transmitted infections), as well as criminal justice ones (e.g. violence; crime), have also been commonly found within APHA presentations (Mino et al. 2008; St. De Lore et al. 2009; Zahnd et al. 2009).

Following these traditions, we convened a symposium at the 2009 annual meeting of the American Sociological Association (ASA) in San Francisco, CA. The symposium was entitled 'Crime, HIV, and Health: Intersections of Criminal Justice and Public Health Concerns'. We personally invited researchers whose work highlighted these intersections and advertised a call for papers in the newsletters of two ASA sections relevant to the topics: Crime, Law and Deviance, and Alcohol, Tobacco and Other Drugs. All ASA members were also invited to the audience at the symposium. The symposium consisted of 13 presentations from approximately 25 different researchers from across the USA, many of whom had previously received funding from the National Institute on Drug Abuse (NIDA), National Institute of Justice (NIJ), Centers for Disease Control and Prevention (CDC), or other Federal agencies.

The impetus for this edited collection grew out of our mutual interests in sociology, criminology, epidemiology and public health, and our research experiences with high-risk youth and risk of exposure to HIV/HCV, especially among marginalized populations, including substance users, ethnic minorities, women, gang members, and the homeless. Under examined crossovers between the fields of criminal justice and public health addressed in the symposium was a subsequent focal area for this collection. Each presenter was invited to submit an original paper based on his or her presentation for inclusion in an edited monograph. Additionally, several researchers whose work we felt reflected the themes of the book were also invited to participate. The book contains 14 chapters written by a total of 52 authors reflecting four different themes.

Our introductory chapter begins by examining two areas common to criminal justice and public health: substance use and violence; and vulnerable populations and incarceration. From here, we briefly outline four general themes on the intersections of criminal justice and public health explored by the chapters in this book: the health of incarcerated populations; health consequences of crime and risk behaviors; crime, space and health; and public health interventions with criminal justice populations. Despite this format, reading the book from beginning to end is not necessary. Rather, each chapter is complete in itself, and the book is designed to allow the reader to jump in at any point.

For the initial theme, three chapters examine the health of incarcerated populations. In the first, researchers from Northwestern University present findings from the Northwest Juvenile Project, a longitudinal study of health and risk behaviors among incarcerated juveniles. In this chapter, the authors report on risky sexual behaviors and exposure to sexually transmitted infections (STIs), including HIV. In the second chapter, researchers from the Integrated Substance Abuse Program at the University of California, Los Angeles, and the Los Angeles County Department of Public Health, Sexually Transmitted Disease Program offer data from a pilot program aimed at increasing screening for STIs among incarcerated female delinquents upon intake and reducing subsequent risky sexual behaviors upon release. In the third chapter, colleagues from Howard University report on disparities in mental health diagnosis and treatment among African Americans and the implications of this for the correctional populations. Here, the authors highlight how various mental health illnesses often go undetected among African Americans, which contributes to their over-representation in jails and prisons.

The second theme is on the health consequences of risk behaviors in the lives of high-risk individuals. The first chapter in this part is based on data from a National Science Foundation project on the use of crystal methamphetamine and other co-occurring risk behaviors. Here, the authors examine the extent that certain personality traits mediate the relationship between methamphetamine users and their participation in violence and risky sexual behaviors. Next, several authors from National Institute on Drug Abuse (NIDA)-funded studies provide data gathered over a 20-year period on substance use, violence, and risky sexual behaviors among gang-identified youth in three major cities: Los Angeles, San Francisco, and San Antonio. Overall, evidence is presented to indicate gang youths' high levels of exposure to negative physical and mental health outcomes. From here, colleagues at the University of Colorado, Boulder, present data on the increases in drug-related mortality in the USA. One interesting finding of this study was that ex-prisoners constituted a significant proportion of these deaths, suggesting that the immediate period upon release is a time when such individuals are particularly vulnerable. Next, data on the overlap of arrest, victimization, substance use, and risky sexual behaviors among young adults in the Miami club scene are presented. An important result that our colleague from the Nova Southeastern University indicates is how many of these behaviors and outcomes appeared to congregate among particular individuals.

The third theme of the book is entitled Crime, Space and Health. The first chapter by researchers at the Pacific Institute for Research and Evaluation examines the growth and spread of crystal methamphetamine in California. Here, the authors present spatial models on how the rise and fall of particular methamphetamine markets paralleled increases and decreases in hospital admissions and arrests for methamphetamine use and manufacture in the same areas. Next, researchers at Ohio State University and the University of Chicago present data to indicate that high crime is related to poor individual health. In particular, the authors highlight how the fear of crime in urban communities leads to heightened levels of stress, which in turn leads to an increase in the risk of developing cardiovascular disease. The final chapter of this part from colleagues at American University examines how incarceration disrupts sexual relationships and how this disruption increases the risk for exposure to HIV among parolees, probationers, and the community.

The final theme of the book is about public health interventions with criminal justice populations. The first chapter, by colleagues affiliated with the CDC's Academic Centers for Excellence, is on the adoption and implementation of a public health model for violence intervention among high risk youth in a couple of cities in California. This model differs from a criminal justice suppression-based approach towards violence in that it focuses on youth violence prevention by using effective violence surveillance tools, identifying and employing successful violence prevention programs, and enhancing community responses to youth violence through mobilization efforts. The second chapter is by researchers at Childrens Hospital Los Angeles, and examines if an intervention that was developed to target one risk behavior among a type of high risk youth can also be applied to reduce other risk behaviors among other types of high risk youth. Specifically, the authors discuss how Project AIM (Adult Identity Mentoring), which was developed to reduce risky sexual behaviors among high-risk middle school-aged students, was implemented towards reducing gang involvement and delinquency among youth in high-risk gang communities. In the final chapter, researchers at the University of Delaware offer an overview of the Criminal Justice Drug Abuse Treatment Study – an ongoing NIDA-sponsored program on the risk of exposure to HIV and HCV among currently incarcerated adults. This research illustrates how HIV/HCV risk reduction messages while incarcerated aim to promote safer sexual behaviors upon post-release. Despite these wonderful contributions by excellent researchers, the book is incomplete. We encourage more research on areas that concern the fields of criminal justice and public health, as well as more dialogue between professionals representing these fields. We also want to thank, profusely, all the contributors to this book who have donated their time and efforts for nothing other than similar desires: to further promote attention and research into the areas discussed within. We are appreciative of Genevieve Vullo's editing assistance as well.

The views and opinions expressed in this report are those of the authors and should not be construed to represent the views of NIDA or any of the sponsoring organizations, agencies, or the US government. We fully assume all responsibility for any errors and omissions and apologize in advance for them. We also invite any and all criticism and suggestions, so as to improve on subsequent editions or potentially another volume. Finally, we wish to thank our friends and, in particular, our families who have provided emotional support and, frankly, put up with us long enough to see this book finished.

Los Angeles, CA B. Sanders
Washington, DC Y. Thomas
Bethesda, MD B. Deeds

References

Block, R. L., Gehlert, S., Masi, C., Tarlov, E., & Zenk, S. (2006, November). *Community crime patterns and health outcomes*. Oral presentation at the annual meeting of the American Society of Criminology, Los Angeles, CA.

Boyington, J. (2007, November). *Politics, policies and prisons: A success story.* Oral presentation at the annual meeting of the American Public Health Association, Washington, DC.

Broussard, B., & Compton, M. (2010, November). *Crisis Intervention Team (CIT): A model multi-agency collaboration between law enforcement, advocacy, and mental health communities to promote improved health outcomes for individuals with mental illnesses.* Oral presentation at the annual meeting of the American Public Health Association, Denver, CO.

DeLone, D. J., & DeLone, M. A. (2008, November). *When is crime a public health problem?* Oral presentation at the annual meeting of the American Society of Criminology, St. Louis, MS.

Gatherer, A. (2007, November). *Lessons from a public health approach to imprisonment rate: Five groups of nations.* Oral presentation at the annual meeting of the American Public Health Association, Washington, DC.

Greifinger, R. (Ed.). (2007). *Public health behind bars: From prisons to communities*. New York: Springer.

Hawkins, J. D., Catalano, R. F., & Miller, J. Y. (1992). Risk and protective factors for alcohol and other drug problems in adolescence and early adulthood: Implications for substance abuse prevention. *Psychological Bulletin, 112*(1), 64–105.

Kawachi, I., & Berkman, L. F. (Eds.). (2003). *Neighborhoods and health.* New York: Oxford University Press.

Koop, C. E. (1986). *Violence and public health: Update*. Retrieved from http://profiles.nlm.nih.gov/QQ/B/B/Q/N/_/qqbbqn.pdf

Krisberg, B. (2005). *Juvenile justice: Redeeming our children*. Thousand Oaks: Sage.

Levy, B. S., & Sidel, V. W. (Eds.). (2006). *Social injustice and public health.* Oxford: New York.

Loeber, R. (2007, November). *Protective and promotive factors for youth violence: Issues, evidence, and public health.* Oral presentation at the annual meeting of the American Society of Criminology, Philadelphia, PA.

Mino, M., Deren, S., & Kang, S-Y. (2008, November). *Criminal justice involvement and injection risk among drug users in NYC and NJ.* Oral presentation at the annual meeting of the American Public Health Association, San Diego, CA.

Moller, L. (2007, November). *A public health approach in prisons.* Oral presentation at the annual meeting of the American Public Health Association, Washington, DC.

St. De Lore, J., Burdon, W. M., & Prendergast, M. L. (2009, November). *HIV risk behaviors and substance abuse/dependence among incarcerated drug-involved offenders: Identifying opportunities for interventions.* Oral presentation at the annual meeting of the American Society of Criminology, Philadelphia, PA.

Taxman, F., & Gallagher, C. (2009, November). *Public health is public safety: Revamping the correctional mission.* Oral presentation at the annual meeting of the American Society of Criminology, Philadelphia, PA.

Webster, D., Mendel, J. S., & Vernick, J. S. (2010, November). *Effects of Baltimore's "Safe Streets" program on gun violence.* Oral presentation at the annual meeting of the American Public Health Association, Denver, CO.

Weinstein, C. (2007, November). *United States: The nations that loves prisons.* Oral presentation at the annual meeting of the American Public Health Association, Washington, DC.

Willison, J. B., & Debus, S. A. (2009, November). *Evaluation of criminal justice interventions for mentally ill offenders: Study overview, court policies, and practices, and baseline participant characteristics.* Oral presentation at the annual meeting of the American Society of Criminology, Philadelphia, PA.

Zahnd, E., Grant, D., Chia, Y. J., Park, Rl., Holtby, S., & Noble, A. (2009, November). *Substance use and intimate partner violence among California's diverse population: Findings from the 2007 California Health Interview Survey.* Oral presentation at the annual meeting of the American Public Health Association, Philadelphia, PA.

Zaitzow, B. H., & Lanier, M. M. (2010, November). *Doing HIV/AIDS time: Health care needs of women prisoners.* Oral presentation at the annual meeting of the American Society of Criminology, San Francisco, CA.

Contents

About the Authors

Karen M. Abram, Ph.D., is an Associate Professor of Psychiatry and Behavioral Sciences at the Feinberg School of Medicine, Northwestern University, where she is also the Associate Director of the Program in Health Disparities and Public Policy. She received her Ph.D. from Northwestern University in 1988. For the past 25 years, the Program in Health Disparities and Public Policy (formerly, the Psycho-Legal Studies Program) has conducted comprehensive studies of the criminalization of the mentally ill, the mental health needs and service use of jail detainees and correlates of violence and HIV/AIDS risk behaviors. Their findings have been used as the basis for changing public health policy nationwide. In addition to publishing papers in widely disseminated journals, their work has been cited in reports of the Surgeon General, used in amicus briefs to the Supreme Court, presented in congressional hearings, and widely disseminated by federal agencies and advocacy groups.

Currently, Prof. Abram is a co-investigator on *the Northwestern Juvenile Project*, the first large scale, longitudinal study of mental health needs and outcomes of juvenile detainees.

Deborah Baskin, Ph.D., received her doctorate in sociology in 1984 from the University of Pennsylvania. She was a National Institute of Mental Health postdoctoral research fellow at the University of Massachusetts-Amherst, Department of Sociology. For 16 years, she was a Professor in the School of Criminal Justice and Criminalistics at California State University, Los Angeles; 11 of which she was the Director of the School. Currently, Dr. Baskin is a Professor and Chairperson of the Department of Criminal Justice and Criminology at Loyola University Chicago.

Dr. Baskin has published on a variety of topics, including female offending, substance abuse and violence, forensic mental health, and community mediation. Dr. Baskin is co-author of *The Social Consequences of Methamphetamine Use* (2004), *Workin' Hard for the Money: The Social and Economic Lives of Female Drug Dealers* (2000) and *Casualties of Community Disorder: Women's Careers in Violent Crime* (1998). She has recently published extensively on the case processing and criminal justice outcomes of violent crimes including homicide, rape, assault, and robbery.

Arielle Baskin-Sommers is a doctoral candidate in clinical psychology at the University of Wisconsin-Madison. She is the 2009 winner of the Cheryl Wynne Hare Award from the Society for the Study of Psychopathy. She received her B.Sc. from Brown University where she graduated with honors and received the Edmund Burke Delabarre Memorial Premium for her fMRI research on behavioral responses to amphetamine.

Substantively, Baskin-Sommers' research interests are concentrated on understanding individual differences in emotion regulation as they relate to vulnerability for maladaptive behaviors. Methodologically, she is interested in integrating a wide range of techniques and technologies to explore this issue. To this end, she has completed research that explored the influence of impulsivity on everyday behaviors (e.g., smoking, risky sexual practices) and on criminal conduct (e.g., illicit drug use, driving under the influence, and criminal violence). Each of these studies employed either survey or neuroimaging techniques. Her current research attempts to provide a more integrated methodological approach to understanding individual differences across more diverse cognitive and emotional domains, again, as they affect the self-regulation of behavior. She has focused her attention on utilizing psychophysiological techniques, such as startle reactivity and event-related potentials in order to examine emotion-cognition interactions among psychopathic and externalizing individuals. Her clinical experience includes work with children at risk for severe mental illness, at an adult inpatient unit, and at a university clinic where she does clinical interviews, therapy, and neuropsychological assessments.

Kim M. Blankenship, Ph.D., is Professor and Chair in the Department of Sociology at American University and also Director of the Center on Health, Risk and Society at American University. Previously, she served on the Sociology faculty at Duke University and at the Duke Global Health Institute (2008–2010) and at Yale University's School of Public Health (YSPH), where from 1998 to Spring 2008, she was the Associate Director of the Center for Interdisciplinary Research on AIDS at YSPH. Her research and publications focus on the social dimensions of health and structural interventions to address health, with an emphasis, over the past 20 years, on HIV/AIDS. She has received funding from NIDA, NIMH, CDC, and the Bill and Melinda Gates Foundation (BMGF).

Current research projects include a mixed methods study of the implementation and impact of community led structural interventions to address HIV risk in female sex workers in India: a mixed methods, longitudinal study of the impact of movement between the criminal justice system and the community (coercive mobility) on HIV related risk of re-entrants and their sexual partners and the extent to which this accounts for race disparities in HIV/AIDS, analysis of secondary data to assess the impact of HIV prevention programming on the dynamics of HIV transmission in Southern India, and a meta analysis of structural interventions in HIV prevention.

Melina R. Boudov, M.A., is the Director of the Infertility Prevention Project at the Sexually Transmitted Disease Program, Los Angeles County Department of Public Health. Boudov coordinates chlamydia and gonorrhea prevention efforts for youth in Los Angeles County in partnership with public, private, and community-based agencies, including middle and high schools, continuation schools, school districts, family planning organizations, juvenile and adult probation departments, gang intervention programs, and other youth-serving agencies. Boudov also directs an STD screening, treatment and case management program for female detainees diagnosed with chlamydia or gonorrhea. In addition, she serves as a project manager for a National Institute of Health-funded study to assess the efficacy of two recommended treatments by the Centers for Disease Control and Prevention for chlamydial infections in high-risk, non-pregnant incarcerated females in juvenile detention settings. This study will measure how a 7-day course of doxycycline compares in effectiveness with a single dose of azythromycin for the successful treatment of chlamydia.

Boudov has published several articles and abstracts pertaining to chlamydia and gonorrhea prevention and control among high risk populations, including juvenile hall detainees, young women in adult detention, family planning clients, and college students. These studies assessed the prevalence and correlates of STD infection among youth and implications for screening policy for youth-serving venues.

Christopher R. Browning, Ph.D, is Professor of Sociology and an affiliate of the Initiative in Population Research at Ohio State University. He received a Ph.D. in Sociology from the University of Chicago in 1997. He has written extensively on the causes and consequences of crime and the role of residential neighborhood contexts in shaping the health and well being of urban adolescents. He is Principal Investigator of a National Institute of Child Health and Human Development-sponsored study exploring the link between features of urban neighborhoods and early adolescent risk-taking behavior using the Project on Human Development in Chicago Neighborhoods data. He has also received funding from the National Institute on Drug Abuse and the WT Grant Foundation for a large-scale data collection effort focused on the consequences of adolescent spatial and social exposures for risk-taking, victimization, and health.

Kathleen A. Cagney, Ph.D., is an Associate Professor in the Departments of Sociology, Health Studies, and Comparative Human Development at the University of Chicago. Her work examines social inequality and its relationship to health with a focus on neighborhood, race, and aging and the life course. She has developed a series of papers on neighborhood social capital and its relationship to outcomes such as self-rated health, asthma prevalence, physical activity, and mortality during the 1995 Chicago heat wave. She also focuses on the validity of such measures and the development of new neighborhood-based metrics that reflect the perceptions and experiences of older residents. Currently she works on two Chicago-based studies of neighborhood context and older adult health, and is examining the role of the social and physical environment in older adult well-being with the National Social Life, Health, and Aging Project. Dr. Cagney is Director of the Population Research Center, Co-Director of the Center on the Demography and Economics of Aging, and a Senior Fellow at the National Opinion Research Center.

Alice Cepeda, Ph.D., is an Assistant Professor in the School of Social Work at the University of Southern California. She was previously in the Department of

Sociology and Associate Director of the Center for Drug and Social Policy Research at the University of Houston. She received her doctoral degree from the City University of New York, Graduate Center. Her work has focused on the social epidemiology of drug use and the related health risk behaviors that disproportionately affect urban Mexican-origin minority populations including violence, HIV/STI infection risks, and mental health conditions. Dr. Cepeda's research has also highlighted the unique gendered experiences encountered by females within this cultural context. Her research publications have explored the complex of social determinants including familial, neighborhood, and socio-ecological factors that contribute to drug use and negative social and health outcomes among vulnerable minority populations.

Dr. Cepeda has been a recipient of several National Institutes of Health federal grants. She currently is Principal Investigator and Co-Investigator, respectively, on two National Institute on Drug Abuse funded studies including (1) a study examining the long term health consequences of adolescent gang membership and (2) the emergence and diffusion of crack use in Mexico City. She has also been a multiple recipient and scholar of the National Center on Minority Health and Health Disparities Loan Repayment Program. Dr. Cepeda received the 2010 National Award of Excellence in Research by a New Investigator from the National Hispanic Science Network on Drug Abuse. She was also a recent recipient of the 2010 Junior Scholar Award presented by the Drinking and Drugs Division of the Society for the Study of Social Problems.

Leslie F. Clark, Ph.D., M.P.H., is the Director of Intervention Science in the Division of Adolescent Medicine, University of Southern California and the Director of the Strengthening Youth Prevention Paradigms Center at Children's Hospital Los Angeles (CHLA). She is also the Evaluation Director for the Substance Abuse and Mental Health Services Administration (SAMSHA) funded CHLA "Community Center for Trauma Informed Services for Runaway Homeless Youth." Her behavioral research, interventions, and community collaborations addresses health, wellness, service needs, risk reduction, and positive youth development among low-income minority youth. Her current work addresses: (a) early and middle adolescents in poverty; (b) runaway homeless youth; (c) male to female transgender youth; (d) young men who have sex with me; and (e) HIV infected youth.

Dr. Clark has been conducting research with at risk adolescents and low-income minority communities for 18 years. Her Project AIM (Adult Identity Mentoring) for middle school youth is designated as an evidence-based HIV prevention program by Center for Disease Control and Prevention Diffusion of Effective Behavioral Interventions and as a pregnancy prevention effective intervention by the Office of Adolescent Health. During the last 15 years, Dr. Clark has designed, implemented, and evaluated several behavioral interventions that focus on reducing risk and promoting positive outcomes for adolescents, young adults, and their families.

Bethany Deeds, Ph.D., M.A., is a Deputy Branch Chief within the Epidemiology Research Branch, Division of Epidemiology, Services and Prevention Research at the National Institute on Drug Abuse (NIDA) where she manages the social epidemiology of drug use portfolio. Prior to joining NIDA, she was an Assistant Professor in the Department of Pediatrics at the University of Maryland Medical School for 4 years where she directed Connect to Protect: Baltimore, one of 13 national sites investigating how community partnerships can reduce adolescent HIV incidence and prevalence by making structural changes to the environment. Her current research interests include the social epidemiology of drug abuse, HIV, and violence; the effects of social environments and their interaction with biological/physiological pathways on health outcomes; and the characterization of modifiable structural factors in communities/neighborhoods. Dr. Deeds' program area covers research related to substance use, HIV, and violence including: social context (e.g., school, workplace, neighborhood/community, institutions); drugs and crime; macro-social determinants of health (e.g., poverty, globalization, urbanicity, etc.); homelessness and housing; violent victimization; drug markets; social networks, climate and norms; and the impact of natural disasters. She is also responsible for the stimulation of new methods in drug abuse epidemiology, measurements of social environment, and public health law and policy research related to substance use.

Brooke Dorsey Holliman is a Ph.D. candidate of the Department of Health and Behavioral Sciences at the University of Colorado Denver. Her work focuses on health disparities by race and ethnicity, particularly disparities among African Americans. In 2008, the National Institutes of Health granted her a research grant to work with Professor Richard Miech in exploring trends in illegal drug use among different socioeconomic populations. Currently, Ms. Dorsey is working with her co-authors on identifying factors contributing to the increase in drug mortality.

Dennis M. Gorman, Ph.D., is a Professor in the Department of Epidemiology and Biostatistics at the Texas A&M Health Science Center School of Rural Public Health. In addition to introductory epidemiology courses, he teaches classes in social epidemiology and psychiatric epidemiology. He earned a B.A. (Hons.) from the Polytechnic of Central London (now the University of Westminster), an M.Sc. from the Bedford College, University of London, and a Ph.D. from the Department of Sociology, Essex University. Gorman's research interests focus on the ecology of alcohol availability and violence, the evaluation of alcohol and drug prevention policies, and the application of evidence-based practice to alcohol, drug and violence prevention. His research has been funded by agencies such as the National Institute of Health, the Robert Wood Johnson Foundation, and the Smith Richardson Foundation. Selected findings from this research have been published in a variety of public health, addiction and evaluation journals, including the *American Journal of Public Health, Preventive Medicine, Addiction, Journal of Studies on Alcohol, Drug and Alcohol Review, Evaluation and Program Planning*, and *Evaluation Review*. His current research interests are focused on the integration of agent-based models into geospatial analyses of alcohol and drug availability and violence, and the processes through which pseudoscientific ideas spread within scientific communities.

Christine E. Grella, Ph.D., is a Professor of Psychiatry and Biobehavioral Sciences at the Integrated Substance Abuse Programs (ISAP), Semel Institute for Neuroscience and Human Behavior, University of California, Los Angeles. Her research focuses on the intersection of multiple service delivery systems, including substance abuse treatment, mental health, child welfare, health services, HIV services, and criminal justice. Her work has examined the relationship of service delivery to treatment outcomes, focusing on treatment for women, adolescents, individuals in the criminal justice system, and individuals with co-occurring mental and substance use disorders. She has published her work widely in the areas of addiction, mental health, health services, and evaluation research.

Dr. Grella is currently conducting an evaluation of a “trauma-informed” substance abuse treatment program at a community correctional facility for women offenders. Previously, she extensively studied the relationship of participation in aftercare treatment for women offenders following their re-entry into the community with substance use, family reunification, and recidivism outcomes. She recently completed a study funded by the National Institute on Drug Abuse (NIDA) in which 25-year follow-up interviews were conducted with a cohort of heroin users sampled in the early 1980s; study analyses focus on gender differences in longitudinal trajectories of heroin and other drug use, treatment participation, and related mental and physical health outcomes among this aging sample of drug users. In addition, Dr. Grella directs the NIDA-funded pre- and postdoctoral training program at ISAP and is a co-investigator on the NIDA-funded Center for Advancing Longitudinal Drug Abuse Research at ISAP.

Paul J. Gruenewald, Ph.D., is Scientific Director and Senior Research Scientist at Prevention Research Center, Pacific Institute for Research and Evaluation, Berkeley, CA. He received his Ph.D. in experimental psychology from Duke University in 1978 and has been active in alcohol and drug research for the past 30 years. His research focuses upon social ecological models of alcohol and drug problems in community settings, mathematical models of alcohol, drug use and related risks, policy evaluation, and methods for community-based preventive intervention research. He served as Component Director and lead evaluator on the National Institute on Alcohol Abuse and Alcoholism (NIAAA) “Community Prevention Trials” environmental prevention intervention project; the first community-based preventive intervention demonstrating the effectiveness of environmental programs for the reduction of alcohol problems.

Dr. Gruenewald received a National Institutes of Health Merit Award to support continued studies of alcohol outlets and violence and an NIAAA advanced research projects contract to design “Ecosystem Models of Alcohol-Related Behaviors,” both projects in which he advanced the application of mathematical models and Bayesian spatial statistics to studies of the ecologies of alcohol and drug problems. Dr. Gruenewald is currently Principal Investigator on the “Environmental Approaches to Prevention” research Center grant from NIAAA and the “Assessing the Development of Drug Markets Using Bayesian Space-Time Models” from the National Institute on Drug Abuse (NIDA). He is also Co-principal Investigator on a NIDA-funded study of “A Community Trial to Prevent Inhalant Use in Alaska.”

Nancy G. Guerra, Ph.D., is a Professor of Psychology at the University of California at Riverside and Director of the Academic Center of Excellence on Youth Violence Prevention. She is an outgoing Associate Editor of the journal *Child Development* and current editor of the *Journal of Research on Adolescence*. Her work emphasizes understanding and preventing aggression and violence in children and youth. She has published numerous research articles examining predictors of aggression and has developed and evaluated several preventive interventions. These interventions include the Metropolitan Area Child Study multi-component, school-based program, Viewpoints cognitive-behavioral program for juvenile offenders, a program based on core competencies for risk prevention and positive youth development, Positive Life Changes, and a new home visitation program for parents of children and teenagers, Child Development Parent Training.

Dr. Guerra has co-edited several related recent books including *Preventing Youth Violence in a Multicultural Society* (American Psychological Association Books, 2005), *Treating the Juvenile Offender* (Guilford Press, 2008), and *Core Competencies to Prevent Problem Behaviors and Promote Positive Youth Development* (Jossey-Bass, 2008). She also has served on numerous study groups, panels, and advisory committees including the President's Council on Juvenile Justice and Delinquency Prevention. Her efforts have involved projects in the USA and internationally, including a recent multi-year study of individual and community level youth violence prevention programs in Jamaica funded by The World Bank.

Mia D. Humphreys, M.S.W., pursued her Masters in Social Work with an emphasis in Community Organization, Planning, and Administration from University of Southern California. She assisted Dr. Clark in the packaging of Project AIM (Adult Identify Mentoring) for community-based organizations as part of her Master's internship. She has been working at the Division of Adolescent Medicine at Children's Hospital Los Angeles (CHLA) fulltime since 2008. She has a strong interest in the intersection of social justice and public health and has worked on numerous community-based research projects involving high-risk youth including homeless/runaway, transgender, and gang-involved youth. She is currently the Capacity Building Assistance Coordinator for the Center for Strengthening Youth Prevention Paradigms (SYPP) at CHLA. Funded by the Center for Disease Control and Prevention, the SYPP Center targets community mobilization around the HIV prevention needs of African American and Latino trans-youth and young gay men.

Geoffrey P. Hunt, Ph.D., is a social and cultural anthropologist who has had nearly 30 years experience in planning, conducting, and managing research in the field of drugs, alcohol, and youth studies. Currently, Dr. Hunt is a Senior Research Scientist at the Institute for Scientific Analysis, the Principal Investigator on two National Institutes Health projects and Professor at the Centre for Alcohol and Drugs Research at the University of Aarhus, Denmark. The first of these projects is on youth gangs in the San Francisco Bay. This study represents the latest project on youth gangs in the San Francisco Bay area, which began in 1990. Since then five additional studies have been completed. The second project that Dr. Hunt is currently directing is on Asian American Gay and Bisexual Men, Club Drugs, and Nightlife. In addition, Dr. Hunt has been involved in two large-scale comparative international projects. The first project focused on the study of alcohol treatment systems in 16 countries and led to the publication of the book *Cure, Care or Control: Alcoholism Treatment in Sixteen Countries* (SUNY 1992). A companion volume *Drugs, Demons and Delinquents: Drug Treatment Systems in an International Perspective* (Sage 1998) examined the drug treatment systems in 20 different countries.

Dr. Hunt has published widely in the field of substance use studies in many of the leading sociology, anthropology, and criminology journals in the USA and the UK. He and his team have just published their latest book *Youth, Drugs and Nightlife* (Routledge, 2010).

James Iveniuk received his B.A. in Anthropology and English literature, with a minor in Semiotics, from the University of Toronto in 2005. He went on to complete a Masters in Anthropology there, writing his thesis on concepts of ethnic authenticity among second-generation Ukrainian-Canadian immigrants. He then spent a year teaching and designing his own courses at a small college in Canada, before beginning a second Masters at the University of Chicago in Comparative Human Development. He is currently working on his Ph.D. in urban sociology, where he is specializing in social statistics, health disparities, and the study of racial segregation. He is also employed as a research assistant at the National Opinion Research Center, and is a participant in several separate projects having to do with neighborhood disorganization, the sociology of religion, survey-based network analysis and the health of America's aging population.

Karen Joe Laidler, Ph.D., is Professor of Sociology and the Director of the Centre for Criminology at the University of Hong Kong. She attained her Ph.D. in sociology from the University of California Davis in 1991. She has been involved in criminological research – applied and theoretical – for nearly 30 years. In the USA, she worked with the National Council on Crime and Delinquency and the California Attorney General's Office on federal, state, and local grants in areas ranging from juvenile detention risk assessment and juvenile court intervention effectiveness to felony sentencing reform and prison crowding to evaluations of drug intervention programs. She has had a longstanding interest in the articulation of gender and ethnicity in gangs, dating back to the late 1980s. In Hong Kong, she has conducted a number of evaluation studies of youth programs and is currently assessing program effectiveness for a drug education project and a drug intervention program.

Dr. Joe Laidler's main research and publications focus on gender, ethnicity, and youth gangs, and alcohol and drug use among women and youth. At present, her research in the USA includes studies on the use patterns and problems associated with club drugs in California; the relationship between alcohol and drug use and violence among female gang members, and alcohol and drug cessation during adolescent pregnancy in the USA. In addition to her work on the sex work industry in Hong Kong, she is also working on a number of drug related studies in Hong Kong including the rise and problems associated with psychotropic drugs, the drug market, the relationship between violence and drug use, Buddhist interventions with heroin users, and generational differences among heroin users.

Fred W. Johnson, Ph.D., received his doctorate from the Quantitative Methods program in Educational Psychology at the University of California, Berkeley in 1990, where he specialized in behavioral genetic research on specific cognitive abilities. He has been an Associate Research Scientist at Prevention Research Center, Pacific Institute for Research and Evaluation, since 1996 after completing a postdoctoral research fellowship under Paul Gruenewald. Working with Dr. Gruenewald, there has been a spatial and often temporal component to much of Dr. Johnson's research. This includes most recently: analyses of drug use in California using spatial panel models; modeling the growth and development of drug markets in the state; and the spatial dynamics of illicit drug availability and rates of drug use at the neighborhood level.

Dr. Johnson's prior work has focused on alcohol-related problems, including spatiotemporal models applied to the relationship between alcohol outlets and suicide. In a series of papers, he helped model the dose–response relationship between individual alcohol consumption and self-reported alcohol-related problems among college drinkers. Dr. Johnson has used multi-level modeling to study the relationship of alcohol availability to motor vehicle crashes and hyperparameter models to model drinking over the life-course within gender and ethnic groups. He has also modeled the relationship between alcohol availability and problematic alcohol-related outcomes such as injuries, motor vehicle accidents, pedestrian accidents, and violence.

Stephen Koester, Ph.D., is Chair of the Department of Anthropology, and a Professor in the Department of Health and Behavioral Sciences at the University of Colorado, Denver. Dr. Koester's research has focused on blood-borne disease transmission among socially and economically marginalized populations. He was the Principal Investigator of a National Institute on Drug Abuse R01 testing a social network focused HIV intervention aimed at injection drug users. His published work has emphasized the risks embedded in the process of drug injection and the contextual factors influencing risk. In 2001, he was a visiting Senior Behavioral Scientist at the Center for Disease Control and Prevention's Division of Viral Hepatitis, and in 2006 he was a Fulbright Scholar at the Hanoi School of Public Health in Vietnam. Currently, Dr. Koester is working with his co-authors on drug mortality and is conducting ethnographic work on the drug economy in the Caribbean.

Steven P. Kurtz, Ph.D., received his doctorate in sociology from Florida International University in 1999. Dr. Kurtz is currently Professor and Co-Director of the Center for Research on Substance Use and Health Disparities at Nova Southeastern University. He is currently the Principal Investigator (PI) of two National Institute on Drug Abuse (NIDA)-funded randomized clinical trials to test the efficacy of novel substance use and sexual risk reduction interventions designed for gay and bisexual men and for young adult polydrug users in the club scene. He is also PI of a NIDA-funded study of prescription drug diversion among diverse populations. Dr. Kurtz has conducted research studies of substance use, sexual risk behaviors, related health and social problems, and intervention approaches among adolescents, young adults, women sex workers, men who have sex with men, and other vulnerable populations since 1995. In addition to these areas, his publications include articles on crime, health disparities, sexual identities, and masculinities, as well as ethnographic accounts of a range of subcultures in which drug use is prevalent.

Dr. Kurtz serves as the alternate member representing South Florida on NIDA's Community Epidemiology Work Group. He is a member of the Under-represented Populations Committee of the College on Problems of Drug Dependence and of the Education Committee of the Gay and Lesbian Medical Association.

Anthony Lawson, Mr. Lawson is a recent graduate with a BA in English from the University of Maryland Eastern Shore. He has been a research assistant at the National Medical Association and the affiliated Cobb Institute. Mr. Lawson has also worked as a research assistant at the Center for Substance Abuse Research at Howard University. He has been a strong advocate for drug abuse prevention programs for minority youth.

William B. Lawson, M.D., Ph.D., D.L F.A.P.A., is currently Professor and Chairman of the Department of Psychiatry and Behavioral Sciences at Howard University Health Sciences, Washington, DC. He is President of the DC chapter of Mental Health America, Past President of the Washington Psychiatric Society, a Distinguished Life Fellow of the American Psychiatric Association, past Chair and E. Y. Williams Clinical Scholar of Distinction Awardee of the Section of Psychiatry and Behavioral Sciences of the National Medical Association, and past president of the Black Psychiatrists of America. He received the National Alliance for the Mentally Ill Exemplary Psychiatrist Award and the National Alliance for the Mentally Ill, Outstanding Psychologist Award. He was twice named one of "America's Leading Black Doctors" by Black Enterprise Magazine, and top doctor by Newsweek magazine. He received the Jeanne Spurlock Award from the American Psychiatric Association and a Multicultural Workplace Award from the Veterans Administration.

Dr. Lawson has over 170 publications and has received federal and foundation funding to study and treat severe mental illness, substance abuse, AIDS, and reduce ethnic disparities in health care. He was among the first to do a controlled psychopharmacological study in a jail. He is now funded to treat HIV positive substance abusers from the correctional system to see if the community risk for AIDS is reduced with that intervention.

Carl Leukefeld, Ph.D., is Professor and Chair of the Department of Behavioral Science and founding Director of the Center on Drug and Alcohol Research at the University of Kentucky. He is also the Bell Alcohol and Addictions Endowed Chair. He came to the University of Kentucky in 1990 to establish the Center on Drug and Alcohol Research from the National Institute on Drug Abuse (NIDA) where he filled administrative and research positions. He was also the Chief Health Services Officer of the United States Public Health Service. Dr. Leukefeld has published over 200 articles, chapters, books, and monographs. He has taught the undergraduate Alcohol and Problem Drinking Course, the Dependency Behavior graduate course, and the Introduction to Clinical Medicine course for medical students. He currently is a reviewer and consulting editor for five journals, grant reviewer, and has been a member of the National Institutes of Health (NIH) Community-Level Health Promotion Study Section and the NIH/NIDA Health Services Initial Review Group. His research interests include treatment interventions, HIV prevention, criminal justice sanctions, and health services.

Steven S. Martin is Senior Scientist and Associate Director at the Center for Drug and Alcohol Studies, University of Delaware. He received his A.B. from Harvard and graduate degrees from the London School of Economics and the University of Michigan. He has been at the University of Delaware since 1988 doing research and teaching. He previously worked at the Center for Prevention Research at the University of Kentucky and at Baylor College of Medicine in Houston. His three main areas of research are evaluation science, youth substance abuse, and the effectiveness of drug and HIV interventions for criminal justice offenders. Martin has been the Evaluator for six Health and Human Services/Substance Abuse and Mental Health Services Administration grants and directs the Delaware School Surveys about substance use and health, the Delaware Youth Risk Behavior Survey, and the Delaware Youth Tobacco Survey. He serves as the state's epidemiologist for substance abuse. In terms of drug and HIV work with offenders, Martin has been involved since 1989 in establishing and evaluating the KEY/CREST drug abuse treatment continuum for offenders in Delaware.

Martin recently completed work as Co-principal Investigator on a long-term National Institute on Drug Abuse (NIDA) study on treatment effectiveness for drug involved offenders and as Principal Investigator on NIDA grants examining HIV prevention interventions among probationers and the validity of self-report of drug use. Currently, he is Co-Investigator on the University of Delaware's part in the National Institutes of Health initiative in criminal justice drug abuse treatment (CJ-DATS2). He is the author/co-author of over 100 articles on substance abuse, treatment effectiveness, delinquency, and methodology.

Jennifer L. Matjasko, Ph.D., is a Behavioral Scientist in the Prevention Development and Evaluation Branch in the Division of Violence Prevention at the Centers for Disease Control and Prevention. She earned her Ph.D. and Masters in Public Policy from the University of Chicago. While there, Dr. Matjasko focused her training in developmental psychology, econometrics, and family/community violence. She has served as an assistant professor in the Department of Human Ecology at the University of Texas at Austin and as a senior researcher at Edvance Research, Inc./REL Southwest. Her research interests focus on the development of at-risk adolescents and the factors that promote their health and well-being. Her research emphasizes the use of ecological, life-course, and person-centered approaches in understanding the relationship between individual, family, school, and community factors, and adolescent functioning in order to inform prevention, intervention, and policy efforts targeted to at-risk youth.

Dr. Matjasko served as a co-investigator on the *Three-City Teacher Study,* a study of academic success among low-income children and adolescents in Boston, Chicago, and San Antonio. Her current projects include program and policy research related to youth violence, the relationship between macroeconomic factors and youth violence, and the development and evaluation of structural interventions on health outcomes.

Gary M. McClelland has a Ph.D. in comparative history from the Northwestern University Department of Sociology. He joined the faculty of the Department of Psychiatry and Behavioral Sciences at the Northwestern University Medical School in June 1989 where he has worked as a methodologist, epidemiologist, and policy analyst. He was Senior Analyst with the Psycho-Legal Studies Program until April of 2006, and has since been the Director of Data Operations at the Mental Health Services and Policy Program. He is also active with the John Howard Association of Illinois and Alliance I-11 where his focus is the improvement of medical care in the Illinois Department of Corrections. He contributes to the Chicago area Prison Industrial Complex Teaching Collaborative on issues of mental health and medical care in correctional settings.

In addition to public policy in general, Dr. McCllelland's research interests include social inequality, mental health, criminal justice, prison reform, juvenile justice, crime and victimization, and child welfare and child trauma. His current work with the Mental Health Services and Policy Program focuses on child trauma in the Illinois child welfare system. In conjunction with the National Child Traumatic Stress Network and the Illinois Department of Children and Family Services he contributes to the development and deployment of trauma informed practice throughout the Illinois State child welfare system.

Richard Miech, Ph.D., M.P.H., is a Professor in the Department of Health and Behavioral Sciences at the University of Colorado Denver. His work focuses on health disparities by socioeconomic status, with a particular emphasis on new disparities that have emerged or widened in recent years. His current work centers on drug-related mortality, which ranks as one of the fastest growing of all major mortality disparities in recent years (see his article in *American Sociological Review*).

Recently, Dr. Miech and colleagues show that the increase in drug-related mortality over the past decade is primarily a "historical period" effect that has affected all cohorts and is not specific to the young or the baby boom generation (Miech, Koester, & Dorsey-Holliman. (2011). He looks forward to working with colleagues to specify the driving force (or forces) behind this trend and, ultimately, to aid in the development of interventions and policies aimed at countering it.

Molly Moloney, Ph.D., is Senior Research Associate at the Institute for Scientific Analysis in Alameda, California. Dr. Moloney is a qualitative sociologist whose work centers on issues of gender and sexuality, ethnic identity, culture, and consumption.

She has published on issues of gender, sexuality, and parenthood among youth street gang members, as well as on identity, consumption, and ethnicity in the rave and club scenes, with particular emphasis on Asian American club drug users. Her work seeks to situate studies of drug and alcohol consumption in the broader context of cultural consumption more generally. Along with Geoffrey Hunt and Kristen Evans she is author of *Youth, Drugs and Nightlife* (Routledge, 2010).

Tanya Nieri, Ph.D. is Assistant Professor of Sociology at the University of California at Riverside (UCR) where she is an affiliate of the Robert Presley Center for Crime and Justice Studies, the Southern California Academic Center of Excellence on Youth Violence Prevention, and the Center for Family Studies. Her research interests include cultural identity and change (including acculturation determinants and consequences, ethnic identity, and discrimination), juvenile delinquency (including school and neighborhood effects), and community-based prevention and health promotion. Her work tends to focus on Latinos, especially Mexican-heritage youth and families in the USA and Mexico and Latin American immigrants in Spain. Current projects include assessing the association between violence experience and migration aspirations and intentions, examining the existence, consequences, and mediators of parent–child acculturation differences, and investigating the effects of a substance use prevention program on youth delinquency.

Prior to coming to UCR, Dr. Nieri was a research coordinator at the Southwest Interdisciplinary Research Center at Arizona State University where she focused on health disparities research among Latinos and American Indians and worked on several randomized controlled trials of youth and family substance use prevention interventions, including *keepin' it REAL*, a model program as designated by the Substance Abuse and Mental Health Services Administration.

Daniel J. O'Connell, Ph.D., earned his doctorate in Criminology form the University of Delaware in 2004, where he remains a Scientist at the Center for Drug and Alcohol Studies. His intellectual interests generally coalesce around the idea that the lives of persons involved in continuing criminal and addictive lifestyles are un-glamorous, un-exciting, un-productive and short. From this, his working interests focus on understanding and improving the lives of persons involved in crime and addiction through research on desistance, prisoner reentry, community based sanctions, and HIV prevention interventions. He has served as Project Director for the Delaware and New Jersey sites of the National Institute on Drug Abuse sponsored Criminal Justice Drugs Abuse Studies project (CJ-DATS), is Co-Principal Investigator of a National Institute of Justice (NIJ) project collecting life history interviews from 300 persons who completed drug treatment in the early 1990s, and is Principal Investigator of the NIJ sponsored evaluation of the Delaware Decide Your Time program, which combines swift, certain, but not severe sanctions with probation officer-administered treatment among a group of drug involved probationers.

Dr. O'Connell has turned a home video hobby into the production of video based HIV prevention/intervention for criminal justice populations. He has authored numerous articles on criminological theory, HIV prevention, and correctional management in addition to the book *Prisoner Reentry and the Life Course*. He currently teaches criminology courses as part of the Inside Out program, bringing together traditional criminal justice students with incarcerated persons to investigate issues of crime and justice.

William R. Ponicki, M.A., is an Associate Research Scientist at Prevention Research Center, Pacific Institute for Research and Evaluation, Berkeley, CA. He received an M.A. in Public Policy Studies from the University of Chicago in 1987 and an M.A. in Economics from the University of California at Berkeley in 1997. He has been active in alcohol and drug research since 1990. His research focuses on statistical analyses explaining the use of addictive substances and the evaluation of policy measures to reduce social problems associated with alcohol and other drugs. Evaluated policy interventions include price and tax changes, minimum legal drinking ages, limitations on alcohol outlets or sales hours, restrictions on precursor chemicals used to manufacture illegal drugs, and creating incentives for store clerks to refuse sales to underage patrons. The outcome measures in these studies include drinking by beverage type, fatalities due to various alcohol-related causes (e.g., traffic crashes, cirrhosis, homicide, or suicide), and hospitalizations or arrests related to illegal drugs.

Ponicki's areas of statistical expertise include methods appropriate to the analysis of panel and hierarchical data, particularly analysis models to address spatial and temporal autocorrelation. His most recent work includes the development of varying-parameter Bayesian space-time models of the spread of methamphetamine use across California.

Lillian G. Remer, M.A., GISP, is an Associate Research Scientist at the Prevention Research Center of Pacific Institute for Research and Evaluation (PIRE) and a certified Geographic Information Systems Professional. She holds a Masters degree in Biology with a specialty in Environmental Toxicology, but for the past 25 years she has focused on social science research involving prevention of substance abuse (alcohol, tobacco, and illegal drugs) and the concomitant problems of violence, traffic crashes, and other public health impacts. Her primary expertise is in the area of database design, development, and manipulation including Geographical Information Systems (GIS), and the acquisition, manipulation, and conflation of data from diverse sources. Her work includes the use of extremely large, state and national archival data sets, and project specific data collection through telephone and in person surveys. She has developed GIS analysis routines in Avenue, VBA, VB, and Python, and co-authored scientific publication of research findings.

Remer has contributed to research projects involving juvenile delinquency interventions, homeless recovery services, substance abuse problem prevention, and computer modeling. She is also the coordinator of the San Francisco Bay Area ArcGIS User's Group, a member of the Bay Area Automated Mapping Association, and an original member of the Spatial Systems Group of PIRE.

Anne Rhodes, M.S., is a senior research associate at George Mason University, who works on data systems and analysis issues for a number of federally funded initiatives related to substance use and the criminal justice system. She has her B.S. and M.S. from Virginia Tech in applied economics. She has worked with the Virginia Department of Health (VDH) for the past 15 years on developing statewide data collection systems for programs funded by the Ryan White CARE Act. She established a statewide system for collection data on HIV prevention activities funded by the Centers for Disease Control and Prevention. She currently provides ongoing data analysis and forecasting for the Ryan White programs, as well as establishing program evaluation processes for a number of VDH initiatives. Rhodes also served as the data coordinator for the Criminal Justice Drug Abuse Treatment Studies I (CJ-DATS1), funded by the National Institute on Drug Abuse. In this role, Rhodes established policies and procedures for data collection, documentation, and analysis for all ten of the multi-site studies conducted under CJ-DATS1 and also served as the CJ-DATS1 liaison to the Data and Safety Monitoring Board. She has presented at annual meetings of academic conferences, including Addiction Health Services Research, the American Society of Criminology, and the College on Problems of Drug Dependence. Rhodes has extensive experience in SAS and SPSS analysis, as well as SEM and multi-level modeling techniques. She has worked in the area of HIV care and prevention for the past 15 years and her dissertation research focuses on the social networks of drug-using probationers.

Erin Gregory Romero, Ph.D., is currently the Coordinator for the Services for Returning Veterans Mental Health Program (SeRV-MH) across the Veterans Administration Maryland Health Care System (VAMHC). The SeRV-MH program focuses on the mental health needs of returning veterans from the *Operation Enduring Freedom/Operation Iraqi Freedom* (OEF/OIF) wars and other combat areas that are part of the Global War on Terrorism. The goal of this program is preventative maintenance. She received her doctoral degree from Northwestern University Feinberg School of Medicine, Department of Psychiatry and Behavioral Sciences, Division of Psychology. She completed a psychology predoctoral internship at the VAMHC and obtained specialized training in substance use, serious mental illness, and posttraumatic stress disorder (PTSD). She received further specialized training in PTSD during her integrated postdoctoral fellowship in traumatic brain injury and PTSD in returning veterans at the VAMHC.

Dr. Romero's research has focused on racial/ethnic health disparities. Her research on the mental health needs and HIV/AIDS risk behaviors of delinquent youth has resulted in many peer-reviewed publications and conference presentations. Her doctoral dissertation investigated the role of incarceration in HIV/AIDS risk behaviors. Since working with veterans during her predoctoral internship, Dr. Romero has increasingly become interested in barriers to mental health care in OEF/OIF veterans. She is currently collaborating on a pilot study on the efficacy of Virtual Reality Exposure Treatment on PTSD symptom reduction in OEF/OIF veterans.

Bill Sanders, Ph.D., is an Associate Professor within the School of Criminal Justice and Criminalistics at California State University, Los Angeles. Dr. Sanders has conducted qualitative research on high-risk behaviors among at risk youth in London,

New York, and Los Angeles. He has published in areas such as substance use, violence, crime, and unsafe sexual practices among young offenders, gang members, injection drug users, and those who experience homelessness. Dr. Sanders has also published on drug selling, club drug use, prescription drug misuse, gang intervention, and qualitative research methods.

Dr. Sanders has been promoting as a public health agenda toward the study and approach of gang youth. Publications that reflect this agenda thus far have included: a public health model for studying risk behaviors among gang youth; the operationalization of a partnership with community-based organizations in order to access and interview active gang youth; evidence that gang youth are a vulnerable population suitable for nursing intervention; the normalized character of marijuana; and epidemiological data on unsafe sexual practices. Dr. Sanders continues research on risk behaviors and health aspects of gang youth, as well as other intersections of criminal justice and public health more generally.

Amy B. Smoyer, M.S.W., is a Ph.D. Candidate in Social Welfare at the City University of New York. Her dissertation, *Cafeteria, Commissary & Cooking: Foodways and Negotiations of Power and Identity in a Women's Prison*, analyzes women's narratives about prison food in order to build knowledge about the lived experience of female incarceration in the USA. From 2003 to 2011, Amy managed HIV prevention research projects at the Yale University School of Public Health's Center for Interdisciplinary Research on AIDS, including the Structures, Health and Risk among Reentrants, Probationers and Partners (SHARPP) Study. Prior to becoming involved in research, Smoyer's practice experience included providing HIV care, prevention and advocacy services in Miami, FL.

Ira Sommers, Ph.D., received his doctorate in Social Work in 1983 from the University of Pennsylvania. He was a National Institute of Mental Health postdoctoral research fellow at the University of Massachusetts-Amherst, Department of Sociology. Most recently, Dr. Sommers was a Professor in the School of Criminal Justice and Criminalistics at California State University, Los Angeles. In addition to teaching a variety of undergraduate and graduate classes, for 11 years, Dr. Sommers was the Director of the CSULA Graduate Masters Program in Criminal Justice. Currently, Dr. Sommers is an Adjunct Professor in the Department of Criminal Justice and Criminology at Loyola University Chicago.

Over the course of his academic career, Dr. Sommers has conducted and published research on a wide range of topics, including female offending, substance abuse and violence, forensic mental health, substance use and risk behaviors, and domestic violence. He is co-author of *The Social Consequences of Methamphetamine Use (2004), Workin' Hard for the Money: The Social and Economic Lives of Female Drug Dealers* (2000) and *Casualties of Community Disorder: Women's Careers in Violent Crime* (1998). In addition, Dr. Sommers published over 50 journal articles and/or book chapters and was either Principal or Co-Principal Investigator on numerous grants including but not limited to the National Institute of Justice, National Science Foundation, National Institute on Drug Abuse, and Guggenheim Foundation, totaling approximately $10 million dollars. Recently, he completed a

National Science Foundation grant studying methamphetamine use and violence and a National Institute of Justice study that assessed the role and impact of forensic evidence on criminal justice outcomes.

Jane K. Steinberg, Ph.D., M.P.H., is the Director of Policy and Programs at the Sexually Transmitted Disease (STD) Program, Los Angeles County Department of Public Health. She also holds two academic appointments: one as an Assistant Adjunct Professor at Occidental College and the other as a lecturer at the University of Southern California's Keck School of Medicine, School of Public Health where she teaches courses on public health and STDs. Her current research focuses on the nexus between substance abuse and sexual risk behaviors in criminal justice settings. Her work has focused on developing health education programs for vulnerable groups and reducing STD risks and improving service delivery to vulnerable populations, including women, adolescents, homeless populations, and performers in the adult film industry. She has recently worked on legislation to improve access to STD screening and treatment for marginalized populations. She has also published her work in the areas of public health and STD research.

In 2001, Dr. Steinberg completed a National Institute on Drug Abuse-funded predoctoral fellowship exploring correlates of drug use and recidivism among California adult jail arrestees. Dr. Steinberg plans on continuing research and developing programs that address sexual health and substance use interventions among marginalized populations.

Hilary L. Surratt, Ph.D., is a Senior Scientist with the Center for Drug and Alcohol Studies at the University of Delaware, and a Guest Professor in the Department of Psychiatry at the Federal University of Rio Grande do Sul in Porto Alegre, Brazil. Before coming to Delaware, she was a Senior Research Associate in the Department of Epidemiology and Public Health at the University of Miami School of Medicine. She is currently the Principal Investigator of a National Institute on Drug Abuse (NIDA)-funded epidemiologic study of antiretroviral medication diversion among HIV positive substance abusers in Miami, Florida; Principal Investigator of a NIDA-funded case management intervention program for African American women at high risk for HIV; and Co-Investigator on two other National Institute of Health-funded studies targeting prescription drug abuse and the diversion of prescription drugs to the illicit market.

Dr. Surratt has substantial experience with cross-cultural research, having previously served as a senior investigator on two HIV prevention/intervention initiatives in Brazil and the US Virgin Islands. She has expertise in the areas of HIV/AIDS, including the development and evaluation of interventions for underserved populations, HIV-related issues among women drug abusers and female sex workers, illicit and prescription drug abuse, and prescription drug diversion. She has published widely in both English and foreign-language journals in the areas of HIV/AIDS, substance abuse, violence, and drug policy.

Holly Swan is a doctoral student in the Sociology and Criminal Justice Department at the University of Delaware. She is currently a research assistant at the Center for Drug and Alcohol Studies where she is involved with the second phase of the Criminal Justice Drug Abuse Treatment Studies project, a project funded by the National Institute on Drug Abuse that is testing strategies for implementing evidence-based practices in criminal justice agencies for substance using offenders. Her interests include the intersection of deviance and health, social problems, and implementation science. She holds an M.A. in Sociology from Kent State University.

Faye S. Taxman, Ph.D., is a Professor in the Criminology, Law and Society Department and Director of the Center for Advancing Correctional Excellence at George Mason University. Dr. Taxman has over 30 years of experience in conducting research in the areas of sentencing, courts, corrections, and organizational change. She is recognized for her work in the development of the seamless systems of care models that link the criminal justice with other service delivery systems, as well as reengineering probation and parole supervision services, and organizational change models. Her most recent work concerns the best strategies to advance the implementation of evidence-based practices in correctional, particularly probation, settings. Her work covers the breadth of the correctional system from jails and prisons to community corrections and adult and juvenile offenders, including all types of interventions and system improvement factors.

Dr. Taxman has had numerous grants from the National Institute on Drug Abuse, National Institute of Justice, National Institute of Corrections, Office of National Drug Control Policy, and Bureau of Justice Assistance. She has active "laboratories" with her nearly 20-year agreement with the Maryland Department of Public Safety and Correctional Services. She has published over 120 articles including translational work such as the *Tools of the Trade: A Guide to Incorporating Science into Practice*, a publication of the National Institute on Corrections that provides guidance to the implementation of science-based concepts into practice.

Linda A. Teplin, Ph.D., is the Owen L. Coon Professor of Psychiatry and Behavioral Sciences at the Feinberg School of Medicine, Northwestern University, where she is also the Vice Chair of Research in the Department of Psychiatry and Director of the Program in Health Disparities and Public Policy (formerly entitled "Psycho-Legal Studies Program"). Since receiving her Ph.D. from Northwestern University in 1975, she has focused on special populations seldom examined in prior studies. She conducted the first large scale epidemiologic studies of psychiatric disorders in incarcerated females and males, examining adults (1983–1995) and juveniles (1995 to present). Other studies have addressed criminalization of the mentally ill, correlates of violence, patterns of crime victimization, health service utilization, and HIV/AIDS risk behaviors. In addition to publishing papers in widely-disseminated professional journals, her work has been cited in reports of the Surgeon General, used in amicus briefs to the Supreme Court, presented in congressional hearings, and widely disseminated by federal agencies and advocacy groups.

Dr. Teplin's national honors include the National Institute of Mental Health MERIT Award (1995), the American Psychological Association's career award for "Distinguished Contributions to Research in Public Policy" (1992), the National

Alliance for the Mentally Ill Young Scientist Award (1990) and the National Commission on Correctional Health Care's Bernard Harrison Award of Merit (2001).

Professor Teplin is currently conducting *the Northwestern Juvenile Project*, the first large-scale longitudinal study of health needs and outcomes of juvenile detainees. In this study, her team tracks and re-interviews 1829 youth who were initially arrested and detained between 1995 and 1998. Published papers have addressed a variety of topics: psychiatric disorders, substance abuse, health services, death rates, child maltreatment, trauma, suicidal ideation, functional impairment, and HIV/AIDS risk behaviors. Her research group is focusing on drug and alcohol abuse, comorbid psychiatric disorders and HIV/AIDS. The Northwestern Juvenile Project provides a unique opportunity to examine how the disproportionate incarceration of African Americans affects health disparities in drug abuse and HIV/AIDS.

Yonette F. Thomas, Ph.D., is currently the Associate Vice President for Research Compliance at Howard University. Prior to joining the staff and faculty of Howard University, she served, for almost a decade, as Program Director for the Sociology Epidemiology Program and Branch Chief of the Epidemiology Research Branch at the National Institute on Drug Abuse, at the National Institutes of Health (NIH). She currently has faculty and research appointments at Howard University and at the Miller School of Medicine, University of Miami. She worked at Howard University as an Associate Professor of Psychiatry and Behavioral Sciences and adjunct Associate Professor of Research and a Senior Research Fellow with the Center for Minority Health Services Research (CMHSR) within the College of Pharmacy at Howard University and at the Miller School of Medicine as a Voluntary Associate Professor in the Department of Epidemiology and Public Health.

Dr. Thomas is a social epidemiologist, with training in epidemiology, medical sociology, and demography. Her primary research and publications have focused on the social epidemiology of drug abuse and HIV/AIDS and the link with geography and Geographic Methods. At the National Institute on Drug Abuse, she was instrumental in the development of the Institute's research focus on the social epidemiology of drug abuse and HIV/AIDS and the role of the social environment. At the NIH, she led a trans-NIH workgroup on the mapping of the social environment as it relates to the social determinants of health, and developed and stimulated a portfolio of science broadly focused on social epidemiology, genetic liability, and phenotypic heterogeneity, and human development across the life course.

Avelardo Valdez, Ph.D., is currently a Professor at the School of Social Work at the University of Southern California. He obtained his Ph.D. in Sociology at the University of California, Los Angeles.

A primary focus of his research has been on the relationship between substance abuse and violence and health issues among high-risk groups. His research projects have been among "hidden populations." He has developed innovative methodologies to examine distinct street populations such as Latino adolescent male gang members and gang affiliated females, female sex workers on the US/Mexico border, Mexican American non-injecting heroin users, Hurricane Katrina evacuees in Houston, Latino immigrant day laborers in post-Katrina New Orleans, and aging

Mexican American injecting heroin users. His publication record includes journal articles, chapters, and academic publications including two books *Mexican American Girls and Gang Violence: Beyond Risk* (Palgrave Press) and *Puro Conjunto* (University of Texas Press).

He is a recipient of federal grants from the National Institutes of Health (NIH), National Institute on Drug Abuse (NIDA), Centers for Disease Control and Prevention, and Substance Abuse and Mental Health Services Administration. His current NIH funded grant focuses on examining the long-term consequences of adolescent gang membership among Mexican Americans in San Antonio, Texas. Dr Valdez is also a recipient of a NIDA R25 training grant entitled "Interdisciplinary Research Training Institute on Hispanic Drug Abuse." His most recent (2011) award is a NIDA grant to examine the emergence and diffusion of crack use in Mexico City.

Christy A. Visher, Ph.D., is Professor of Sociology and Criminal Justice at the University of Delaware and Director of the Center for Drug and Alcohol Studies. The Center operates as part of the Department of Sociology and Criminal Justice and facilitates collaborative research and publication on substance abuse, HIV, and health risk behaviors among faculty, professional staff, and graduate students. Prior to joining the University of Delaware, she was Principal Research Associate with the Justice Policy Center at the Urban Institute in Washington, DC. From 1993 to 2000, she was Science Advisor to the Director of the National Institute of Justice, the research arm of the US Department of Justice. Her research interests focus on substance use, criminal careers, communities and crime, the role of social factors in criminal desistance, and the evaluation of strategies for crime control and prevention. She is currently one of nine principal investigators in the National Institute of Drug Abuse's Criminal Justice Drug Abuse Treatment Studies research collaborative that is focused on improving the implementation of evidence-based practices for substance-using populations. One of the aims of the collaboration is to develop implementation strategies for improving HIV services and treatment for offenders and the continuity of their care from prison to the community.

Dr. Visher has over 25 articles in refereed journals and co-edited *Prisoner Reentry and Crime in America* with Jeremy Travis. Dr. Visher received her M.A. (1980) and Ph.D. (1982) in Sociology from Indiana University, Bloomington.

Lance A. Waller, Ph.D., is Rollins Professor and Chair of the Department of Biostatistics and Bioinformatics, Rollins School of Public Health at Emory University in Atlanta, GA. He received his doctorate in Operations Research from Cornell University in 1991 and has been actively developing and applying statistical analytic methods for spatially-referenced data since that time. His research focuses on the analysis of spatial patterns in the environmental sciences ranging from environmental epidemiology to disease ecology to alcohol epidemiology. Recent projects include the development of methods to assess environmental justice, assess health impacts of air pollution, quantify impacts of construction projects on sea turtle nesting patterns, assess ecologic impacts on neglected tropical diseases, and describe the impact of landscape features on the spread of raccoon rabies. Most recently, Dr. Waller's research addresses links between mathematical and statistical models of the spread of epidemics of infectious disease. This area of research provides an emerging toolbox for the analysis of spatiotemporal patterns of illegal drug use and crime.

Dr. Waller is a co-author with Dr. Carol Gotway of the text "Applied Spatial Statistics for Public Health Data." Dr. Waller is the Principal Investigator of the project "Spatial Statistics for Disease Ecology" funded by the National Institute of Environmental Health Sciences, and serves as Principal Investigator of multiple training programs in Biostatistics funded by the National Institutes of Health.

Jason J. Washburn, Ph.D., ABPP, received his M.A. and Ph.D. in clinical psychology from DePaul University, specializing in child and adolescent psychology. He completed his clinical internship at the University of Washington School of Medicine in community/correctional child psychology and a postdoctoral fellowship in clinical child and adolescent psychology at the University of Michigan Medical School. He was a Robert Wood Johnson Research Scholar at Northwestern University Feinberg School of Medicine. He is currently the Director of Education and Clinical Training for the Division of Psychology at Northwestern University Feinberg School of Medicine. He is also the Director of the Center for Evidence-Based Practice at Alexian Brothers Behavioral Hospital. He is a board certified specialist in clinical child and adolescent psychology and a fellow of the Academy of Clinical Child and Adolescent Psychology.

Leah J. Welty, Ph.D., earned a B.S. in mathematics from the University of Chicago, an M.A. in mathematics from Washington University in St. Louis, and a Ph.D. in statistics from the University of Chicago. Following a postdoctoral fellowship in the Department of Biostatistics at Johns Hopkins University, she joined the Department of Preventive Medicine at Northwestern University as an Assistant Professor. She is also a biostatistician for the Biostatistics Collaboration Center, and holds an adjunct appointment in the Department of Psychiatry and Behavioral Sciences. Dr. Welty's research interests include applications of statistics to psycho-social, medical, and environmental sciences, and in particular the formulation of statistical models for outcomes correlated over time and space.

Kirk R. Williams received his Ph.D. from The University of Arizona and was a Post-Doctoral Fellow at Yale University. He has held faculty appointments at The University of Memphis and The University of New Hampshire, where he maintained an affiliation with the Family Research Laboratory. He also was a Professor at The University of Colorado at Boulder, where he was the founding Associate Director of the Center for the Study and Prevention of Violence. Dr. Williams currently is a Professor of Sociology, Co-Director of the Robert Presley Center for Crime and Justice Studies, and Co-Principal Investigator for the Southern California Center of Academic Excellence in Youth Violence Prevention at The University of California, Riverside.

Dr. Williams has published widely on the causes and prevention of violence, particularly involving youth or adult intimate partners, with the most recent publications addressing bullying, juvenile offending, and domestic violence risk assessment. He has received numerous grants from federal and state funding sources, in addition to private foundations to support his research. His most recent federal grant is from the National Institute of Justice, supporting a study of youth homicide in the nation's 100 largest cities from 1984 to 2006. He also has worked extensively with community-based groups, schools, and agencies in violence prevention planning, implementation, and evaluation.

Li Zhu, Ph.D., is a mathematical statistician in the Statistics Methodology and Applications Branch, Division of Cancer Control and Population Sciences, National Cancer Institute, National Institutes of Health. Dr. Zhu received a Bachelor of Sciences degree in Geography from Peking University in China. She came to the USA to pursue advanced study in the area of statistics. She received her Ph.D. in biostatistics from the School of Public Health, University of Minnesota, in 2000. After that she served as visiting assistant professor in the Department of Health Evaluation Sciences, College of Medicine, Penn State University, before moving to Texas A&M University as a tenure-track Assistant Professor. She held a joint appointment in the Department of Epidemiology and Biostatistics, School of Rural Public Health, and in the Department of Statistics, College of Science at Texas A&M. She was promoted to tenured Associate Professor there. She joined the National Cancer Institute in August 2009.

Dr. Zhu's main research interests include spatiotemporal model development via hierarchical Bayesian approaches, disease mapping, and spatial epidemiology. She is currently working on projects that combine advanced statistical hierarchical modeling and computing with Geographic Information System tools to understand the impact of cancer control interventions, and geographic or spatial-temporal, economic, social, behavioral, and other factors on the cancer burden.

Chapter 1
Crime and Public Health in the United States

Bill Sanders, Bethany Deeds, and Yonette F. Thomas

Abstract *The fields of criminal justice and public health intersect in various ways in the United States. Certain criminal behaviors, criminal and delinquent rehabilitation, and the fear of crime have public health implications to the extent they shape exposure to immediate and long-term negative health outcomes, overall access to health care, and intervention strategies towards high-risk populations. As such, the study of criminality and particular types of 'offenders' remain a concern for both criminal justice and public health researchers and policy makers. This introductory chapter first reviews certain 'intersections' of areas pertinent to the fields of criminal justice and public health, particularly substance use and violence, vulnerable populations, negative health outcomes and incarceration, and interventions that crossover both public health and criminal justice initiatives. From here, the chapter provides a brief overview of the four themes examined within the book: Incarceration and health risks; health risk behaviors among high-risk youth; crime, space, and health; and public health interventions towards traditional criminal justice populations.*

B. Sanders, Ph.D. (✉)
School of Criminal Justice and Criminalistics, California State University, Los Angeles, CA, USA
e-mail: bsander2@calstatele.edu

B. Deeds, Ph.D., M.A.
Division of Epidemiology, Services and Prevention Research, National Institute on Drug Abuse (NIDA), Bethesda, MD, USA

Y.F. Thomas, Ph.D.
Office of Regulatory Research Compliance, Howard University, Washington, DC, USA

B. Sanders et al. (eds.), *Crime, HIV and Health: Intersections of Criminal Justice and Public Health Concerns*, DOI 10.1007/978-90-481-8921-2_1,

1.1 Substance Use and Violence

Substance use and violence are significant criminal justice concerns in the United States, but also have importance within the public health community. For instance, the prevalence of substance use disorders among juvenile and adult offenders remain high (Chassin 2008; Johnson et al. 2004; Teplin et al. 2002), with substantial rates of co-morbid mental health disorders documented in a variety of studies (Abram et al. 2003; Regier et al. 1990; Rowe et al. 2004; Washburn et al. 2008). Concomitantly, substance use is associated with a host of morbidities in correctional populations, including infections like human immunodeficiency virus (HIV), Hepatitis B virus (HBV), and Hepatitis C virus (HCV) as well (Chandler et al. 2009; Rhodes et al. 2008; Weinbaum et al. 2005). Violence is also a leading cause of injury, disability and death in the United States, where the homicide and suicide rates are significantly higher than comparable Western countries (Centers for Disease Control and Prevention [CDC] 2010; Krug et al. 1998). Acts of violence, such as robbery, assault, and homicide, are very serious offences that carry strong community penalties.

Drug cases clog the judicial system and billions of dollars are spent on the 'war on drugs' on an annual basis (Bewley-Taylor et al. 2005). The significant incarceration increases in the United States during the past decades have been largely attributed to stricter penalties for drug-related crime (Chandler et al. 2009; Jensen et al. 2004). Violence and drugs also interact. For instance, data indicate that a large percentage of State (53%) and Federal (45%) prisoners met DSM-IV criteria for drug dependence or abuse and that one in four violent offenders committed their offense while using drugs and one in three property offenders indicated drug money as their motive (Mumola and Karberg 2006). A recent systematic literature review and meta-analysis of 30 studies reported that the odds of offending were three to four times greater for drug users than non-drug users for a variety of offences including burglary, robbery, shoplifting, and prostitution (Bennett et al. 2008). In working towards keeping communities 'safe' regarding drug-related and violent behaviors, criminal justice and public health share common ground.

1.2 Vulnerable Populations, Negative Health Outcomes, and Incarceration

Groups of high-risk populations, including young offenders, gang members, and the homeless, have elevated levels of substance use, violence perpetration and victimization, and involvement in other health risk behaviors, such as unsafe sexual practices. Studies have indicated that such populations are also exposed to the negative health outcomes associated with these behaviors, such as contact with sexually transmitted infections (e.g. HIV, HCV), addiction, symptoms of mental health disorders, overdose, injury, disability, and death (Abram et al. 2003, 2004; Belenko et al. 2009; Ennett et al. 1999; Teplin et al. 2005; Uman et al. 2006).

A prospective longitudinal study, the Northwestern Juvenile Project, which investigated the health needs and outcomes of delinquent youth, examined mortality rates among the 1,829 youth enrolled and found that the overall mortality rate of delinquent youth was four times greater than the general-population rate (Teplin et al. 2005). This mortality link was even stronger for cities where gang activity is high. In Los Angeles and Chicago, for instance, approximately 50% of homicides have been 'gang related' for over a decade (Egley et al. 2010). If gang members largely target and kill other gang members (Sanders 1994), then the victim of every other homicide in these two cities for more than 10 years has been a gang member. Gang membership is thus an indicator of an individual at an increased risk of premature violent death.

Also, and importantly, the distribution of young offenders, gang members, and the homeless is not even across society. Ethnic minority populations, particularly African Americans and Latinos/Hispanics, are disproportionately represented within such groups, further contributing to negative effects in their communities and families (Bagett et al. 2010; Teplin et al. 2005). In the Northwestern Juvenile Project African American male detained youth had the highest mortality rate reported at 887 deaths per 100,000 person-years (Teplin et al. 2005).

Furthermore, inmates generally experience poorer health than comparable, non-incarcerated adults. About nine million people are incarcerated around the world, of which approximately two million are in the United States. While the United States constitutes about 6% of the world's population, it contains approximately 22% of the world's prisoners. While prisons might serve to punish the guilty, they can also expose inmates to elevated health risks and exacerbate current health disorders. For instance, in comparison to the general population, prisoners have an increased exposure to deadly viral infections, such as HIV, HCV, and active tuberculosis (Greifinger 2006; Hammett 2006; Massoglia 2008; Okie 2007; Weinbaum et al. 2005). Moreover, prison inmates are at an increased risk of violent victimization, particularly sexual assault, whereby as many as one in five male prisoners reported being raped by other inmates (Mariner 2001).

Mental health disorders are also common among prisoners, with research indicating that more than half off all prisoners report symptoms of various conditions, some of which are very serious (James and Glaze 2006). Data from a national survey of jail inmates also indicated that recent homelessness was 7.5–11.3 times more common among jail inmates than in the general population (Greenberg and Rosenheck 2008) while another national prison study indicated that one in seven drug dependent or abusing inmates in State prison were homeless within a year before their entrance (Mumola and Karberg 2006). While incarceration is intended to deter or rehabilitate the guilty, an apparent side effect is that such institutions may, however inadvertently, decrease the quality of prisoners' overall immediate and future health prospects and produce negative social consequences for certain communities (i.e. family disorganization, unemployment; Freudenberg 2001; Golembeski and Fullilove 2005). Incarceration also disproportionately impacts ethnic minority populations, with African Americans about six times more likely as whites and Hispanic/Latinos about two times more likely as whites to experience incarceration during their lifetimes (Mauer and King 2007).

The sociologist Emile Durkheim (1895/1982) noted that crime is an inevitable part of all healthy societies. Certain forms of crime, however, such as gun violence, robbery, and substance abuse, and particular 'criminals', such as drug sellers, gang youth, and street walking prostitutes, are not distributed evenly across society. Rather, such individuals are often concentrated in certain sections, particularly urban, inner-city areas containing a high percentage of ethnic minority and/or immigrant populations. Within such areas, the fear of crime may be elevated to such an extent that everyday residents refuse to leave their homes for general purposes. Due to these seriously perceived threats, such residents may not engage in regular physical exercise, fail to go a physician's office for particular examinations, and have difficulty obtaining prescription medications. Fear of crime thus reduces neighborhood mobility to an extent that it may impact overall health or access to health care (Block et al. 2006; Crank et al. 2003; Ross and Mirowsky 2001). In a similar vein, residents who live in areas with high rates of crime and violence might also suffer from other negative health outcomes, such as high blood pressure and stress, in relation to their proximity to such behaviors (Block et al. 2006; Chap. 10 by Browning, Cagney and Iveniuk, this volume). Living around crime and disorder has negative consequences for an individual's physical and mental health.

1.3 Exploring Common Ground: Criminal Justice and Public Health

How does a public health approach towards crime differ from a criminal justice one? Researchers in the United States have moved forward with interventions on traditional criminal justice populations that are driven from a public health perspective. These interventions may include a multi-agency collaboration in which hospitals play a central role, a more concentrated focus on the prevention of risk behaviors, harm reduction (such as needle exchange programs), the implementation of programs that focus on behavioral change over time, and the adoption of treatment delivery systems in criminal justice settings (Chandler, Fletcher and Volkow 2009; Chap. 13 by Clark and Humphreys, this volume; Sanders et al. 2009; Taxman et al. 2009; Watters et al. 1994). This direction is in accordance with the current National Drug Control Strategy that focuses both on the public health and public safety aspects of drug use and addiction (Office of National Drug Control Policy 2010, 2011).

Public health approaches towards crime and delinquency cannot replace criminal and juvenile justice initiatives; law enforcement services are still needed to protect public safety. However, public health approaches could complement such initiatives by preventing high-risk individuals from entering the criminal justice system, reducing the reentry number of offenders, and linking vulnerable populations to needed treatments for drug abuse and HIV infection. In concert, public health and criminal justice programs may better accomplish mutual aims. Below, four themes covered in this book where the fields of criminal justice and public health intersect in the United Sates are briefly discussed: Incarceration; health risk behaviors among high-risk youth; crime, space, and health; and public health interventions towards traditional criminal justice populations.

1.3.1 Incarceration

Incarceration affects the health of prisoners in the United States in at least four ways: Contact with life-threatening infectious diseases; exposure to violence; lack of treatment for symptoms of mental health disorders; and years of life lost.

Prisoners in the United States are in contact with various infections during incarceration that affect their health. For instance, in 2007, 1.5% of prison inmates were HIV-positive or had confirmed AIDS; AIDS cases among prisoners are about two and a half times the estimated rate of the general population (Maruschak and Beavers 2009). Annually, estimates indicate that about 25% of all HIV-infected persons, 33% of HCV-infected persons, and 40% of those with active tuberculosis in the United States will spend time in a correctional facility (Okie 2007). It remains largely unclear, however, whether such infections are contracted while incarcerated or whether inmates become aware of them during incarceration (Hammett 2006). In addition, incarceration can disrupt stable sex partnerships, which can be protective against high-risk sex partnerships and increase STI/HIV risk. A recent study using the 2002 National Survey of Family Growth showed that incarceration among adult men resulted in disproportionate levels of concurrent partnerships and higher levels of unprotected sex, which were even more elevated for illicit drug users (Khan et al. 2009). Other harmful infections, such as HCV, tuberculosis and Methicillin-resistant *Staphylococcus aureus* (MRSA), have also been problematic in jails and prisons (Clark 2009; Parvez 2007; Weinbaum and Hennessey 2007). For instance, in California between 1999 and 2007, the largest increase of individuals with resistant strains of MRSA was attributable to patients admitted to hospitals from jails and prisons (Clark 2009).

Suicide and homicide are the third and fourth leading causes of death among inmates respectively and, in comparison to the general population, jail and prison inmates are significantly more likely to be a victim of either form of violence (Mumola 2005). Prisoners are at risk of others forms of violent victimization, such as rape. *No Escape*, a Human Rights Watch publication, indicated that around 20% of men within some state prisons had experienced coerced sexual occasions, and that shy, physically weak, and effeminate men are often the targets of prison rape (Mariner 2001). Research in California has estimated that thousands of male inmates have been sexually assaulted, and that such incidents were higher among transgendered individuals (Jenness et al. 2007). Qualitative accounts among prisoners about rape in prison – either committed by staff or fellow inmates – also indicate that 22% of men believed that at least one rape had occurred in an institution in which they were housed at one point during their lifetimes (Fleisher and Krienert 2006).

Symptoms of mental health disorders are a significant concern among incarcerated populations (Chap. 4 by Lawson and Lawson, this volume). Approximately three times as many seriously mentally ill people are in prison than in mental health hospitals, and the rate of serious mental health illness is between two and four times higher in prison when compared to the general population (Fellner 2006). Similar to infectious diseases, correctional facilities often serve as way stations where individuals first learn of their mental health symptoms (Hoge et al. 2009). While incarceration is often a traumatic experience for healthy individuals, it remains much more so for those with mental health illnesses (Hoge et al. 2009). Such mental health conditions are likely to be related to reasons why such inmates are incarcerated in the first place, and, moreover, the process of incarceration itself is likely to aggravate such conditions (Hoge et al. 2009). A United States Department of Justice report indicates that, as of June 2000, approximately 90% of State public and private correctional facilities offer mental health services to inmates (Beck and Maruschak 2001). However, proper clinically indicated treatment of serious mental health conditions among inmates may not always align with prison policies (Fellner 2006). In such cases, inmates with serious mental health conditions will fail to have their symptoms correctly addressed, leading not only to an exasperation of their condition, but also potentially lengthening their time at the correctional facility.

Years of life lost (YLL) or years of potential life lost are metrics used to determine the influence of harmful events upon populations, particularly as they affect younger individuals. In recent years, researchers have treated years incarcerated as 'lost life' in order to examine the impact of incarceration upon various populations, particular as they relate to ethnic minority communities (Drucker 2002; Hogg et al. 2008). For instance, Drucker (2002) examined the population impact of mass incarceration under New York's Rockefeller Drug Laws. In doing so, Drucker estimated that the life expectancy of those incarcerated for drug charges to be 68 years, several years less than those within the general population. By examining all of the inmates currently incarcerated under such laws, Drucker calculated that 325,000 person years have been spent incarcerated, which is equivalent to the 'deaths' of 9,848 people. Drucker concluded by indicating that YLL due to incarceration has similar impacts on particular populations as disease epidemics, wars, and terrorist attacks, but that drug law incarcerations have a disproportionate impact on ethnic minority communities, particularly African American males (Hogg et al. 2008; Williams 2007). Drucker (2002) expanded the YLL methodology to examine the impact of those incarcerated due to drug offences across the United States, and estimated that the incarceration of over half a million of such individuals equates to approximately 15,000 'deaths' annually and more than 200,000 'deaths' over the 30-year 'war on drugs' – approximately twice the number of service personal killed in the Korean and Vietnam wars.

1.3.2 Health Risk Behaviors Among High-Risk Youth

Three categories of high-risk youth that straddle the fields of criminal justice and public health are discussed here: Young offenders, gang youth, and the homeless.

Young people in the United States are responsible for a disproportionate amount of the nation's crime. While many youth 'age out' of crime as they enter adulthood, for others the committal of various offences remains an integral part of their lives (Laub and Sampson 1993). For these 'high risk' youth, elevated rates of recidivism and overall participation in crime often place them more firmly within the arms of the criminal justice system and further away from active roles in conventional society. Such young offenders have also reported other negative health outcomes that are often considered 'co-morbidities.' For instance, in comparison to their peers, young offenders have reported higher levels of symptoms of mental health disorders, higher rates of sexually transmitted infections, and higher rates of violent victimization (Abram et al. 2003, 2004; Belenko et al. 2009; Palmer and Farmer 2002; Rivara et al. 1995; Chap. 2 by Romero et al., this volume). A young adult polydrug user study in urban club settings found these higher levels in tandem – three-quarters of study participants met DSM-IV diagnostic criteria for substance dependence, over two-thirds reported emotional, physical or sexual victimization, and 40% reported being arrested at least once (Chap. 8 by Kurtz, this volume). Such outcomes may be a byproduct of participation in crime and delinquency, part of their etiology, or somewhere in between.

Gang members are one particular category of young offenders at an elevated risk for negative health outcomes. Strong evidence has suggested that gang youth, in comparison to their non-gang peers, are involved in significantly higher levels of crime, violence, and substance use (Battin-Pearson et al. 1998; Gordon et al. 2004; Hill et al. 1999). Additional research reports that gang youth are also likely to participate in risky sexual behaviors and have sexually transmitted infections, symptoms of mental health disorders, and injuries from violence victimization (Cepeda and Valdez 2003; Harper et al. 2008; MacDonald et al. 2007; Salazar et al. 2007; Voisin et al. 2004). Moreover, available epidemiological data on substance use among gang members indicates significantly higher levels than those reported in national youth sentinel data,[1] as well as injection drug use and drug addiction (De La Rosa et al. 2006; Mata et al. 2002). The combination of these negative health outcomes in relation to health risk behaviors (i.e. substance use, violence, unsafe sex) indicates gang youth also require public health-related services (Knox and Tromanhauser 1999; Sanders and Lankenau 2006; Chap. 6 by Sanders et al., this volume). As such, public health approaches towards gang youth could complement criminal justice efforts, with the idea that, together, such approaches could help better alleviate the gang activity.

Homelessness poses numerous health risks, including injuries from criminal and violent victimization (Fitzpatrick et al. 1993; Kipke et al. 1997). High rates of symptoms of mental health disorders are also evident among homeless populations, as well as problems with substance abuse, including addiction and exposure to HIV and HCV (Ennett et al. 1999; Folsom et al. 2005; Nyamathi et al. 2005). Mental

[1] e.g. Monitoring the Future; National Survey on Drug Use and Health; Youth Risk Behavioral Survey.

health disorders, in particular, appear to contribute to both prolonged episodes of homelessness, as well as further victimization while homeless (Perron et al. 2008). A report by the National Coalition for the Homeless & National Law Center on Homelessness and Poverty (2006) indicates that while homeless people are in need of help and care, homelessness has also been criminalized. The report discusses how, in many respects, simply being homeless is illegal; loitering, trespassing, begging, and public nuisance are law-breaking actions for which homeless people have been arrested and charged.

1.3.3 Crime, Health, and Space

Neighborhoods characterized by high crime and violence also expose those who live in such communities to greater health care risks. Some of these stem from the fear created by the elevated levels of crime and violence, such as a reluctance to visit health care professionals or increases in anxiety, stress and/or depression, which, in turn, lead to further detrimental health outcomes (Block et al. 2006; Chap. 10 by Browning, Cagney and Iveniuk, this volume; Ross and Mirowsky 2001). Furthermore, certain crimes are strongly related to one another, such as drug selling and violence, both of which significantly impact communities. Drug markets are also mobile, and when they move from one community to the next, they bring with them the problems associated with substance use and violence (Chap. 9 by Gruenewald et al., this volume). In all of these respects, crime, health, and space are interconnected.

As mentioned earlier, evidence suggests that people living in poorer neighborhoods in close proximity to disorder and crime may suffer from negative mental and physical health outcomes in direct relation to living such conditions. For instance, Kim (2010) reported that rates of symptoms of psychological distress, such as depression, were significantly linked to neighborhood disorder. Other studies have reported on how fear of crime contributes to health risks. For instance, a theoretical model offered by Ross and Mirowsky (2001) proposes the interrelationship between neighborhood disadvantage, disorder, fear and health. In this model, crime leads to fear, which leads to a lack of taking regular exercise, such as walking, which, in turn, leads to a decreased level of health (see Fig. 1.1).

Block et al. (2006) offer tentative support of this model in a report on how robbery was negatively associated with frequency of walking among men involved in an exercise program in Chicago. Moreover, Block et al (2006) presented data that indicated that reluctance among women to attend annual mammogram checkups, and thus receive less favorable reports when they do, may be related to an elevated fear of crime generated largely by high rates of violent offences in their neighborhoods. The compounding effects of stress brought on from high crime rates unnecessarily contribute to lower qualities of life among individuals already residing in marginalized communities.

Shifts in drug markets are related to shifts in the health risks a community is exposed to. For example, crack cocaine emergence within inner city areas in the

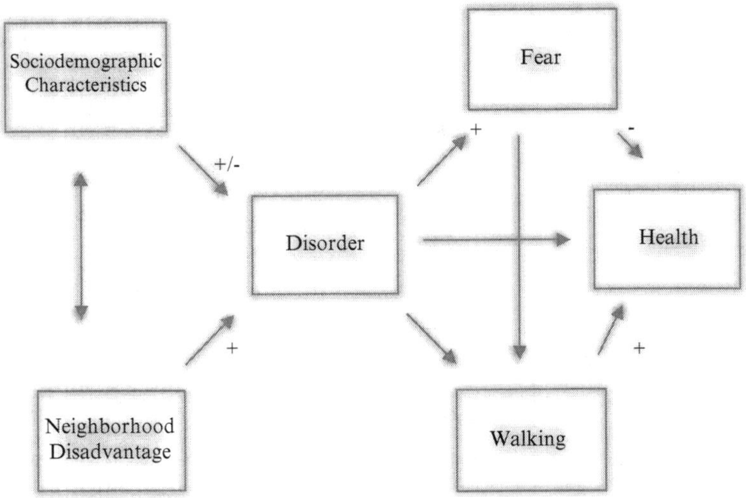

Fig. 1.1 Theoretical model of the processes by which neighborhood disadvantage affects health (Ross and Mirowsky 2001)

1980s, particularly those within ethnic minority communities, was associated with not only increases in assaults and deadly violence, but also increases in sexually transmitted infections, including HIV, addiction, and pregnancy-related complications, including the birth of children born addicted to crack cocaine (Watkins et al. 1998; Watkins and Fullilove 1999). A similar pattern of health risks emerged in relation to increases in use of crystal methamphetamine. In California, for instance, shifts in the location of crystal methamphetamine markets are significantly associated with increases in violence within those same geographic areas (Chap. 9 by Gruenewald et al., this volume). While crystal methamphetamine has long been found within Western states, as the drug moved. Eastward, so too did public health related problems. For instance, the local production of crystal methamphetamine can be a very dangerous endeavor, and when things go wrong the results can be powerful explosions that emit burning chemical compounds. When crystal methamphetamine markets reached the 'heartland' of the United States, the increase in victims of such explosions began to strain the annual budgets of local burn units (Jefferson 2005).

A focus on illicit substance use markets in relation to crime and disorder takes the spotlight off what is arguably the most commonly associated substance with such behaviors: alcohol. The consistent significant findings that associate alcohol consumption with a wide range of violent behaviors – assault, rape, intimate partner violence, and homicide – are strong evidence that this drug more than any others should be the focus on substance control policy. Moreover, studies have provided evidence for a potential affect of the density of alcohol availability outlets and the frequency of violent incidents, from common assaults to gang-related homicides to other forms of violence (Gruenewald and Remer 2006; Parker et al. 2007). In other words, the more places within an area that sell alcohol, the more violent incidents that are likely to occur in that same area. Alcohol is a strong indicator of violence potential, which is a reason that this substance remains an important concern for public health and criminal justice professionals.

1.3.4 Public Health Interventions and Criminal Justice Populations

Substance use is a risk behavior that has been discussed in each public health/criminal justice scenario presented, and work between the fields appears to have generated some promising results. Syringe exchange programs, whereby injection drug users (IDUs) are able to obtain free clean needles to replace their used ones, as well as clean injection paraphernalia, have been found to significantly reduce the sharing of needles and, consequently, the spread of HIV and HCV (Bluthenthal et al. 2000), particularly when a part of a comprehensive HIV prevention program. Opponents of such exchange programs, though, argue that they encourage more drug use and do not address core reasons associated with addiction (Christoffersen 2007).

In addition, state and federal prisons have increased treatment provision to drug-involved offenders, though the estimated need for treatment among this vulnerable population is still out-pacing the services provided. Current research emphasizes the use of evidence –based treatment approaches and aims to elucidate the effectiveness of both correctional and community based treatments for drug-abusing offenders and to better understand the organizational factors that integrate activities and improve service delivery (Grella et al. 2007; Lehman et al. 2009; Taxman et al. 2007). Furthermore, diversion programs for offenders arrested for drug-related charges, such as California's Proposition 36 – the Substance Abuse and Crime Prevention Act of 2000 are also being implemented and evaluated. This approach suggests that a treatment program in comparison to incarceration would contribute to reductions in recidivism for substance-related offences. Though this program has received mixed reviews due to a lack of funding, high dropout rates, and statewide increases in drug-related arrests (Urada et al. 2008), new research findings are suggesting methods for optimizing the effectiveness (Evans et al. 2012).

Public health approaches have also targeted violence and specifically gang violence. Findings from the Chicago-based *Ceasefire* program, for instance, report positive results. *Ceasefire*, created by epidemiologist Gary Slutkin, was informed by his research on tuberculosis and AIDS conducted in Africa and other countries. The program utilized community mobilization approaches – galvanizing local participation from youth groups, community-based organizations, faith based organizations, and public services – in conjunction with public education campaigns and trained street-level out-reach workers which made significant reductions in violent crimes in the Chicago area (Ritter 2009; Skogan et al. 2009). Another violence intervention effort in Boston, called *Operation Ceasefire* (not related to the Chicago example) also showed positive results, but its approach centered more on firearm trafficking and the use of video surveillance by law enforcement (Braga et al. 2001; Braga and Pierce 2005).

Interventions aimed at reducing one risk behavior may also be relevant to the reduction of other risk behaviors and/or the encouragement of pro-social activities. Project AIM (Adult Identity Monitoring), is one such program (Chap. 13 by Clark and Humphreys, this volume). Project AIM was developed to target risky sexual behaviors among middle school students. While results indicated that it accomplished this task, the intervention was also related to reductions in violent behaviors and increases in school attendance and other positive activities (Clark et al. 2005). Due to its success, Project AIM has also been applied to reduce substance use among high school students, risk behaviors among transgender youths, and crime, violence, and substance use among gang members (see Chap. 13 by Clark and Humphreys, this volume).

Project AIM follows a tradition of public health-initiated interventions that have also been shown to reduce levels of offending and participation in high-risk behaviors. For instance, in the late 1970s David Olds, a pediatrician, developed an idea to intervene in the lives of poor teenage mothers by having nurses provide in-home counseling on the proper care of their children during the first few difficult years. Years later, evidence indicated that these children not only had lower rates of sickness, but they also had lower rates of offending and participation in the juvenile justice system, as well as lower levels of substance use compared to similar children who did not receive services (Kitzman et al. 2010; Olds et al. 1998). The intervention, Nurse-Family Partnership (NFP), capitalizes on the often-touted idea that 'prevention is the best cure', or, in other words, that the best way to intervene in the lives of high risk youth is to prevent them from becoming high risk in the first place. Though NFP is now operating in over half of all states in the US and receives millions of dollars in Federal funding each year, questions still remain regarding how to scale up the program (Kleinman 2009).

The material presented in this introductory chapter has covered a range of topics where the fields of public health and criminal justice intersect. Much collaboration has existed between these fields for many years, and, at times, antagonism exists as to which are the most appropriate approaches to pursue. Are substance users best suited to be placed in treatment programs or should they be institutionalized for lengthy terms? Are gang members a public health concern or liability to society? Should rehabilitation be based on corrections or care? In collaboration, criminal justice and public health professionals can work together to help effectively resolve these issues that are pertinent to both their respective fields. More research at the intersection of criminal justice and public health concerns is imperative to reduce violence and improve health outcomes for vulnerable populations.

References

Abram, K. M., Teplin, L. A., McClelland, G. M., & Dulcan, M. K. (2003). Comorbid psychiatric disorders in youth in juvenile detention. *Archives of General Psychiatry, 60*(11), 1097–1108.

Abram, K. M., Teplin, L. A., Charles, D. R., Longworth, S. L., McClelland, G. M., & Dulcan, M. K. (2004). Postraumatic stress disorder and trauma in youth in juvenile detention. *Archives of General Psychiatry, 61*, 403–410.

Bagett, T. P., O'Connell, J. J., Singer, D. E., & Rigotti, N. A. (2010). The unmet health care needs of homeless adults: A national study. *American Journal of Public Health, 100*(7), 1326–1333.

Battin-Pearson, S. R., Thornberry, T. P., Hawkins, J. D., & Krohn, M. D. (1998). *Gang membership, delinquent peers, and delinquent behavior*. Washington, DC: Office of Juvenile Justice and Delinquency Prevention.

Beck, A. L., & Maruschak, L. M. (2001). *Mental health treatment in state prisons, 2000*. Washington, DC: Bureau of Justice Statistics.

Belenko, S., Dembo, R., Rollie, M., Childs, K., & Salvatore, C. (2009). Detecting, preventing, and treating sexually transmitted diseases among adolescent arrestees: An unmet public health need. *American Journal of Public Health, 99*(6), 1032–1041.

Bennett, T., Holloway, K., & Farrington, D. (2008). The statistical association between drug misuse and crime: A meta-analysis. *Aggression and Violent Behavior, 13*(2), 107–118.

Bewley-Taylor, D., Trace, M., & Stevens, A. (2005). *Incarcerations of drug offenders: Costs and impacts: Briefing Paper No 7*. Oxford: The Beckley Foundation Drug.

Block, R. L., Gehlert, S., Masi, C., Tarlov, E., & Zenk, S. (2006, October 31–November 4) *Community crime, environment and individual health*. Presented at the American Society of Criminology Annual Meeting, Los Angeles, CA.

Bluthenthal, R. N., Kral, A. H., Gee, L., Erringer, E. A., & Edlin, B. R. (2000). The effect of syringe exchange use on high-risk injection drug users: A cohort study. *AIDS, 14*(5), 605–611.

Braga, A. A., & Pierce, G. L. (2005). Disrupting illegal firearms markets in Boston: The effects of Operation Ceasefire on the supply of new handguns to criminals. *Criminology & Public Policy, 4*, 717–749.

Braga, A. A., Kennedy, D. M., Waring, E. J., & Piehl, A. M. (2001). Problem-oriented policing, deterrence, and youth violence: An evaluation of Boston's Operation Ceasefire. *Journal of Research in Crime and Delinquency, 38*, 195–225.

Centers for Disease Control and Prevention (CDC). (2010). *Youth violence*. Retrieved from http://www.cdc.gov/ViolencePrevention/pdf/yv-datasheet-a.pdf

Cepeda, A., & Valdez, A. (2003). Risk behaviors among young Mexican American gang-associated females: Sexual relations, partying, substance use, and crime. *Journal of Adolescent Research, 18*(1), 90–107.

Chandler, R. K., Bennett, F. W., & Volkow, N. D. (2009). Treating drug abuse and addiction in the criminal justice system: Improving public health and safety. *Journal of the American Medical Association, 301*(2), 183–190.

Chassin, L. (2008). Juvenile justice and substance. *The Future of Children, 18*(2), 143–164.

Christoffersen, J. (2007, March 11). Needle exchange programs struggle with funding despite positive studies. *USA Today*. Retrieved from http://www.usatoday.com/news/health/2007-03-11-needleexchange_N.htm

Clark, C. L. (2009, December 16). MRSA cases in California skyrocket. *Health Leaders Media*. Retrieved from http://www.healthleadersmedia.com/print/COM-243619/MRSA-Cases-in-California-Skyrocket

Clark, L. F., Miller, K. S., Nagy, S. S, Avery, J., Roth, D. L., Liddon, N., & Mukherjee, S. (2005). Adult identity mentoring: Reducing sexual risk for African-American seventh grade students. *Journal of Adolescent Health, 37*(4), 337.e1–337.e10.

Crank, J. P., Giaconmazzi, A., & Heck, C. (2003). Fear of crime in a nonurban setting. *Journal of Criminal Justice, 31*, 249–263.

De La Rosa, M., Rugh, D., & Rice, C. (2006). An analysis of risk domains associated with drug transitions of active Latino gang members. *Journal of Addictive Diseases, 25*(4), 81–90.

Drucker, E. (2002). Population impact of mass incarceration under New York's Rockefeller drug laws: An analysis of years of life lost. *Journal of Urban Health, 79*(3), 1–10.

Durkheim, E (1982 [1895]). *The rules of the sociological method* (W. D. Halls, Trans.). New York: The Free Press

Egley, A., Jr., Howell, J. C., & Moore, J. P. (2010). *Highlights of the 2008 National Youth Gang Survey*. Washington, DC: Office of Juvenile Justice and Delinquency Prevention.

Ennett, S. T., Bailey, S. L., & Federman, E. B. (1999). Social network characteristics associated with risky behaviors among runaway and homeless youth. *Journal of Health and Social Behavior, 40*(1), 63–78.

Evans, E., Jaffe, A., Urada, D., & Anglin, M. D. (2012). Differential outcomes of court-supervised substance abuse treatment among California parolees and probationers. *International Journal of Offender Therapy and Comparative Criminology, 56*, 539–556.

Fellner, J. (2006). A corrections quandary: Mental illness and prison rules. *Harvard Civil Rights-Civil Liberties Law Review, 41*, 391–412.

Fitzpatrick, K. M., La Gory, M. E., & Ritchey, F. J. (1993). Criminal victimization among the homeless. *Justice Quarterly, 10*(3), 353–368.

Fleisher, M. S., & Krienert, J. L. (2006). *The culture of prison sexual violence*. Washington, DC: National Institute of Justice.

Folsom, D. P., Hawthorne, W., Lindamer, L., Gilmer, T., Bailey, A., Golshan, S., Garcia, P., Unutzer, J., Hough, R., & Jeste, D. V. (2005). Prevalence and risk factors for homeless and utilization of mental health services among 10, 340 patients with serious mental illness in a large public mental health system. *American Journal of Psychiatry, 162*, 370–376.

Freudenberg, N. (2001). Jails, prisons, and the health of urban populations: A review of the impact of the correctional system on community health. *Journal of Urban Health, 78*, 214–235.

Golembeski, C., & Fullilove, R. (2005). Criminal (in)justice in the city and its associated health consequences. *American Journal of Public Health, 95*, 1701–1706.

Gordon, R. A., Lahey, B. B., Kawai, E., Loeber, R., Stouthamer-Loeber, M., & Farrington, D. P. (2004). Antisocial behaviors and youth gang membership: Selection and socialization. *Criminology, 42*(1), 55–87.

Greenberg, G. A., & Rosenheck, R. A. (2008). Jail incarceration, homelessness, and mental health: A national study. *Psychiatric Services, 59*, 170–177.

Greifinger, R. B. (2006). Inmates as public health sentinels. *Washington University Journal of Law and Policy, 22*, 253–264.

Grella, C. E., Greenwell, L., Prendergast, M., Farabee, D., Hall, D., Cartier, J., & Burdon, W. (2007). Organizational characteristics of drug abuse treatment programs for offenders. *Journal of Substance Abuse Treatment, 32*(3), 291–300.

Gruenewald, P. J., & Remer, L. (2006). Changes in outlet densities affect violence rates. *Alcoholism: Clinical & Experimental Research, 30*, 1184–1193.

Hammett, T. (2006). HIV in prison: Editorial introduction. *Criminology & Public Policy, 5*(1), 109–112.

Harper, G. W., Davidson, J., & Hosek, S. G. (2008). Influence of gang membership on negative affects, substance use, and antisocial behavior among homeless African American male youth. *American Journal of Men's Health, 2*, 229–243.

Hill, K. G., Howell, J. C., Hawkins, J. D., & Battin-Pearson, S. R. (1999). Childhood risk factors for adolescent gang membership: Results from the Seattle Social Development Project. *Journal of Research in Crime and Delinquency, 36*, 300–322.

Hoge, S. K., Buchanan, A. W., Kovasznay, B. M. & Roskes, E. J. (2009). *Outpatient services for the mentally ill involved in the criminal justice system*. A report of the task force on outpatient forensic services. American Psychiatric Association. October, Retrieved from http://www.law.uchicago.edu/files/file/outpatient-crimjustice.pdf

Hogg, R. S., Druyts, E. F., Burris, S., Drucker, E., & Strathdee, S. A. (2008). Years of life lost to prison: Racial and gender gradients in the United States of America. *Harm Reduction Journal, 5*(4), 1–5.

James, D. J., & Glaze, L. E. (2006). *Mental health problems of prison and jail inmates*. Washington, DC: Department of Justice.

Jefferson, D. J. (2005, August 8). Meth: America's most dangerous drug. *Newsweek*. Retrieved from http://www.newsweek.com/2005/08/08/america-s-most-dangerous-drug.html

Jenness, V., Maxson, C. L., Matsuda, K. N., & Sumner, J. M. (2007). *Violence in California correctional facilities: An empirical examination of sexual assault*. Irvine: University of California, Irvine, Center for Evidence-Based Corrections.

Jensen, E. L., Gerber, J., & Mosher, C. (2004). Social consequences of the war on drugs: The legacy of failed policy. *Criminal Justice Policy Review, 5*(1), 100–121.

Johnson, T., Cho, Y. I., Fendrich, M., Graf, I., Kelly-Wilson, L., & Pickup, L. (2004). Treatment need and utilization among youth entering the juvenile corrections system. *Journal of Substance Abuse Treatment, 26*(3), 117–128.

Khan, M., Doherty, I., Schoenbach, V., Taylor, E., Epperson, M., & Adimora, A. (2009). Incarceration and high-risk sexual partnerships among men in the United States. *Journal of Urban Health, 86*(4), 584–601.

Kim, J. (2010). Neighborhood disadvantage and mental health: The role of neighborhood disorder and social relationships. *Social Science & Medicine, 3*(2), 260–271.

Kipke, M., Simon, T., Montgomery, S., Unger, J., & Iversen, E. (1997). Homeless youth and their exposure to and involvement in violence while living on the streets. *Journal of Adolescent Health, 20*(5), 360–367.

Kitzman, H. J., Olds, D. L., Cole, R. E., Hanks, C. A., Anson, E. A., Arcoleo, K. J., Luckey, D. W., Knudtson, M. D., Henderson, C. R., Jr., & Holmberg, J. R. (2010). Enduring effects of prenatal and infancy home visiting by nurses on children. *Archives of Pediatric Adolescent Medicine, 164*(5), 412–418.

Kleinman, M. A. R. (2009, September 12). How health care reform could combat crime. *Newsweek*. Retrieved from http://www.newsweek.com/2009/09/11/how-health-care-reform-could-combat-crime.html

Knox, G. W., & Tromanhauser, E. D. (1999). Juvenile gang members: A public health perspective. *The Journal of Gang Research, 6*(3), 49–60.

Krug, E. G., Powell, K. E., & Dahlberg, L. L. (1998). Firearm-related deaths in the United States and 35 other high-and upper-middle-income countries. *International Journal of Epidemiology, 27*, 214–221.

Laub, J. H., & Sampson, R. J. (1993). Turning points in the life course. Why change matters to the study of crime. *Criminology, 31*(3), 301–325.

Lehman, W. E., Fletcher, B. W., Wexler, H. K., & Melnick, G. (2009). Organizational factors and collaboration and integration activities in criminal justice and drug abuse treatment agencies. *Drug and Alcohol Dependence, 103S*, S65–S72.

MacDonald, J., Ridgeway, G., Gover, A. R., & Jennings, W. G. (2007). *Assessing the effects of gang membership on victimization using doubly robust propensity score modeling*. Retrieved from http://www.crim.upenn.edu/faculty/papers/macdonald/Gang%20Membership%20and%20Victimization.pdf

Mariner, J. (2001). *No escape: Male rape in prisons*. New York: Human Rights Watch.

Maruschak, L. M., & Beavers, R. (2009). *HIV in prisons, 2007–08*. Washington, DC: Department of Justice.

Massoglia, M. (2008). Incarceration as exposure: The prison, infectious disease, and other stress-related illnesses. *Journal of Health and Social Behavior, 49*, 56–71.

Mata, A., Valdez, A., Alvarado, J., Cepeda, A., Cervantes, R., & Kaplan, C. D. (2002). Drug related violence among Mexican American youth in Laredo, Texas: Preliminary findings. *Free Inquiry in Creative Sociology, 30*, 25–39.

Mauer, M., & King, R. S. (2007) *Uneven justice: State rates of incarceration by race an ethnicity*. Available at http://www.sentencingproject.org/doc/publications/rd_stateratesofincbyraceandethnicity.pdf

Mumola, C. (2005). *Suicide and homicide in state prisons and local jails*. Washington, DC: Bureau of Justice Statistics.

Mumola, C. J., & Karberg, J. C. (2006). *Drug use and dependence, state and federal prisoners, 2004*. Washington, DC: Bureau of Justice Statistics.

National Coalition for the Homeless and the National Law Center on Homelessness and Poverty. (2006). *A dream denied: The criminalization of homelessness in U.S. cities*. Retrieved from http://www.nlchp.org/content/pubs/ADreamDenied1-11-06.pdf

Nyamathi, A. M., Christiani, A., Windokun, F., Jones, T., Strehlow, A., & Shoptaw, S. (2005). Hepatitis C virus infection, substance use and mental illness among homeless youth: A review. *AIDS, 19*, S34–S40.

Office of National Drug Control Policy. (2010). *National drug control strategy*. Washington, DC: Executive Office of the President of the United States. Retrieved from http://www.whitehouse.gov/sites/default/files/ondcp/policy-and-research/ndcs2010.pdf

Office of National Drug Control Policy. (2011). *National drug control strategy*. Washington, DC: Executive Office of the President of the United States. Retrieved from http://www.whitehouse.gov/sites/default/files/ondcp/ndcs2011.pdf

Okie, S. (2007). Sex, drugs, prisons, and HIV. *The New England Journal of Medicine, 356*(2), 105–108.

Olds, D., Henderson, C. R., Jr., Cole, R., Eckenrode, J., Kitzman, H., Luckey, D., Pettitt, L., Sidora, K., Morris, P., & Powers, J. (1998). Long-term effects of nurse visitation on children's criminal and antisocial behavior: Fifteen-year follow-up of a randomized controlled trial. *Journal of the American Medical Association, 280*, 1238–1244.

Palmer, E. J., & Farmer, S. (2002). Victimizing behaviour among juvenile and young offenders: How different are perpetrators? *Journal of Adolescence, 25*(5), 469–481.

Parker, R. N., Luther, K., & Murphy, L. (2007). Availability, gang violence and alcohol policy: Gaining support for alcohol regulation via harm reduction strategies. *Contemporary Drug Problems, 34*, 611–634.

Parvez, F. M. (2007). Prevention and control of tuberculosis in correctional facilities. In R. Greifinger (Ed.), *Public health behind bars* (pp. 174–211). New York: Springer.

Perron, B. E., Alexander-Eitzman, B., Gillespie, D. F., & Pollio, D. (2008). Modeling the mental health effects of victimization among homeless persons. *Social Science & Medicine, 67*, 1475–1479.

Regier, D. A., Farmer, M. E., Rea, D. S., Locke, B. Z., Keith, S. J., Judd, L. J., & Goodwin, F. K. (1990). Comorbidity of mental disorders with alcohol and other drug abuse: Results from the Epidemiologic Catchment Area (ECA) study. *Journal of the American Medical Association, 264*(19), 2511–2518.

Rhodes, A. G., Taxman, F. S., Friedmann, P. D., & Cropsey, K. L. (2008). HCV in incarcerated populations: An analysis of gender and criminality on risk. *Journal of Psychoactive Drugs, 40*(4), 493–501.

Ritter, N. (2009). CeaseFire: A public health approach to reduce shootings and killings. *National Institute of Justice Journal, 264*, 20–25.

Rivara, F. P., Shepherd, J. P., Farrington, D. P., Richmond, P. W., & Cannon, P. (1995). Victim as offender in youth violence. *Annuals of Emergency Medicine, 26*(5), 609–614.

Ross, C. E., & Mirowsky, J. (2001). Neighborhood disadvantage, disorder and health. *Journal of Health and Social Behavior, 42*, 258–276.

Rowe, C., Liddle, H. A., Greenbaum, P. E., & Henderson, C. E. (2004). Impact of psychiatric comorbidity on treatment of adolescent drug abusers. *Journal of Substance Abuse Treatment, 26*(2), 129–140.

Salazar, L. F., Crosby, R. A., DiClemente, R. J., Wingood, G. M., Rose, E., Sales, J. M., & Caliendo, A. M. (2007). Personal, relational, and peer-level risk factors for laboratory confirmed STD prevalence among low-income African American adolescent families. *Sexually Transmitted Diseases, 334*(10), 761–766.

Sanders, W. B. (1994). *Gangbangs and drive-bys: Grounded culture and juvenile gang violence*. New York: Aldine de Gruyter.

Sanders, B., & Lankenau, S. E. (2006). A public health model for studying gangs. In J. J. Short & L. A. Hughes (Eds.), *Studying youth gangs* (pp. 117–128). Lanham: Altamira Press.

Sanders, B., Schneiderman, J. U., Loken, A., Lankenau, S. E., & Jackson Bloom, J. (2009). Gang youth as a vulnerable population for nursing intervention. *Public Health Nursing, 26*(4), 346–352.

Skogan, W. G., Hartnett, S. M., Bump, N., & Dubois, J. (2009). *Evaluation of ceasefire-Chicago*. Washington, DC: National Institute of Justice.

Taxman, F. S., Perdoni, M. L., & Harrison, L. D. (2007). Drug treatment services for adult offenders: The state of the state. *Journal of Substance Abuse Treatment, 32*(3), 239–254.

Taxman, F. S., Henderson, C. E., & Belenko, S. (2009). Organizational context, systems change, and adopting treatment delivery systems in the criminal justice system. *Drug and Alcohol Dependence, 103*(1), S1–S6.

Teplin, L. A., Abram, K. M., McClelland, G. M., Dulcan, M. K., & Mericle, A. A. (2002). Psychiatric disorders in youth in juvenile detention. *Archives of General Psychiatry, 59*, 1133–1143.

Teplin, L. A., McClelland, G. M., Abram, K. M., & Mileusnic, D. (2005). Early violent death among delinquent youth: A prospective longitudinal study. *Pediatrics, 115*, 1586–1593.

Uman, G. C., Urman, H. N., Malloy, C. L., Martinez, B., & DeMorst, L. (2006). *Pilot study on HIV among gang members*. Los Angeles: City of Los Angeles AIDS Coordinator's Office.

Urada, D., Hawken, A., Conner, B. T., Evans, E., Anglin, M. D., Yang, J., Teruya, C., Herbeck, D., Fan, J., Rutkowski, B., Gonzales, R., Rawson, R., Grella, C., Prendergast, M., Hser, Y.-I., Hunter, J., & Poe, A. (2008). *Evaluation of proposition 36: The Substance Abuse and Crime Prevention Act of 2000: 2008 report*. Los Angeles: University of California, Los Angeles, Integrated Substance Abuse Programs.

Voisin, D. R., Salazar, L. F., Crosby, R., DiClemente, R. J., Yarber, W. L., & Staples-Horne, M. (2004). The association between gang involvement and sexual behaviours among detained adolescent males. *Sexually Transmitted Infections, 80*, 440–442.

Washburn, J. J., Teplin, L. A., Voss, L. S., Simon, C. D., Abram, K. M., & McClelland, G. M. (2008). Psychiatric disorders among detained youths: A comparison of youths processed in juvenile court and adult criminal court. *Psychiatry Services, 59*, 965–973.

Watkins, B. X., & Fullilove, M. T. (1999). Crack cocaine and Harlem's health. *Souls: A Critical Journal of Black Politics, Culture, and Society, 1*(1), 1548–3843.

Watkins, B. X., Fullilove, R. E., & Fullilove, M. T. (1998). Arms against illness: Crack cocaine and drug policy in the United States. *Health and Human Rights, 2*(4), 43–58.

Watters, J. K., Estilo, M. J., Clark, G. L., & Lorvick, J. (1994). Syringe and needle exchange as HIV/AIDS prevention for injection drug users. *Journal of the American Medical Association, 271*, 115–120.

Weinbaum, C., & Hennessey, K. A. (2007). Prevention of viral hepatitis. In R. Greifinger (Ed.), *Public health behind bars* (pp. 127–155). New York: Springer.

Weinbaum, C. M., Sabin, K. M., & Santibanez, S. S. (2005). Hepatitis B, hepatitis C, and HIV in correctional populations: A review of epidemiology and prevention. *AIDS, 19*(3), S41–S46.

Williams, N. H. (2007). *Where are the men? The impact of incarceration and reentry on African-American men and their children and families*. Atlanta: Morehouse University, National Center for Primary Center.

Part I
The Health of Incarcerated Populations

Chapter 2
A Longitudinal Study of the Prevalence, Development, and Persistence of HIV/STI Risk Behaviors in Delinquent Youth: Implications for Health Care in the Community

Erin Gregory Romero, Linda A. Teplin, Gary M. McClelland, Karen M. Abram, Leah J. Welty, and Jason J. Washburn

Abstract *Our goal was to examine the prevalence, development, and persistence of drug and sex risk behaviors that place delinquent youth at risk for HIV and other sexually transmitted infections. At the baseline interview, HIV/sexually transmitted infection drug and sex risk behaviors were assessed in a stratified random sample*

This work was supported by National Institute of Mental Health grants R01MH54197 and R01MH59463 (Division of Services and Intervention Research and Center for Mental Health Research on AIDS) and Office of Juvenile Justice and Delinquency Prevention grants 1999-JE-FX-1001 and 2005-JL-FX-0288. Major funding was also provided by the National Institute on Drug Abuse, the Substance Abuse and Mental Health Services Administration (Center for Mental Health Services, Center for Substance Abuse Prevention, and Center for Substance Abuse Treatment), the National Institutes of Health Center on Minority Health and Health Disparities, the Centers for Disease Control and Prevention (National Center on Injury Prevention and Control and National Center for HIV, STD and TB Prevention), the National Institute on Alcohol Abuse and Alcoholism, the National Institutes of Health Office of Research on Women's Health, the National

E.G. Romero, Ph.D.
Trauma Recovery Program, Veterans Administration Maryland Health Care System (VAMHC), Baltimore, MD, USA

L.A. Teplin, Ph.D. (✉) • G.M. McClelland • K.M. Abram, Ph.D.
Department of Psychiatry and Behavioral Sciences, Feinberg School of Medicine, Northwestern University, 710 N. Lakeshore Drive, Suite 900, Chicago, IL 60611, USA
e-mail: healthdisparities@northwestern.edu

L.J. Welty, Ph.D.
Department of Preventive Medicine, Feinberg School of Medicine, Northwestern University, Chicago, IL, USA

J.J. Washburn, Ph.D.
Division of Psychology, Feinberg School of Medicine, Northwestern University, Chicago, IL, USA

B. Sanders et al. (eds.), *Crime, HIV and Health: Intersections of Criminal Justice and Public Health Concerns*, DOI 10.1007/978-90-481-8921-2_2,
Reproduced with permission from Pediatrics, Vol. 119, Pages e1126-e1141

of 800 juvenile detainees aged 10–18 years. Participants were re-interviewed approximately 3 years later. The final sample in these analyses (n = 724) included 316 females and 408 males; there were 393 African American participants, 198 Hispanic participants, 131 non-Hispanic white participants, and two participants who self-identified their race as "other." More than 60% of youth had engaged in ≥10 risk behaviors at their baseline interview, and nearly two thirds of them persisted in ≥10 risk behaviors at follow-up. Among youth living in the community, many behaviors were more prevalent at follow-up than at baseline. Among incarcerated youth, the opposite pattern prevailed. Compared with females, males had higher prevalence rates of many HIV/sexually transmitted infection risk behaviors and were more likely to persist in some behaviors and develop new ones. Yet, injection risk behaviors were more prevalent among females than males and were also more likely to develop and persist. Overall, there were few racial and ethnic differences in patterns of HIV/sexually transmitted infection risk behaviors; most involved the initiation and persistence of substance use among non-Hispanic whites and Hispanics. Because detained youth have a median stay of only 2 weeks, HIV/sexually transmitted infection risk behaviors in delinquent youth are a community public health problem, not just a problem for the juvenile justice system. Improving the coordination among systems that provide HIV/sexually transmitted infection interventions to youth – primary care, education, mental health, and juvenile justice – can reduce the prevalence of risk behaviors and substantially reduce the spread of HIV/sexually transmitted infection in young people.

Adolescents and young adults are disproportionately affected by HIV and other sexually transmitted infections (STIs). Youth aged 15–24 years old represent approximately 25% of sexual active persons in the United States but accounted for nearly 50% of new STI cases (9.1 million) in 2000 (Weinstock et al. 2004). Between

Institutes of Health Office on Rare Diseases, Department of Labor, the William T. Grant Foundation, and the Robert Wood Johnson Foundation. Additional funds were provided by the John D. and Catherine T. MacArthur Foundation, the Open Society Institute, and the Chicago Community Trust. We thank all of our agencies for their collaborative spirit and steadfast support.

Many more people than the authors contributed to this project. This study could not have been accomplished without the advice of Ann Hohmann, PhD, Kimberly Hoagwood, PhD, Heather Ringeisen, PhD, and Eugene Griffin, PhD. Jacques Normand, PhD, Helen Cesari, MS, Richard Needle, PhD, Robert Booth, PhD, David Huizinga, PhD, and David Ostrow, MD, PhD, generously offered their expertise in developing our instruments. David Stoff, PhD, Grayson Norquist, MD, and Delores Parron, PhD, provided support and encouragement. Celia Fisher, PhD, guided our human subject procedures. We thank Frank Palella, Jr, MD, and the anonymous reviewers for their many helpful comments. We also thank all of the project staff, especially Amy Mericle, PhD, for instrumentation development and project leadership and Lynda Carey, MA, for her superb data management. We thank Kate Elkington, PhD, for literature review. We also greatly appreciate the cooperation of everyone working in the Cook County and State of Illinois systems. Without their cooperation, this study would not have been possible. Finally, we thank the participants for their time and willingness to participate and our field interviewers for their commitment to excellence.

2001 and 2005, HIV/AIDS diagnoses increased more than 20% in persons aged 13–24 years old (Centers for Disease Control and Prevention (CDC) 2006a). Advances for treating AIDS have slowed mortality (CDC 2006b; Kochanek et al. 2004). Still, among persons aged 25–34 years, HIV is the sixth leading cause of death among non-Hispanic whites and Hispanics, the third leading cause of death among African Americans, and the leading cause of death in African American women (Anderson et al. 2005).

HIV/AIDS and other STIs are increasingly diseases of racial/ethnic minorities and youth (CDC 2006b, c). The National Longitudinal Study of Adolescent Health, which sampled more than13 000 young adults, found that the rate of HIV infection in African Americans was 4.9 cases per 1,000 persons, compared with 0.22 cases per 1,000 in other racial/ethnic groups (CDC 2005a; Morris et al. 2006). The most recent statistics compiled by the CDC indicate that more than three quarters of persons younger than 25 years diagnosed with HIV/AIDS are African American or Hispanic (CDC 2006d). Young minority females are at particular risk. African American and Hispanic females account for approximately 80% of HIV/AIDS diagnoses in females aged 13–24 years old (CDC 2006d). Minorities have greater exposure to risk factors than do other groups, including low socioeconomic status, urban living, substance abuse, and limited access to health care (Fisher et al. 2002; Jemmott et al. 1992; Kaiser Family Foundation 2006a, b; Karon et al. 2001).

Minorities are also overrepresented in the juvenile justice system, where HIV/STI risk behaviors are prevalent (Canterbury et al. 1995; DiClemente et al. 1991; Magura et al. 1994; Morris et al. 1995; Snyder and Sickmund 2006; Teplin et al. 2002). Detained youth report more risk behaviors and initiate them at younger ages than do youth in the community (Teplin et al. 2003). Detained youth are likely to be at continued risk for HIV infection as they age. Adults in prison have higher rates of HIV/STI risk behaviors (Hammett and Daugherty 1991; Horsburgh et al. 1990; Magura et al. 1993; Mahon 1996; McClelland et al. 2002) and HIV infection (1.8%) than the general population (0.2%; Maruschak 2006). Sound public policy and effective interventions require data on the developmental course of HIV/STI risk behaviors. Because youth are detained for an average of only 2 weeks (Snyder and Sickmund 2006), their behaviors place persons in the community at risk.

There are, however, few comprehensive studies of HIV/STI risk behaviors in delinquent youth (Canterbury et al. 1995, 1998; Catania et al. 1990; Devieux et al. 2002; Kingree and Phan 2001; Lucenko et al. 2003; Magura et al. 1994; Otto-Salaj et al. 2002; Rolf et al. 1990; Teplin et al. 2003), and, to our knowledge, no longitudinal studies. Even after expanding our literature review to include "high-risk" youth, such as inner city youth and other impoverished populations, we found only four epidemiological studies with follow-up periods greater than 6 months (Brook et al. 2004; Capaldi et al. 2002; Katz et al. 2001; Stiffman et al. 1995). Only one of these studies collected comprehensive information on HIV/STI sex and drug risk behaviors (Stiffman et al. 1995). None of these studies investigated how the development and persistence of HIV/STI risk behaviors differ by gender, race/ethnicity, and age (Brook et al. 2004; Capaldi et al. 2002; Katz et al. 2001; Stiffman et al. 1995).

To our knowledge, this is the first large-scale longitudinal study of HIV/STI risk behaviors in delinquent youth. Our study has two methodological strengths: a stratified random sample, large enough ($n = 724$) to generate reliable rates of HIV/STI risk behaviors for key demographic subgroups (e.g., females and Hispanics) and comprehensive measures of HIV/STI drug and sex risk behaviors.

In this article, we address three questions:

- Prevalence: among youth in the sample, what proportion reported each HIV/STI behavior?
- Development: among youth who did not report a specific HIV/STI behavior at baseline, what proportion reported that behavior at follow-up?
- Persistence: among youth who did report a specific HIV/STI behavior at baseline, what proportion persisted in that behavior at follow-up?

We examine differences according to incarceration status and demographic variables (gender, race/ethnicity, and age).

2.1 Methods

2.1.1 Sampling Procedures

Our data are from the Northwestern Juvenile Project, a longitudinal study of health needs and outcomes of delinquent youth (Abram et al. 2003; Teplin et al. 2002, 2003). We recruited a stratified random sample of 1,829 detained youth initially arrested and detained awaiting the adjudication and/or disposition of their case between November 20, 1995, and June 14, 1998, at the Cook County Juvenile Temporary Detention Center (CCJTDC) in Chicago, IL. To ensure adequate representation of key subgroups, we stratified our sample by age (10–13 years or ≥14 years), gender, race/ethnicity (African American, non-Hispanic white, and Hispanic), and legal status (processed as a juvenile or an adult). The CCJTDC is used for pretrial detention and for offenders sentenced for less than 30 days. Consistent with juvenile detainees nationwide (Snyder and Sickmund 2006), more than 80% of detainees at CCJTDC were male, and most were racial/ethnic minorities. Additional information on our methods has been published elsewhere (Teplin et al. 2002, 2003).

2.1.2 Procedures to Obtain Assent and Consent

This research was approved by the institutional review boards of Northwestern University, the CDC, and the United States Office of Protection from Research Risks. At the baseline and follow-up interviews, participants signed either an assent form (if they were <18 years) or a consent form (if they were ≥18 years). The Northwestern University Institutional Review Board and the CDC Institutional

Review Board waived parental consent, consistent with federal regulations regarding research with minimal risk (45 Code of Federal Regulations [CFR] 46.116[c], 45 CFR 46.116[d], and 45 CFR 46.408[c]; Federal Register 1991). We nevertheless tried to contact parents to provide them information and offer an opportunity to decline participation. Despite repeated attempts to contact the parent or guardian, for 43.8% of the participants, none could be found. In lieu of parental consent, an independent participant advocate representing the interests of the participants oversaw youth assent. Federal regulations allow for a participant advocate if parental consent is not feasible (45 CFR 46.116[d]; Federal Register 1991).

2.1.3 Participants

Collection of the baseline HIV/STI data began when funding became available, from February 1997 through June 1998. Among the 1,052 youth sampled during this period, 3.9% ($n=41$) refused to participate (Teplin et al. 2003, 2005). There were no significant differences in refusal rates according to gender, race/ethnicity, or age. Fourteen participants did not complete the HIV/STI questions because of the interviewer's error. One participant was released from detention before finishing the interview; 196 participants left the detention center while we were locating their caretakers to obtain consent or before we could schedule an interview. The final number of youth who received the HIV/STI interview was 800; of these, 769 (96.1%) were interviewed at follow-up; 12 (1.5%) died before the follow-up; 3 (0.4%) withdrew from the study; and 16 (2.0%) were lost to follow-up. Time to follow-up was between 2.9 and 7.9 years (mean [SD] follow-up: 3.3 [0.6] years; median follow-up: 3.1 years).

Forty-five of the 769 participants were excluded from our analyses: 5 (0.7%) did not receive the HIV/STI risk behavior assessment at follow-up (because of time constraints or the interviewer's error); and 40 (5.2%) received their follow-up interview more than 4.5 years after their baseline interview. We chose 4.5 years for the cutoff, because, in this high-risk and highly mobile sample, participants can be difficult to track; using a stricter cutoff would restrict the generalizability of the sample. To ensure that our cutoff did not bias the findings, we compared the demographic characteristics (gender, race/ethnicity, and age) of participants who were interviewed between 3.5 and 4.5 years ($n=81$; 11% of the sample) after baseline with those interviewed within 3.5 years after baseline; there were no significant differences. In addition, we examined whether our findings were affected by including these participants. We repeated all analyses using only participants interviewed within 3.5 years; the findings were substantially the same.

The final sample in these analyses ($n=724$) included 316 females and 408 males; there were 393 African American participants, 198 Hispanic participants, 131 non-Hispanic white participants, and 2 participants who self-identified their race as "other." At baseline, 113 youth were processed as adults, and 611 were processed as juveniles. The median length of stay at CCJTDC was 15 days (range: 1–686 days;

mean [SD] days: 40.7 [75.3]). At baseline, participants were aged 10–18 years old (mean [SD] age: 14.8 [1.4]; median age: 15). At follow-up, participants were aged 13–22 years old (mean [SD] age: 18.1 [1.4]; median age: 18). Time to follow-up was 2.9–4.5 years (mean [SD] time to follow-up: 3.2 [0.3] years; median: 3.1 years).

2.1.4 Procedures for Data Collection

At the baseline interview, face-to-face, structured interviews were conducted at the detention center in a private area; most interviews took place within 2 days of intake (Abram et al. 2003; Teplin et al. 2002, 2003). At the follow-up, the same participants were interviewed, irrespective of where they lived. Participants were interviewed in the community (66.2%), at correctional facilities (26.2%), at residential placement facilities (2.5%), or by telephone if they lived in a community more than 2 h away (5.1%). Baseline and follow-up interviews took 2–4 h to complete (Abram et al. 2003; Teplin et al. 2002, 2003). We used both male and female interviewers; female participants were interviewed only by female interviewers. Most interviewers had advanced degrees in psychology or an associated field and had experience interviewing at-risk youth. All of the interviewers were trained for more than a month by one of the authors (Dr. Abram) and other supervisory staff. One third of the interviewers were fluent in Spanish (Abram et al. 2003; Teplin et al. 2002, 2003).

2.1.5 Measures

We examined behaviors associated with increased risk for HIV/STI, including sex risk behaviors and injection risk behaviors (sharing needles or "works" for drug injection, piercings, or tattoos) (Carroll et al. 2002; D'Angelo and DiClemente 1996; Kipke et al. 1996; Long and Rickman 1994; Valois et al. 1999). We also examined antecedents to HIV/STI risk behaviors, such as alcohol and other drug use, because they may indirectly lead to HIV/STIs by increasing high-risk sexual behaviors.

HIV/STI risk behaviors were assessed using the National Institute on Drug Abuse (NIDA) Risk Behavior Assessment (RBA; Needle et al. 1995). Although designed for adults, we chose the RBA because instruments designed for adolescents and young adults did not assess the breadth, frequency, and severity of HIV/AIDS risk behaviors common in our sample. A report issued by the Substance Abuse and Mental Health Services Administration recommends the RBA for the comprehensive assessment of HIV/AIDS among drug-using adolescents (Winters 1999). The RBA is a reliable and valid measure of drug and sex risk behaviors (Dowling et al. 1994; Needle et al. 1995; Weatherby et al. 1994). We supplemented the RBA with items from the Adolescent Health Survey from NIDA's Study of Street Youth at Risk for AIDS (Watters 1994) and Yale's AIDS Risk Inventory (Chawarski et al. 1996). Experts reviewed our measure at baseline, and we pilot-tested

58 participants. At baseline, lifetime drug use was assessed using screen items (1 for each substance) from the Diagnostic Interview Schedule 2.3 (Shaffer et al. 1996). At baseline and follow-up, recency and frequency of drug use were assessed using NIDA's RBA.

2.1.6 *Missing Data*

2.1.6.1 Missing Cases

To assess the effect of attrition on generalizability, we compared participants who provided follow-up data with those who did not on the following variables: demographic characteristics (gender, race/ethnicity, and age) and HIV/STI risk behaviors reported at baseline. There were no significant differences except those who died were more likely to be male ($P < .05$), and those lost to follow-up were more likely to be non-Hispanic white or Hispanic ($P < .05$) and were less likely to have had sex with more than one partner ($P < .05$). Potential bias from demographic differences in attrition was adjusted by weighting the statistical analyses by sampling strata (see Sect. 2.1.8).

2.1.6.2 Missing Data from Interviews Conducted by Telephone

Because telephone interviews needed to be shorter than face-to-face interviews, they are missing the following variables at follow-up ($n = 37$; 5.1%): use of specific drugs, types of sex with a high-risk partner, sex and unprotected sex while drunk or high, and trading sex and drugs. Comparing participants interviewed by telephone with those interviewed face-to-face revealed the following: (1) no significant demographic differences (gender, race/ethnicity, or age); (2) no significant differences in the prevalence of HIV/STI risk behaviors reported at baseline; and (3) no significant differences in the prevalence of other HIV/STI risk behaviors reported at follow-up.

2.1.7 *Independent Variables*

We compared HIV/STI risk behaviors by gender, race/ethnicity, and age. We also examined incarceration status since baseline. For behaviors assessed "since the last interview," participants were considered incarcerated if they self-reported that they had been "mostly in correctional facilities" since the baseline interview (21.4% of sample; 126 males and 29 females). For behaviors assessed "in the past 3 months" or less, participants were considered incarcerated if they self-reported that they had been "mostly in correctional facilities in the past 3 months" (23.1% of sample; 138 males and 29 females).

2.1.8 *Statistical Analysis*

All of the data were weighted to reflect the population at the CCJTDC. Because selected strata were oversampled, we used sample weights, based on CCJTDC's population, to estimate descriptive statistics and model parameters that reflect CCJTDC's population. Taylor series linearization was used to estimate SEs (Cochran 1977; Levy and Lemeshow 1999). Only statistically significant findings with $P<.05$ are noted in the text.

Changes in the prevalence of behaviors between the baseline and follow-up interviews were assessed using paired differences with an adjusted Wald F statistic (Korn and Graubard 1990). Logistic regression was used to assess demographic differences in the prevalence (Tables 2.1 and 2.2), development (Tables 2.3 and 2.4), and persistence (Tables 2.5 and 2.6) of individual risk behaviors (Hosmer and Lemeshow 2000). The independent variables in the regression models were incarceration status only (Tables 2.1 and 2.2), incarceration status and gender (Tables 2.2, 2.3 and 2.5), incarceration status and race/ethnicity (Tables 2.4 and 2.6), and incarceration status and age. We tested for differences between specific groups (e.g., African American versus Hispanic) only when the overall model was significant at the $P<.05$ level. We controlled for incarceration status in all of the analyses by either computing separate prevalence rates for those incarcerated and those in the community or including incarceration status in logistic regression models.

2.2 Results

2.2.1 *Prevalence of HIV/STI Risk Behaviors*

2.2.1.1 Comparing the Baseline and Follow-up Interviews

Males

Table 2.1 shows that prevalence of the following behaviors increased at follow-up: oral sex, anal sex (receptive and/or insertive), sex while drunk or high, and unprotected sex while drunk or high. In contrast, multiple sex partners (>1 and >3 in the past 3 months), recent use of marijuana, and frequent use of marijuana decreased at follow-up.

Table 2.1 also shows differences according to incarceration status. Among males in the community, most behaviors were more prevalent at follow-up. Only two behaviors, recent and frequent use of marijuana, were significantly less prevalent. Among incarcerated males, the opposite pattern prevailed; many behaviors were less prevalent at follow-up. Only one behavior, oral sex with a high-risk partner, was significantly more prevalent.

Table 2.1 Prevalence of HIV/STI sex and drug risk behaviors in male juvenile detainees at the baseline and follow-up interviews ($n=408$)

Variable	Total males ($n=408$)			Living situation at follow-up[a]: Community			Incarcerated			Significant difference between incarcerated and community at follow-up, *P*
	Baseline prevalence, %	Follow-up prevalence, %	Significant change, *P*	Baseline prevalence, %	Follow-up prevalence, %	Significant change, *P*	Baseline prevalence, %	Follow-up prevalence, %	Significant change, *P*	
Sex risk behaviors										
Sexually active	90.6	92.9	NS	90.1	99.0	<.001	91.7	80.3	NS	<.001
Multiple partners: >1 in past 3 months	61.7	36.8	<.001	63.7	53.4	NS	57.7	3.2	<.001	<.001
Multiple partners: >3 in past 3 months	35.2	15.5	<.01	33.5	22.2	NS	38.8	2.1	<.001	<.001
Vaginal sex	90.3	92.3	NS	89.6	98.6	<.01	91.7	79.9	NS	<.001
Recent (past 3 months) unprotected vaginal sex	36.4	44.4	NS	35.1	62.2	<.01	38.9	8.9	<.001	<.001
Vaginal sex with high-risk partner[b]	25.1	37.9	NS	21.7	36.6	NS	31.3	40.4	NS	NS
Oral sex	43.1	58.8	<.05	39.5	63.2	<.01	50.0	50.4	NS	NS
Recent (past 3 months) unprotected oral sex	32.9	35.1	NS	32.1	47.9	<.01	34.6	8.1	<.05	<.01
Oral sex with high-risk partner[b]	8.1	16.3	NS	11.4	13.1	NS	1.7	22.4	<.05	NS

(continued)

Table 2.1 (continued)

	Living situation at follow-up[a]									
	Total males ($n=408$)			Community			Incarcerated			
Variable	Baseline prevalence, %	Follow-up prevalence, %	Significant change, *P*	Baseline prevalence, %	Follow-up prevalence, %	Significant change, *P*	Baseline prevalence, %	Follow-up prevalence, %	Significant change, *P*	Significant difference between incarcerated and community at follow-up, *P*
Anal sex (receptive and/ or insertive)	9.7	22.3	<.05	9.8	17.3	NS	9.6	31.9	NS	NS
Receptive anal sex	1.6	0.5	NS	2.3	0.7	NS	0.0	0.1	NS	NS
Insertive anal sex (males only)	9.7	22.1	NS	9.8	17.0	NS	9.6	31.9	NS	NS
Recent (past 3 months) unprotected anal sex	3.2	7.1	NS	4.1	10.5	NS	1.4	0.1	<.05	<.001
Anal sex with high-risk partner[b]	2.5	6.3	NS	3.5	1.6	NS	0.7	14.9	NS	<.001
Sex while drunk or high	65.8	80.2	<.05	64.6	85.0	<.01	67.8	71.8	NS	NS
Unprotected sex while drunk or high	36.0	54.9	<.01	33.6	53.8	<.05	40.0	56.9	NS	NS
Traded sex and drugs	2.8	6.8	NS	1.2	9.9	NS	5.9	1.1	NS	<.01
Drug and injection risk behaviors										
Used alcohol	89.2	89.1	NS	88.0	91.5	NS	91.5	84.5	NS	NS
Recent (past month) use of alcohol	56.7	47.8	NS	62.0	64.7	NS	45.9	13.6	<.01	<.001

Frequent use of alcohol (>3 times past month)	30.8	29.1	NS	31.5	38.4	NS	29.4	10.1	NS	<.05
Used marijuana	93.4	88.5	NS	93.8	96.1	NS	92.8	74.4	<.05	<.001
Recent (past month) use of marijuana	77.5	46.1	<.001	84.9	62.7	<.01	62.9	13.1	<.001	<.001
Frequent use of marijuana (>3 times past month)	60.4	37.4	<.001	67.0	50.0	<.05	47.2	12.2	<.01	<.01
Used other substance[c]	14.2	15.1	NS	17.2	17.9	NS	8.8	9.9	NS	NS
Recent (past month) use of other substance[c]	7.0	3.7	NS	8.8	4.7	NS	3.4	1.8	NS	NS
Frequent use of other substance (>3 times past month)[c]	1.4	1.2	NS	1.7	1.2	NS	1.0	1.1	NS	NS
Injected drugs	0.1	0.1	NS	0.2	0.1	NS	0.0	0.0	–[d]	–[e]
Tattooed	43.8	43.8	NS	39.5	41.8	NS	52.5	48.1	NS	NS
Shared needle(s) or equipment (injection drug use/tattooing)	3.5	0.3	NS	4.9	0.4	NS	0.4	0.1	NS	NS
Shared needle(s) in a risky location (injection drug use/tattooing)[f]	1.6	0.0	NS	2.3	0.0	NS	0.0	0.0	–[d]	–[e]

(continued)

Table 2.1 (continued)

				Living situation at follow-up[a]						
	Total males ($n=408$)			Community			Incarcerated			
Variable	Baseline prevalence, %	Follow-up prevalence, %	Significant change, *P*	Baseline prevalence, %	Follow-up prevalence, %	Significant change, *P*	Baseline prevalence, %	Follow-up prevalence, %	Significant change, *P*	Significant difference between incarcerated and community at follow-up, *P*
Shared needle(s) without cleaning (injection drug use/tattooing)	1.6	0.0	NS	2.3	0.0	NS	0.0	0.1	NS	–[e]

This table uses all of the cases that have baseline and follow-up data for each variable. Follow-up data are measured "since the last interview" unless noted. Data are weighted to reflect the actual population of the CCJTDC

NS not significant

[a]For variables measured "since the last interview," the number of "incarcerated participants" is composed of those who self-reported they had "been mostly in correctional facilities" since the baseline interview (126 males and 29 females). For variables measured "in the last 3 months" or less, the number of incarcerated participants is composed of those that self reported they had been "mostly in correctional facilities in the past 3 months" (138 males and 29 females)

[b] "High-risk partners" include persons who have ever worked as a prostitute, persons with HIV/AIDS, persons who inject drugs, and persons whose sexual history is not well known

[c] "Other substance" includes substances other than alcohol or marijuana

[d] Tests of significance could not be computed, because baseline and follow-up prevalence rates were 0

[e] Tests of significance could not be computed because ≥1 cell size was 0

[f] "Risky locations" include a park, street, alley, abandoned building, car, public bathroom, and crack house/shooting gallery

Table 2.2 Prevalence of HIV/STI sex and drug risk behaviors in female juvenile detainees at the baseline and follow-up Interviews ($n=316$)

Variable	Total females ($n=316$)			Living situation at follow-up[a]						Significant difference between incarcerated and community at follow-up, *P*	Odds ratios (95% confidence intervals for follow-up prevalence, males to females (adjusted for incarceration status)[a]
				Community			Incarcerated				
	Baseline prevalence, %	Follow-up prevalence, %	Significant change, *P*	Baseline prevalence, %	Follow-up prevalence, %	Significant change, *P*	Baseline prevalence, %	Follow-up prevalence, %	Significant change, *P*		
Sex risk behaviors											
Sexually active	87.0	94.6	<.001	86.4	96.6	<.001	93.3	73.6	<.05	<.001	2.2 (1.0–5.0)
Multiple partners: >1 in past 3 months	26.9	13.3	<.001	26.2	12.3	<.01	33.9	23.2	NS	NS	6.7 (3.6–12.3)[b]
Multiple partners: >3 in past 3 months	5.1	2.3	NS	4.8	1.8	<.05	7.6	7.6	NS	NS	11.1(4.1–30.0)[b]
Vaginal sex	83.7	94.0	<.001	83.1	95.8	<.001	90.3	72.0	NS	<.001	2.4 (1.1–5.2)[c]
Recent (past 3 months) unprotected vaginal sex	50.8	61.9	<.01	50.9	65.2	<.001	49.1	23.4	<.05	<.01	0.8 (0.5–1.5)
Vaginal sex with high-risk partner[d]	19.2	25.4	NS	19.5	24.4	NS	16.1	38.5	NS	NS	1.7 (0.9–3.2)

(continued)

Table 2.2 (continued)

Variable	Total females ($n=316$)			Living situation at follow-up[a]						Significant difference between incarcerated and community at follow-up, P	Odds ratios (95% confidence intervals for follow-up prevalence, males to females (adjusted for incarceration status)[a]
				Community			Incarcerated				
	Baseline prevalence, %	Follow-up prevalence, %	Significant change, P	Baseline prevalence, %	Follow-up prevalence, %	Significant change, P	Baseline prevalence, %	Follow-up prevalence, %	Significant change, P		
Oral sex	31.6	48.4	<.001	33.1	47.7	<.001	14.8	56.0	<.01	NS	1.7 (1.0–3.2)
Recent (past 3 months) unprotected oral sex	23.7	35.9	<.001	24.3	36.1	<.01	17.3	34.6	NS	NS	1.4 (0.8–2.7)
Oral sex with high-risk partner[d]	3.4	6.3	NS	3.7	6.4	NS	0.0	5.1	NS	NS	2.4 (1.0–5.8)[c]
Anal sex (receptive and/or insertive)	7.7	9.8	NS	8.4	9.7	NS	0.0	11.0	NS	NS	2.1 (1.1–4.1)[c]
Anal sex (receptive)	7.7	9.8	NS	8.4	9.7	NS	0.0	11.0	NS	NS	0.1 (0.02–0.2)[b]
Recent (past 3 months) unprotected anal sex	1.8	3.6	NS	1.9	3.5	NS	0.0	5.4	NS	NS	2.8 (0.9–8.8)
Anal sex with high-risk partner[d]	3.5	0.3	NS	3.8	0.3	NS	0.0	0.0	–[e]	–[f]	10.7 (1.3–86.7)[c]

Sex while drunk or high	53.0	58.7	NS	52.2	59.7	<.05	60.5	48.8	NS	NS	3.7 (1.8–7.6)[b]
Unprotected sex while drunk or high	34.6	45.7	<.01	34.1	46.4	<.01	39.4	39.4	NS	NS	1.4 (0.8–2.5)
Traded sex and drugs	3.1	8.0	<.01	3.0	8.0	<.01	3.7	7.5	NS	NS	1.1 (0.4–3.4)
Drug and injection risk behaviors											
Used alcohol	90.9	85.6	<.05	90.8	86.8	NS	92.2	74.3	NS	NS	1.7 (0.7–4.1)
Recent (past month) use of alcohol	53.7	48.8	NS	52.0	52.2	NS	72.1	14.0	<.001	<.001	1.6 (0.9–3.0)
Frequent use of alcohol (>3 times past month)	26.3	23.1	NS	24.6	24.9	NS	44.5	3.8	<.001	<.05	1.9 (1.1–3.4)[c]
Used marijuana	90.4	81.9	<.001	89.8	82.2	<.01	96.3	79.8	NS	NS	3.7 (2.2–6.2)[b]
Recent (past month) use of marijuana	67.4	52.3	<.001	66.0	56.8	<.01	82.2	6.3	<.001	<.001	1.3 (0.7–2.3)
Frequent use of marijuana (>3 times past month)	44.2	38.0	NS	43.3	41.4	NS	53.5	3.8	<.001	<.01	1.5 (0.8–2.6)
Used other substance[g]	21.5	24.6	NS	20.4	23.2	NS	32.3	38.8	NS	NS	0.6 (0.4–1.1)
Recent (past month) use of other substance[g]	8.4	5.1	NS	7.8	5.4	NS	14.8	2.5	NS	NS	0.9 (0.5–1.6)

(continued)

Table 2.2 (continued)

Variable	Total females ($n=316$)			Living situation at follow-up[a]						Significant difference between incarcerated and community at follow-up, P	Odds ratios (95% confidence intervals for follow-up prevalence, males to females (adjusted for incarceration status)[a]
				Community			Incarcerated				
	Baseline prevalence, %	Follow-up prevalence, %	Significant change, P	Baseline prevalence, %	Follow-up prevalence, %	Significant change, P	Baseline prevalence, %	Follow-up prevalence, %	Significant change, P		
Frequent use of other substance (>3 times past month)[g]	2.7	1.9	NS	1.7	2.1	NS	12.3	0.0	<.05	–[f]	0.6 (0.2–1.9)
Injected drugs	1.0	0.9	NS	0.7	1.0	NS	3.8	0.0	NS	–[f]	0.1 (0.01–0.9)[c]
Tattooed	46.2	42.0	NS	45.4	41.9	NS	54.0	43.5	NS	NS	1.0 (0.6–1.7)
Shared needle(s) or equipment (injection drug use/tattooing)	1.3	1.0	NS	1.1	0.8	NS	3.0	3.0	NS	NS	0.3 (0.05–2.3)
Shared needle(s) in a risky location (injection drug use/tattooing)[h]	0.0	0.2	NS	0.0	0.2	NS	0.0	0.0	–[e]	–[f]	–[f]
Shared needle(s) without cleaning (injection drug use/tattooing)	0.3	0.4	NS	0.0	0.5	NS	3.1	0.0	NS	–[f]	–[f]

This table uses all of the cases that have baseline and follow-up data for each variable. Follow-up data are measured "since the last interview" unless noted. Data are weighted to reflect the actual population of the CCJTDC

NS not significant

[a]For variables measured "since the last interview," the number of "incarcerated participants" is composed of those who self-reported they had "been mostly in correctional facilities" since the baseline interview (126 males and 29 females). For variables measured "in the last 3 months" or less, the number of incarcerated participants is composed of those who self reported they had been "mostly in correctional facilities in the past 3 months" (138 males and 29 females)

[b]$P < .001$

[c]$P < .05$

[d]"High-risk partners" include persons who have ever worked as a prostitute, persons with HIV/AIDS, persons who inject drugs, and persons whose sexual history is not well known

[e]Tests of significance could not be computed because baseline and follow-up prevalence rates were 0

[f]Tests of significance could not be computed because ≥1 cell size was 0

[g]"Other substance" includes substances other than alcohol or marijuana

[h]"Risky locations" include a park, street, alley, abandoned building, car, public bathroom, and crack house/shooting gallery

Table 2.3 Development of HIV/STI sex and drug risk behaviors in juvenile detainees between the baseline and follow-up interviews according to gender ($n=724$)

Variable	Males ($n=408$)		Females ($n=316$)		Odds ratios (95% confidence intervals) for developing, males to females (adjusted for incarceration status)[a,b]
	% Absent at baseline	% Developing[a]	% Absent at baseline	% Developing[a]	
Sex risk behaviors					
Sexually active	9.4	92.9	13.0	80.7	2.8 (0.8–9.7)
Multiple partners: >1 in past 3 months	38.3	28.9	73.1	10.8	5.7 (2.3–13.7)[c]
Multiple partners: >3 in past 3 months	64.8	11.2	94.9	2.1	8.0 (2.4–26.5)[c]
Vaginal sex	9.7	91.0	16.3	80.7	2.1 (0.6–6.9)
Recent (past 3 months) unprotected vaginal sex	63.6	38.7	49.2	54.9	0.8 (0.4–1.8)
Vaginal sex with high-risk partner[d]	74.9	36.5	80.8	18.8	2.3 (1.1–4.6)[e]
Oral sex	56.9	52.5	68.4	39.6	1.8 (0.9–3.7)
Recent (past 3 months) unprotected oral sex	67.1	23.3	76.3	29.9	0.9 (0.4–1.8)
Oral sex with high-risk partner[d]	91.9	14.7	96.6	5.1	2.4 (1.0–6.0)
Anal sex (receptive and/or insertive)	90.3	22.6	92.3	9.6	2.1 (1.0–4.4)[e]
Receptive anal sex	98.4	0.5	92.3	9.6	0.1 (0.02–0.2)[c]
Insertive anal sex (males only)	90.3	22.6	NA	NA	NA
Recent (past 3 months) unprotected anal sex	96.8	7.2	98.2	3.7	2.9 (0.9–9.0)

Anal sex with high-risk partner[d]	97.5	6.4	96.5	0.3	10.6 (1.3–86.2)[e]
Sex while drunk or high	34.2	65.5	47.0	43.7	2.8 (1.1–7.0)
Unprotected sex while drunk or high	64.0	43.6	65.4	39.1	1.2 (0.6–2.4)
Traded sex and drugs	97.2	6.8	96.9	7.1	1.3 (0.4–3.9)
Drug and injection risk behaviors					
Used alcohol	10.8	76.3	9.1	54.6	8.0 (2.0–32.0)[f]
Recent (past month) use of alcohol	43.3	32.7	46.3	34.9	1.5 (0.6–3.6)
Frequent use of alcohol (>3 times past month)	69.2	26.3	73.7	18.0	2.1 (1.0–4.3)[e]
Used marijuana	6.6	51.9	9.6	42.5	4.5 (1.0–21.0)
Recent (past month) use of marijuana	22.5	24.7	32.6	37.6	0.9 (0.3–2.9)
Frequent use of marijuana (>3 times past month)	39.6	27.2	55.8	26.4	1.3 (0.5–3.7)
Used other substance[g]	85.8	5.3	78.5	12.3	0.4 (0.3–0.8)[f]
Recent (past month) use of other substance[g]	93.0	2.3	91.6	4.8	0.5 (0.3–1.1)
Frequent use of other substance (>3 times past month)[g]	98.6	1.1	97.3	1.7	0.6 (0.2–2.1)
Injected drugs	99.9	0.1	99.0	0.9	0.1 (0.01–0.9)[e]
Tattooed	56.2	28.1	53.8	31.6	1.0 (0.5–2.3)
Shared needle(s) or equipment (injection drug use/tattooing)	96.5	0.3	98.7	0.7	0.5 (0.1–3.7)

(continued)

Table 2.3 (continued)

Variable	Males ($n=408$)		Females ($n=316$)		Odds ratios (95% confidence intervals) for developing, males to females (adjusted for incarceration status)[a,b]
	% Absent at baseline	% Developing[a]	% Absent at baseline	% Developing[a]	
Shared needle(s) in a risky location (injection drug use/tattooing)[h]	98.4	0.0	100.0	0.2	–[i]
Shared needle(s) without cleaning (injection drug use/tattooing)	98.4	0.0	99.7	0.4	–[i]

This table uses all of the cases that have baseline and follow-up data for each variable. Follow-up data are measured "since the last interview" unless noted. Data are weighted to reflect the actual population of the CCJTDC

NA not applicable

[a]"Development" is defined as follows: among youth who did not report a specific HIV/STI behavior at baseline, what proportion reported that behavior at follow-up?

[b]Tests of significant are adjusted for incarceration status (yes/no). For variables measured "since the last interview" participants are considered incarcerated if they self-reported that they had "been mostly in correctional facilities" since the baseline interview (126 males and 29 females). For variables measured "in the last 3 months" or less, participants are considered incarcerated if they self-reported they had been "mostly in correctional facilities in the past 3 months" (138 males and 29 females)

[c]$P<.001$

[d]"High-risk partners" include persons who have ever worked as a prostitute, persons with HIV/AIDS, persons who inject drugs, and persons whose sexual history is not well known

[e]$P<.05$

[f]$P<.01$

[g]"Other substance" includes substances other than alcohol or marijuana

[h]"Risky locations" include a park, street, alley, abandoned building, car, public bathroom, and crack house/shooting gallery

[i]Odds ratios and tests of significance could not be computed because ≥1 cell size was 0

Table 2.4 Development of HIV/STI sex and drug risk behaviors in juvenile detainees between the baseline and follow-up interviews according to race/ethnicity (n=722)

Variable	African American, % ($n=393$)		Non-Hispanic White, % ($n=131$)		Hispanic, % ($n=198$)		Overall test of racial/ethnic differences for developing (adjusted for incarceration status), p[a,b,c]	Odds ratios (95% confidence intervals) for developing (adjusted for incarceration status)[a,c]		
	% Absent at baseline	% Developing[a]	% Absent at baseline	% Developing[a]	% Absent at baseline	% Developing[a]		African American vs non-Hispanic White	African American vs Hispanic	Non-Hispanic White vs Hispanic
Sex risk behaviors										
Sexually active	7.9	91.3	21.1	86.9	14.0	95.0	NS			
Multiple partners: >1 in past 3 months	37.0	29.4	64.3	29.0	49.9	14.2	NS			
Multiple partners: >3 in past 3 months	62.5	12.0	85.2	3.8	79.8	6.9	NS			
Vaginal sex	8.5	88.3	21.1	86.9	14.2	94.9	NS			
Recent (past 3 months) unprotected vaginal sex	64.1	41.8	62.6	44.8	58.1	28.3	NS			
Vaginal sex with high-risk partner[d]	74.5	33.6	84.6	43.0	76.6	38.9	NS			

(continued)

Table 2.4 (continued)

Variable	African American, % ($n=393$)		Non-Hispanic White, % ($n=131$)		Hispanic, % ($n=198$)		Overall test of racial/ethnic differences for developing (adjusted for incarceration status), p[a,b,c]	Odds ratios (95% confidence intervals) for developing (adjusted for incarceration status)[a,c]		
	% Absent at baseline	% Developing[a]	% Absent at baseline	% Developing[a]	% Absent at baseline	% Developing[a]		African American vs non-Hispanic White	African American vs Hispanic	Non-Hispanic White vs Hispanic
Oral sex	57.4	48.2	47.2	64.5	64.1	59.8	NS			
Recent (past 3 months) unprotected oral sex	66.8	23.1	60.1	43.2	75.9	21.8	<.05	0.4 (0.2–1.0)[e]	0.9 (0.3–2.3)	2.1 (1.0–4.5)
Oral sex with high-risk partner[d]	90.7	12.5	93.6	24.6	98.4	16.9	NS			
Anal sex (receptive and/or insertive)	91.0	19.2	89.6	16.9	89.5	33.4	NS			
Receptive anal sex	97.8	0.8	98.7	2.9	99.9	1.9	NS			
Insertive anal sex (males only)	90.7	20.0	89.6	16.5	88.8	35.5	NS			
Recent (past 3 months) unprotected anal sex	97.0	5.0	94.1	4.4	97.5	16.1	<.05	1.4 (0.3–7.0)	0.2 (0.04–1.2)	0.2 (0.03–0.7)[e]

Anal sex with high-risk partner[d]	97.4	5.8	97.0	4.0	98.9	7.2	NS			
Sex while drunk or high	33.3	65.0	38.0	65.6	42.6	57.5	NS			
Unprotected sex while drunk or high	66.3	43.7	62.0	42.7	58.0	41.1	NS			
Traded sex and drugs	96.9	8.2	98.5	4.5	98.0	2.3	NS			
Drug and injection risk behaviors										
Used alcohol	13.2	75.5	5.2	65.9	2.3	66.9	NS			
Recent (past month) use of alcohol	44.9	24.8	37.4	66.9	39.0	64.0	<.001	0.2 (0.1–0.5)[f]	0.1 (0.03–0.5)[f]	0.6 (0.1–2.8)
Frequent use of alcohol (>3 times past month)	69.8	21.2	73.4	38.9	67.7	41.6	NS			
Used marijuana	5.9	70.6	6.5	27.4	10.8	11.0	NS			
Recent (past month) use of marijuana	23.4	25.8	22.9	38.0	23.5	23.4	NS			
Frequent use of marijuana (>3 times past month)	39.1	25.7	38.3	38.3	48.9	27.0	NS			

(continued)

Table 2.4 (continued)

Variable	African American, % ($n=393$)		Non-Hispanic White, % ($n=131$)		Hispanic, % ($n=198$)		Overall test of racial/ethnic differences for developing (adjusted for incarceration status), p[a,b,c]	Odds ratios (95% confidence intervals) for developing (adjusted for incarceration status)[a,c]		
	% Absent at baseline	% Developing[a]	% Absent at baseline	% Developing[a]	% Absent at baseline	% Developing[a]		African American vs non-Hispanic White	African American vs Hispanic	Non-Hispanic White vs Hispanic
Used other substance[g]	97.2	1.6	41.4	52.2	50.4	24.7	<.001	0.02 (0.01–0.04)[h]	0.04 (0.02–0.10)[h]	2.5 (1.0–6.4)
Recent (past month) use of other substance[g]	97.8	0.4	67.9	14.5	79.9	8.5	<.001	0.02 (0.01–0.07)[h]	0.04 (0.01–0.13)[h]	1.6 (0.6–4.4)
Frequent use of other substance (>3 times past month)[g]	99.9	0.3	87.5	4.3	95.7	2.4	<.001	0.1 (0.01–0.25)[h]	0.1 (0.02–0.7)[e]	2.0 (0.4–10.2)
Injected drugs	100.0	0.0	97.6	2.3	99.8	0.0	–[i]			
Tattooed	59.9	27.4	61.7	35.8	37.9	31.6	NS			
Shared needle(s) or equipment (injection drug use/tattooing)	96.0	0.0	99.7	1.7	98.4	1.1	–[i]			

Shared needle(s) in a risky location (injection drug use/ tattooing)[j]	98.1	0.0	100.0	0.3	100.0	0.0	–[i]
Shared needle(s) without cleaning (injection drug use/ tattooing)	98.1	0.0	100.0	0.6	99.9	0.1	–[i]

One male and 1 female who self-identified as "other" race/ethnicity were not included in this analysis. This table uses all of the cases that have baseline and follow-up data for each variable. Follow-up data are measured "since the last interview" unless noted. Data are weighted to reflect the actual population of the CCJTDC

NS not significant

[a]"Development" is defined as follows: among youth who did not report a specific HIV/STI behavior at baseline, what proportion reported that behavior at follow-up?

[b]We tested for differences between specific groups (eg, African American versus Hispanic) only when the overall model was significant at the $<.05$ level

[c]Tests of significant are adjusted for incarceration status (yes/no). For variables measured "since the last interview," participants are considered incarcerated if they self-reported they had "been mostly in correctional facilities" since the baseline interview (126 males and 29 females). For variables measured "in the last 3 months" or less, participants are considered incarcerated if they self-reported that they had been "mostly in correctional facilities in the past 3 months" (138 males and 29 females)

[d]"High-risk partners" include persons who have ever worked as a prostitute, persons with HIV/AIDS, persons who inject drugs, and persons whose sexual history is not well known

[e]$P<.05$

[f]$P<.01$

[g]"Other substance" includes substances other than alcohol or marijuana

[h]$P<.001$

[i]Odds ratios and tests of significance could not be computed because ≥1 cell size was 0

[j]"Risky locations" include a park, street, alley, abandoned building, car, public bathroom, and crack house/shooting gallery

Table 2.5 Persistence of HIV/STI sex and drug risk behaviors in juvenile detainees between the baseline and follow-up interviews according to gender ($n=724$)

Variable	Males, % ($n=408$)		Females, % ($n=316$)		Odds ratios (95% confidence intervals) for persisting, males to females (adjusted for incarceration status)[a,b]
	% Present at baseline	% Persisting[a]	% Present at baseline	% Persisting[a]	
Sex risk behaviors					
Sexually active	90.6	92.9	87.0	96.6	1.6 (0.5–5.1)
Multiple partners: >1 in past 3 months	61.7	41.7	26.9	20.0	5.0 (1.9–12.9)[c]
Multiple partners: >3 in past 3 months	35.2	23.6	5.1	6.7	6.6 (0.6–73.4)
Vaginal sex	90.3	92.4	83.7	96.6	1.9 (0.6–6.3)
Recent (past 3 months) unprotected vaginal sex	36.4	54.2	50.8	68.7	1.1 (0.4–3.2)
Vaginal sex with high-risk partner[d]	25.1	42.1	19.2	53.3	0.8 (0.2–3.8)
Oral sex	43.1	67.1	31.6	67.4	1.4 (0.4–4.4)
Recent (past 3 months) unprotected oral sex	32.9	59.2	23.7	55.3	5.0 (1.0–25.6)
Oral sex with high-risk partner[d]	8.1	35.2	3.4	40.3	0.9 (0.1–10.2)
Anal sex (receptive and/or insertive)	9.7	19.4	7.7	11.8	2.3 (0.3–16.1)
Receptive anal sex	1.6	0.0	7.7	11.8	–[e]
Insertive anal sex (males only)	9.7	17.4	NA		NA
Recent (past 3 months) unprotected anal sex	3.2	2.8	1.8	0.0	–[e]
Anal sex with high-risk partner[d]	2.5	3.6	3.5	0.0	–[e]

Sex while drunk or high	65.8	87.8	53.0	72.0	4.7 (1.3–17.3)[f]
Unprotected sex while drunk or high	36.0	75.2	34.6	58.2	2.0 (0.7–6.4)
Traded sex and drugs	2.8	6.2	3.1	34.6	0.2 (0.01–3.2)
Drug and injection risk behaviors					
Used alcohol	89.2	90.7	90.9	88.7	1.3 (0.5–3.7)
Recent (past month) use of alcohol	56.7	59.4	53.7	60.8	1.5 (0.7–3.4)
Frequent use of alcohol (>3 times past month)	30.8	35.3	26.3	37.2	1.4 (0.5–4.0)
Used marijuana	93.4	91.1	90.4	86.1	3.6 (1.9–6.7)[c]
Recent (past month) use of marijuana	77.5	52.3	67.4	59.4	1.1 (0.6–2.2)
Frequent use of marijuana (>3 times past month)	60.4	44.1	44.2	52.8	1.0 (0.5–2.1)
Used other substance[g]	14.2	73.9	21.5	69.5	1.2 (0.3–4.7)
Recent (past month) use of other substance[g]	7.0	23.2	8.4	8.4	3.4 (0.7–15.3)
Frequent use of other substance (>3 times past month)[g]	1.4	8.9	2.7	10.0	0.6 (0.04–9.2)
Injected drugs	0.1	0.0	1.0	0.0	–[e]
Tattooed	43.8	64.1	46.2	54.2	1.1 (0.5–2.6)
Shared needle(s) or equipment (injection drug use/tattooing)	3.5	0.7	1.3	20.5	0.04 (0.0004–4.8)

(continued)

Table 2.5 (continued)

Variable	Males, % ($n=408$)		Females, % ($n=316$)		Odds ratios (95% confidence intervals) for persisting, males to females (adjusted for incarceration status)[a,b]
	% Present at baseline	% Persisting[a]	% Present at baseline	% Persisting[a]	
Shared needle(s) in a risky location (injection drug use/tattooing)[h]	1.6	0.0	0.0	–	–[e]
Shared needle(s) without cleaning (injection drug use/tattooing)	1.6	0.0	0.3	0.0	–[e]

This table uses all cases that have baseline and follow-up data for each variable. Follow-up data are measured "since the last interview" unless noted. Data are weighted to reflect the actual population of the CCJTDC

NA not applicable

[a]"Persistence" is defined as follows: among youth who engaged in a behavior at the baseline interview, what proportion persisted in that behavior at the follow-up interview?

[b]Tests of significant are adjusted for incarceration status (yes/no). For variables measured "since the last interview," participants are considered incarcerated if they self-reported that they had "been mostly in correctional facilities" since the baseline interview (126 males and 29 females). For variables measured "in the last 3 months" or less, participants are considered incarcerated if they self-reported they had been "mostly in correctional facilities in the past 3 months" (138 males and 29 females)

[c]$P < .001$

[d]"High-risk partners" include persons who have ever worked as a prostitute, persons with HIV/AIDS, persons who inject drugs, and persons whose sexual history is not well known

[e]Odds ratios and tests of significance could not be computed because ≥1 cell size was 0

[f]$P < .05$

[g]"Other substance" includes substances other than alcohol or marijuana

[h]"Risky locations" include a park, street, alley, abandoned building, car, public bathroom, and crack house/shooting gallery

Table 2.6 Persistence of HIV/STI sex and drug risk behaviors in juvenile detainees between the baseline and follow-up interviews according to race/ethnicity ($n=722$)

Variable	African American, % ($n=393$)		Non-Hispanic White, % ($n=131$)		Hispanic, % ($n=198$)		Overall test of racial/ethnic differences for persisting (adjusted for incarceration status), $P^{a,b,c}$	Odds ratios (95% confidence intervals) for persisting (adjusted for incarceration status)[a,c]		
	% Present at Baseline	% Persisting[a]	% Present at Baseline	% Persisting[a]	% Present at Baseline	% Persisting[a]		African American vs non-Hispanic White	African American vs Hispanic	Non-Hispanic White vs Hispanic
Sex risk behaviors										
Sexually active	92.1	94.2	78.9	96.0	86.0	87.5	NS			
Multiple partners: >1 in past 3 months	63.0	41.9	35.7	34.2	50.1	38.7	NS			
Multiple partners: >3 in past 3 months	37.5	24.6	14.8	14.5	20.2	16.0	NS			
Vaginal sex	91.5	93.8	78.9	93.9	85.8	87.0	NS			
Recent (past 3 months) unprotected vaginal sex	35.9	52.4	37.4	64.1	41.9	61.9	NS			
Vaginal sex with high-risk partner[d]	25.5	40.8	15.4	72.6	23.4	47.8	NS			

(continued)

Table 2.6 (continued)

Variable	African American, % ($n=393$)		Non-Hispanic White, % ($n=131$)		Hispanic, % ($n=198$)		Overall test of racial/ethnic differences for persisting (adjusted for incarceration status), P[a,b,c]	Odds ratios (95% confidence intervals) for persisting (adjusted for incarceration status)[a,c]		
	% Present at Baseline	% Persisting[a]	% Present at Baseline	% Persisting[a]	% Present at Baseline	% Persisting[a]		African American vs non-Hispanic White	African American vs Hispanic	Non-Hispanic White vs Hispanic
Oral sex	42.6	60.4	52.8	89.0	35.9	88.1	<.05	0.2 (0.1–0.8)[e]	0.2 (0.04–0.8)[e]	0.8 (0.2–4.0)
Recent (past 3 months) unprotected oral sex	33.2	51.8	39.9	84.6	24.1	81.9	NS			
Oral sex with high-risk partner[d]	9.3	35.1	6.4	57.9	1.6	12.4	NS			
Anal sex (receptive and/or insertive)	9.0	13.6	10.4	36.7	10.5	35.4	NS			
Receptive anal sex	2.2	1.9	1.3	50.0	0.1	0.0	–[f]			
Insertive anal sex (males only)	9.3	13.5	10.4	34.9	11.2	26.2	NS			
Recent (past 3 months) unprotected anal sex	3.0	0.0	5.9	17.9	2.5	5.0	–[f]			

Anal sex with high-risk partner[d]	2.6	4.2	3.0	0.0	1.1	0.0	–[f]			
Sex while drunk or high	66.7	85.0	62.0	89.3	57.4	94.1	NS			
Unprotected sex while drunk or high	33.7	70.9	38.0	68.2	42.0	83.5	NS			
Traded sex and drugs	3.1	10.2	1.5	0.0	2.0	0.0	–[f]			
Drug and injection risk behaviors										
Used alcohol	86.8	88.9	94.8	95.8	97.7	94.7	NS			
Recent (past month) use of alcohol	55.1	55.2	62.6	74.5	61.0	70.2	<.05	0.44 (0.2–1.1)	0.20 (0.04–0.9)[e]	0.4 (0.1–2.0)
Frequent use of alcohol (>3 times past month)	30.2	29.6	26.6	52.5	32.3	51.7	NS			
Used marijuana	94.1	89.8	93.5	92.1	89.2	93.7	NS			
Recent (past month) use of marijuana	76.6	49.9	77.1	69.0	76.5	58.2	NS			
Frequent use of marijuana (>3 times past month)	60.9	42.4	61.7	61.7	51.1	47.2	NS			

(continued)

Table 2.6 (continued)

Variable	African American, % ($n=393$)		Non-Hispanic White, % ($n=131$)		Hispanic, % ($n=198$)		Overall test of racial/ethnic differences for persisting (adjusted for incarceration status), P[a,b,c]	Odds ratios (95% confidence intervals) for persisting (adjusted for incarceration status)[a,c]		
	% Present at Baseline	% Persisting[a]	% Present at Baseline	% Persisting[a]	% Present at Baseline	% Persisting[a]		African American vs non-Hispanic White	African American vs Hispanic	Non-Hispanic White vs Hispanic
Used other substance[g]	2.8	11.4	58.6	86.4	49.6	82.7	<.01	0.02 (0.002–0.2)[h]	0.02 (0.002–0.2)[i]	1.2 (0.4–3.5)
Recent (past month) use of other substance[g]	2.2	5.5	32.1	44.7	20.1	18.2	NS			
Frequent use of other substance (>3 times past month)[g]	0.1	0.0	12.5	16.9	4.3	2.5	–[f]			
Injected drugs	0.0	–	2.4	0.0	0.2	0.0	–[f]			
Tattooed	40.1	56.4	38.3	63.4	62.1	83.8	<.05	0.57 (0.2–1.7)	0.25 (0.08–0.8)[e]	0.4 (0.1–1.2)
Shared needle(s) or equipment (injection drug use/tattooing)	4.0	0.0	0.3	0.0	1.6	14.9	–[f]			

Shared needle(s) in a risky location (injection drug use/tattooing)[j]	1.9	0.0	0.0	–	0.0	–	–[f]
Shared needle(s) without cleaning (injection drug use/tattooing)	1.9	0.0	0.0	–	0.1	0.0	–[f]

One male and 1 female who self-identified as "other" race/ethnicity were not included in this analysis. This table uses all of the cases that have baseline and follow-up data for each variable. Follow-up data are measured "since the last interview" unless noted. Data are weighted to reflect the actual population of the CCJTDC

NS not significant

[a]"Persistence" is defined as follows: among youth who engaged in a behavior at the baseline interview, what proportion persisted in that behavior at the follow-up interview?

[b]We tested for differences between specific groups (eg, African American versus Hispanic) only when the overall model was significant at the $<.05$ level

[c]Tests of significant are adjusted for incarceration status (yes/no). For variables measured "since the last interview," participants are considered incarcerated if they self-reported they had "been mostly in correctional facilities" since the baseline interview (126 males and 29 females). For variables measured "in the last 3 months" or less, participants are considered incarcerated if they self-reported that they had been "mostly in correctional facilities in the past 3 months" (138 males and 29 females)

[d]"High-risk partners" include persons who have ever worked as a prostitute, persons with HIV/AIDS, persons who inject drugs, and persons whose sexual history is not well known

[e]$P<.05$

[f]Odds ratios and tests of significance could not be computed because ≥1 cell size was 0

[g]"Other substance" includes substances other than alcohol or marijuana

[h]$P<.001$

[i]$P<.01$

[j]"Risky locations" include a park, street, alley, abandoned building, car, public bathroom, and crack house/shooting gallery

Females

Table 2.2 shows that the prevalence of the following behaviors increased at follow-up: sexual activity, vaginal sex, recent unprotected vaginal sex, oral sex, recent unprotected oral sex, unprotected sex while drunk or high, and trading sex and drugs. In contrast, multiple sex partners (>1 in the past 3 months), use of alcohol, use of marijuana, and recent use of marijuana were less prevalent at follow-up.

Table 2.2 also reports differences by incarceration status. Among females in the community, many behaviors were more prevalent at follow-up. Only four behaviors, multiple sex partners (>1 and >3 in the past 3 months), use of marijuana, and recent use of marijuana, were significantly less prevalent. Among incarcerated females, the opposite pattern prevailed; only one behavior, oral sex, was significantly more prevalent.

2.2.1.2 Prevalence at Follow-up

Males

Table 2.1 shows that at follow-up, nearly all of the males were sexually active, had vaginal sex, and used alcohol and marijuana. The prevalence of unprotected sex in the past three months was also notable: nearly half had recent unprotected vaginal sex, more than one third had recent unprotected oral sex, 7% had recent unprotected anal sex, and more than half had unprotected sex while drunk or high.

Table 2.1 also shows that, at follow-up, more males in the community than incarcerated males reported the following behaviors: sexually active, multiple sex partners (>1 and >3 in the past 3 months), vaginal sex, recent unprotected vaginal sex, recent unprotected oral sex, recent unprotected anal sex, traded sex and drugs, recent use of alcohol, frequent use of alcohol, use of marijuana, recent use of marijuana, and frequent use of marijuana. In contrast, more incarcerated males engaged in anal sex with a high-risk partner than those in the community.

Females

Table 2.2 shows that, at follow-up, nearly all of the females were sexually active and had vaginal sex; more than four fifths used alcohol and marijuana. The prevalence of unprotected sex in the past 3 months was also notable: nearly two thirds had recent unprotected vaginal sex, more than one third had recent unprotected oral sex, nearly 4% had recent unprotected anal sex, and nearly half had unprotected sex while drunk or high.

Table 2.2 also shows that, at follow-up, more females in the community than incarcerated females reported the following behaviors: sexually active, vaginal sex, recent unprotected vaginal sex, recent use of alcohol, frequent use of alcohol, recent use of marijuana, and frequent use of marijuana.

2.2.1.3 Gender Differences

There were many gender differences, which are reported in Table 2.2. More males than females reported the following behaviors: multiple sex partners (>1 and >3 in the past 3 months), vaginal sex, oral sex with a high-risk partner, anal sex (receptive and/or insertive), anal sex with a high-risk partner, sex while drunk or high, frequent use of alcohol, and use of marijuana. In contrast, more females than males reported the following behaviors: receptive anal sex and injection drugs.

2.2.1.4 Age Differences (Data Not Shown)

More youth 18 years or older ($n=502$) than youth younger than 18 years ($n=222$) reported the following behaviors: recent unprotected anal sex (prevalence rate: 2.0% vs. 7.9%; $P<.05$), recent use of alcohol (prevalence rate: 28.9% vs. 52.9%; $P<.05$), and tattooing (prevalence rate: 19.8% vs. 50.1%; $P<.001$).

2.2.2 *Development of HIV/STI Risk Behaviors*

Table 2.3 shows that many participants who had not reported risk behaviors at baseline had developed them by follow-up. For example, among those who had not previously reported unprotected vaginal sex, nearly 40% of males and more than half of females reported such behavior at follow-up. More than 40% of males and nearly 40% of females began engaging in unprotected sex while drunk or high at follow-up.

2.2.2.1 Gender Differences

Table 2.3 shows that, at follow-up, more males than females had begun engaging in the following behaviors: multiple sex partners (>1 and >3 in the past 3 months), vaginal sex with a high-risk partner, anal sex (receptive and/or insertive), anal sex with a high-risk partner, use of alcohol, and frequent use of alcohol. In contrast, at follow-up more females than males had begun engaging in receptive anal sex, use of substances other than alcohol and marijuana, and injection drugs.

2.2.2.2 Racial/Ethnic Differences

Table 2.4 shows that there were few racial and ethnic differences in the development of risk behaviors; most involved the initiation of substance use among non-Hispanic whites and Hispanics. More non-Hispanic whites and Hispanics than African Americans had begun engaging in recent use of alcohol, use of substances other than alcohol or marijuana, recent use of substances other than alcohol or marijuana, and frequent use of substances other than alcohol or marijuana. More non-Hispanic whites than African Americans had begun having recent unprotected oral sex. More Hispanics than non-Hispanic whites had begun having recent unprotected anal sex.

2.2.3 Persistence of HIV/STI Risk Behaviors

Table 2.5 shows that persistence of sex and drug risk behaviors was common for both males and females. For example, among youth who had engaged in unprotected vaginal sex at baseline, more than half of males and nearly 70% of females persisted in this behavior at follow-up. More than three quarters of males and nearly 60% of females persisted in unprotected sex while drunk or high at follow-up. More than 70% of males and nearly 70% of females persisted in using substances other than alcohol and marijuana at follow-up.

2.2.3.1 Gender Differences

There were few gender differences in the tendency for risk behaviors to persist. At follow-up, more males than females had persisted in the following sex risk behaviors: multiple sex partners (>1 in the past 3 months), sex while drunk or high, and use of marijuana.

2.2.3.2 Racial/Ethnic Differences

Table 2.6 shows that there were few racial or ethnic differences in the tendency for behaviors to persist. More non-Hispanic whites and Hispanics than African Americans persisted in the following behaviors: oral sex and use of substances other than alcohol and marijuana. More Hispanics than African Americans persisted in recent use of alcohol and tattooing.

2.3 Discussion

Our findings show that youth involved in the juvenile justice system continue to be at great risk for HIV/STIs as they age. Nearly three quarters of youth engaged in one or more unprotected sexual risk behavior at follow-up. More than 60% had engaged in ten or more risk behaviors at their baseline interview (Teplin et al. 2003), and nearly two thirds of them persisted in ten or more risk behaviors at follow-up.

Irrespective of gender, race/ethnicity, or age, sex risk behaviors were prevalent and likely to persist and develop. At follow-up, more than one third of males and one fourth of females reported engaging in vaginal sex with a high-risk partner. At baseline, more than one third of males and more than half of females reported engaging in recent unprotected vaginal sex. At follow-up, more than half of youth persisted in this behavior, and more than one third developed this behavior. These findings underscore the importance of providing early HIV/STI interventions, continued outreach, and long-term interventions that focus on sex risk behaviors.

Injection risk behaviors were uncommon at baseline and at follow-up. However, our findings on risk behaviors related to non-injection drug use are of great concern. One half of our participants had a substance use disorder at baseline (Teplin et al. 2002), and more than 80% of youth reported using alcohol and marijuana at follow-up. At baseline, more than one third of participants engaged in unprotected sex while drunk or high. At follow-up, approximately three fifths of the youth persisted in this behavior, and two fifths of the youth developed this behavior. Substance abuse can lead to high-risk sexual behaviors by affecting decision making, compromising judgment, decreasing the likelihood of condom use, and increasing the likelihood of sex-for-drug exchanges and injection drug use (Chaisson et al. 1989; Chitwood et al. 1995; Cooper et al. 1994; Edlin et al. 1992, 1994; Fullilove et al. 1990; Inciardi et al. 1991; Keller et al. 1991; McBride et al. 1992; Schoenbaum et al. 1989; Shafer et al. 1993; Shrier et al. 1997; Weatherby et al. 1992; Williams 1993; Zule 1992). Yet, research on non-injection drug use and HIV/STIs has lagged, considering its importance in the current HIV/STI epidemic.

Taken together, these findings mirror the changing patterns of transmission of HIV/STIs in the general population. In the early stages of the HIV/STI epidemic, the most common patterns of transmission were injection drug use (approximately one quarter of AIDS cases) and male-to-male sex (two thirds of AIDS cases) (CDC 1987). Male-to-female sexual contact at that time accounted for only 4% of AIDS cases (CDC 1987); it now accounts for one third of reported HIV/AIDS cases (CDC 2005b).

We found a number of gender differences, even after adjusting for incarceration status. Compared with females, males had higher prevalence rates of many HIV/STI risk behaviors and were more likely to persist in some behaviors and develop new ones. Yet, injection risk behaviors were more prevalent among females than males and were also more likely to develop and persist. Our findings emphasize the need to develop interventions tailored to specific patterns of risk and transmission (CDC 2005b). For example, nearly 80% of females contract HIV/AIDS from vaginal sex compared with only 16% of males (CDC 2005b). Gender-specific interventions are especially important now that females comprise nearly 20% of juvenile detainees (Snyder and Sickmund 2006) and 26% of AIDS cases (CDC 2006a) (compared with 7% during the early years of the epidemic (CDC 1987)).

Incarceration status was an important variable. Among youth in the community, many behaviors were more prevalent at follow-up than at baseline. Among incarcerated youth, the opposite pattern prevailed. Our findings add to the growing debate on the role of incarceration in the HIV/STI epidemic. One view is that correctional facilities are "breeding grounds" for HIV/AIDS (Hammett 2006). Others suggest that the disproportionately high prevalence of HIV/AIDS in correctional facilities occurs because behaviors that put persons at risk for HIV/AIDS (e.g., drug use, prostitution) also put them at risk for incarceration (Hammett 2006).

Although risk behaviors may be less common in correctional facilities than in the community, they may carry substantially greater risk. For example, to prevent HIV/STI transmission, prisoners may use plastic gloves and hand lotion instead of lubricated condoms (CDC 2006e; Mahon 1996). Similarly, to inject drugs, inmates may share needles or "works" or use dirty equipment if sterilization is unavailable (CDC 2006e; Hammett et al. 1995; Kantor 2003; Mahon 1996). Moreover, the probability of infection is also higher, because more persons in prisons than in the community are infected with HIV (Maruschak 2006).

Overall, there were few racial and ethnic differences in patterns of HIV/STI risk behaviors; most involved the initiation and persistence of substance use among non-Hispanic whites and Hispanics. There were surprisingly few racial/ethnic differences in sex risk behaviors. Yet, because of the disproportionate numbers of African Americans who cycle through correctional facilities (Harrison and Beck 2006; Reynolds et al. 2001), the pediatrics community must focus on implementing culturally appropriate interventions for African American youth and young adults. More than any other racial/ethnic group, African Americans are disproportionately incarcerated and affected by HIV/AIDS (Belenko et al. 2005). Although African Americans comprise only 13% of the general population (United States Census Bureau 2006), and juvenile crime rates are relatively similar across race/ethnicity (Huizinga and Elliott 1987), African Americans compose about 40% of incarcerated youth and adults (Harrison and Beck 2005, 2006; Snyder and Sickmund 2006) and 49% of new cases of HIV/AIDS (42% among men and 66% among women) (CDC 2006a).

The prevalence of HIV/STI risk behaviors in our sample is similar to that of other high-risk youth: those living on the street, drug users, and those living in the inner city (Brook et al. 1998; Clements et al. 1997; Deas-Nesmith et al. 1999; DiClemente et al. 1996; Stanton et al. 1994; Stiffman et al. 1994). Primary risk reduction interventions may not reach these youth. Although most schools now provide HIV/STI education (CDC 1988, 1996), youth who are frequently truant, such as delinquent and homeless youth, are unlikely to receive school-based interventions (Dembo 1996). Moreover, delinquent youth are overrepresented in groups that are uninsured (including the poor (Brindis et al. 2003)), youth living in central cities (Holahan et al. 2003), and older adolescents (Collins et al. 2004; Holahan et al. 2003; Newacheck et al. 1999; Short and Graefe 2003), reducing the likelihood that they will have a primary care physician from whom they could receive primary interventions (Feinstein et al. 1998; Hughes and Ng 2003; Zuvekas and Weinick 1999). Public clinics and emergency services are often the primary source of health care for high-risk youth (Christakis et al. 2001; Hedberg et al. 1996). As recently recommended by the American Academy of Pediatrics (American Academy of Pediatrics Committee on Pediatric AIDS 2006), public clinics should integrate HIV prevention, especially sex education and substance abuse treatment, into primary medical care. HIV/STI interventions should also be provided in detention centers and in juvenile courts that, based on recent statistics, could reach as many as 1.6 million youth annually (Snyder and Sickmund 2006).

2.4 Limitations

It was not possible to assess actual HIV/STI risk behaviors, such as having unprotected sex with an infected partner and sharing injection/piercing equipment with an infected partner. Moreover, it was not feasible to obtain biological outcome measures, such as HIV or STI tests. Thus, our measures of HIV/STI risk are proximal. Findings might have been slightly different had follow-up data been available for participants who died, withdrew from the study, or were lost to follow-up. We examined HIV/STI risk behaviors during two periods of our subjects' lives. Our analyses do not address causal mechanisms underlying HIV/STI risk. Our findings, drawn from one site, may pertain only to youth who were detained during adolescence in urban detention centers of similar demographic composition. Our sample (though larger than most previous investigations) limited our analyses of demographic subgroups that are less common in detention centers, such as young, non-Hispanic white females. Finally, the data are subject to the limitations of self-reporting. Participants may have underreported some behaviors and exaggerated others.

2.5 Conclusions

HIV infection and disproportionate minority confinement are among the most critical racial/ethnic disparities in our nation. Future studies must explore the causes and correlates of the increased risk of HIV/STIs faced by minority youth. To develop appropriate public policy initiatives, future studies must also disentangle the role of incarceration in the transmission of HIV/STIs. Because most detained youth return to their communities, HIV/STI risk behaviors in delinquent youth are a community public health problem, not just a problem for the juvenile justice system. Improving the coordination among systems that provide HIV/STI interventions to youth – primary care, education, mental health, and juvenile justice – can reduce the prevalence of risk behaviors and substantially reduce the spread of HIV/STIs in young people. The Surgeon General will soon issue a "Call to Action on Correctional Health." By targeting HIV/STI risk behaviors in delinquent youth, we have the opportunity to redress significant health disparities and threats to public health.

References

Abram, K. M., Teplin, L. A., McClelland, G. M., & Dulcan, M. K. (2003). Comorbid psychiatric disorders in youth in juvenile detention. *Archives of General Psychiatry, 60*(11), 1097–1108.

American Academy of Pediatrics Committee on Pediatric Aids. (2006). Reducing the risk of HIV infection associated with illicit drug use. *Pediatrics, 117*(2), 566–571.

Anderson, R., Smith, B. L., & Division of Vital Statistics. (2005). Deaths: Leading causes 2002. *National Vital Statistics Reports, 53*(17), 1–92.

Belenko, S. R., Shedlin, M., & Chaple, M. (2005). HIV risk behaviors, knowledge, and prevention service experiences among African American and other offenders. *Journal of Health Care for the Poor and Underserved, 16*(4 Suppl B), 108–129.

Brindis, C., Morreale, M., & English, A. (2003). The unique health care needs of adolescents. *The Future of Children, 13*(1), 117–135.

Brook, J. S., Cohen, P., & Brook, D. W. (1998). Longitudinal study of co-occurring psychiatric disorders and substance use. *Journal of the American Academy of Child & Adolescent Psychiatry, 37*(3), 322–330.

Brook, J. S., Adams, R. E., Balka, E. B., Whiteman, M., Zhang, C., & Sugerman, R. (2004). Illicit drug use and risky sexual behavior among African American and Puerto Rican urban adolescents: The longitudinal links. *Journal of Genetic Psychology, 165*(2), 203–220.

Canterbury, R. J., McGarvey, E. L., Sheldon-Keller, A. E., Waite, D., Reams, P., & Koopman, C. (1995). Prevalence of HIV-related risk behaviors and STDs among incarcerated adolescents. *Journal of Adolescent Health, 17*(3), 173–177.

Canterbury, R. J., Clavet, G. J., McGarvey, E. L., & Koopman, C. (1998). HIV risk-related attitudes and behaviors of incarcerated adolescents: Implications for public school students. *High School Journal, 82*(1), 1–10.

Capaldi, D. M., Stoolmiller, M., Clark, S., & Owen, L. D. (2002). Heterosexual risk behaviors in at-risk young men from early adolescence to young adulthood: Prevalence, prediction, and association with STD contraction. *Developmental Psychology, 38*(3), 394–406.

Carroll, S. T., Riffenburgh, R. H., Roberts, T. A., & Myhre, E. B. (2002). Tattoos and body piercings as indicators of adolescent risk-taking behaviors. *Pediatrics, 109*(6), 1021–1027.

Catania, J. A., Gibson, D. R., Marin, B. V., Coates, T. J., & Greenblatt, R. M. (1990). Response bias in assessing sexual behaviors relevant to HIV transmission. *Evaluation & Program Planning, 13*(1), 19–29.

Centers for Disease Control and Prevention. (1987). *AIDS weekly surveillance report-United States.* AIDS Program, Center for Infectious Diseases. December 29, 1986. *Surveillance Report.* Retrieved from http://www.cdc.gov/hiv/stats/surveillance86.pdf

Centers for Disease Control and Prevention. (1988). Guidelines for effective school health education to prevent the spread of AIDS. *Morbidity & Mortality Weekly Report, 37*(S-2), 1–14.

Centers for Disease Control and Prevention. (1996). School-based HIV-prevention education United States, 1994. *Morbidity & Mortality Weekly Report, 45*(35), 760–765.

Centers for Disease Control and Prevention. (2005a). Cases of HIV infection and AIDS in the United States, 2004. *HIV/AIDS Surveillance Report, 16*, 1–46.

Centers for Disease Control and Prevention. (2005b). *HIV/AIDS surveillance – general epidemiology (through 2004)*, Slide series. Retrieved from http://www.cdc.gov/hiv/topics/surveillance/resources/slides/general/index.htm

Centers for Disease Control and Prevention. (2006a). Cases of HIV infection and AIDS in the United States, 2005. *HIV/AIDS Surveillance Report, 17*, 1–54.

Centers for Disease Control and Prevention. (2006b). *A glance at the HIV epidemic.* Retrieved from http://www.cdc.gov/hiv/PUBS/Facts/At-A-Glance.pdf

Centers for Disease Control and Prevention. (2006c). *HIV/AIDS among African Americans.* Retrieved from http://www.cdc.gov/hiv/topics/aa/resources/factsheets/pdf/aa.pdf

Centers for Disease Control and Prevention. (2006d). Cases of HIV infection and AIDS in the United States, by race/ethnicity, 2000–2004. *HIV/AIDS Surveillance Supplemental Report, 12*, 1–36.

Centers for Disease Control and Prevention. (2006e). HIV Transmission among male inmates in a state prison system – Georgia 1992–2005. *Morbidity & Mortality Weekly Report, 55*(15), 421–426.

Chaisson, R. E., Bacchetti, P., Osmond, D., Brodie, B., Sande, M. A., & Moss, A. R. (1989). Cocaine use and HIV infection in intravenous drug users in San Francisco. *Journal of the American Medical Association, 261*(4), 561–565.

Chawarski, M. C., Schottenfeld, R. S., Pakes, J., & Avants, K. (1996). AIDS risk inventory (ARI): A structured interview for assessing risk of HIV infection in a population of drug abusers.

In *Problems of drug dependence 1996: Proceedings of the 58th Annual Scientific Meeting. NIDA research monograph 174*. Washington, DC: US Department of Health and Human Services.

Chitwood, D. D., Griffin, D. K., Comerford, M., Page, J. B., Trapido, E. J., Lai, S., & McCoy, C. B. (1995). Risk factors for HIV-1 seroconversion among injection drug users: A case–control study. *American Journal of Public Health, 85*(11), 1538–1542.

Christakis, D. A., Mell, L., Koepsell, T. D., Zimmerman, F. J., & Connell, F. A. (2001). Association of lower continuity of care with greater risk of emergency department use and hospitalization in children. *Pediatrics, 107*(3), 524–529.

Clements, K., Gleghorn, A., Garcia, D., Katz, M., & Marx, R. (1997). A risk profile of street youth in northern California: Implications for gender-specific human immunodeficiency virus prevention. *Journal of Adolescent Health, 20*(5), 343–353.

Cochran, W. (1977). *Sampling techniques* (3rd ed.). New York: Wiley.

Collins, S. R., Schoen, C., Tenney, K., Doty, M. M., & Ho, A. (2004). Rite of passage? Why young adults become uninsured and how new policies can help. *Issue Brief (Commonwealth Fund), 649*, 1–8.

Cooper, M. L., Peirce, R. S., & Huselid, R. F. (1994). Substance use and sexual risk taking among black adolescents and white adolescents. *Health Psychology, 13*(3), 251–262.

D'Angelo, L., & DiClemente, R. (1996). Sexually transmitted diseases including human immunodeficiency virus infection. In R. DiClemente, W. Hansen, & L. Ponton (Eds.), *Handbook of adolescent health risk behavior* (pp. 333–367). New York: Plenum Press.

Deas-Nesmith, D., Brady, K. T., White, R., & Campbell, S. (1999). HIV-risk behaviors in adolescent substance abusers. *Journal of Substance Abuse Treatment, 16*(2), 169–172.

Dembo, R. (1996). Problems among youths entering the juvenile justice system, their service needs and innovative approaches to address them. *Substance Use & Misuse, 31*(1), 81–94.

Devieux, J., Malow, R., Stein, J. A., Jennings, T. E., Lucenko, B. A., Averhart, C., & Kalichman, S. (2002). Impulsivity and HIV risk among adjudicated alcohol- and other drug-abusing adolescent offenders. *AIDS Education & Prevention, 14*(5 Suppl B), 24–35.

DiClemente, R. J., Lanier, M. M., Horan, P. F., & Lodico, M. (1991). Comparison of AIDS knowledge, attitudes, and behaviors among incarcerated adolescents and a public school sample in San Francisco. *American Journal of Public Health, 81*(5), 628–630.

DiClemente, R. J., Lodico, M., Grinstead, O. A., Harper, G., Rickman, R. L., Evans, P. E., & Coates, T. J. (1996). African-American adolescents residing in high-risk urban environments do use condoms: Correlates and predictors of condom use among adolescents in public housing developments. *Pediatrics, 98*(2 Pt 1), 269–278.

Dowling, S., Johnson, M. E., & Fisher, D. G. (1994). Reliability of drug users' self-reported recent drug use. *Assessment, 1*, 382–392.

Edlin, B. R., Irwin, K. L., Ludwig, D. D., McCoy, H. V., Serrano, Y., Word, C., Bowser, B. P., Faruque, S., McCoy, C. B., Schilling, R. F., & The Multicenter Crack Cocaine and HIV Infection Study Team. (1992). High-risk sex behavior among young street-recruited crack cocaine smokers in three American cities: an interim report. *Journal of Psychoactive Drugs, 24*(4), 363–371.

Edlin, B. R., Irwin, K. L., Faruque, S., McCoy, C. B., Word, C., Serrano, Y., Inciardi, J. A., Bowser, B. P., Schilling, R. F., Holmberg, S. D., & The Multicenter Crack Cocaine and HIV Infection Study Team. (1994). Intersecting epidemics – crack cocaine use and HIV infection among inner-city young adults. *New England Journal of Medicine, 331*(21), 1422–1427.

Federal Register. (1991, June 18). *Federal policy for the protection of human subjects: Notices and Rules. Part 2, 56*(117): 28002–32 (56 FR 28002).

Feinstein, R. A., Lampkin, A., Lorish, C. D., Klerman, L. V., Maisiak, R., & Oh, M. K. (1998). Medical status of adolescents at time of admission to a juvenile detention center. *Journal of Adolescent Health, 22*(3), 190–196.

Fisher, J. D., Fisher, W. A., Bryan, A. D., & Misovich, S. J. (2002). Information-motivation-behavioral skills model-based HIV risk behavior change intervention for inner-city high school youth. *Health Psychology, 21*(2), 177–186.

Fullilove, R. E., Fullilove, M. T., Bowser, B. P., & Gross, S. A. (1990). Risk of sexually transmitted disease among black adolescent crack users in Oakland and San Francisco, Calif. *Journal of the American Medical Association, 263*(6), 851–855.

Hammett, T. M. (2006). HIV/AIDS and other infectious diseases among correctional inmates: transmission, burden, and an appropriate response. *American Journal of Public Health, 96*(6), 974–978.

Hammett, T. M., & Daugherty, A. (1991). Epidemiology of HIV disease in correctional facilities and the population at large. In T. M. Hammett & A. L. Daugherty (Eds.), *1990 Update: AIDS in correctional facilities* (pp. 9–24). Washington, DC: US Department of Justice, National Institute of Justice.

Hammett, T. M., Widom, R., Epstein, J., Gross, M., Sifre, S., & Enos, T. (1995). *1994 Update: HIV/AIDS and STDs in correctional facilities*. Washington, DC: US Department of Justice.

Harrison, P. M., & Beck, A. J. (2005). *Prison and jail inmates at midyear 2004*. (NCJ Publication No. 208801). Washington, DC: US Department of Justice.

Harrison, P. M., & Beck, A. J. (2006). *Prison and jail inmates at midyear 2005*. (NCJ Publication No. 213133). Washington, DC: US Department of Justice.

Hedberg, V. A., Byrd, R. S., Klein, J. D., Auinger, P., & Weitzman, M. (1996). The role of community health centers in providing preventive care to adolescents. *Archives of Pediatrics & Adolescent Medicine, 150*(6), 603–608.

Holahan, J., Dubay, L., & Kenney, G. (2003). Which children are still uninsured and why. *The Future of Children, 13*(1), 55–79.

Horsburgh, C., Jarvis, J. Q., McArther, T., Ignacio, T., & Stock, P. (1990). Seroconversion to human immunodeficiency virus in prison inmates. *American Journal of Public Health, 80*(2), 209–210.

Hosmer, D. W., & Lemeshow, S. (2000). *Applied logistic regression* (2nd ed.). New York: Wiley.

Hughes, D. C., & Ng, S. (2003). Reducing health disparitites among children. *The Future of Children, 13*(1), 153–167.

Huizinga, D., & Elliott, D. S. (1987). Juvenile offenders: prevalence, offender incidence, and arrest rates by race. *Crime and Delinquency, 33*(2), 206–223.

Inciardi, J., Pottieger, A., Forney, M., Chitwood, D., & McBride, D. (1991). Prostitution, IV drug use, and sex-for-crack exchanges among serious delinquents: risks for HIV infection. *Criminology, 29*, 221–235.

Jemmott, J. B., Jemmott, L. S., & Fong, G. T. (1992). Reductions in HIV risk-associated sexual behaviors among black male adolescents: Effects of an AIDS prevention intervention. *American Journal of Public Health, 82*(3), 372–377.

Kaiser Family Foundation. (2006a). *HIV/AIDS policy fact sheet: African Americans and HIV/AIDS*. Retrieved from http://www.kff.org/hivaids/upload/6089-03.pdf

Kaiser Family Foundation. (2006b, February). *HIV/AIDS policy fact sheet: Latinos and HIV/AIDS*. Retrieved from http://www.kff.org/hivaids/upload/6007-03.pdf

Kantor, E. (2003). *HIV transmission and prevention in prisons, HIV InSite Knowledge Base Chapter* [online text]. Retrieved from http://hivinsite.ucsf.edu/InSite?page=kb-07&doc=kb-07-04-13

Karon, J. M., Fleming, P. L., Steketee, R. W., & De Cock, K. M. (2001). HIV in the United States at the turn of the century: an epidemic in transition. *American Journal of Public Health, 91*(7), 1060–1068.

Katz, B. P., Fortenberry, J. D., Tu, W., Harezlak, J., & Orr, D. P. (2001). Sexual behavior among adolescent women at high risk for sexually transmitted infections. *Sexually Transmitted Diseases, 28*(5), 247–251.

Keller, S. E., Bartlett, J. A., Schleifer, S. J., Johnson, R. L., Pinner, E., & Delaney, B. (1991). HIV-relevant sexual behavior among a healthy inner-city heterosexual adolescent population in an endemic area of HIV. *Journal of Adolescent Health, 12*(1), 44–48.

Kingree, J. B., & Phan, D. L. (2001). Marijuana use and HIV risk among adolescent offenders: the moderating effect of age. *Journal of Substance Abuse, 13*(1–2), 59–71.

Kipke, M. D., Unger, J. B., Palmer, R. F., & Edgington, R. (1996). Drug use, needle sharing, and HIV risk among injection drug-using street youth. *Substance Use & Misuse, 31*(9), 1167–1187.

Kochanek, K. D., Sherry, M., Anderson, R., Scott, C., & Division of Vital Statistics. (2004). Deaths: Final data for 2002. *National Vital Statistics Report, 53*(5), 1–116.

Korn, E. L., & Graubard, B. I. (1990). Simultaneous testing of regression coefficients with complex survey data: Use of Bonferroni t statistics. *American Statistician, 44*, 270–276.

Levy, P., & Lemeshow, S. (1999). *Sampling of populations: Methods and applications* (3rd ed.). New York: Wiley.

Long, G. E., & Rickman, L. S. (1994). Infectious complications of tattoos. *Clinical Infectious Diseases, 18*(4), 610–619.

Lucenko, B. A., Malow, R. M., Sanchez-Martinez, M., Jennings, T., & Devieux, J. G. (2003). Negative affect and HIV risk in alcohol and other drug (AOD) abusing adolescent offenders. *Journal of Child & Adolescent Substance Abuse, 13*(1), 1–17.

Magura, S., Kang, S. Y., Shapiro, J., & O'Day, J. (1993). HIV risk among women injecting drug users who are in jail. *Addiction, 88*(10), 1351–1360.

Magura, S., Kang, S. Y., & Shapiro, J. L. (1994). Outcomes of intensive AIDS education for male adolescent drug users in jail. *Journal of Adolescent Health, 15*(6), 457–463.

Mahon, N. (1996). New York inmates' HIV risk behaviors: The implications for prevention policy and programs. *American Journal of Public Health, 86*(9), 1211–1215.

Maruschak, L. M. (2006). *HIV in prisons, 2004, Bureau of Justice Statistics Bulletin* (NCJ Publication No. 213897). Washington, DC: US Department of Justice.

McBride, D. C., Inciardi, J. A., Chitwood, D. D., McCoy, C. B., & The National AIDS Research Consortium. (1992). Crack use and correlates of use in a national population of street heroin users. *Journal of Psychoactive Drugs, 24*(4), 411–416.

McClelland, G., Teplin, L. A., Abram, K. M., & Jacobs, N. (2002). HIV and AIDS risk behaviors among female jail detainees: Implications for public heath policy. *American Journal of Public Health, 92*(5), 818–825.

Morris, R. E., Harrison, E. A., Knox, G. W., Tromanhauser, E., Marquis, D. K., & Watts, L. L. (1995). Health risk behavioral survey from 39 juvenile correctional facilities in the United States. *Journal of Adolescent Health, 17*(6), 334–344.

Morris, M., Handcock, M. S., Miller, W. C., Ford, C. A., Schmitz, J. L., Hobbs, M. M., Cohen, M. S., Harris, K. M., & Urdy, J. R. (2006). Prevalence of HIV infection among young adults in the United States: results from the Add Health Study. *American Journal of Public Health, 96*(6), 1091–1097.

Needle, R., Fisher, D., Weatherby, N., Chitwood, D., Brown, D., Cesari, H., Booth, R., Williams, M. L., Watters, J., Andersen, M., & Braunstein, M. (1995). The reliability of self-reported HIV risk behaviors of drug users. *Psychology of Addictive Behaviors, 9*(4), 242–250.

Newacheck, P. W., Brindis, C. D., Cart, C. U., Marchi, K., & Irwin, C. E. (1999). Adolescent health insurance coverage: Recent changes and access to care. *Pediatrics, 104*(2 Pt 1), 195–202.

Otto-Salaj, L., Gore-Felton, C., McGarvey, E., & Canterbury, R. (2002). Psychiatric functioning and substance use: Factors associated with HIV risk among incarcerated adolescents. *Child Psychiatry & Human Development, 22*, 91–106.

Reynolds, A. J., Temple, J. A., Robertson, D. L., & Mann, E. A. (2001). Long-term effects of an early childhood intervention on educational achievement and juvenile arrest: A 15-year follow-up of low-income children. *Journal of the American Medical Association, 285*(18), 2339–2346.

Rolf, J., Nanda, J., Baldwin, J., Chandra, A., & Thompson, L. (1990). Substance misuse and HIV/AIDS risks among delinquents: A prevention challenge. *International Journal of the Addictions, 25*(4A), 533–559.

Schoenbaum, E. E., Hartel, D., Selwyn, P. A., Klein, R. S., Davenny, K., Rogers, M., et al. (1989). Risk factors for human immunodeficiency virus infection in intravenous drug users. *New England Journal of Medicine, 321*(13), 874–879.

Shafer, M., Hilton, J. F., Ekstrand, M., Keogh, J., Gee, L., Digiorgio-Haag, L., Shalwitz, J., & Schachter, J. (1993). Relationship between drug use and sexual behaviors and the occurence of sexually transmitted diseases among high-risk male youth. *Sexually Transmitted Diseases, 20*, 307–313.

Shaffer, D., Fisher, P., Dulcan, M. K., Davies, M., Piacentini, J., Schwab-Stone, M. E., Lahey, B. B., Bourdon, K., Jensen, P. S., Bird, H. R., Canino, G., & Regier, D. A. (1996). The NIMH diagnostic interview schedule for children version 2.3 (DISC-2.3): Description, acceptability, prevalence rates, and performance in the MECA study: Methods for the epidemiology of child and adolescent mental disorders study. *Journal of the American Academy of Child & Adolescent Psychiatry, 35*(7), 865–877.

Short, P. F., & Graefe, D. R. (2003). Battery-powered health insurance? Stability in coverage of the uninsured. *Health Affairs, 22*(6), 244–255.

Shrier, L. A., Emans, S. J., Woods, E. R., & DuRant, R. H. (1997). The association of sexual risk behaviors and problem drug behaviors in high school students. *Journal of Adolescent Health, 20*(5), 377–383.

Snyder, H. N., & Sickmund, M. (2006). *Juvenile offenders and victims: 2006 national report.* Washington, DC: US Department of Justice, Office of Juvenile Justice Programs, Office of Juvenile Justice and Delinquency Prevention.

Stanton, B., Li, X., Black, M., Ricardo, I., Galbraith, J., Kaljee, L., & Feigelman, S. (1994). Sexual practices and intentions among preadolescent and early adolescent low-income urban African-Americans. *Pediatrics, 93*(6 Pt 1), 966–973.

Stiffman, A. R., Dore, P., & Cunningham, R. M. (1994). Inner-city youths and condom use: Health beliefs, clinic care, welfare, and the HIV epidemic. *Adolescence, 29*(116), 805–820.

Stiffman, A. R., Dore, P., Cunningham, R. M., & Earls, F. (1995). Person and environment in HIV risk behavior change between adolescence and young adulthood. *Health Education Quarterly, 22*(2), 211–226.

Teplin, L. A., Abram, K. M., McClelland, G. M., Dulcan, M. K., & Mericle, A. A. (2002). Psychiatric disorders in youth in juvenile detention. *Archives of General Psychiatry, 59*(12), 1133–1143.

Teplin, L. A., Mericle, A. A., McClelland, G. M., & Abram, K. M. (2003). HIV and AIDS risk behaviors in juvenile detainees: Implications for public health policy. *American Journal of Public Health, 93*(6), 906–912.

Teplin, L. A., Elkington, K. S., McClelland, G. M., Abram, K. M., Mericle, A. A., & Washburn, J. J. (2005). Major mental disorders, substance use disorders, comorbidity, and HIV-AIDS risk behaviors in juvenile detainees. *Psychiatric Services, 56*(7), 823–828.

US Census Bureau. (2006). Resident population, by race, hispanic origin, and age: 2000 to 2005. *The 2007 Statistical Abstract*, Table 14. Retrieved from http://www.census.gov/compendia/statab/population/

Valois, R. F., Oeltmann, J. E., Waller, J., & Hussey, J. R. (1999). Relationship between number of sexual intercourse partners and selected health risk behaviors among public high school adolescents. *Journal of Adolescent Health, 25*(5), 328–335.

Watters, J. (1994). *Street youth at risk for AIDS.* Paper presented at the Final Report Rockville, MD.

Weatherby, N. L., Shultz, J. M., Chitwood, D. D., McCoy, H. V., McCoy, C. B., Ludwig, D. D., et al. (1992). Crack cocaine use and sexual activity in Miami, Florida. *Journal of Psychoactive Drugs, 24*(4), 373–380.

Weatherby, N. L., Needle, R., & Cesari, H. (1994). Validity of self-reported drug use among injection drug users and crack cocaine users recruited through street outreach. *Evaluation and Program Planning, 17*, 347–355.

Weinstock, H., Berman, S., & Cates, W. (2004). Sexually transmitted diseases among American youth: Incidence and prevalence estimates, 2000. *Perspectives on Sexual & Reproductive Health, 36*(1), 6–10.

Williams, M. (1993). HIV infection among a national sample of adolescent intravenous drug abusers. *Alcohol Treatment Quarterly, 10*, 107–121.

Winters, K. C. (1999). *TIP 31: Screening and assessing adolescents for substance use disorders* (DHHS Publication No. SMA 99-3282, Vol. 2006). Retrieved from http://www.ncbi.nlm.nih.gov/books/bv.fcgi?rid=hstat5.chapter.54841

Zule, W. A. (1992). Risk and reciprocity: HIV and the injection drug user. *Journal of Psychoactive Drugs, 24*(3), 243–249.

Zuvekas, S. H., & Weinick, R. M. (1999). Changes in access to care, 1977–1996: The role of health insurance. *Health Services Research, 34*(1 Pt 2), 271–279.

Chapter 3
Risky Sexual Behavior and Negative Health Consequences Among Incarcerated Female Adolescents: Implications for Public Health Policy and Practice

Jane K. Steinberg, Christine E. Grella, and Melina R. Boudov

Abstract *Young female offenders are at a heightened risk of participating in unsafe sexual behaviors. Juvenile detention facilities are important venues for screening such youth for sexually transmitted diseases (STD) and other preventable health conditions. Recognition of sexual risk behaviors and their health consequences increases the need to provide interventions that address sex-linked risk behaviors. However, detection and treatment of STDs within juvenile correctional facilities are often lacking or non-existent, and youth often suffer from such conditions prior to, during and after their incarceration. This chapter describes a pilot STD case management program to identify risk factors for Chlamydia and gonorrhea among a sample of 540 case records of STD positive, incarcerated female adolescents who completed a health risk assessment in a California juvenile detention facility between January 2006 and June 2007. The chapter first reviews some of the specific risk factors for female delinquency and participation in risky sexual behaviors. From here, STDs among incarcerated juvenile females are discussed, as well as some challenges in delivering health-related services to this population. The chapter then provides an overview of the pilot STD program, including data about the participants. Finally, the implications for policy and prevention programming among incarcerated female adolescents in terms of their sexual risk behaviors are discussed.*

The authors acknowledge the work of case managers Kirsten Wilson and Kimberly Coffee, who conducted intake interviews. We also thank Elizabeth Teshome and Kris Langabeer, who assisted with manuscript preparation, and Christine Wells of the University of California, Los Angeles Academic Technology Services who provided statistical support.

J.K. Steinberg, Ph.D., M.P.H. (✉) • M.R. Boudov, M.A.
Sexually Transmitted Disease (STD) Program, 2615 South Grand Avenue, Suite 500, Los Angeles, CA 90007, USA
e-mail:jsteinberg@ph.lacounty.gov

C.E. Grella, Ph.D.
Integrated Substance Abuse Programs, Semel Institute for Neuroscience and Human Behavior, University of California, Los Angeles, CA, USA

B. Sanders et al. (eds.), *Crime, HIV and Health: Intersections of Criminal Justice and Public Health Concerns*, DOI 10.1007/978-90-481-8921-2_3,

Approximately 12,000 females are housed in the juvenile justice system in the United States, representing approximately 15% of the total population of detained juveniles (Sickmund 2010). Incarcerated female adolescents are at significantly increased risk of adverse health outcomes relative to their incarcerated male counterparts and to non-incarcerated adolescent females in the community (Cromwell et al. 2002; Staples-Horne 2007; Zahn et al. 2008). Such outcomes include: depression, anxiety, reproductive health problems due to high-risk sexual behaviors, and unmet drug treatment needs (Abram et al. 2003; Farabee et al. 2001; Staples-Horne 2007). Incarcerated female adolescents also have a host of complex health, educational and treatment needs, which differ significantly from those of incarcerated males, and necessitate tailored interventions (Amaro et al. 2001; Timmons-Mitchell et al. 1997).

Research has indicated that risk factors for delinquency that impact female differently from males include sexual and physical abuse, difficulty in school, prior delinquency, gang-related activities, early puberty, and romantic partners involved with crime (Zahn et al. 2008). However, research has identified significant gaps in knowledge regarding the identification of at-risk girls prior to their contact with juvenile justice system, as well effective prevention and intervention strategies for them (Zahn 2007). As Krisberg (2005, p. 115) has noted, delinquency intervention programs are not really geared specifically for incarcerated females:

> [T]here are few, if any, specialized programs for young women. A popular comment is that current girls' programs involve little more than taking a boys' program and 'painting it pink.' Such programs are often guided by gross stereotypes about the adolescent development of young women (e.g., girls like tea parties, young women are inherently deceitful, the principal focus of girls' programs should be helping them find an acceptable mate, and girls need to learn to control their sexual urges.) Moreover, girls' programs are often given fewer budgetary resources, and young women are given second-class access to educational, vocational, and recreational resources in juvenile corrections system.

Other researchers have examined evaluation evidence for nine programs targeting girls and six programs for both boys and girls in custody, and found that comprehensive programs targeting multiple risk factors appeared to work best in reducing subsequent delinquency, irrespective of sex (Zahn et al. 2009). The authors added that this finding did not necessarily mean that female-specific programs are unnecessary, but that more well designed, female-specific programs are needed in order to encourage further evaluations.

The Juvenile Justice and Delinquency Prevention Act of 1974 specified that programs should be established to meet the full range of health needs (e.g., mental health, general health care, substance abuse, physical and sexual assault) experienced by female offenders (Trupin et al. 2002). However, the evidence suggests that many juvenile correctional facilities do not offer sexual or reproductive health services or those related to substance abuse or mental health for detained girls (Gallagher et al. 2007; Otto et al. 1992; Pajer et al. 2007). Thus, detained females adolescents not only often fail to be provided delinquency intervention services, but also basic health-related services.

This chapter first reviews some of the literature on pathways into delinquency for adolescent females, and how risk factors impact females in distinct ways from males.

Then, sexually transmitted diseases (STDs) among incarcerated female adolescents are discussed, as well as some of the challenges in delivering health services to detained female adolescents. Then, the chapter will provide an overview of an STD case management intervention program for girls in a detention center in California, including components of the intervention, descriptive statistics on the population, and qualitative data extracted from case files. Finally, the implications of this program for policy and prevention programming among incarcerated female adolescents are discussed.

3.1 Pathways into Delinquency for Female Adolescents

A great deal of research has examined the factors involved in male delinquency, but the factors involved in female delinquency are still not fully known (Zahn et al. 2008). In an effort to understand the causes of female delinquency, the Office of Juvenile Justice and Delinquency Prevention convened a group of researchers and practitioners called the *Girls Study Group*. Through extensive literature reviews, several factors were identified that increase girl's risks of delinquency more than a boy's, including early puberty, sexual abuse, depression and anxiety, conflict with parents and involvement with delinquent (and often older) male partners (Zahn et al. 2008, 2010).

Early puberty. Females generally reach puberty before males. Early onset of puberty in females is associated with other risk-taking behaviors, such as dating at younger ages and affiliating with older males involved in delinquency or crime (Stattin and Magnusson 1990). Interest in the opposite sex at earlier ages also leads to delinquency indirectly through increased conflict with parents over dating (e.g. curfew, running away, dating 'older' guys) and conflict with other girls (e.g. violence over boyfriends) (Heimer and De Costa 2010; Paikoff and Brooks-Gunn 1991).

Sexual abuse. Studies have also examined how various forms of abuse are associated with risky sexual behaviors. For example, sexual abuse has been associated with earlier maturation and age of sexual debut (Kendler et al. 2000). Early age of sexual initiation, in turn, is generally associated with participating in other unsafe sexual behaviors, such as sex with multiple partners, sex without contraception, sex with older males, sex with coercion or violence, and sex while intoxicated (Baumgartner et al. 2009; Sanfort et al. 2008; Sneed 2009).

Several studies have reported differences between males and females in the impact of childhood sexual abuse on future delinquency. For instance, Herrera and McCloskey (2001) conducted a prospective study of 299 children who were interviewed with their mothers about forms of abuse in the family. At 5 year follow up, a search of juvenile court records was performed for these same children. Exposure to marital violence in childhood predicted referral to juvenile court for both sexes. While no sex differences emerged in overall referral rates to juvenile court, boys were more likely than girls to be referred for property, felony, and violent offenses.

Girls with a history of physical child abuse were arrested for violent offenses more than boys with similar histories, but the context of violent offenses differed dramatically by sex: nearly all referrals for a violent offense for girls were for domestic violence. The authors concluded that it may take more severe abuse to prompt violence in girls than is necessary to explain boys' violent offending.

McCormack and colleagues (1986) reported that sexually abused female runaways were significantly more likely than their non-abused counterparts to engage in delinquency, such as substance abuse, petty theft, and prostitution, whereas sexually abused male runaways did not show a different pattern of delinquency than non-abused male runaways. Also, Dembo et al. (1995) noted that females' problem behavior relates to an abusive and traumatizing home life, whereas males' law-violating behavior reflects their involvement in a delinquent life style. Other theorists also have related female delinquency in general to experiences of sexual abuse in the home (Chesney-Lind 2010; Siegal and Williams 2003).

Prostitution, substance use, and sexual abuse. Sexual abuse has also been linked with entry into specific forms of delinquency for females, such as prostitution. McClanahan et al. (1999), for instance, examined pathways into prostitution in a sample of 1,142 female jail detainees. The authors measured the effects of childhood sexual abuse, running away, and early drug use on entry into prostitution and their differential effects over the life-course. Two distinct pathways were identified: running away had an effect on entry into prostitution in early adolescence, but little effect later in life; and childhood sexual assault nearly doubled the odds of entry into prostitution throughout the lives of females. Although the prevalence of drug use was higher among prostitutes than among non-prostitutes, drug abuse alone did not explain entry into prostitution.

Wilson and Widom (2010) examined adolescent problem behaviors (e.g., early sexual initiation, running away, delinquency, school problems, and early substance use) as potential mediators of the relationship between childhood maltreatment and involvement in prostitution. Using a prospective cohort design, abused and neglected children were matched with non-abused, non-neglected children ($n = 1,196$) and followed into young adulthood. Individuals with a history of child abuse and neglect were at increased risk for all problem behaviors except substance use. In the full model, only early sexual initiation remained significant as a mediator in the pathway from child abuse and neglect to prostitution. The authors noted that previous findings with this sample suggest that substance use may in fact represent a separate pathway to prostitution, independent of child abuse and neglect (Wilson and Widom 2009).

Depression and anxiety. Several studies have documented that symptoms of depression, anxiety, suicidality, and post-traumatic stress disorder (PTSD) are more prevalent among incarcerated adolescent girls compared to boys (Abram et al. 2004, 2008; Teplin et al. 2002; Timmons-Mitchell et al. 1997). Moreover, PTSD and substance use disorders are more strongly linked among girls than boys in juvenile detention (Abram et al. 2003).

Although the causal relationship of psychological distress and mental disorders with the onset of risk behaviors cannot be determined from these observational studies, some longitudinal research suggests that depressive disorders precede involvement in antisocial behaviors for girls. For instance, a longitudinal study of girls aged 12–15 years old from inner-city neighborhoods in Chicago ($n=754$) found that mild to moderate symptoms of depression were associated with later involvement in antisocial behavior (Obeidallah and Earls 1999). Using data from the National Longitudinal Survey of Youth, Vaske and Gehring (2010) examined whether the mechanisms underlying the relationship between depression and delinquency varied between male and female adolescents. The authors found that depression increased the odds of peer rejection for males, which subsequently increased males' involvement in delinquency. Conversely, substance abuse mediated the relationship between depression and delinquency for female adolescents.

Washburn and colleagues (2007) have suggested that chronic depression and its associated symptoms of hopelessness, pessimism, low self-esteem, and poor coping skills, put youth at risk for antisocial behavior by increasing their willingness to engage in self-destructive and risky behaviors. In contrast, the increased levels of fearfulness associated with anxiety disorders may inhibit involvement in antisocial behaviors. However, the authors also suggested that these relationships may vary by sex. In a longitudinal study of over 1,100 youth in juvenile detention, they found that dysthymia (chronic depression) increased the odds whereas generalized anxiety disorder decreased the odds of developing antisocial personality disorder for males, but not females (Washburn et al. 2007). The lower prevalence of antisocial personality disorder among females may have limited the predictive relationship with other mental disorders, yet others have proposed that the same mechanisms that lead from childhood disorders to later adolescent and early adult antisocial behaviors may have different developmental trajectories for boys and girls (Silverthorn and Frick 1999).

Romantic partners and delinquency. Studies have indicated that when a girl's boyfriend commits an offense, she may also commit an offense (Zahn et al. 2008, 2010). Haynie et al. (2005) found that a romantic partner's delinquency influenced the likelihood of delinquency in the other partner, but that this dynamic had more relevancy for girls' delinquency than for boys'. Girls may also adopt antisocial behaviors such as substance use to cope with partner abuse, to win their partner's approval, or to fit in with peers (Giordano et al. 2002). Additionally, violence related to jealousy and other relationship problems may also contribute to girls' delinquency (Heimer and De Costa 2010; Miller and White 2003).

3.2 Health Service Needs and Service Gaps among Incarcerated Female Adolescents

Both male and female incarcerated adolescents are often medically underserved because they tend to be economically impoverished, lack health insurance and are less likely to have access to routine health care (Staples-Horne 2007). Compared to their male counterparts, however, incarcerated female adolescents have reported higher rates of reproductive and sexually-linked health issues, such as unprotected sex while intoxicated, unintended pregnancy, and early age of sexual initiation (Gallagher et al.

2007; Morris et al. 1995; Chap. 2 by Romero et al., this volume; Stiffman et al. 1995). Incarcerated females also have higher rates of STDs than their male counterparts (Bauer et al. 2004). This is due primarily to increased biological susceptibility to infection (Centers for Disease Control and Prevention [CDC] 2010).

In the United States, Chlamydia and gonorrhea rates are highest in adolescent females aged 15–19 years old and in males aged 20–24 years old (CDC 2003). Chlamydia prevalence monitoring in juvenile detention settings has reported rates of up to 16% among females screened in detention facilities in the United States, compared to 7% among females screened in family planning clinics (CDC 2009; Kahn et al. 2005). In contrast, among incarcerated adolescent boys, Chlamydia positivity has ranged from 5.9 to 14.4% and gonorrhea positivity from 0.6 to 6.7% (Belenko et al. 2009).

Chlamydia is often asymptomatic, and adolescent females have a disproportionate burden of serious sequelae from other STDs, including increased risks of exposure to HIV (CDC 1998; Cohen et al. 1999; Gaydos et al. 2003). Unrecognized, untreated or inadequately treated STDs in adolescent females can lead to long-term morbidity and mortality associated with pelvic inflammatory disease, ectopic pregnancy, infertility, perinatal infections and poor birth outcomes (CDC 2006). Given the high rate of STD morbidity among incarcerated female adolescents, screening for Chlamydia and gonorrhea has been shown to be a cost-effective strategy for preventing adverse reproductive health consequences (Kraut et al. 2002) and the CDC recommends annual screening for sexually active adolescents.

Despite increased health risks for detained females, research suggests that sexual health and other reproductive health services are generally lacking within incarceration facilities. Gallagher and colleagues (2007) conducted a national study of juvenile justice facilities and found that universal (full population) testing for pregnancy and STDs occurred in less than 18% of all facilities surveyed. Likewise, Pajer et al. (2007) found that, while 25% of all facilities reported housing at least one pregnant adolescent, an equal number of facilities offered no obstetric services. A report in Los Angeles found that sex-specific health care and reproductive health services were lacking and were needed among incarcerated females (Los Angeles County Juvenile Justice Coordinating Committee 2001).

Other studies have reported that mental health and substance abuse treatment services were lacking in detention settings despite the significant percentage of youth in the juvenile justice system that exhibited serious mental or emotional problems with a co-occurring substance use disorder (Otto et al. 1992; Pajer et al. 2007; Trupin et al. 2002). These findings are particularly alarming, given that correctional health care is often the primary source of care for incarcerated adolescents (American Academy of Pediatrics 2001). In short-term facilities, such as juvenile hall settings, continuity of care is often compromised because newly arrested youths spend less than 24 h in custody and are often released before receiving a medical exam (Snyder and Sickmund 2006). In addition, the high volume of juveniles in many facilities restricts staff's ability to provide health or mental health services, along with individual health education or risk reduction counseling (Austin et al. 2000). Once detainees leave the juvenile justice system, they often lose access to an organized system of referrals due to limited discharge planning. Incarceration thus offers a critically important opportunity to address the physical and mental health care and needs of female adolescents.

3.3 STD Screening and Treatment in Juvenile Detention Settings in California

Juvenile detention facilities are important venues for screening high-risk youth who may not otherwise access care (McDonnell et al. 2009). A pilot program sought to identify risk factors for Chlamydia and gonorrhea among incarcerated adolescents in a county in California juvenile detention facilities that began an STD screening and case management program in 1996. This project began as one of 14 CDC-funded pilot project youth programs across the United States. The goals of this project were to: develop innovative, locally relevant approaches to adolescent STD prevention and control; expand the range and access of services beyond clinic-based facilities; and increase commitment of local resources (DeLisle and Wasserheit 1999). Operated by employees of the health department, a key program goal was to establish contact with high-risk females who were either in juvenile hall or recently released to ensure timely treatment to reduce the impact of STD morbidity and sequelae. Prior to the inception of this pilot project, high rates of STD re-infection were reported among detainees due to the lack of partner services offered (DeLisle and Wasserheit 1999).

Since its inception in 1996, the pilot project has become a fully developed program with ongoing funding. All female detainees in this county's juvenile detention center are now screened for STDs within two hours of admission. After initial processing, juveniles are then taken to the medical unit for a health screening that includes the collection of a urine specimen for Chlamydia and gonorrhea testing, and a blood specimen for syphilis testing. Upon receipt of a positive STD diagnosis (usually within 5 days of admission), clinical staff members at the juvenile halls initiate STD treatment for all positive female detainees. At the same time, two public health case managers from the program follow up with these and any other STD-positive female clients to ensure that treatment was completed (single dose oral antibiotic) and provide partner services (e.g., staff elicit names of partners to encourage them to get treated in a clinic or staff will provide field-based treatment to the partner). In addition, case managers provide individualized STD/HIV risk assessment counseling and offer referrals to appropriate ancillary services. The risk assessment includes information on demographics, arrest charge, sexual risk behaviors, reproductive health status, prior STDs, substance use, sexual/physical abuse history, education, and housing needs. For those clients who are released from custody prior to receiving treatment, staff provide extensive field follow-up. Over 90% of all clients initially released untreated have completed treatment following discharge.

3.3.1 Profiles of Project Participants and Qualitative Findings

To illustrate the risk profiles of adolescent girls in the juvenile justice system, data are described from case records of a sample ($n = 540$) of female detainees who completed a risk assessment between January 2006 and June 2007. All detainees had confirmed Chlamydia and gonorrhea reported to the local health department and were receiving case management through this project.

Demographics, substance use, and sexual risk behaviors among the sample are summarized in Table 3.1. The sample ranged in age from 12 to 18 years old, with a mean age of 15.8 years. Almost half of the sample were African American (49.3%), followed by Hispanic (37.4%), "other" ethnic group (7.4%), and White (7%). Over two-fifths of the sample (42.2%) received an arrest charge for a warrant or violation of probation (e.g., lack of school attendance, no show for court date); 18% were arrested for a property-related crime; 16.3% for a violent crime; 12% for a prostitution-related charge (including loitering with intent); and 11% for a drug-related arrest (including violating terms of drug parole). While the majority of the sample lived with an adult (80%), in most cases they lived with their mother, grandmother, aunt or friend's parent. About one in five (19%) of the sample lived away from home, which consisted of living with friends, relatives, a partner or pimp, on the streets/runaway or in a foster home, group home or other placement.

Significant participation in high-risk behaviors characterized the sample. Respondents reported an average of nine lifetime sexual partners, and their average age of sexual initiation was 14 years old, which is 3.5 years younger than the national average for females (Gates and Sonenstein 2000). Moreover, 61% of the sample reported having not using condoms at their last sexual encounter, and 18% had a history of exchanging sex for money or drugs. Over one-fourth reported a pregnancy reported a prior pregnancy and 7% were pregnant upon admission to juvenile hall. Lifetime STD infections were reported by 27% of the sample, and 20% reported prior sexual abuse. Half of the sample reported that prior to becoming incarcerated, they used alcohol or drugs on a daily basis. Marijuana was the most frequently reported drug (37%), followed by alcohol (21%), and crystal methamphetamine (16%). One-fifth (20.2%) reported polydrug use, the sequential and simultaneous combination of two or more substances.

3.3.2 Qualitative Findings: Condom Use

One of the risk assessment questions asked the client why they did not use condoms at their last sexual encounter. Representative themes that emerged from the data were: 'We've known each other long time' and 'We already have a child together', sexual partner is a boyfriend, pimp or the baby's daddy; pimp refuses to use condoms;

Table 3.1 Socio-demographic characteristics, drug use and sexual risk behaviors

	% or mean
Mean age (range: 12–18)	15.8
Ethnicity	
African American	49.3
Hispanic	37.0
Other	7.4
White	7.0
Place of residence	
Parent	80.0
Friends/relatives/partner	8.0
Foster/group home or placement	6.0
Streets, runaway	6.0
Criminal justice charge	
Warrant/violation	42.2
Property	18.0
Violence	16.3
Prostitution-related	12.0
Any drug-related charge	11.0
Substance use	
Any drug use	50.0
Marijuana	37.0
Alcohol	21.0
Polydrug use	20.2
Methamphetamine	16.0
Sexual behavior	
Mean (SD) age first sex (Range: 9–17)	14.0 (1.2)
Mean (SD)/median number lifetime partners (Range: 1–300)	9.0(20.7)/4.0
Regular condom use	63.1
Condom use last sex	39.1
Prior STD infection	27.0
Prior pregnancy	26.0
Ever sexually assaulted	20.0
Ever trade sex	18.0
Have children	11.0
Currently pregnant	7.0
STD diagnosis at arrest	
Chlamydia	72.0
Gonorrhea	12.0
Both	17.0

only uses condoms with 'dates' and not private partners; partner does not like condoms; rape; was drunk or high; wanted to get pregnant; did not have any or did not know where to get them; condom broke; he took off condom; receive more money from 'dates' if 'I didn't use condoms'.

3.3.3 *Qualitative Findings: Family Life*

Family situation and history were also noted in case manager notes. Representative themes included: running away; living in foster care or being removed from their home by social service agencies due to parental abuse, neglect and or/substance use; being homeless; having older male partners who are in jail; living with pimp; being unaware of where their parents lived; parental incarceration or death; and having young children who lived with other caretakers. Among these themes are the interconnectedness of abuse, family upheaval, parental substance use, and parent and partner incarceration. Case manager notes below provide specific examples:

> Was in "the system" (Department of Social Services) for three years, abuse history, diagnosed with Chlamdyia, gonorrhea, trichomoniasis, genital warts and is homeless.
>
> Doesn't know the number of sex partners. As of 2007 had STDs 6 times. Prostitution is her only way to survive. Mom on drugs, physically abused her. Raped as a child by trick.
>
> Placement since age 9. Drinks/smokes weed daily.
>
> Smoked marijuana daily since age 9 and hard alcohol a few times per week. Was sexually abused at age 10.
>
> Client is pregnant and a heavy methamphetamine user.
>
> Client has an 11-month old daughter and wants another one. She was kicked out of the house for drug use.
>
> Daily marijuana user when not pregnant (currently pregnant) and has a 1-year old, living with friend and was released from the system where client lived entire life; physical and sexual abuse history.
>
> AWOL'd placement two years ago and is now in the system. Partner in jail, mom is heavy crack user.
>
> Lived in the system for a time, then grandpa, now on her own. At age 10 mom sold her for crack to a dealer. Started hooking at age 12. She learned this from mom.
>
> Ran away from aunt's home. Client is trying to get pregnant for someone to love.
>
> Multiple foster homes. Mom uses drugs; has no relationship with client, who is pregnant, homeless and prostitutes to survive.
>
> Prostituted since age 13; says she was a call girl with elderly men but never had sex with them.
>
> Partner is in adult jail; client lives on own. Mom is homeless, dad in jail, siblings use drugs like mom so client feels better off on own.
>
> Mom paroled from state prison; wants meth treatment for self and mom, client was homeless earlier.
>
> Both parents dead, DCFS (Dept of Children and Family Services) since age 2; removed mother due to drug use, was with grandmother until age 14, removed due to abuse.

3.3.4 *Overlap of Family Conflict, Substance Use and Risky Sexual Behaviors*

As noted from the case manager notes, substance use and risky sexual decision-making appeared to be interconnected, which mirror findings from other studies. For instance, Castrucci and Martin's (2002) study of incarcerated adolescents reported that regular use of substances was associated with inconsistent condom use, having sex with multiple partners, and exchanging sex for money or drugs. Likewise, Romero et al.'s longitudinal study of HIV/STD risk behaviors among delinquent youth found that at follow up, nearly two thirds had recent unprotected vaginal sex, approximately half of which had unprotected sex while drunk or high (Chap. 2 by Romero et al., this volume).

As also noted in the case manager notes, significant traumatic experiences and family fragmentation may also have contributed to participation in risk behaviors. The common themes of separation from parents due to abuse/neglect, living in foster care or social services, parental or partner incarceration, homelessness and high-risk behaviors such as prostitution and pregnancy characterized this group of adolescents. Similar findings were noted by Acoca and Dedel (1998) and Patino and colleagues (2006). The authors examined family issues and risk behaviors among 512 incarcerated girls in California and Florida. Over 40% of the sample in both states experienced an out-of-home placement, 77% were chronic runaways, between 48 and 88% had experienced sexual, physical or emotional abuse, over one-half had a parent who was incarcerated, and 29% had a former pregnancy. Among the California sample, 75% reported using any drug or alcohol on a regular basis and 72% reported the same for methamphetamine use. Overall, qualitative data about family life from the detained females in the pilot program closely mirrored findings from prior research that has indicated that ineffective parental supervision, frequent parent/child conflict, parental incarceration, older male partners and other family problems are overwhelmingly linked with girls' delinquency (National Council on Crime and Delinquency 2009).

3.4 Discussion

Understanding the social worlds of incarcerated female adolescents and the meanings attached to their substance use and sexual risk behaviors can inform the development of interventions targeted to this population (Belenko et al. 2004; Blake et al. 2001). Incarcerated female adolescents with an STD diagnosis represent a group with significant reproductive health and substance use needs, as was reported among the pilot project participants. Recognition of sexual risk behaviors and their health consequences increases the need to provide interventions that address sex-linked risk behaviors in correctional settings. Given the significant traumatic events that often lead up to incarceration for at-risk females, community-based prevention and early intervention efforts for young adolescents and their families are needed before multiple problems compromise health and lead to their involvement in the juvenile justice system (Acoca and Dedel 1998).

The primary outcome measure of this project is the number of individuals treated for an STD, either in custody or following release to the field. Over 90% of all STD positive arrestees now receive STD treatment, either while in custody or during field follow-up. Among those screened before the pilot program began, 15% were released from custody without receiving any treatment; that number has been reduced to 8%.

These treatment rates are noteworthy given the transient nature of a female arrestees and their extremely high risk of exposure to STDs. In addition, partner services are now offered, where STD treatment is provided to arrestees to give to their partners, or where staff provide direct treatment to partners in the field. Such service provision is important for community members who lack a regular source of health care or who rely on publicly financed health care. For instance, 62% of project respondents reported receiving health insurance benefits.

Prior to the implementation of the pilot project, public health staff observed that diverse dispositions and movement of youth within the juvenile justice system dictated that most female detainees did not encounter STD screening, treatment, risk reduction counseling, and partner elicitation interviews while in custody. In addition, the lack of single-dose treatment prior to the project's inception, as well as a 1-week turnaround period for Chlamydia test results, caused many individuals to be lost to treatment.

Another key gap identified by the pilot project was the lack of a coordinated data system and the insufficient coordination of custody staff to accurately assess and track detainees with current STD infections while in custody and during post-release. Discussions with program staff and youth also highlighted problems in case management services. These included a lack of systematic attention to the immediate priority needs of currently infected detainees; lack of individualized education; and no systems of linkage to assure continuity of care for those who did not complete medication. Staff noted that once detainees leave juvenile hall, they often lost further access to medical staff and any organized system of referrals. Initial barriers to program implementation were the lack of medical staff within the juvenile halls to screen all female inmates and initiate treatment for those found to be positive. Health department staff were hired to assist probation medical and nursing staff, which remedied the problem.

The pilot project has filled critical gaps in health services delivery for female juvenile offenders in through the development of a seamless system of care for STD screening, treatment, and intensive case management to reduce the rates of re-infection with Chlamydia and other STDs among a population at extremely high risk for these diseases.[1] Program activities and staff have been fully integrated into the fully integrated into the probation department's system of care. Staff were funded through local county funds and federal infertility prevention funding, providing a stable funding base. Other jurisdictions in California were looking to adapt this project in youth detention settings.

Although following project participants upon treatment completion was not possible, the public health case managers do provide an extensive packet of referrals for each participating client, along with health education counseling about the importance of regular pap smears, use of condoms and other barrier methods, and other health concerns. Through these conversations, issues of substance abuse and mental health concerns are also raised and addressed. Staff have reported encountering returning arrestees with repeated STD diagnoses and have established a trusting

[1] Due to issues of confidentiality, the names and locations of the project has been omitted.

relationship with them and other clients. These staff have been able to continue assisting detainees with linkages to health care, drug treatment, mental health and related social service needs that were not available to these arrestees prior to the pilot program's inception.

While other juvenile justice programs in California and the United States offer STD screening to incarcerated female adolescents, this project remains only one of a few programs in the country to utilize public health workers who provide in-custody and field-based STD treatment, case management and partner services to incarcerated female adolescents. In 2005, this project received a national adolescent health epidemiology award for effective practice at the community level. The primary purpose of this award was to recognize and promote excellence in MCH epidemiology through research, practice and leadership. The CDC has also identified this project as an innovative public health model for probation departments nationwide who serve populations at risk for STDs.

Public health workers in correctional settings such as juvenile halls represent an important and often untapped resource for addressing health-related needs of incarcerated adolescents through the provision of STD/HIV screening, treatment and follow up, health education and risk reduction counseling. Given the significant level of co-morbid conditions such as substance abuse and psychiatric impairments among incarcerated adolescents, brief interventions for these conditions with linked referrals upon release are well within the range of skill sets of public health workers and should be maximized. Additionally, juvenile detention policies should support collaborations with these and other community based providers to address the significant, ongoing health-related concerns of young female detainees. The time that youth spend incarcerated often represents their only significant contact with a health care provider outside of an emergency setting (Golzari et al. 2006). As such, health care providers should utilize the opportunity to educate and connect these youth with community resources to facilitate their access to health care upon their re-entry into the community.

References

Abram, K. M., Teplin, L. A., McClelland, G. M., & Dulcan, M. K. (2003). Comorbid psychiatric disorders in youth in juvenile detention. *Archives of General Psychiatry, 60*(11), 1097–1108.

Abram, K. M., Teplin, L. A., Charles, D. R., Longworth, S. L., McClelland, G. M., & Dulcan, M. K. (2004). Posttraumatic stress disorder and trauma in youth in juvenile detention. *Archives of General Psychiatry, 61*, 403–410.

Abram, K. M., Choe, J. Y., Washburn, J. J., Teplin, L. A., King, D. C., & Dulcan, M. K. (2008). Suicidal ideation and behaviors among youths in juvenile detention. *Journal of the American Academy of Child and Adolescent Psychiatry, 47*(3), 291–300.

Acoca, L., & Dedel, K. (1998). *No place to hide. Understanding and meeting the needs of girls in the California Juvenile Justice System. National Council on Crime and Delinquency.* Retrieved from http://www.justiceforallgirls.org/resources/No%20Place%20To%20Hide.pdf

Amaro, H., Blake, S. M., Schwartz, P. M., & Flinchbaugh, L. J. (2001). Developing theory-based substance abuse prevention programs for young adolescent girls. *Journal of Early Adolescence, 21*(3), 256–293.

American Academy of Pediatrics. (2001). Health care for children and adolescents in the juvenile correctional care system. *Pediatrics, 197*(4), 799–803.

Austin, J., Johnson, K. D., & Gregoriou, M. (2000). *Juveniles in adult prisons and jails. A national assessment* (NCJ Publication No. 182503). Washington, DC: Bureau of Justice Assistance.

Bauer, H. M., Chartier, M., Kessell, E., Packel, L., Brammeier, M., Little, M., & Bolan, G. (2004). Chlamydia screening of youth and young adults in non-clinical settings throughout California. *Sexually Transmitted Diseases, 31*(7), 409–414.

Baumgartner, J. M., Geary, C. W., Tucker, H., & Wedderburn, M. (2009). The influence of early sexual debut and sexual violence on adolescent pregnancy: A matched case–control study in Jamaica. *International Perspectives on Sexual and Reproductive Health, 35*(1), 21–28.

Belenko, S., Sprott, J. B., & Petersen, C. (2004). Drug and alcohol involvement among minority and female juvenile offenders: Treatment and policy issues. *Criminal Justice Policy Review, 15*(1), 3–26.

Belenko, S., Dembo, R., Rollie, M., Childs, K., & Salvatore, C. (2009). Detecting, preventing, and treating sexually transmitted diseases among adolescent arrestees: An unmet public health need. *American Journal of Public Health, 99*(6), 1032–1041.

Blake, S. M., Amaro, H., Schwartz, P. M., & Flinchbaugh, L. J. (2001). A review of substance abuse prevention interventions for young adolescent girls. *Journal of Early Adolescence, 21*(3), 294–324.

Castrucci, B. C., & Martin, S. L. (2002). The association between substance use and risky sexual behaviors among incarcerated adolescents. *Maternal and Child Health Journal, 6*(1), 43–47.

Centers for Disease Control and Prevention. (1998). HIV prevention through early detection and treatment of other sexually transmitted diseases: United States recommendations of the advisory committee for HIV and STD prevention. *Morbidity and Mortality Weekly Report, 47*, 1–24.

Centers for Disease Control and Prevention. (2003). *Sexually transmitted disease surveillance, 2002.* Retrieved from http://www.cdc.gov/std/

Centers for Disease Control and Prevention. (2006). Sexually transmitted diseases treatment guidelines. *Morbidity and Mortality Weekly Recommendation Report, 55*(RR-11), 1–94.

Centers for Disease Control and Prevention. (2009). *Sexually transmitted disease surveillance, 2008.* Retrieved from http://www.cdc.gov/std/

Centers for Disease Control and Prevention. (2010). *STD facts-Chlamydia.* Retrieved from http://www.cdc.gov/std/

Chesney-Lind, M. (2010). A feminist theory of female delinquency. In F. T. Cullen & R. Agnew (Eds.), *Criminological theory: Past to present* (4th ed., pp. 341–347). New York: Oxford University Press.

Cohen, D. A., Nsuami, M., Martin, D. H., & Farley, T. A. (1999). Repeated school-based screening for sexually transmitted diseases: A feasible strategy for reaching adolescents. *Pediatrics, 104*(6), 1281–1285.

Cromwell, P. F., Risser, W. L., & Risser, J. M. (2002). Prevalence and incidence of pelvic inflammatory disease in incarcerated adolescents. *Sexually Transmitted Diseases, 29*(7), 391–396.

deLisle, S., & Wasserheit, J. N. (1999). Accelerated campaign to enhance STD services (ACCESS) for youth. *Sexually Transmitted Diseases, 26*(4), S28–S43.

Dembo, R., Schmeidler, J., Sue, C. C., Borden, P., & Manning, D. (1995). Gender differences in service needs among youths entering a juvenile assessment center: A replication study. *Journal of Correctional Health Care, 2*, 191–216.

Farabee, D., Shen, H., Hser, Y. I., Grella, C. E., & Anglin, M. D. (2001). The effect of drug treatment on adolescent criminal behavior. *Journal of Adolescent Research, 16*(6), 679–696.

Gallagher, C. A., Dobrin, A., & Douds, A. S. (2007). A national overview of reproductive health care services for girls in juvenile justice residential facilities. *Womens Health Issues, 17*(4), 217–226.

Gates, G. J., & Sonenstein, F. L. (2000). Heterosexual genital sexual activity among adolescent males: 1988 and 1995. *Family Planning Perspectives, 32*(6), 295–297, 304.

Gaydos, C. A., Howell, M. R., Quinn, T. C., McKee, K. T., Jr., & Gaydos, J. C. (2003). Sustained high prevalence of Chlamydia trachomatis infections in female army recruits. *Sexually Transmitted Diseases, 30*(7), 539–544.

Giordano, P. C., Cernkovich, S. A., & Rossel, J. (2002, August). *Emotion, cognition, and crime.* Paper presented at the annual meeting of the American Sociological Association, Chicago, IL.

Golzari, M., Hunt, S. J., & Anoshiravani, A. (2006). The health status of youth in juvenile detention facilities. *Journal of Adolescent Health, 38*(6), 776–782.

Haynie, D. L., Giordano, P. C., Manning, W., & Longmore, M. A. (2005). Adolescent romantic relationships and delinquency involvement. *Criminology, 43*(1), 177–210.

Heimer, K., & De Costa, S. (2010). The gendering of violent delinquency. In F. T. Cullen & R. Agnew (Eds.), *Criminological theory: Past to present* (4th ed., pp. 348–356). New York: Oxford University Press.

Herrera, V. M., & McCloskey, L. (2001). Gender differences in the risk for delinquency among youth exposed to family violence. *Child Abuse & Neglect, 25*(8), 1037–1051.

Kahn, R. H., Mosure, D. J., Blank, S., Kent, C. K., Chow, J. M., Boudov, M. R., Brock, J., & Tulloch, S. (2005). Chlamydia trachomatis and Neisseria gonorrhoeae prevalence and coinfection in adolescents entering selected US juvenile detention centers, 1997–2002. *Sexually Transmitted Diseases, 32*(4), 255–259.

Kendler, K. S., Bulik, C. M., Silberg, J., Hettema, J. M., Myers, J., & Prescott, C. A. (2000). Childhood sexual abuse and adult psychiatric and substance use disorders in women: An epidemiological and cotwin control analysis. *Archives of General Psychiatry, 57*(10), 953–959.

Kraut, J., Haddix, A. C., Carande-Kulis, V., & Greifinger, R. B. (2002). Cost-effectiveness of routine screening for sexually transmitted diseases among inmates in United States prisons and jails. In National Commission on Correctional Health Care (Ed.), *The health status of soon-to-be-released inmates: A report to Congress* (Vol. II, pp. 1–105). Chicago: National Commission on Correctional Health Care.

Krisberg, B. (2005). *Juvenile justice: Redeeming our children.* Thousand Oaks: Sage.

Los Angeles County Juvenile Justice Coordinating Council. (2001). *Comprehensive multi-agency juvenile justice plan.* Retrieved from http://probation.co.la.ca.us/schiff_cardenas/schiffcardenas.pdf

McClanahan, S. F., McClelland, G. M., Abram, K. M., & Teplin, L. A. (1999). Pathways into prostitution among female jail detainees and their implications for mental health services. *Psychiatric Services, 50*(12), 1606–1613.

McCormack, A., Janus, M. D., & Burgess, A. W. (1986). Runaway youths and sexual victimization: Gender differences in an adolescent runaway population. *Child Abuse & Neglect, 10*(3), 387–395.

McDonnell, D. D., Levy, V., & Morton, T. J. (2009). Risk factors for chlamydia among young women in a Northern California juvenile detention facility: Implications for community intervention. *Sexually Transmitted Diseases, 36*(2), S29–S33.

Miller, J., & White, N. A. (2003). Gender and adolescent relationship violence. *Criminology, 41*(4), 1207–1248.

Morris, R. E., Harrison, E. A., Knox, G. W., Tromanhauser, E., Marquis, D. K., & Watts, L. L. (1995). Health risk behavioral survey from 39 juvenile correctional facilities in the United States. *Journal of Adolescent Health, 17*(6), 334–344.

National Council on Crime and Delinquency, Center for Girls and Young Women. (2009). *Getting the facts straight about girls in the juvenile justice system.* Retrieved from http://www.justiceforallgirls.org/advocacy/CenterFactSheet.pdf

Obeidallah, D. A., & Earls, F. J. (1999). *Adolescent girls: The role of depression in the development of delinquency.* Rockville: US Department of Justice, National Institute of Justice.

Otto, R. K., Greenstein, J. J., Johnson, M. K., & Friedman, R. M. (1992). Prevalence of mental disorders among youth in the juvenile justice system. In J. J. Cocozza (Ed.), *Responding to the mental health needs of youth in the juvenile justice system* (pp. 7–48). Seattle: The National Coalition for the Mentally Ill in the Criminal Justice System.

Paikoff, R. L., & Brooks-Gunn, J. (1991). Do parent–child relationships change during puberty? *Psychological Bulletin, 110*(1), 47–66.

Pajer, K. A., Kelleher, K., Gupta, R. A., Rolls, J., & Gardner, W. (2007). Psychiatric and medical health care policies in juvenile detention facilities. *Journal of the American Academy of Child and Adolescent Psychiatry, 46*(12), 1660–1667.

Patino, V., Ravoira, L., & Wolf, A. (2006). *A rallying cry for change: Charting a new direction in the state of Florida's response to girls in juvenile justice*. Oakland: National Council on Crime and Delinquency.

Sanfort, T. G. M., Orr, M., Hirsch, J. S., & Santelli, J. (2008). Long-term health correlates of timing of sexual debut: Results from a national US study. *American Journal of Public Health, 98*(1), 155–161.

Sickmund, M. (2010). *OJJDP Bulletin: Juveniles in residential placement, 1997–2008* (NCJ Publication No. 229379). Washington, DC: U.S. Department of Justice, Office of Justice Programs, Office of Juvenile Justice and Delinquency Prevention.

Siegal, J. A., & Williams, L. M. (2003). The relationship between child sexual abuse and female delinquency and crime: A prospective study (2003). *Journal of Research in Crime and Delinquency, 40*(1), 71–94.

Silverthorn, P., & Frick, P. J. (1999). Developmental pathways to antisocial behavior: The delayed-onset pathway in girls. *Development and Psychopathology, 11*, 101–126.

Sneed, C. D. (2009). Sexual risk behavior among early initiators of sexual intercourse. *AIDS Care, 21*(11), 1395–1400.

Snyder, H. N., & Sickmund, M. (2006). *Juvenile offenders and victims: 2006 National Report*. Washington, DC: U.S. Department of Justice, Office of Justice Programs, Office of Juvenile Justice and Delinquency Prevention.

Staples-Horne, M. (2007). Addressing the specific health care needs of female adolescents. *Corrections Today*, 42–46. Retrieved from http://www.aca.org/publications/pdf/Staples-Horne.pdf

Stattin, H., & Magnusson, D. (1990). *Pubertal maturation in female development: Paths through life*. Hillsdale: Erlbaum.

Stiffman, A. R., Dore, P., Cunningham, R., & Earls, M. F. (1995). Person and environment in HIV risk behavior change between adolescence and young adulthood. *Health Education Quarterly, 22*(2), 211–226.

Teplin, L. A., Abram, K. M., McClelland, G. M., Dulcan, M. K., & Mericle, A. A. (2002). Psychiatric disorders in youth in juvenile detention. *Archives of General Psychiatry, 59*, 1133–1143.

Timmons-Mitchell, J., Brown, C., Schulz, S. C., Webster, S. E., Underwood, L. A., & Semple, W. E. (1997). Comparing the mental health needs of female and male incarcerated juvenile delinquents. *Behavioral Sciences & the Law, 15*(2), 195–202.

Trupin, E. W., Stewart, D. B., Beach, B., & Boesky, L. (2002). Effectiveness of a dialectical behaviour therapy program for incarcerated female juvenile offenders. *Child and Adolescent Mental Health, 7*(3), 121–127.

Vaske, J., & Gehring, K. (2010). Mechanisms linking depression to delinquency for males and females. *Feminist Criminology, 5*(1), 8–28.

Washburn, J. J., Romero, E. G., Welty, L. J., Abram, K. M., Teplin, L. A., McClelland, G. M., & Paskar, L. D. (2007). Development of antisocial personality disorder in detained youths: The predictive value of mental disorders. *Journal of Consulting and Clinical Psychology, 75*(2), 221–231.

Wilson, H. W., & Widom, C. S. (2009). A prospective examination of the path from child abuse and neglect to illicit drug use in middle adulthood: The potential mediating role of four risk factors. *Journal of Youth and Adolescence, 38*(3), 340–354.

Wilson, H. W., & Widom, C. S. (2010). The role of youth problem behaviors in the path from child abuse and neglect to prostitution: A prospective examination. *Journal of Research on Adolescence, 20*(1), 210–236.

Zahn, M. A. (2007). The causes of girls' delinquency and their program implications. *Family Court Review, 45*(3), 456–465.

Zahn, M. A., Hawkins, S. R., Chiancone, J., & Whitworth, A. (2008). *The girls study group: Charting the way to delinquency prevention for girls* (NCJ Publication No. 223434). Washington, DC: U.S. Department of Justice, Office of Justice Programs, Office of Juvenile Justice and Delinquency Prevention.

Zahn, M. A., Day, J. C., Mihalic, S. F., & Tichavsky, L. (2009). Determining what works for girls in the juvenile justice system: A summary of evaluation evidence. *Journal of Crime and Delinquency, 55*(2), 266–293.

Zahn, M. A., Agnew, R., Fishbein, D., Miller, S., Winn, D. M., Dakoff, G., Kruttschnitt, C., Giordano, P., Gottfredson, D. C., Payne, A. A., Feld, B. C., Chesney-Lind, M. (2010). *The girls study group: Causes and correlates of girls' delinquency* (NCJ Publication No. 226358). Washington, DC: U.S. Department of Justice, Office of Justice Programs, Office of Juvenile Justice and Delinquency Prevention.

Chapter 4
Disparities in Mental Health Diagnosis and Treatment Among African Americans: Implications for the Correctional Systems

William B. Lawson and Anthony Lawson

Abstract *African Americans are more likely to show such disparities in mental health as misdiagnosis, lack of treatment access, and poorer outcomes. Due in part to stigma in African American communities, schizophrenia, post-traumatic stress disorder, depression and bipolar illness are often missed. Mental health disparities in diagnosis and treatment have contributed significantly to the overrepresentation of African Americans in correctional settings. The lack of mental health services in such settings has implications for the course of mental illness and overall recidivism. Screening for mental health illness, awareness of substance abuse, recognition of new treatment approaches, and an appreciation of the importance of culture and communications in a comprehensive diagnosis and treatment must be developed for African Americans within correctional populations.*

Epidemiological studies report that African Americans experience the full range of psychiatric disorders (Kessler et al. 2005). Disparities in such disorders have been well documented for African Americans even though racial/ethnic differences in prevalence of mental disorders are uncommon (Kessler et al. 2005; Primm 2006). Moreover, clinicians continue to grossly over diagnose relatively uncommon disorders such as schizophrenia at the expense of much more familiar ones such as mood and anxiety disorders (Lawson 2002; Strakowski et al. 2003). This under recognition of some mental disorders and excessive misdiagnoses contributes to treatment disparities among African Americans (US Department of Health and Human Services [USDHHS] 2001). Such disparities also contribute to their incarceration, as mentally ill underrepresented minorities are often not recognized as such and are instead arrested (Foulks 2004).

W.B. Lawson, M.D., Ph.D., D.L.F.A.P.A. (✉) • A. Lawson
Department of Psychiatry and Behavioral Sciences, Howard University Health Sciences, Washington, DC, USA
e-mail: wblawson@howard.edu

B. Sanders et al. (eds.), *Crime, HIV and Health: Intersections of Criminal Justice and Public Health Concerns*, DOI 10.1007/978-90-481-8921-2_4,

In an otherwise laudable attempt to offer an alternative to hospitalization, many severely mentally ill individuals were deinstitutionalized (Foulks 2004; McNiel et al. 2005). The assumption was that closing large mental hospitals would be replaced by cheaper outpatient care as funds followed the patient (USDHHS 2001). Unfortunately, African Americans often received the least desirable and more punitive care (Lawson 2008a). Rather than day hospitals and intensive outpatient treatment, African Americans often ended up without sustained treatment and emergency care (Foulks 2004; USDHHS 2001). Many made up the homeless population and others were incarcerated, having been jailed for stealing food, vagrancy, or loitering (McNiel et al. 2005). Incarceration may also be viewed as the best option for individuals with mental illness due to the perceived absence of other services (McNiel et al. 2005; Sabol et al. 2007). Jails and prisons are now the largest provider of mental health services in the country, serving more mentally ill then any public mental health hospital or clinic (Diamond et al. 2001). Given this, some have referred to the correctional system as the "new asylum" (Baillargeon et al. 2009). Once incarcerated, inmates often have little chance of accessing mental health services (Baillargeon et al. 2010; Olley et al. 2009). The lack of services contributes to recidivism, trapping individuals in an endless cycle of mental illness and incarceration. This cycle appears particularly prominent among African Americans (Primm and Lawson 2010). For instance, African Americans are more likely to be underserved in correctional settings compared to other racial/ethnic groups (Hartwell 2001). Moreover, African American youth with similar behavioral problems are more likely to end up in correctional systems than white youth (Cohen et al. 1990; Gunter-Justice and Ott 1997; Lewis et al. 1980).

This chapter provides an overview of disparities in mental health diagnosis and treatment among African Americans, as well as how such disparities may increase their likelihood of incarceration. From here, recommendations for culturally sensitive correctional-based interventions that target mental health among African Americans are offered.

4.1 Disparities in Mental Health Diagnoses and Treatment

4.1.1 Anxiety

Lower rates of anxiety disorder have been observed for African Americans diagnosed by clinicians not using assessment instruments, which are related to misdiagnosis and under-recognition of symptoms (Lawson 2002). In contrast, anxiety disorders such as generalized anxiety disorder or post-traumatic stress disorder (PTSD) are among the most common mental disorders and may show a higher prevalence among African Americans. PTSD in particular has been found to be more prevalent in African Americans (Lawson 2002). PTSD is widespread in inner cities where African Americans are over-represented (Alim et al. 2006). Yet PTSD often is both under diagnosed or misdiagnosed, as those with the disorder tend to be hyper-vigilant, and show autonomic hyperactivity and emotional numbness (Lawson 2009). Such individuals are often perceived as callous and their behavior as aggressive and malicious (Lawson et al. 2002). They are at risk of being perceived as guilty or troublemakers and quickly are perceived as criminals (Hicks 2004).

Many in the African American community stigmatize mental illness and often believe that it is better to be perceived as 'bad' rather then 'mad' (Williams 2008). For instance, youth exposed to violence or in gangs who have symptoms of PTSD may deal with their related concerns and fears by being tougher and engaging in more violence. Subsyndromal symptoms (i.e. symptoms that are not severe enough for diagnostic purposes) may be deemed culturally acceptable responses to environmental stress. The individual may not show frank anxiety symptoms or may mask them to appear tough and invulnerable, a positively perceived behavior on the street and in prison, but one that could risk arrest in questionable circumstances. In such cases, arrest and incarceration becomes a badge of honor while receiving mental health services may be considered evidence of weakness. Subsequent incarceration is likely to worsen or exacerbate PTSD (Crisanti and Frueh 2011).

4.1.2 Depression

Among African Americans, mood disorders, including major depression are often under diagnosed (Williams et al. 2007). Major depressive disorder in is typically overlooked, undiagnosed, untreated, inadequately treated, more severe, and/or associated with greater disability (Williams et al. 2007). For instance, only 45% of African Americans reporting symptoms of major depressive disorders receive any treatment (Williams et al. 2007). Among the underlying reasons for unmet need for depression care among African Americans is the presentation of depressive symptoms other then sadness, such as irritability, hostility, and somatic symptoms that the clinician may interpret as another psychiatric disorder or even a general medical condition (Lawson 2002; Primm 2006). Law enforcement agents may interpret such behavior in young people as attempting to start trouble, or preludes to criminal activity (Hicks 2004).

The problem is further enhanced by the failure of many African Americans to recognize depression when they are suffering from it (Primm 2006). This phenomenon is demonstrated in the book *Black Pain* by Terri Williams (2008). She notes that as a trained social worker, she did not recognize her own severe depression. She also quotes gang members who cope with their depression by 'acting out' and committing antisocial or violent acts. Again, such youth feel that being perceived as 'bad' rather then as 'mad' is more appropriate. Suicide is an important consequence of depression and is a reminder that depression can be a mortal illness. In the past, suicide was thought to be rare among African Americans (Primm and Lawson. 2010). Recent studies, however, have reported that young African American males do not differ in rates from their white counterparts (Joe et al. 2006).

4.1.3 Bipolar Disorder

Racial/ethnic differences have never been found in the rates of bipolar disorder or manic-depressive illness in epidemiological studies (Kessler et al. 2005; Lawson 2005). Nevertheless, many clinicians have believed that bipolar disorder was rare among African Americans (Primm and Lawson 2010). Misdiagnosis of bipolar disorder when it first presents itself is common in any population (Lawson 2005). African Americans, however, are much more likely to be under or misdiagnosed at rates of 90% with first presentation (Lawson 2005). The preference for service by primary care providers over mental health specialists also contributes to misdiagnoses since primary care providers often are not familiar with the many ways that bipolar disorder may be present, and believe it is rare outside of psychiatric settings (Graves et al. 2007). Yet, recent studies show that bipolar disorder may make up 10–20% of patients in primary care settings (Graves et al. 2007).

More alarming, many individuals with bipolar disorder may also be perceived as being sociopaths because both conditions are characterized by impulsivity, pleasurable high-risk behavior, and irritability. Impulsive violent behavior, drug use, overspending, sexual assault, gambling and disregard for the rights of others are all common in a manic episode. As a result, individuals suffering from bipolar disorder may end up being incarcerated as opposed to being treated. Up to 33% of inmates may have unrecognized bipolar disorder (Kemp et al. 2008). Moreover, bipolar disorder may be the most single important factor in recidivism in jails, substance abuse, and suicide attempts (Quanbeck et al. 2005a, b). The increased likelihood of under diagnosis among African Americans makes the risk for arrest far greater rather than the likelihood for treatment. Cultural factors within African American communities may also mask symptoms of bipolar disorder (Primm et al. 2005). For instance, indicators of bipolar disorder, such as having multiple sex partners and heavy drug use and gambling may be valued rather than being seen as an illness (Lawson 2004)

4.1.4 Schizophrenia

Consistent misdiagnosis of schizophrenia for African Americans has been reported for decades (Lawson 2005; Strakowski et al. 2003). African Americans have been regarded as having an increased risk of schizophrenia, and severe mental disorders. However, studies have reported no differences in the prevalence of schizophrenia among African Americans when socioeconomic status was controlled, and that African Americans were less likely than European Americans to have non-affective psychosis, primarily schizophrenia (Kessler et al. 2005; Robins et al. 1991). Nevertheless, many people with schizophrenia are not diagnosed or misdiagnosed as antisocial, sometimes with the initial diagnosis being made in the correctional system (Rautanen and Laura 2011). For African Americans, such symptoms as impulsivity, poor judgment, callousness, a blunted affect, command hallucinations and delusions may be interpreted as antisocial or criminal (Hicks 2004). Once in the correctional system, individuals with schizophrenia are at great risk for being victimized (Blitz et al. 2008).

4.1.5 Treatment Disparities

The scientific literature is replete with examples of psychiatric treatment disparities experienced by African Americans (Lawson 2002; USDHHS 2001). Multiple studies have shown that less than a quarter of African Americans receive evidence-based treatment for most mental disorders in any setting (Primm and Lawson 2010; Wang et al. 2000). When African Americans do receive psychiatric care, they tend to be more invasive and potentially with less benign forms of treatment (Primm and Lawson 2010). African Americans are also more likely to be involuntarily committed, placed in seclusion and restraint, or given higher doses of medication (Lawson 2008a, b). Moreover, when given medication, African Americans are more likely to be prescribed antipsychotics and are less likely to be prescribed newer antipsychotics or antidepressants (Lawson 2007). African Americans are also less likely to be offered different types of psychotherapy (Chermack et al. 2008). These differences are due to misdiagnosis, lack of availability, stereotypical beliefs about African Americans being more hostile, providers' attitudes, and unwillingness by providers to be therapeutically engaged or culturally aware (Primm and Lawson 2010; Segal et al. 1996). Moreover, African Americans often show mistrust of physicians and psychiatrists, stigmatize mental illness, and have concerns about addictiveness of medication (Chermack et al. 2008).

Many clinicians are unaware of potential racial/ethnic differences in pharmacological response (Lawson 2008b). For example, many anticipate that African Americans will respond to medication similar to the way other racial/ethnic groups do since considerable genetic similarity exists across such groups (Lawson 2008b). Many also feel that African Americans require more medication based on the misconception that African American males are more hostile (Lawson 2002). However, the evidence suggests that African Americans may require if anything, less medication due to differential pharmacological response (Bradford 2002). For instance, African Americans may require lower doses of antipsychotic and antidepressant medications than whites. For instance, cytochrome P 450 enzymes metabolize over 90% of drugs in clinical use including antipsychotic and antidepressant medications, and individuals with relatively inactive CYP2D6 alleles (which account for 25% of metabolism of commonly used drugs) tend to have higher plasma levels of antipsychotics and antidepressants (Bradford 2002). However, 50% of people of African ancestry have reduced functioning or non-functioning alleles, which lead to slower metabolism of older antipsychotics or tricyclic antidepressants and higher plasma levels. Chronically higher plasma levels may be associated with an increased risk of side effects, such as intolerance of the medication, which in turn can lead to poorer adherence to treatment (Lawson 2008a, b). African Americans are also more likely to develop tardive dyskinesia when receiving first generation antipsychotics (Lawson 2007). However, African Americans are less likely to receive *newer* generation antipsychotic medications that are associated with less extrapyramidal symptoms, can ameliorate negative symptoms of schizophrenia, and have lower risk of tardive dyskinesia. The caveat is that newer generation antipsychotics pose higher risks of type-2 diabetes and significant weight gain, for which African Americans are at great risk (Lawson 2008a, b).

4.2 Implications for Correctional Settings

Individuals with mental disorders are now more likely to be arrested and sent to the correctional system, often because the mental disorder is unrecognized or lack of services in the community (McNiel et al. 2005; Sabol et al. 2007). Once incarcerated, those with mentally illness are eight times more likely to be abused then other inmates (Crisanti and Frueh 2011).

Moreover, individuals are often under-referred for mental health services (USDHS 2001) and correctional systems often lack the professional staff to address mental disorders, such as providing any evidence-based psychotherapy (Foulks 2004; Hicks 2004). The culture of corrections further complicates the problem (Frailing 2010). For instance, African American are far more likely to be given medication rather than psychotherapies or both, which is very likely due to the focus on behavioral control rather than the resolution of intrapsychic issues or symptom relief (Thornburg 1995). Many correctional systems heavily use older medications because of cost, which particularly impacts African Americans due to possible differences in drug treatment response (Primm and Lawson 2010). Comorbid substance abuse adds an additional complication that may require specialized treatment (Foulks 2004; Lawson et al. 2011). The consequence is often poor mental health outcomes and recidivism. Moreover, former inmates can be excluded from jobs, public assistance, subsidized housing programs, and may not qualify for many health services (Pager 2007). As a consequence, treatments for mental disorders are even less available. Numerous other factors such as homelessness, support systems, affordability, cultural norms, and medication side effects are exacerbated in those released from corrections and affect initiation, maintenance, and adherence to treatment for mental disorders and substance abuse (Friedmann et al. 2012; Foulks 2004).

The recognition of mental disorders among correctional staff is important first step and all personnel from the arresting officer to parole officers should have some training and awareness. Support groups such as National Alliance on Mental Illness have worked with police departments to address this problem (Parker 2009). Collaborative relationships with public departments of mental health and academic facilities have also been beneficial (Rich et al. 2011). Such approaches are necessary to increase awareness, reduce stigma, and change the culture. Screening is also important and primary care settings have successfully used various instruments to identify mental health illness (Gilbody et al. 2005). These instruments can be very brief and self-administered and often have good validity and reliability, although not all have been standardized in ethnic minority populations (Hicks 2004). Similar screening instruments have been used in correctional settings for research and diagnoses (Kemp et al. 2008).

Mental health and drug courts are a valuable and effective source for early detection, referral and navigation of services (Gallagher et al. 2011). They offer a fresh insight into the potentially beneficial and detrimental effects of legal decisions and views one of the roles of law as that of a healing agent (Frailing 2010). At present, many states have instituted mental health courts based on these concepts, incorporating previous drug court experiences (Gallagher et al. 2011). Their goal is to avoid the criminalization of the mentally ill and their recidivism through the creation of special programs (Palermo 2010). One program reported a significant drop in psychiatric hospitalization days for mentally ill participants and a decrease in positive drug and alcohol tests (Palermo 2010). A non-adversarial atmosphere in which participants interact directly with the judge and in which praise and encouragement are issued far more often than sanctions (Frailing 2010). A mental health court program in Nevada, reported successfully keeping mentally ill offenders out of the correctional system while concomitantly improving their mental condition. In so doing, the program has lightened the load of the overburdened courts and has greatly diminished the financial burden incurred for court trials and jail and prison stays (Frailing 2010). Moreover mental health courts have been found to lower post treatment arrest rates and days of incarceration (Steadman et al. 2011). While mental health and drug courts may be limited by the need for extended incarceration, the failure to integrate services, or the absence of services in the community, they are an important first step to providing services to reduce disparities (Wren 2010).

Issues concerning culture, racial/ethnic disparities, attitudes about mental illness, and language must be addressed (Hicks 2004; Primm and Lawson 2010). Patients who speak English as a second language are more likely to be misdiagnosed as having schizophrenia when they have depression (Lawson 2002). Limited English proficient individuals may be misdiagnosed, ignored, or victimized in the correctional system, may not adhere to treatment, or may not receive appropriate and necessary treatment (Foulks 2004). A growing number of people of African descent living in the US are facing this potential barrier to treatment (Dove et al. 2006). Among such immigrant and refugee populations, languages including Haitian Creole, French, Portuguese, and Spanish are common. Providing mental health services in the language that the patient speaks at home by making available bilingual psychiatric clinicians or at least trained translators or interpreters is important. The National Standards for Culturally and Linguistically Appropriate Services, promulgated by the Office of Minority Health, also urge the provision of signage and written materials in the languages spoken by patient populations. The correlated concept of cultural competence entails engagement of patients as partners in problem solving and decision-making, holistic consideration of social and cultural context, and the consequences of patients' experiences with illnesses (Hicks 2004). Moreover, social and cultural barriers between health care providers and patients may affect the quality of health care (Primm and Lawson 2010). African Americans may harbor distrust of mental health care providers based on historical or ongoing experiences of discrimination (Lawson 2002). Distrust of the correctional system has been longstanding in the African American community and could influence willingness to accept treatment. Awareness of these issues are an important step towards addressing them.

Treatment in the correctional system must address the complex problem of substance use comorbidity (Conway et al. 2006). Because drugs of abuse affect similar brain circuits or receptor mechanisms proposed for mental disorders, they can cause drug abusers to experience one or more symptoms of mental illness (Lawson et al. 2011). When substance abusers present with similar symptoms of mental disorders, an underlying mental disorder may be missed and a drug abuser may be incarcerated rather then get adequate treatment (Caspi et al. 2005; Conway et al. 2006). The result could be misdiagnosis and inappropriate treatment. Additionally, individuals with overt, mild, or even subclinical mental disorders may abuse drugs as a form of self-medication (Lawson et al. 2011). As a result, the mental disorder is considered yet another symptom of substance abuse and treatment for the mental disorder might be delay or never provided, especially in the correctional settings (Hicks 2004; Lawson et al. 2011). Furthermore, substance abuse adds to the burden by exacerbating mental illness and leading to a poorer outcome (Lawson et al. 2011). In correctional systems, co-occurring disorders greatly exacerbate the rate of recidivism (Baillargeon et al. 2010). Moreover, those with co-occurring substance abuse are more likely to be held in jail longer than other inmates charged with similar crimes (McNiel et al. 2005). The combination of mental illness contributes to a revolving door of incarceration. Treatment for comorbidity is inherently more difficult and often requires specialized services (Hicks 2004; Lawson et al. 2011). In the correctional system, such treatment is even less accessible especially when the diagnosis is overlooked.

Integrated treatment approaches combined with mental health courts can provide the effective outcomes necessary. Dual diagnosis program have now been introduced in many settings often with excellent results (Wexler 2003). However, many of those with comprehensive services in the correctional system discontinue them when released (Foulks 2004). Providing early detection, personnel education, alternatives to incarceration, evidence base treatment in corrections, and strong aftercare will be economically feasible and may make a substantial dent in the health and mental health disparities seen in African Americans. Identification and treatment could contribute to reducing the high return rate of African Americans to correctional facilities and return potentially productive people back to society.

References

Alim, T. N., Graves, E., Mellman, T. A., Aigbogun, N., Gray, E., Lawson, W., & Charney, D. S. (2006). Trauma exposure, posttraumatic stress disorder and depression in an African-American primary care population. *Journal National of the Medical Association, 98*, 1630–1636.

Baillargeon, J., Binswanger, I. A., Penn, J. V., Williams, B. A., & Murray, O. J. (2009). Psychiatric disorders and repeat incarcerations: The revolving prison door. *American Journal of Psychiatry, 166*, 103–109.

Baillargeon, J., Penn, J. V., Knight, K., Harzke, A. J., Baillargeon, G., & Becker, E. A. (2010). Risk of reincarceration among prisoners with co-occurring severe mental illness and substance use disorders. *Administration Policy and Mental Health, 37*, 367–374.

Blitz, C. L., Wolff, N., & Shi, J. (2008). Physical victimization in prison: The role of mental illness. *International Journal of Law and Psychiatry, 31*, 385–393.

Bradford, L. D. (2002). CYP2D6 allele frequency in European Caucasians, Asians, Africans and their descendants. *Pharmacogenomics, 3*, 229–243.

Caspi, A., Moffitt, T. E., Cannon, M., et al. (2005). Moderation of the effect of adolescent-onset cannabis use on adult psychosis by a functional polymorphism in the catechol-O-methyltransferase gene: Longitudinal evidence of a gene×environment interaction. *Biological Psychiatry, 57*, 1117–1127.

Chermack, S. T., Zivin, K., Valenstein, M., Ilgen, M., Austin, K. L., Wryobeck, J., & Blow, F. C. (2008). The prevalence and predictors of mental health treatment services in a national sample of depressed veterans. *Medical Care, 46*, 813–820.

Cohen, R., Parmelee, D. X., Irwin, L., Weisz, J. R., Howard, P., Purcell, P., & Best, A. M. (1990). Characteristics of children and adolescents in a psychiatric hospital and a corrections facility. *Journal of the American Academy of Child and Adolescent Psychiatry, 29*(6), 909–913.

Conway, K. P., Compton, W., Stinson, F. S., & Grant, B. F. (2006). Lifetime comorbidity of DSM-IV mood and anxiety disorders and specific drug use disorders: Results from the Conway national epidemiologic survey on alcohol and related conditions. *Journal of Clinical Psychiatry, 67*, 247–257.

Crisanti, A. S., & Frueh, B. C. (2011). Risk of trauma exposure among persons with mental illness in jails and prisons: What do we really know? *Current Opinion in Psychiatry, 24*, 431–435.

Dove, H. W., Anderson, T. R., & Bell, C. C. (2006). In D. Satcher & R. Pamies (Eds.), *Mental health in multicultural medicine and health disparities.* (pp. 295–304). New York: McGraw Hill.

Diamond, P. M., Wang, E. W., Holzer, C. E., III, Thomas, C., & Cruser, D. A. (2001). The prevalence of mental illness in prison. *Administration Policy in Mental Health, 29*, 21–40.

Foulks, E. F. (2004). Commentary: Racial bias in diagnosis and medication of mentally ill minorities in prisons and communities. *American Academy of Psychiatry and Law, 32*, 34–35.

Frailing, K. (2010). How mental health courts function: Outcomes and observations. *International Journal of Law and Psychiatry, 33*, 207–213.

Friedmann, P. D., Hoskinson, R., Gordon, M., Schwartz, R., Kinlock, T., Knight, K., Flynn, P. M., Welsh, W. N., Stein, L. A., Sacks, S., O'Connell, D. J., Knudsen, H. K., Shafer, M. S., Hall, E., Frisman, L. K., & Mat Working Group of CJ-Dats. (2012). Medication-assisted treatment in criminal justice agencies affiliated with the criminal justice-drug abuse treatment studies (CJ-DATS): Availability, barriers, and intentions. *Substance Abuse, 33*, 9–18.

Gallagher, M., Skubby, D., Bonfine, N., Munetz, M. R., & Teller, J. L. (2011). Recognition and understanding of goals and roles: The key features of mental health court teams. *International Journal of Law and Psychiatry, 34*, 406–413.

Gilbody, S., House, A. O., & Sheldon, T. A. (2005, Oct). Screening and case finding instruments for depression. *Cochrane Database of Systematic Reviews, 19(4)*, CD002792 (Review). .

Graves, R. E., Alim, T. A., Aigbogun, N., Chrishon, C., Mellman, T., Charney, D., & Lawson, W. B. (2007). Diagnosing bipolar disorder in primary care clinics. *Bipolar Disorder, 9*, 318–323.

Gunter-Justice, T. D., & Ott, D. A. (1997). Who does the family court refer for psychiatric services? *Journal of Forensic Science, 42*, 1104–1106.

Hartwell, S. (2001). An examination of racial differences among mentally ill offenders in Massachusetts. *Psychiatric Services, 52*, 234–236.

Hicks, J. W. (2004). Ethnicity, race, and forensic psychiatry: Are we color-blind? *Journal of American Academic Psychiatry and Law, 32*, 21–33.

Joe, S., Baser, R. E., Breeden, G., Neighbors, H. W., & Jackson, J. S. (2006). Prevalence of and risk factors for lifetime suicide attempts among blacks in the United States. *Journal of the American Medical Association, 296*, 2112–2123.

Kemp, D. E., Hirschfeld, R. M., Ganocy, S. J., Elhaj, O., Slembarski, R., Bilali, S., Conroy, C., Pontau, J., Findling, R. L., & Calabrese, J. R. (2008). Screening for bipolar disorder in a county jail at the time of criminal arrest. *Journal of Psychiatric Research, 42*, 778–786.

Kessler, R. C., Berglund, P., Demler, O., Jin, R., Merikangas, K. R., & Walters, E. E. (2005). Lifetime prevalence and age-of-onset distributions of DSM-IV disorders in the National Comorbidity Survey Replication. *Archives of General Psychiatry, 62*, 593–602.

Lawson, W. B. (2002). Mental health issues for African Americans. In B. Guillermo, J. E. Trimble, A. K. Burlow, & F. T. I. Leong (Eds.), *Handbook of racial and ethnic minority psychology* (pp. 561–570). Thousand Oaks: Sage.

Lawson, W. B. (2004). The spectrum of bipolar disorder. *Psychiatric Annals, 34*, 6.

Lawson, W. B. (2005). Bipolar disorder in African Americans in perspective. In A. M. Georgiopoulos & J. M. Rosenbaum (Eds.), *Cross-cultural psychiatry* (pp. 135–142). Philadelphia: Lippincott Williams and Wilkins.

Lawson, W. B. (2007). Schizophrenia in African Americans. In K. T. Mueser & D. V. Jeste (Eds.), *Clinical handbook of schizophrenia* (pp. 616–623). New York: Guilford Publications.

Lawson, W. B. (2008a). Identifying interethnic variations in psychotropic response in African-Americans and other ethnic minorities. In C. H. Ng, K.-M. Lin, B. S. Singh, & E. Chiu (Eds.), *Ethno-psychopharmacology advances in current practice* (pp. 111–117). New York: Cambridge University Press.

Lawson, W. B. (2008b). Schizophrenia in African Americans. In K. T. Mueser & V. Di Jeste (Eds.), *Clinical handbook of schizophrenia* (pp. 616–623). New York: Guilford Press.

Lawson, W. B. (2009). Anxiety disorders in African Americans and other ethnic minorities. In G. Andrews, D. S. Charney, P. J. Sirovatka, & D. A. Regier (Eds.), *Stress-induced and fear circuitry disorders: Advancing the research agenda for DSM-V* (pp. 139–144). Arlington: American Psychiatric Publishing.

Lawson, W. B., Cunningham, J., & Lawson, V. (2002). Violence prevention in African American youth. In J. C. Chun (Ed.), *The health, behavioral change imperative: Theory, education, and practice in diverse populations* (pp. 61–72). New York: Kluwer/Plenum Publishers.

Lawson, W. B., Herrera, J., & Lawson, R. G. (2011). African Americans: Alcohol and substance abuse. In P. Ruiz & E. C. Strain (Eds.), *Substance abuse: A comprehensive textbook* (pp. 813–818). Baltimore: Wolters Kluver/Lippincott Williams & Wilkins.

Lewis, D. O., Shanok, S. S., Cohen, R. J., Kligfeld, M., & Frisone, G. (1980). Race bias in the diagnosis and disposition of violent adolescents. *American Journal of Psychiatry, 137*, 1211–1216.

McNiel, D. E., Binder, R. L., & Robinson, J. C. (2005). Incarceration associated with homelessness, mental disorder, and co-occurring substance abuse. *Psychiatric Services, 56*, 840–846.

Olley, M. C., Nicholls, T. L., & Brink, J. (2009). Mentally ill individuals in limbo: obstacles and opportunities for providing psychiatric services to corrections inmates with mental illness. *Behavioral Science Law, 27*, 811–831.

Pager, D. (2007). *Race, crime, and finding work in an era of mass incarceration*. Chicago: University of Chicago Press.

Palermo, G. B. (2010). The Nevada mental health courts. *International Journal of Law Psychiatry, 33*, 214–219.

Parker, G. F. (2009). Impact of a mental health training course for correctional officers on a special housing unit. *Psychiatric Services, 60*, 640–645.

Primm, A. (2006). Cultural issues in assessment and treatment: African American patients. In R. F. Lim (Ed.), *Clinical manual of cultural psychiatry*. (pp. 35–68). Washington, DC: American Psychiatric Publishing, Inc.

Primm, A. B., Ogden, F. C., & Gomez, M. B. (2005). Race and ethnicity, mental health services and cultural competence in the criminal justice system: Are we ready to change? *Community Mental Health Journal, 41*, 557–569.

Primm, A. B., & Lawson, W. B. (2010). Disparities among ethnic groups: African Americans. In P. Ruiz & A. Primm (Eds.), *Disparities in psychiatric care: Clinical and cross-cultural perspectives* (pp. 19–29). Baltimore: Wolters Kluver/Lippincott Williams & Wilkins.

Quanbeck, C. D., McDermott, B. E., & Frye, M. A. (2005a). Clinical and legal characteristics of inmates with bipolar disorder. *Current Psychiatry Reports, 7*, 478–484.

Quanbeck, C. D., Stone, D. C., McDermott, B. E., Boone, K., Scott, C. L., & Frye, M. A. (2005b). Relationship between criminal arrest and community treatment history among patients with bipolar disorder. *Psychiatric Services, 56*, 847–852.

Rautanen, M., & Laura, H. (2011). Imprisonment and diagnostic delay among male offenders with schizophrenia. *Criminal Behavior and Mental Health, 21*(4), 259–264.

Rich, J. D., Wohl, D. A., Beckwith, C. G., Spaulding, A. C., Lepp, N. E., Baillargeon, J., Gardner, A., Avery, A., Altice, F. L., & Springer, S. (2011). HIV-Related research in correctional populations: Now is the time. *Current HIV/AIDS Reports, 8*, 288–296.

Robins, L. N., Locke, B., & Regier, D. A. (1991). An overview of psychiatric disorders in America. In L. N. Robins & D. A. Regier (Eds.), *Psychiatric disorders in America: The epidemiologic catchment area study* (pp. 328–366). New York: The Free Press.

Sabol, W. J., Minton, T. D., & Harrison, P. M. (2007). *Prison and jail inmates at midyear*. Washington, DC: U.S. Department of Justice.

Segal, S. P., Bola, J. R., & Watson, M. A. (1996). Race, quality of care, and antipsychotic prescribing practices in psychiatric emergency services. *Psychiatric Services, 47*, 282–286.

Steadman, H. J., Redlich, A., Callahan, L., Robbins, P. C., & Vesselinov, R. (2011). Effect of mental health courts on arrests and jail days: A multisite study. *Archives of General Psychiatry, 68*, 167–172.

Strakowski, S. M., Keck, P. E., Jr., Arnold, L. M., Collins, J., Wilson, R. M., Fleck, D. E., Corey, K. B., Amicone, J., & Adebimpe, V. R. (2003). Ethnicity and diagnosis in patients with affective disorders. *Journal of Clinical Psychiatry, 64*, 747–754.

Thornburg, K. M. (1995). Health care in correctional facilities. *Western Journal of Medicine, 163*, 560–564.

US Department of Health and Human Services (USDHHS). (2001). *Mental health: Culture, race, and ethnicity – A supplement to mental health: A report of the Surgeon General*. Rockville: US Department of Health and Human Services.

Wang, P. S., Berglund, P., & Kessler, R. C. (2000). Recent care of common mental disorders in the United States: Prevalence and conformance with evidence-based recommendations. *Journal of General Internal Medicine, 15*, 284–292.

Wexler, H. K. (2003). The promise of prison-based treatment for dually diagnosed inmates. *Journal of Substance Abuse Treatment, 25*, 223–231.

Williams, T. (2008). *Black pain: It just looks like we're not hurting*. New York: Scribner.

Williams, D. R., Gonzalez, H. M., Neighbors, H., Nesses, R., Abelson, J. M., Sweetman, J., & Jackson, J. S. (2007). Prevalence and distribution of major depressive disorder in African Americans, Caribbean blacks, and non-Hispanic whites: Results from the National Survey of American Life. *Archives of General Psychiatry, 64*, 305–315.

Wren, G. L. (2010). Mental health courts: Serving justice and promoting recovery. *Annals of Health Law, 19*(3), 577–593.

Part II
Health Consequences of Crime and Risk Behaviors

Chapter 5
Methamphetamine Use, Personality Traits, and High-Risk Behaviors

Deborah Baskin, Ira Sommers, and Arielle Baskin-Sommers

Abstract *This study explored the relationships among methamphetamine use and violent behavior, methamphetamine use and risky sexual conduct, as well as the role of personality traits as moderating variables. The sample was comprised of 339 respondents, aged 16–30 years old and included comparison groups of alcohol only users, methamphetamine users, and non-substance users. The results indicated that during the 6 months prior to data collection, individuals who used alcohol or methamphetamines were more likely to be involved in violence and high-risk sex than non-substance users. Perhaps most important, methamphetamine users were more likely to be involved in assault and unprotected sex than alcohol-only users. In addition, the results suggest that personality trait differences, specifically volatile temper, accounted for the overwhelming majority of explained variance in the prevalence of assault. In fact, when controlling for personality traits, substance use ceased to be a significant predictor of the prevalence of assault. While volatile temper was the key predictor of the prevalence of violence, it was not associated significantly with the co-occurrence of substance use and violence. However, the co-occurrence of substance use and assault was significantly greater for respondents who used methamphetamines as compared to alcohol-only users. With regard to risky sexual behavior, the findings indicate that substance use, alcohol-only, and methamphetamines heightened the risk for unprotected sexual intercourse even when controlling for demographics and personality traits.*

D. Baskin, Ph.D. (✉) • I. Sommers, Ph.D.
Department of Criminal Justice and Criminology,
Loyola University Chicago, Chicago, IL, USA
e-mail: dbaskin@luc.edu

A. Baskin-Sommers, M.S.
Harvard Medical School, McClean Hospital, Belmont, MA

B. Sanders et al. (eds.), *Crime, HIV and Health: Intersections of Criminal Justice and Public Health Concerns*, DOI 10.1007/978-90-481-8921-2_5,

In 2007, 13 million Americans reported having ever used methamphetamines (Office of National Drug Control Policy 2007). Although this number represents a tapering off of a decade of steep growth, it remains of grave public health concern. For that matter, despite the stabilization of use, between 2002 and 2004, rates of dependence rose from 10.6 to 22.3% (American Academy of Family Physicians 2007). Research documents substantial increases in emergency room visits and admissions to drug treatment by methamphetamine users (Crevecoeur et al. 2007). Surveys indicate that between 5 and 25% of men who have sex with men use methamphetamines and report significant health and social consequences (Schrem and Halkitis 2008; Semple et al. 2004). Furthermore, between 1994 and 2006, the number of pregnant women seeking treatment for methamphetamine dependence tripled (National Library of Medicine 2009).

Although methamphetamines were initially used almost exclusively by Whites, their use has spread to Hispanic and Asian communities (Hunt et al. 2005; Sommers and Baskin 2004). Methamphetamine use in the United States has expanded from its origin in the West to the Midwest and now to many parts of the East (Maxwell and Rutkowski 2008), and is currently an urban, suburban, and rural phenomenon (Borders et al. 2008; Sexton et al. 2009; Simons et al. 2005), with increasing globalization (Hall et al. 1996; Humeniuk and Ali 2004; Isralowitz and Rawson 2006; Pinhey and Wells 2007; Pluddemann et al. 2008; Sekine et al. 2006). The staying power of methamphetamine use seems to rest on the ease of its production and procurement, its low cost, and its functional uses, as a diet aid, an energy and mood booster, and as a way to stay awake for employment and recreational activities. Nonetheless, methamphetamine use has not been without its individual and societal costs. Some estimates have been given for 2005 that suggest $48 billion in economic costs, $4.2 billion in crime and criminal justice loss and expenditures and $545 million in drug treatment (Nicosia et al. 2005). Methamphetamine use has also been associated with mortality, disability, employment loss, child maltreatment, divorce, and psychiatric distress (Baskin-Sommers and Sommers 2006; Darke et al. 2008; Nicosia et al. 2005; Sommers et al. 2006; Zweben et al. 2004).

Research on the societal and health risks of methamphetamine use identifies violence and risky sexual behavior as two major correlates. Recent reviews of the literature document the strength of these associations across a wide variety of studies and cross-cultural contexts (Hoeken and Stewart 2003; Maxwell 2005; McKetin et al. 2006; Meredith et al. 2005; Tyner and Fremouw 2008). A correlation between methamphetamine use and criminal violence is found in national data base surveys, treatment and criminal justice samples, and community studies. For instance, Stretsky (2008), using the National Household Survey on Drug Abuse and the Survey of Inmates in State and Federal Correctional Facilities, finds that methamphetamine users are nine times more likely to commit homicide than their non-using counterparts. Cartier et al.'s study (2006) of male parolees also uncovers a significant association between methamphetamine use and violent behavior.

These results are replicated among other samples, as well. Pinhey and Wells (2007), in an analysis of data from the Youth Risk Survey in Guam, demonstrate that methamphetamine use increases involvement in violence for both males and females. Similarly, Wright and Klee (2001) and Brecht et al. (2004) report that in their treatment samples of methamphetamine users, 47 and 57%, respectively, were involved in criminal violence, with no differences based on gender. The absence of gender differences in methamphetamine use and violence is corroborated in a treatment sample studied by von Mayrhauser et al. (2001). And, in Zweben et al.'s (2004) research, 45% of the treatment sample was involved in violent behavior. These findings appear in community studies, too well (Hall et al. 1996; Sekine et al. 2006; Sexton et al. 2009). Thus, research consistently points to a strong correlation between use and violent behavior.

Much the same can be said about the correlation between methamphetamine use and high-risk sexual behaviors. From research related to men who have sex with men (Bolding et al. 2006; Bonell et al. 2010; Drumright et al. 2006; Schrem and Halkitis 2008; Semple et al. 2004) to those involving youth (Pinhey and Wells 2007; Cheng-Fang and Mian-Moon 2006), and heterosexual adults (Darke et al. 2008; Lorvick et al. 2006; Molitor et al. 1998; Zule and Desmond 1999) studies, time and again, demonstrate that methamphetamine use increases participation in risky sex. One study of heterosexual men from low-income California neighborhoods finds a significant relationship between recent methamphetamine use and having multiple partners (Centers for Disease Control and Prevention [CDC] 2006), although no significant relationship was found for condom use after controlling for demographic characteristics and use of *other* substances. Yet, a study by Iritani et al. (2007) shows no unique relationship to sexual risk among men but did find an association for women. Therefore, much like the literature on the social consequences of methamphetamine use, i.e. violence, there may be an association with risky sexual conduct, as well.

Nonetheless, some studies do not find such a widespread presence of risky behavior among methamphetamine users (Lende et al. 2007; Sommers and Baskin 2004). Instead, it could be that the grievous social and individual consequences documented in many studies exist only for certain *subgroups* of users. In other words, there may be particular factors that moderate the relationship between methamphetamine use and risky behaviors. For instance, researchers have identified certain stable personality traits as being correlated with methamphetamine use and its social consequences (Borders et al. 2008; Brecht et al. 2004; Herman-Stahl et al. 2007; Iritiani et al. 2007; Stretsky 2008).

Personality traits represent internal factors that affect individual life histories and social interactions and influence cognitions, opinions, attitudes, behavior, and direct experiences (Zillmann and Weaver 1997). They develop in early childhood and remain constant throughout the lifecourse (Romero et al. 2003). Traits such as impulsivity, volatile temper, and sensation seeking have been associated with the development of risky behaviors (Gottfredson and Hirschi 1990; Donovan and Jessor 1985) and act to release the individual from social restraints. This results in an inability to control behavior, thereby producing myriad psychosocial problems (Cauffman and Steinberg 2000; Silk et al. 2003).

Impulsivity refers to behavior performed with little or inadequate forethought (Whiteside and Lynam 2003), and has long been considered a key correlate of violence risk and substance abuse, as well as an explanation for many other uncontrolled behaviors (Lynam and Miller 2004; Ramoutar and Farrington 2006; Wiebe 2006). Dickman (1990) proposes that impulsivity is related to aggression in two distinct forms. The first is functional impulsivity, which is an appropriate response to situations that require quick decisions. The second is dysfunctional impulsivity and is related to speedy and non-reflexive decisions. This form often brings about negative consequences for the individual which may result in violence.

Volatile temper, the inability of an individual to regulate their own expression of annoyance, irritation, antagonism, resentment, or rage, is also identified as a personality trait related to substance abuse and violence (Huang et al. 2001; Nichols et al. 2008; Swaim et al. 1989; Weiner et al. 2001). Poor anger control and substance use both may function to produce violence by reducing the inhibition of aggressive impulses (Parrott and Giancola 2004). Furthermore, their combination may synergistically reduce the inhibition of aggressive impulses more than either alone.

Anderson and Bushman (2002) propose that volatile temper may influence violence in three ways. First, temper may reduce prohibitions against aggression, either by justifying the aggressive response or by disrupting normal cognitive processes that would otherwise suppress aggression. Second, over time, episodes of anger become information cues and primes for aggressive "scripts." Thus, certain thoughts, images, and memories become closely associated with an anger experience such that each new episode of anger arousal activates the same processes and motivational sets that call forth an aggressive response. As a result, aggressive individuals behave violently, in part, because they have effortlessly accessed a highly routinized script that dictates how that individual should think, feel, and respond to that particular type of situation. Third, anger energizes behavior by increasing arousal levels. Excitation-transfer models (Zillmann and Weaver 1997) demonstrate how individuals experiencing increased anger arousal from one source will transfer that arousal to a temporally related second source and then mistakenly ascribe the cause of the arousal to the second source.

A third personality trait that has been linked to the substance use-violence nexus is that of sensation seeking (Butler and Montgomery 2004; Dauman et al. 2001; Puente et al. 2008; Yanovitzky 2006). According to Zuckerman (1979, p. 10), sensation seeking is a biologically based personality trait that represents "the need for varied, novel, and complex sensations and experiences and the willingness to take physical and social risks for the sake of such experiences." Research suggests that high sensation seekers are more aggressive (Zuckerman et al. 1993), more curious about morbid events (Zuckerman and Litle 1986), and more attracted to dangerous behaviors than low sensation seekers (Romero et al. 2003). Thus, sensation seeking, much like impulsivity and volatile temper, may act as a pathway to methamphetamine use and/or moderate the relationship between use and a variety of outcomes.

The present study explores the relationships among methamphetamine use and violent behavior, methamphetamine use and risky sexual conduct, as well as the role of personality traits as moderating variables. Additionally, the research examines the temporal relationship of methamphetamine use and two high-risk behaviors: assault and unprotected sex.

5.1 Research Methods

5.1.1 Sample Recruitment

A non-random community sample of 339 respondents, aged 16–30 years old, was recruited from various Los Angeles County locations. Recruitment flyers were posted at four universities and three high schools (with principals' permission). The flyers described the research as a study on health and social behaviors and included a telephone number to call for more information. In addition, potential respondents were recruited from neighborhood venues, such as coffee shops and bookstores. Individuals who expressed interest were screened systematically for eligibility. Specifically, a brief interview that focused on demographic characteristics and substance use patterns was used to monitor the selection of the sample. In this way, the sample reflected the demographic diversity of Los Angeles and, most importantly, included comparison groups of substance users: alcohol only, methamphetamines, and non-substance users. In light of the age structure of methamphetamine use, risk behaviors, and violence, the present study targeted individuals 16–30 years old. All questionnaires were completed in a private university office and were anonymous.

5.1.2 Measures

Demographics. (1) *Sex* was a dichotomy of male and female. (2) *Age* was coded originally as a continuous variable and then recoded into three categories: *teens* (16–19 years old), *young adults* (20–24 years old) and *adults* (25–30 years old). (3) *Race* included White, Black, Latino, and Asian.

Substance use. The study sample included three subgroups: alcohol users only, methamphetamine users, and non-substance users. Each respondent was screened prior to acceptance into the study. The subgroup of methamphetamine users was asked if they had ever used (i.e., yes/no) other substances including alcohol, marijuana, ecstasy, cocaine, or heroin during the previous 6 months. For each substance used, the methamphetamine users reported the frequency of use.

Violence. Respondents reported the frequency (continuous variable) of committing assault (stranger and intimate partner) during the previous 6 months.

Sexual risk-taking. Study participants reported the number of times that they had sexual intercourse without a condom outside of a long-term monogamous (i.e., a minimum of 12 months) relationship during the prior 6 months.

Co-occurrence of substance use and assault. To ensure that substance use and violence occurred together, participants were asked to report on the use of specific substances while engaging in assaultive behavior. For each time the participants engaged in assault, they were asked to specify if they used alcohol, methamphetamines, and/or other substances prior to and/or during involvement in assault.

Co-occurrence of substance use and high risk sex. To ensure that substance use and sexual risk behaviors occurred together, participants were asked to report on the use of specific substances while engaging in risky sexual behaviors. For each time the participants engaged in unprotected sex, they were asked to specify if they used alcohol, methamphetamines, and/or other substances prior to and/or during involvement in the behavior.

Personality traits. The study used the impulsivity and temper subscales developed by Grasmick et al. (1993). The following items were measured on a four-point Likert scale (Strongly Disagree to Strongly Agree):

Impulsivity (Cronbach's alpha = .903)
"I often act on the spur of the moment."
"I don't devote much thought and effort to preparing for the future."
"I often do whatever brings me pleasure here and now, even at the cost of some distant goal."
"I'm more concerned about what happens to me in the short run than in the long run."
Volatile Temper (Cronbach's alpha = .815)
"I lose my temper pretty easily."
"Often, when I am angry at people I feel more like hurting them than talking to them about why I am angry."
'When I have a serious disagreement with someone, it is usually hard for me to talk about it without getting upset."
Sensation seeking. Sensation seeking was measured using the brief sensation seeking scale developed by Stephenson et al. (2003). The following three items were measured on a three-point Likert scale (Strongly Disagree to Strongly Agree; Cronbach's Alpha = .835):
"I like to explore strange places."
"I like to do frightening things."
"I like new and exciting experiences, even if I have to break the rules."

5.2 Study Results

5.2.1 Sample

The sample was comprised of 159 male (46.9%) and 180 female (53.1%) respondents (Table 5.1). The majority of participants were Latino (47.8%) and in their teens (16–19 years old, 52.2%). A total of 174 (51.3%) respondents used only alcohol during the 6 month time period, 63 (18.6%) respondents used methamphetamines and 102 (30.1%) sample members did not use any substances during the 6-month period. Importantly, all of the study subjects who used methamphetamines also used alcohol and marijuana.

Of the 339 people in the study, 23.0% ($n = 78$) committed assault at least once in the previous 6 months. All of the 78 participants who committed assault used alco-

Table 5.1 Sample characteristics and involvement in high risk behaviors

	Total (N=339)	No drug use (N=102)	Alcohol only (N=174)	Meth (N=63)
		(30.1%)	(51.3%)	(18.6%)
Sex				
% Male	46.9	41.2	37.9	81.0***
Race/ethnicity				
% White	30.1	39.2	23.6	33.3*
% Black	8.8	5.9	8.6	14.2
% Latino	47.8	35.3	55.2	47.6**
% Asian	13.3	19.6	12.6	4.8*
Age				
% 16–19	52.2	57.8	43.1	68.3**
% 20–24	23.0	23.5	23.0	22.2
% 25–30	24.8	18.6	33.9	9.5***
Personality traits (mean scores)				
Impulsive	2.17	1.85	2.10	2.88***
Sensation seeking	2.21	1.85	2.06	3.14***
Volatile temper	1.52	1.09	1.36	2.65***
Assault (prevalence):				
% Yes	23.0	0	17.2	76.2***
% Co-occurrence of drug use and assault:	18.6	NA	6.9	80.1***
Risky sex (prevalence):				
% Yes	53.4	9.8	63.2	96.8***
% Co-occurrence of drug use and risky sex:	14.2	NA	12.1	42.9***

*p<.05; **p<.01; ***p=.000

hol or methamphetamines during the 6 month period. Of the 78 respondents who engaged in assault, 63 (80.8%) reported that they committed at least one act of assault while using alcohol or methamphetamines (18.6% of the total sample).

A total of 244 of the 339 (72.3%) people in the sample had sexual intercourse during the prior 6 months. Of the 245 sexually active respondents, 181 (73.9%) reported that they did not use condoms at least once during the past 6 months. The data indicate that substance use co-occurred with high-risk sexual behavior in 28.1% ($n=48$) of the respondents who engaged in unprotected sex as compared to 9.8% of non-substance users who engaged in high-risk sex.

5.2.2 *Predictors of Violence*

Logistic regression analyses were performed in order to test the effects of substance use and personality traits on the prevalence of violence, as well as on the co-occurrence of substance use and violence. Prevalence of violence and the co-occurrence

Table 5.2 Hierarchical logistic regression of the prevalence of assault

	B	S.E.	Odds	B	S.E.	Odds	B	S.E.	Odds
Males	2.76	.420	15.84***	1.97	.444	7.17***	2.20	.620	9.04***
Teens	.697	.429	2.01	.191	.471	1.21	−.172	.573	.842
Young adults	−.491	.559	.612	−1.16	.680	.314	−1.56	.966	.210
Black	1.69	.695	5.43*	1.36	.790	3.89	2.19	1.07	8.98*
Latino	.735	.411	2.09	1.14	.488	3.13*	2.21	.690	9.12**
Asian	−19.93	7115	.000	−19.29	7362	.000	−17.81	7719	.000
Meth use				2.58	.508	13.18***	1.09	.672	2.98
Impulsive							.377	.334	1.46
Sensation seek							.789	.496	2.20
Volatile temper							1.84	.500	6.27***
R^2			.345			.429			.519

*p<.05; **p<.01; ***p=.000

Table 5.3 Hierarchical logistic regression of the co-occurrence of substance use and assault

	B	S.E.	Odds	B	S.E.	Odds	B	S.E.	Odds
Males	1.51	.850	4.54	−.713	1.03	.490	−2.42	1.53	.089
Teens	2.65	.843	14.18**	1.81	1.08	6.12	2.38	1.15	10.78*
Young adults	22.29	13466	.000	20.05	13579	.000	18.91	13274	.000
Black	20.46	12544	.000	18.50	12839	.000	20.01	12281	.000
Latino**	.398	.682	1.49	.288	.987	1.33	1.24	1.26	3.44
Asian	constant (0)			constant (0)			constant (0)		
Meth use				3.70	.896	40.44***	4.20	1.17	66.93***
Impulsive							−.461	.763	.631
Sensation seek							2.27	1.43	9.68
Volatile temper							−1.02	.763	.360
R^2			.337			.507			.535

*p<.05; **p<.01; ***p=.000

of substance use and violence were coded as dichotomous variables (yes or no). Since no violent events for the non-substance users were reported, the analyses excluded this group. Each model included controls for age, sex, and race. Table 5.2 indicates the results for the hierarchical regression models on the prevalence of violence. The data demonstrate a strong relationship between personality traits, specifically volatile temper (e.g., anger), and having committed assault over the 6-month period. When personality trait factors were eliminated from the model, methamphetamine users were approximately 13 times more likely to commit assault than alcohol only users. However, the significance of this association disappeared when controlling for personality traits. In addition, males and Blacks and Latinos were more likely to commit assault than females and White participants.

The analysis in Table 5.3 focused on the co-occurrence of substance use and assault. The results were different when analyzing the subgroup of participants who engaged in violence ($n=78$) with respect to the co-occurrence of substance use and

Table 5.4 Hierarchical logistic regression of the prevalence of unprotected sex

	B	S.E.	Odds	B	S.E.	Odds	B	S.E.	Odds
Males	.772	.239	2.16**	.138	.315	1.15	.178	.339	1.20
Teens	−.711	.288	.491*	−.882	.364	.440*	−.970	.399	.379*
Young adults	.290	.337	1.34	.464	.427	1.59	.518	.464	1.68
Black	.180	.436	1.20	−1.17	.603	.309*	−.996	.680	.369
Latino	.198	.270	1.22	−.399	.388	.671	−.308	.435	.735
Asian	−.744	.384	.475*	−.880	.509	.415	−.941	.557	.390
Alcohol only				2.95	.408	19.03***	2.89	.431	17.90***
Meth use				6.08	.845	435.65***	5.55	.966	58.11***
Impulsive							.058	.242	1.06
Sensation seek							.241	.361	1.27
Volatile temper							.497	.353	1.64
R^2			.071			.405			.416

*p<.05; **p<.01; ***p=.000

violence as compared to the results for the prevalence of assault. Two variables were significant predictors of the co-occurrence of substance use and assault: age and methamphetamine use. For instance, teens were approximately 11 times more likely to commit assault while under the influence of drugs than adults. Respondents who used methamphetamines were approximately 67 times more likely than alcohol only users to commit assault while intoxicated. Personality traits were not significant predictors of the co-occurrence of drug use and assault. In fact, unlike the results for the prevalence model, the odds of committing assault increased for methamphetamine users when controlling for personality traits.

5.2.3 *Predictors of Risky Sexual Behavior*

Logistic regression analyses were performed in order to test the effects of substance use and personality traits on the prevalence of risky sex as well as on the co-occurrence of substance use and risky sex. Table 5.4 reports the results for the hierarchical regression models on the prevalence of risky sexual behavior. The data indicate that respondents who used alcohol only (odds=17.90) or methamphetamines (odds=258.11) were significantly more likely to engage in risky sex over the 6 month period than non-substance users even when controlling for personality traits and demographic differences. Furthermore, methamphetamine users were 14 times more likely to engage in risky sex than alcohol only users (data not shown). Personality traits were not related significantly to high risk sexual behavior. Teens were less likely to engage in risky sex than adults. Contrary to previous findings (Benda and Corwyn 1999; CDC 2006), no significant differences between males and females emerged with regard to the prevalence of unprotected sex. Finally, the logistic regression results indicated no race/ethnic differences in the use of condoms.

Table 5.5 Hierarchical logistic regression of the co-occurrence of substance use and unprotected sex

	B	S.E.	Odds	B	S.E.	Odds	B	S.E.	Odds
Males	−.981	.446	.375*	−2.32	.650	.099***	−2.09	.694	.124**
Teens	2.59	.678	13.27***	2.38	.706	10.78**	2.09	.718	8.06**
Young adults	.454	.736	1.58	−.083	.783	.920	−.074	.861	.929
Black	1.93	.687	6.91**	1.52	.734	4.57*	.773	.820	2.17
Latino	.430	.475	1.54	.613	.544	1.85	.149	.580	1.16
Asian	−19.11	9182	.000	−20.20	8312	.000	−19.79	9054	.000
Meth use				1.86	.612	6.42**	1.48	.690	4.37*
Impulsive							.009	.275	1.01
Sensation seek							−.461	.547	.631
Volatile temper							1.28	.424	3.61**
R^2			.245			.314			.356

*p<.05; **p<.01; ***p=.000

The odds of the co-occurrence of substance use and being involved in unprotected sexual intercourse are shown in Table 5.5. The data indicate a significant relationship between methamphetamine use and condom use, even when controlling for demographics and personality traits. The odds of not using a condom were significantly higher for individuals who used methamphetamines compared to respondents who only used alcohol (odds=4.37). The results also indicate that individuals with higher scores on the volatile temper scale were more likely to engage in unprotected sex than individuals with lower scores (odds=3.61). Unlike the findings for the prevalence of unprotected sex, a significant gender difference emerged for the co-occurrence of substance use and risky sex: males were less likely than females to have unprotected sex while using drugs. Also, teens were more likely to have high risk sex while using drugs than adults.

5.3 Discussion

The objective of the present study was to gain an understanding of the temporal relationship of substance use and high-risk behaviors (assault and unprotected sex) within a 6-month time frame. During the 6 months prior to data collection, individuals who used alcohol or methamphetamines were more likely to be involved in violence and high-risk sex than non-substance users. Perhaps most important, methamphetamine users were more likely to be involved in assault and unprotected sex than alcohol-only users.

The present study also explored the possibility that the drug-risky behavior connection is spurious. Studies emanating from developmental psychology suggest that traits related to emotion dysregulation may play a key role in poor judgment and risk taking behaviors (Cauffman and Steinberg 2000; Steinberg 2004). For instance, some studies have demonstrated that sensation seeking is related to emotional regulation and its converse, impulsivity (Boyer 2006; Cauffman and Steinberg 2000;

Loeber 1988). The logic of this perspective is that individuals who lack regulation skills hastily engage in more goal-defeating, sensation-seeking behaviors, especially in frustrating or anger provoking situations.

Along the lines suggested by the research cited above, the current study attempted to disentangle the many intersecting factors that may link substance use with high risk behaviors by including three personality traits that underlie emotion regulation: impulsivity, sensation seeking and volatile temper. The results suggest, clearly, that personality trait differences, specifically volatile temper, accounted for the overwhelming majority of explained variance in the prevalence of assault. In fact, when controlling for personality traits, substance use ceased to be a significant predictor of the prevalence of assault. Thus, the findings suggest that the relationship between substance use and the prevalence of assault may be spurious.

Importantly, however, the relationship among personality traits, substance use, and involvement in violence varied based on the outcome measure of association. Volatile temper was the key predictor of the *prevalence* of violence, but was not associated significantly with the *co-occurrence* of substance use and violence. However, the co-occurrence of substance use and assault was significantly greater for respondents who used methamphetamines as compared to alcohol-only users.

Similarly, Fals-Stewart et al. (2003) collected detailed diaries over a 15 month time frame from male partners with a history of intimate partner violence (IPV), entering either an alcoholism or domestic violence treatment program, and from their female partners. The diaries contained information not only about the occurrence of male-to-female aggression, but also about the time of day these episodes happened, whether the male partner drank alcohol during the same day the violence occurred, and what time of day the drinking occurred. This allowed for a detailed examination of the daily temporal relationship between male-to-female physical aggression and alcohol consumption. Importantly, in both samples, over 80% of all IPV episodes occurred within 4 h following drinking by the male partner. Similar results were found for the temporal association between cocaine and episodes of IPV in a sample of patients who primarily abused drugs other than alcohol (Fals-Stewart et al. 2003). These findings suggest the need for future research that examines the concurrent and simultaneous relationship of substance use and violence.

With regard to risky sexual behavior, the findings indicate that substance use, alcohol- only, and methamphetamines heightened the risk for unprotected sexual intercourse even when controlling for demographics and personality traits. The findings are similar to those of other studies that indicate that both the frequency of substance use and use at last intercourse were strongly associated with the likelihood of condom use (Santelli et al. 2001; Tapert et al. 2001).

Contrary to general deviance models, which imply that risk behaviors are unidimensional, current results support a multidimensional model for risk-taking behaviors (Boyer 2006; Romero et al. 2003). Although volatile temper was related to both risk behaviors, its predictive value varied by measure of association and by type of risk behavior. However, the reverse association was found for risky sexual behavior. Volatile temper was not associated with the prevalence of unprotected sex but was a significant predictor of the co-occurrence of drug use and high risk sex.

The complexity of the interaction of substance use, personality traits, and high risk behaviors suggests the need for longitudinal research that can trace their mutual development and interaction across time (Romero et al. 2003). So as to reconstruct the key influences on the development of high risk behaviors, such research should include the following: severity, frequency, timing, and recency of high risk behavior; precipitating life events, location, context, and consequences; presence of individual-level mental health problems and active symptoms; substance use and intoxication at the time the behavior occurs; and subjects' interpretations of these episodes.

In addition, future investigations in this area should assess the consistency of the findings by exploring the dynamic interplay of the occurrence and timing of drug use on different violent behaviors, not just assault. Finally, the current study compared individuals who only used alcohol to methamphetamine users. However, all of the respondents in the methamphetamine group were polydrug users, both concurrently and simultaneously. Thus, future research should explore the role that polydrug use plays with regard to risky behaviors.

Aside from the acute effects associated with intoxication and impairment, little research has examined simultaneous polydrug drug use in relation to behavioral outcomes. Some evidence indicates that the use of multiple substances increases the risk of violence. For instance, polydrug abusers in treatment obtained significantly higher scores on self-report measures of hostility and aggression than did single-substance abusers, regardless of the particular types of drugs and drug combinations used (McCormick and Smith 1995). In addition, Bennett (2000) reported an exponential relationship between the number of drug types that arrestees used during a 1-year period and the number of acquisitive offenses that occurred during that same period. It may be that polydrug users have personality traits (particularly antagonism and impulsiveness) that predispose them toward violence (McCormick et al. 1998), that polydrug use prompts more instrumental violence and acquisitive crime to maintain a multiple-drug habit (Bennett and Holloway 2005; Smith and Polsenberg 1992), or that polydrug use coincides with heavier involvement in a deviant, problematic, and "excessive" lifestyles than does single-substance abuse.

Alternatively, the use of multiple drugs may interact to increase intoxication, which places one at greater risk for violence than does single drug use (Hammersley and Morrison 1987). One reason for this is that particular drug combinations might create unique metabolites with greater toxicity than those formed when the drugs are used individually. For instance, Pennings et al. (2002) suggest that alcohol and cocaine each elevate extraneuronal dopamine and serotonin levels, which may lead to deficits in impulse control and then to violent behavior.

Much drug research is often limited by its reliance on a simple checklist of drugs used by respondents without elaborating on whether it was single, combined, or polydrug use that characterized consumption (Grob 2000; Pedersen and Skrondal 1999; Reid et al. 2007). However, when polydrug use is considered, its definition is so variable as to make comparisons across studies difficult. Some research defines polydrug use as having ingested more than one drug during over the course of the respondent's life (Montgomery et al. 2005; Scholey et al. 2004; Sneed et al. 2004; Wu et al. 2006) over the 6 months prior to the study, the prior 90 or 30 days, the week before, or 1 or 2 days prior to data collection (Carlson et al. 2005; Copeland et al. 2006; Hunt et al. 2005; Isralowitz and Rawson 2006; Sterk et al. 2000). These studies often ignore the frequency of use and the differences between combined and sequential use.

Complicating studies on polydrug use is the fact that substances are co-used in different ways for different reasons. Some users, for example, may inject cocaine and heroin simultaneously in the form of a speedball to experience the effects of both drugs at the same time. Some may use the speedball to achieve a greater level of euphoria, especially when they have insufficient quantities of either drug. Other users might mix cocaine with heroin with the goal of gradually reducing heroin consequently eliminating their physical reliance upon opioids. Heroin users often report co-use of cocaine in a sequential manner either to enhance euphoria or to reduce the withdrawal symptoms commonly experienced during their typical day or when they decide to detoxify from opioid drugs (Leri et al. 2003). Therefore, future research must incorporate these relevant dimensions if a more complete understanding of the relationships among substance use and risky behaviors is to be attained.

References

American Academy of Family Physicians. (2007). Retrieved July 14, 2009, from www.aafp.org/afp/20071015/1169/html

Anderson, C. I., & Bushman, B. J. (2002). Human aggression. *Annual Review of Psychology, 53*, 27–51.

Baskin-Sommers, A., & Sommers, I. (2006). The co-occurrence of substance use with high-risk behaviors. *Journal of Adolescent Health, 38*, 609–611.

Benda, B., & Corwyn, R. (1999). Developmental differences in theories of sexual behavior among rural adolescents residing in AFDC families. *Deviant Behavior, 20*, 359–386.

Bennett, T. (2000). *Drugs and crime: The results of the second developmental stage of the NEWADAM programme* (Home Office Research Study No. 205). London: Home Office.

Bennett, T., & Holloway, K. (2005). The association between multiple drug misuse and crime. *International journal of Offender Therapy and Comparative Criminology, 49*, 63–81.

Bolding, G., Hart, G., Sherr, L., & Elford, J. (2006). Use of crystal methamphetamine among gay men in London. *Addiction, 101*, 1622–1630.

Bonell, C., Hickson, F., Weatherburn, P., & Reid, D. (2010). Methamphetamine use among gay men aross the UK. *The International Journal of Drug Policy, 21*, 244–246.

Borders, T., Booth, B., Han, X., Wright, P., Falck, R., & Carlson, R. (2008). Longitudinal changes in methamphetamine and cocaine use in untreated rural stimulant users: Racial differences and the impact of methamphetamine legislation. *Addiction, 103*, 800–808.

Boyer, T. (2006). The development of risk-taking; a multi-perspective review. *Developmental Review, 26*, 291–345.

Brecht, M., O'Briena, A., von Mayrhauser, C., & Anglin, M. (2004). Methamphetamine use behaviors and gender differences. *Addictive Behaviors, 29*, 89–106.

Butler, G., & Montgomery, A. (2004). Impulsivity, risk taking and recreational ecstasy (MDMA) use. *Drug and Alcohol Dependence, 76*, 55–62.

Carlson, R., Wang, J., Falck, R., & Siegal, H. (2005). Drug use practices among MDMA/Ecstasy users in Ohio: A latent class analysis. *Drug and Alcohol Dependence, 79*, 167–179.

Cartier, J., Farabee, D., & Predergast, M. (2006). Methamphetamine use, self-reported violent crime, and recidivism among offenders in California who abuse substances. *Journal of Interpersonal Violence, 21*, 435–445.

Cauffman, E., & Steinberg, L. (2000). (Im)maturity of judgment in adolescence: Why adolescents might be less culpable than adults? *Behavioral Sciences and the Law, 18*, 741–760.

Centers for Disease Control and Prevention. (2006). Youth risk behavior surveillance system 2005. *Morbidity & Mortality Weekly Report, 55*(SS-5), 1–108.

Cheng-Fang, Y., & Mian-Moon, C. (2006). Cormorbid psychiatric disorders, sex, and methamphetamine use in adolescents: A case control study. *Comprehensive Psychiatry, 47*, 215–220.

Copeland, J., Dillon, P., & Gascoigne, M. (2006). Ecstasy and the concomitant use of pharmaceuticals. *Addictive Behaviors, 57*, 367–370.

Crevecoeur, D., Rutkowski, B., & Rawson, R. (2007). The rise in treatment admissions for methamphetamine use in Los Angeles County from 2001–2005. *Journal of Psychoactive Drugs, 4*, 383–392.

Darke, S., Kaye, S., McKetin, R., & Duflou, J. (2008). Major physical and psychological harms of methamphetamine use. *Drug and Alcohol Review, 27*, 253–262.

Dauman, J., Pelz, S., Becker, S., Tuchtenhagen, F., & Gouzoulis-Mayfrank, E. (2001). Psychological profile of abstinenet recreational Ecstasy (MDMA) users and significance of concomitant cannabis use. *Human Psychopharmacology: Clinical and Experimental, 16*, 627–633.

Dickman, S. J. (1990). Functional and dysfunctional impulsivity: Personality and cognitive correlates. *Journal of Personality and Social Personality, 58*(1), 95–102.

Donovan, J., & Jessor, R. (1985). Structure of problem behavior in adolescence and young adulthood. *Journal of Consulting and Clinical Psychology, 53*, 890–904.

Drumright, L., Patterson, T., & Strathdee, S. (2006). Club drugs as causal risk factors for HIV acquisition among MSM: A review. *Drug Alcohol Dependence, 83*, 225–232.

Fals-Stewart, W., Golden, J., & Schumacher, J. A. (2003). Intimate partner violence and substance use: A longitudinal day-to-day examination. *Addictive Behaviors, 28*, 1555–1574.

Gottfredson, M., & Hirschi, T. (1990). *A general theory of crime*. Stanford: Stanford University Press.

Grasmick, H., Tittle, C., Bursik, R., & Arneklev, B. (1993). Testing the core empirical implications of Gottfredson and Hirschi's general theory of crime. *Journal of Research in Crime and Delinquency, 30*, 5–29.

Grob, C. (2000). Deconstructing ecstasy: The politics of MDMA research. *Addiction Research, 8*, 549–588.

Hall, W., Hando, J., Darke, S., & Ross, J. (1996). Psychological morbidity and route of administration among amphetamine users in Sydney, Australia. *Addiction, 91*, 81–87.

Hammersley, R., & Morrison, V. (1987). Effects of polydrug use on the criminal activities of heroin users. *British Journal of Addiction, 82*, 899–906.

Herman-Stahl, M., Krebs, C., Kroutil, L., & Heller, D. (2007). Protective and risk factors for methamphetamine use and nonmedical use of prescription stimulants among young adults aged 18–25. *Addictive Behaviors, 32*, 1003–1015.

Hoeken, P., & Stewart, S. (2003). Drugs of abuse and the elicitation of human aggressive behavior. *Addictive Behaviors, 28*, 1533–1554.

Huang, B., White, H., Kosterman, R., Catalano, R., & Hawkins, J. (2001). Developmental associations between alcohol and interpersonal aggression during adolescence. *Journal of Research in Crime Delinquency, 38*, 64–83.

Humeniuk, R., & Ali, R. (2004). Amphetamines in Asia: The value of information networks. *Drug and Alcohol Review, 23*, 235–237.

Hunt, G., Evans, K., Wu, E., & Reyes, A. (2005). Asian American youth, the dance scene, and club drugs. *Journal of Drug Issues, 35*(4), 695–732.

Iritiani, B., Hallfors, D., & Bauer, D. (2007). Crystal methamphetamine use among young adults in the USA. *Addiction, 102*, 1102–1113.

Isralowitz, R., & Rawson, R. (2006). Gender differences in prevalence of drug use among high risk adolescents in Israel. *Addictive Behaviors, 31*, 355–358.

Lende, D., Leonard, T., Sterk, C., & Elifson, K. (2007). Functional methamphetamine use: The insider's perspective. *Addiction Research and Theory, 15*, 465–477.

Leri, F., Bruneau, J., & Stewart, J. (2003). Understanding polydrug use: Review of heroin and cocaine co-use. *Addiction, 98*, 7–22.

Loeber, R. (1988). Natural histories of conduct problems, delinquency, and associated substance use: Evidence for development progressions. In B. Lahey & A. Kazdin (Eds.), *Advances in clinical child psychology* (pp. 73–124). New York: Plenum.

Lorvick, J., Martinez, A., Gee, L., & Kral, A. (2006). Sexual and injection risk among women who inject methamphetamine in San Francisco. *Journal of Urban Health, 83*, 497–505.

Lynam, D., & Miller, J. (2004). Personality pathways to impulsive behavior and their relations to deviance: Results from three samples. *Journal of Quantitative Criminology, 20*, 319–341.

Maxwell, J. (2005). Emerging research on methamphetamine. *Current Opinion in Psychiatry, 18*, 235–242.

Maxwell, J., & Rutkowski, B. (2008). The prevalence of methamphetamine and amphetamine abuse in North America. *Drug and Alcohol Review, 27*, 229–235.

McCormick, R. A., & Smith, M. (1995). Aggression and hostility in substance abusers: The relationship to abuse patterns, coping style, and relapse triggers. *Addictive Behaviors, 20*, 555–562.

McCormick, R., Dowd, T., Quirk, S., & Zegarra, J. (1998). The relationship of neo-PI performance to coping styles, patterns of use, and triggers for use among substance abusers. *Addictive Behaviors, 23*, 497–507.

McKetin, R., McLaren, J., Ridell, S., & Robins, L. (2006). The relationship between methamphetamine use and violent behaviour. *Crime and Justice Bulletin, 9*, 1–16.

Meredith, C., Jaffe, C., Ang-Lee, K., & Saxon, A. (2005). Implications of chronic methamphetamine use: A literature review. *Harvard Review of Psychiatry, 13*, 141–154.

Molitor, F., Truax, S., Ruiz, J., & Sun, R. (1998). Association of methamphetamine us during sex with risky sexual behaviors and HIV infection among non-injecting drug users. *The Western Journal of Medicine, 168*, 93–97.

Montgomery, C., Fisk, J., Newcombe, R., & Murphy, P. (2005). The differential effects of ecstasy/polydrug use on executive components: Shifting, inhibition, updating and access to semantic memory. *Psychopharmacology, 18*, 262–267.

National Library of Medicine. (2009). Retrieved from www.nlm.nih.gov/medlineplus/news/fullstory-84586.html

Nichols, T., Mahadeo, M., Bryant, K., & Botvin, G. (2008). Examining anger as a predictor of drug use among multiethnic middle school students. *Journal of School Health, 78*, 480–486.

Nicosia, N., Pacula, R., Kilmer, B., Lundberg, R., & Chiesa, J. (2005). *The economic cost of methamphetamine use in the United States, 2005*. Santa Monica: RAND Institute.

Office of National Drug Control Policy. (2007). Retrieved from www.whitehousedrugpolicy.gov/drugfact/methamphetamine.methamphetamine_ff.html

Parrott, D., & Giancola, P. (2004). A further examination of the relation between trait anger and alcohol-related aggression: The role of anger control. *Alcoholism: Clinical & Experimental Research, 28*(6), 855–864.

Pedersen, W., & Skrondal, A. (1999). Ecstasy and new patterns of drug use: A normal population study. *Addiction, 94*, 1695–1706.

Pennings, J. M., Leccese, A. P., & De Wolff, F. A. (2002). Effects of concurrent use of alcohol and cocaine. *Addiction, 97*, 773–783.

Pinhey, T., & Wells, R. (2007). Asian Pacific Islander adolescent methamphetamine use: Does "ice" increase aggression and sexual risks. *Substance Use & Misuse, 42*, 801–809.

Pluddemann, A., Myers, B., & Parry, C. (2008). Surge in treatment admissions related to methamphetamine use in Cape Town, South Africa: Implications for public health. *Drug and Alcohol Review, 27*, 185–189.

Puente, C., Guiterrez, J., Abellan, I., & Lopez, A. (2008). Sensation seeking, attitudes toward drug use, and actual use among adolescents: Testing a model for alcohol and ecstasy use. *Substance Use & Misuse, 43*, 1618–1630.

Ramoutar, K., & Farrington, D. (2006). Are the same factors related to participation and frequency of offending by male and female prisoners? *Psychology, Crime & Law, 12*, 557–572.
Reid, L., Elifson, K., & Sterk, C. (2007). Ecstasy and gateway drugs: Initiating the use of ecstasy and other drugs. *Annals of Epidemiology, 17*, 74–80.
Romero, E., Gomez-Fraguela, J. A., Luengo, M. A., & Sobral, J. (2003). The self-control construct in the general theory of crime: An investigation in terms of personality psychology. *Psychology, Crime & Law, 9*, 61–86.
Santelli, J., Robin, L., Brener, N., & Lowry, R. (2001). Timing of alcohol and other drug use and sexual risk behaviors among unmarried adolescents and young adults. *Family Planning Perspectives, 33*, 200–205.
Scholey, A. B., Parrott, A. C., Buchanan, T., Heffeman, T. M., Ling, J., & Rodgers, J. (2004). Increased intensity of ecstasy and polydrug usage in the more experienced recreational ecstasy/MDMA users: A WWW study. *Addictive Behaviors, 29*, 743–752.
Schrem, M., & Halkitis, P. (2008). Methamphetamine abuse in the United States: Contextual, psychological and sociological considerations. *Journal of Health Psychology, 13*, 669–679.
Sekine, Y., Ouchi, Y., Akei, N., Yoshikawa, E., Nakamura, K., Futatsubashi, M., Okada, H., Minabe, Y., Suzuki, K., Iwata, Y., Tsuchiya, K. J., Tsukada, H., Iyo, M., & Mori, N. (2006). Brain serotonin transporter density and aggression in abstinent methamphetamine abusers. *General Psychiatry, 63*, 90–100.
Semple, S., Patterson, T., & Grant, I. (2004). A comparison of injection and non-injection methamphetamine-using HIV positive men who have sex with men. *Drug and Alcohol Dependence, 76*, 203–212.
Sexton, R., Carlson, R., Leukefeld, C., & Booth, B. (2009). An ethnographic exploration of self-reported violence among rural methamphetamine users. *Journal of Ethnicity in Substance Abuse, 8*, 35–53.
Silk, J., Steinberg, L., & Morris, A. S. (2003). Adolescents' Emotion regulation in daily life: Links to depressive symptoms and problem behavior. *Child Development, 74*, 1869–1880.
Simons, J., Olivera, M., Gahera, R., & Ebel, G. (2005). Methamphetamine and alcohol abuse and dependence symptoms: Associations with affect lability and impulsivity in a rural treatment population. *Addictive Behaviors, 30*, 1370–1381.
Smith, D., & Polsenberg, C. (1992). Specifying the relationship between arrestee drug test results and recidivism. *The Journal of Criminal Law and Criminology, 83*, 364–377.
Sneed, C., Morisky, D., Rotheram-Borus, M. J., Lee, S., & Ebin, V. (2004). Indices of lifetime polydrug use among adolescents. *Journal of Adolescence, 27*, 239–249.
Sommers, I., & Baskin, D. (2004). *The social consequences of methamphetamine use*. New York: The Edward Mellen Press.
Sommers, I., Baskin, D., & Baskin-Sommers, A. (2006). Methamphetamine use among young adults: Health and social consequences. *Addictive Behaviors, 31*, 1469–1476.
Steinberg, L. (2004). Risk taking in adolescence: What changes, and why? *Annals of the New York Academy of Sciences, 102*, 51–58.
Stephenson, M., Hoyle, R., Palmgreen, P., & Slater, M. (2003). Brief measures of sensation seeking for screening and large scale surveys. *Drug & Alcohol Dependence, 72*, 279–286.
Sterk, C., Elifson, K., & Theall, K. (2000). Women and drug treatment experiences: A generational comparison of mothers and daughters. *Journal of Drug Issues, 30*, 839–862.
Stretsky, P. (2008). National case–control study of homicide offending and methamphetamine use. *Journal of Interpersonal Violence, 24*, 911–924.
Swaim, R., Oetting, E., Edwards, R., & Beauvais, F. (1989). Links from emotional distress to adolescent drug use: A path model. *Journal of Consulting Clinical Psychology, 57*, 227–231.
Tapert, S., Aarons, G., Sedlar, G., & Brown, S. (2001). Adolescent substance use and sexual risk-taking behavior. *Journal of Adolescent Health, 28*, 181–189.
Tyner, E., & Fremouw, W. (2008). The relation of methamphetamine use and violence: A critical review. *Aggression and Violent Behavior, 13*, 285–297.

von Mayrhauser, C., Brecht, M., & Anglin, M. (2001). Use ecology and drug use motivations of methamphetamine users admitted to substance abuse treatment facilities in Los Angeles. *Journal of Addictive Diseases, 21*, 45–60.

Weiner, M., Pentz, M., Turner, G., & Dwyer, J. (2001). From early to late adolescence: Alcohol use and anger relationships. *Journal of Adolescent Health, 28*, 450–457.

Whiteside, S. P., & Lynam, D. R. (2003). Understanding the role of impulsivity and externalizing psychopathology in alcohol abuse: Application of the UPPS impulsive behavior scale. *Experimental and Clinical Psychopharmacology, 11*, 210–217.

Wiebe, R. (2006). Using an expanded measure of self-control to predict delinquency. *Psychology, Crime & Law, 12*, 519–536.

Wright, S., & Klee, H. (2001). Violent crime, aggression and amphetamine: What are the implications for drug treatment services? *Drugs: education, prevention and policy, 8*, 73–90.

Wu, Z. H., Hölzer, C. E., III, Breitkopf, C. R., Grady, J. J., & Berenson, A. B. (2006). Patterns and perceptions of ecstasy use among young, low-income women. *Addictive Behaviors, 31*, 676–685.

Yanovitzky, I. (2006). Sensation seeking and alcohol use by college students: Examining multiple pathways of effects. *Journal of Health Communication, 11*, 269–280.

Zillmann, D., & Weaver, J. (1997). Psychoticism in the effect of prolonged exposure to gratuitous media violence on the acceptance of violence as a preferred means of conflict resolution. *Personality & Individual Differences, 22*, 613–627.

Zuckerman, M. (1979). *Sensation seeking: Beyond the optimal level of arousal*. Hillsdale: Lawrence Erlbaum.

Zuckerman, M., & Litle, P. (1986). Personality and curiosity about morbid sexual events. *Personality and Individual Differences, 7*, 49–56.

Zuckerman, M., Kuhlman, D. M., Joireman, J., Teta, P., & Kraft, M. (1993). A comparison of the three structural models for personality: The big three, the big five, and the alternative five. *Journal of Personality and Social Psychology, 65*, 757–768.

Zule, W., & Desmond, D. (1999). An ethnographic comparison of HIV risk behaviors among heroin and methamphetamine injectors. *American Journal of Drug and Alcohol Abuse, 25*, 1–23.

Zweben, J., Cohen, J., Christian, D., Galloway, G., Pham, D., Salinardi, M., Parent, D., & Iguchi, M. (2004). Psychiatric symptoms in methamphetamine users. *The American Journal on Addictions, 13*, 181–190.

Chapter 6
Gang Youth, Risk Behaviors, and Negative Health Outcomes

Bill Sanders, Avelardo Valdez, Geoffrey P. Hunt, Karen Joe Laidler, Molly Moloney, and Alice Cepeda

Abstract *Gang youth have been a perennial issue with criminologists for nearly a century. Much evidence suggests that something about participation within a gang leads youth to commit more crime when compared to non-gang youth. Gang youth are at an increased risk of arrest and incarceration for serious offences in comparison to other delinquent youth. Gang youth also are more likely to report participation in what are described as 'health risk behaviors', which include substance use, violence, and unsafe sexual practices. Consequently, gang youth are at an elevated risk of exposure to the negative health outcomes related to such behaviors, including addiction, overdose, infection, injury, disability, and death. This chapter offers data gathered in three cities over a 20-year period to provide a descriptive epidemiology of substance use, violence and unsafe sexual practices among gang-identified youth. We conclude with a discussion on how public health approaches towards other high-risk categories of youth could compliment current criminal justice efforts aimed at curbing the influence or impact of youth gangs.*

B. Sanders, Ph.D. (✉)
School of Criminal Justice and Criminalistics,
California State University, Los Angeles, CA, USA
e-mail: bsander2@calstatela.edu

A. Valdez, Ph.D. • A. Cepeda, Ph.D.
School of Social Work, University of Southern
California, Los Angeles, CA, USA

G.P. Hunt, Ph.D.
Centre for Alcohol and Drugs Research, University
of Aarhus, Aarhus, Denmark

K.J. Laidler, Ph.D.
Centre for Criminology, University of Hong Kong,
Pokfulam, Hong Kong

M. Moloney, Ph.D.
Institute for Scientific Analysis, Alameda, CA, USA

B. Sanders et al. (eds.), *Crime, HIV and Health: Intersections of Criminal Justice and Public Health Concerns*, DOI 10.1007/978-90-481-8921-2_6,

Gang members are a demonized category of hyper-offenders that perennially fascinate the general public, the media, and academics. A focus of much research on gang youth is their increased contribution to crime and delinquency. Strong evidence from North America and Europe suggests that gang youth, in comparison to their non-gang peers, are more likely to report crime, violence and substance use (Bendixen et al. 2006; Gatti et al. 2005; Gordon et al. 2004; Hall et al. 2006; Sharp et al. 2006). Even among offenders, gang-identified youth are more likely to commit felonies and other serious offences (Howell 1998). For instance, for many years, approximately half of all homicides in Los Angeles and Chicago have been considered 'gang related' (Egley and O'Donnell 2008). Moreover, research on recidivism has suggested that gang membership is one of the strongest predictors of returning to jail or prison (Huebner et al. 2007). In concert, these studies propose that gang membership is an indicator of a youth at increased risk of arrest and incarceration – the domains of criminal justice.

The consequences of gang membership and gang youths' detrimental health-related issues are topics that have received less attention. For instance, some studies have indicated that gang youth are more likely than non-gang youth to experience violence victimization and injuries (DuRant et al. 2000; MacDonald et al. 2007; Peterson et al. 2004). Likewise, studies have reported that gang youth have engaged in risky sexual behaviors that have significantly increased their exposure to HIV, Hepatitis C (HCV) and STIs (Brooks et al. 2009; Salazar et al. 2007; Uman et al. 2006; Voisin et al. 2004; Wingood et al. 2002). Evidence also indicates that gang members are also more likely to report symptoms of mental health disorders, including anxiety, depression, and stress (Hamrin et al. 2004; Harper et al. 2008; Li et al. 2002). Overall, these studies suggest that gang youth have an increased exposure to risk and a decreased quality of life – the domains of public health. However, research that examines public health-related issues among gang youth appear to be in their infancy (Juarez 1992; Sanders and Lankenau 2006).

The aim of this chapter is to offer an overview of what may best be called 'public health research' on gang youth collected over a 20-year period (1990–2010) from three different research teams: San Antonio, Texas and San Francisco and Los Angeles, California. Funded by the National Institutes of Health (NIH),[1] these studies employed qualitative research methods to focus on what are described as 'health risk behaviors' – substance use, violence, and unsafe sexual practices – specifically among gang youth. First, a brief overview of the methodologies utilized in these studies is provided. From here, data on substance use, violent, and risky sexual behaviors among each sample is offered, including some information on the interrelationship

[1] Data from the Los Angeles site: NIDA grant # 1R03DA020410-01; PI: B. Sanders; References: Sanders et al. 2008, 2009, 2010. Data from the San Francisco site: NIDA grant # R01DA06487; NIAA grant # R01 AA 10819 and R01AA11971; PIs: G. Hunt; K. Joe-Laidler; References: Hunt et al. 2002, 2005; Joe and Hunt 1997; MacKenzie et al. 2005; Schalet et al. 2003; Moloney et al. 2009, 2010. Data from the San Antonio site: NIDA grant # R01 DA086 PI: A. Valdez; and Center for Disease Control and Prevention, National Center for Injury Prevention and Control grant # R49/CCRR621048. References: Cepeda and Valdez 2003; Valdez et al. 2000, 2006, 2009.

between risk behaviors and their associated negative health outcomes. A discussion of the potential of public health approach towards gang participation concludes the chapter.

6.1 Qualitative Research on Gang Youth

The use of qualitative methods in the public health studies stemmed from three general consistencies across sites: (1) the exploratory nature of the research aims (i.e. to capture the meaning and significance of risk behaviors); (2) the hidden nature of the non-incarcerated gang population (Valdez and Kaplan 1999); and (3) the research strengths and experiences of the investigators. A technique long employed in the ethnographic tradition of gang research is the utilization of detached youth workers or social workers – often associated with a community-based organization (CBO) – that work directly with youth currently involved in gangs. Detached youth workers in each site helped introduce current gang youth to members of the research teams, and were able to validate the youths' age and self-nomination as gang members.

In San Francisco, data were collected between 1990–2004 and included 1024 in-depth interviews with gang males ($n=383$) and females ($n=641$) (including a sub-sample of 350 gang members who were pregnant or mothers) from three different funded studies. The studies employed a 'snowball' sampling technique, with one interview leading to the next and so on. The interviewers were trained in qualitative techniques, but also had what were described as 'street experiences,' including previous gang involvement or had worked on the 'frontline' with gang members. In this respect, the interviewers were somewhat savvy as to gang culture, which helped facilitate interviews with members of the sample.

For San Antonio, data were collected on 160 male gang members between 1991 and 1995 and on 150 'gang affiliated' females between 1998 and 2001. Data collection included observations, focus groups, in-depth interviews with male gang members. Field workers who provided observational data and linked interviewers to subjects were indigenous to the area, and their histories within the community helped gain trust and rapport with the gang members.

For Los Angeles, data were collected between 2006 and 2007 through in-depth interviews with 60 mostly male gang youth in various locations throughout the city. A detached youth worker introduced each of the gang youth to the principal investigator. Access to gang youth in this site was a constant negotiating process, where the investigator had to gain the trust of detached youth workers from various parts of the city that worked with different gangs. In total, 14 detached youth workers from 11 different CBOs linked the investigator to the sample. Each of the gang specialists were former gang members or current ones who had stopped offending, and often worked with young people involved in the same gang they once were an active member of.

Other similarities between each of the three sites included a reflexive approach towards the projects. For instance, researchers in each project did not disconnect from the detached youth workers and their CBOs, but rather remained in area,

Table 6.1 Lifetime and 30-day illicit substance use frequencies[a]

Drug/site (lifetime/30 day)	San Antonio (%)	San Francisco: Males (%)	San Francisco: Females (%)	Los Angeles[b] (%)
Marijuana	98/75	96/77	96/62	98/56
Methamphetamine	29/7	17/3	38/12	35
Heroin	57/26	9/3	13/4	7
Powder cocaine	90/53	36/3	57/16	32
Crack cocaine	26/6	14/3	32/9	33
Speedball	44/14	NA	NA	2
Ecstasy	NA	30/0	14/2	35
LSD	NA	21/1	57/11	10
Phencyclidine	NA	12/0	48/11	25
Psilocybin	NA	NA	NA	22
Glue/Inhalants	35/4	10/0	38/9	22
Prescription drugs	74/28	10/3	5/2	33

[a]Frequencies rounded to the nearest tenth
[b]30-day substance use data not recorded except for marijuana

available to them as needed. Such practices proved invaluable for each of the research teams because they helped facilitate future access to gang youth. Moreover, these connections also helped legitimize agencies that work with gangs through cooperation with criminal justice researchers and professors at academic institutions (Sanders et al. 2010).

6.2 Involvement in Risk Behaviors

6.2.1 Illicit Substance Use

By a wide margin in all three sites, marijuana use among the samples was the most pervasive, with lifetime rates of use ranging from 96 to 98% and previous 30-day use ranging from a low of 56% in Los Angeles to a high of 77% in San Francisco (see Table 6.1). Marijuana use was highly normalized and perceived as relatively harmless, as illustrated below in excerpts from two different youth from Los Angeles[2]:

> Marijuana is really not a drug…they are giving [it] away to people now [at] the doctor. [Marijuana] don't do nothing to you.

> Like marijuana, its like whatever, its just a plant, you can dry it out.

The uses of other, 'hard' drugs among the gang youth were varied. Powder cocaine and heroin use were much higher in San Antonio, where 90 and 57% of the sample reported, respectively, lifetime rates of use. In the California sites, about a

[2] For a more detailed discussion of marijuana and gang membership see MacKenzie et al. 2005.

third of each of the samples reported powder cocaine use, but less than 10% in each reported heroin and/or the use of speedballs. Lifetime rates of crystal methamphetamine and crack use were similar between the Los Angeles and San Antonio, as well as among the females in the San Francisco sample, where a third to a quarter of each reported the use of these drugs. In the San Francisco male sample, however, about half as many reported crystal methamphetamine (17%) and/or crack use (14%). The California sites indicated that about a third of each sample reported lifetime rates of ecstasy use. Between a quarter to a third of the samples in the San Antonio and Los Angeles samples reported lifetime use of inhalants (e.g. 'spray cans'; 'markers'). Other drugs reported only in the California samples included: phencyclidine (PCP), LSD, psilocybin ('magic') mushrooms and 'poppers' (i.e. amyl/butyl nitrate).

Each of the three sites also recorded details on the non-medical uses of prescription drugs. Such rates were highest in San Antonio, where about three-fourths of the sample reported lifetime usage of drugs such as Valium, Xanax, and Rohyphnol. Approximately one-third of the Los Angeles sample reported the lifetime use of various prescription opiates, particularly Vicodin and Oxycontin. Between 5 and 10% of the San Francisco samples reported the lifetime use of Quaaludes or opiates, such as Percodan and Vicodin, referred to as 'dans'.

6.2.2 *Violence*

In Los Angeles, half of the sample said that they 'put in work' on a daily basis – a euphemism for committing criminal, often violent acts on behalf of the gang. Likewise, in San Antonio, gang youth reported a mean number of five fights in the previous 30-days – more than one fight per week per gang youth. Gang youth in both the Los Angeles and San Antonio samples (42 and 56%) have been arrested for at least one violent offence, including murder. The San Antonio sample, in particular, reported involvement in homicides, which was related to gang type. For instance, young people in the 'criminal youth gang' type, which was distinguished by having a distinct hierarchy and leadership intending to protect the best interests of individual gang members, were much more likely to be involved in homicides than the lesser organized gangs (Valdez et al. 2009).

Violence was pervasive among the San Francisco gang members as well. Of the male gang members, one-third admitted to robbing victims by force or threat of violence and more than 40% said that they had perpetrated violence against someone with a weapon, in the previous year. Almost half (49%) of the men said they carried a gun, and close to that number (41%) carried knives.

A qualitative difference was observed between juvenile and adult gang members in the San Francisco sample. For instance, a sense of self-preservation emerged among the males as they got older. Older gangsters tended not to hang out in public as much and were less likely to engage in street drug sales, preferring to make them by via cell phones and private settings. Generally, older gang members were more interested in moneymaking endeavors, primarily from drug sales, and tended to avoid violent crimes or activities that put them at risk of being arrested. The exception was when other dealers tried to 'move in' on their drug selling territory. In comparison, juvenile gang members were more likely to be violent and 'do dirt' in order to gain status and enhance their reputations.

Gang violence occurred in various contexts. For instance, youth in all sites mentioned getting 'jumped in' to their gangs as a form of initiation, which involved the beating of the initiate by several current members for a period of time. Gang fighting occurred both a one-on-one basis and within a group context, and for different reasons. In Los Angeles, for instance, individual fighting often occurred among members of the same gang over issues of being 'disrespected.' Collective forms of fighting in each site included group 'rumbles' or 'riots', as well as 'jumping' others or 'getting jumped' – surprise attacks involving multiple attackers upon fewer individuals. The motivation for these incidents stemmed from long-held inter-gang rivalries and issues of territoriality. One youth from Los Angeles discussed how he was jumped:

> Respondent: Ten other fools just jumped me.
> *Interviewer. Wow. Were they from a rival gang?*
> R. Yeah, they were rival gang members. I was on my way walking, so when they heard where I was from, I had to go from my enemies' neighborhood to get to my neighborhood. And I fucked up cuz I was walking by the riverbed, and I found the spot where they kick it at. And they fuckin' mopped [beat] me up.

Firearms were common. In San Antonio, two-thirds of the sample had firearms and 83% fired them at rivals during a gang fight. Outside of firearms, homicides were also facilitated by the use of knives, bricks, and metal/glass objects. Likewise, the Los Angeles sample reported the use of a wide range of weapons, from items found on the ground (e.g. stones; metal poles) to a wide-array of sophisticated weaponry, including military-issue hardware (e.g. M-16 rifles; grenades; rocket launchers). About half (49%) of male gang members in the San Francisco sample said they carried guns on their person daily, and many more said they had access to guns. In one incident, a young male gang member borrowed a gun from a friend on his 16th birthday, intending to give it back the next day. He was on his way to return it to the owner and was accompanied by a friend who was on probation. Due to his gang affiliation, the police had a right to search both young men, and afterwards he was arrested and charged for possession of a concealed weapon and resisting arrest.

> So they searched me. I knew I had the gun. I knew I had to run. I ran. I had shorts on. And the shit fell. Right in front of the cops. Motherfuckers seen me. I kept running. Police came down hella fast.

6.3 Female Gang Violence

Gang girls were also involved in violence, not only as victims but also as instigators and perpetrators. The San Francisco data provide a unique insight into violence among female gang members. Two thirds of respondents (66%) reported violence in their lives, particularly during their teens, including domestic or partner abuse, family violence, fighting and bullying in school, gang violence (including internal violence such as jumping in), and violence between gangs. In inter-gang violence, women primarily fought women from other gangs.

As with the San Antonio data, the organizational level and overall objectives of the gang determined the levels of violence experienced by its members. Two types of gang emerged in the San Francisco site: independent, all female gangs and 'separate but together' gangs that had male counterparts. In this case, the former type potentially experienced more types of violence. For instance, the girls from the independent gangs faced violence from selling drugs (e.g. robbery), assaults from other girls in gangs over men, domestic violence from boyfriends, and 'turf' related violence regarding the control over drug sales. As such, many girls in these gangs carried knives or guns for protection. Girls in 'separate but together' gangs faced other forms of violence, including initiation; inter-gang conflict involving males (i.e. gang females assisting gang males in the process of being jumped, conflict with girls from other gangs, conflict with homegirls/homeboys in the same gang, and conflicts with boyfriends). For instance, 20% were 'jumped in' – beaten as part of the gang initiation process, but this process was limited to the Latino gangs in San Francisco. Most women (63%) in other ethnic gangs did not mention anything like us, but rather that reported growing up in the neighborhood or in a specific housing project provided their entree into their gang. About half (47%) ranked their group as extremely violent, and about a third reported both involvement in gang fights (35%) and in neighborhood fights (37%). Reasons for all female gang violence were primarily attributed to disrespect, including territorial issues, insults, and "colors" – a particular style identifying members with their gang.

6.3.1 Risky Sexual Behaviors

Early sexual initiation was common among youth in the samples. For instance, in Los Angeles, 93% of the sample was sexual active, and the mean age of sexual initiation was 13.5 years. Likewise, most of the female gang members in San Antonio and San Francisco reported their first sexual experience by the early teenage years.

Other risky sexual behaviors were also common. For instance, in Los Angeles, about one-third of the sample had not used condoms or any other form of sexual protection at sexual initiation, with one mentioning using a plastic shopping bag as a makeshift condom while having sex with a prostitute in an alley. Gang youth in Los Angeles also mentioned many sexual partners, with a range or 1–100 during their lifetimes and between 0 and 9 within the previous 30-days. About a quarter of that sample also reported group sex, which involved one or two females and several males. One male gang youth from Los Angeles briefly referred to group sex as 'the train' or 'training':

> Training them, like gang banging, like one after the other: three guys in one room with a girl naked right there. One goes, and when he is done, the next one just jumps right in.

During the course of conducting the fieldwork for the study in San Antonio, the research team reported repeated incidents of sexual victimization incidents associated with young girls associated with gang members. Reports from the young girls of sexual victimization at the hands of boyfriends were common. Gloria Ana, 17 years old and the girlfriend of one of the leaders of the criminally oriented, Varrio La Paloma gang, described one incident:

> We were all kicking back at a party. At first she was acting like if she didn't want to have sex with any of the guys. But then the bitch got all fucked up. I guess they put something in her drink. They got her all fucked up and they just threw a train on her.

In San Francisco, condom use was sporadic. Among a study of 350 gang women who were pregnant or mothers, only 58 (17%) said that they *had* used condoms, but admitted this was inconsistent.

> *Interviewer: Did you ever use anything besides condoms? You [said you] used condoms, right?*
> Respondent: Yeah, I have, but not all the time. I mean, I've only two sexual partners.

6.3.2 Interrelationship Between Risk Behaviors

In all sites, illicit substance use, especially crystal methamphetamine and cocaine – often in combination with alcohol – were related in increased participation in violence and risky sexual behaviors. For instance, about 50% of all violent or aggressive behaviors in the San Francisco male sample involved alcohol. At times, such violence was also perpetrated against homegirls who used 'hard' drugs by homeboys who believed such behaviors were inappropriate. Regarding the co-occurrence of substance use and risky sex, about three-fourths of the Los Angeles sample who reported such sessions mentioned having used alcohol, cocaine, marijuana and/or crystal methamphetamine use prior and during.

Substance use was linked to risky sexual behaviors in the San Antonio sample, with their extent of sexual risk taking related to their position within the gang, both in terms of how they perceived themselves and how the homeboys perceived them. For gang females in the San Antonio sample, substance use, risky sex and homeboy perception were all interrelated. The 'hoodrats' who engaged in frequent promiscuous sex, for instance, were viewed as being less loyal to their gang, and therefore less respected. Concomitantly, the 'hoodrats' in San Antonio were those who were the most likely in the sample to report usage of a wide variety of drugs, which, in some cases, preceded engagement in risky sexual behaviors.

The simultaneous or sequential use of various substances, often referred to as polydrug use, was also common among the three sites. For instance, in Los Angeles, approximately 75% of the sample reported the sequential or simultaneous use of two or more substances. Popular drug combinations for the San Antonio site included 'speedballs' (e.g. the simultaneous use of heroin and cocaine). At times, several drugs were combined together. For instance, one youth at the Los Angeles site talked about what he referred to as a 'ghost buster' joint:

> Respondent. You know what you should put on there?
> *Interviewer: What?*
> *R:* Ghost buster.
> *I: What is that?*
> R. It's a [marijuana] joint, with glass [meth], heroin, coke, some cavi [crack], roll it up and dipped in sherm, dipped in PCP.

In Los Angeles, 'p-dogs' – marijuana joints containing crack – were common. In this case, 'p' stands for 'piedra', which is a Spanish word for 'rock' – a colloquialism for crack cocaine. However, gang youth in Los Angeles did not always associate smoking a p-dog with using crack, as the below interview except illustrates:

> *Interviewer: Have you ever used crack?*
> Respondent: No.
> *I: Have you ever smoked a p-dog?*
> R: No, I smoked sherm sticks.
> *I: Okay. That is something. That is PCP.*
> R: Okay. P-dogs. Yeah, I smoked a p-dog.
> *I: Did you smoke a p-dog?*
> R: Yeah. I did not mean to, but you know?

The use of alcohol and drugs was a constant factor in the sexual victimization and violence perpetuation (and victimization) situations in San Antonio among gang members. For instance, almost all reports of the young females' sexual victimization include accounts of drinking alcohol. One respondent described how she saw a 17-year-old girl from the neighborhood get 'gang raped' after a party:

> Everyone had been drinking and smoking [weed]. She always wanted to be around the guys. After almost everyone had left, three members of the TMA [gang] took her into the back room and 'pulled a train' on her. She was all fucked up.

6.3.3 Negative Health Outcomes

6.3.3.1 Illicit Substance Use

The gang youth reported various negative outcomes in relation to their substance use. For instance, four youths in the Los Angeles sample were in a substance use treatment program. Entry into such programs, however, was not voluntary, but mandated by state legislation requiring such treatment for drug-related offenders. More directly, approximately one third of this sample self-reported that their substance use had 'caused them problems', particularly PCP, crystal methamphetamine, and powder cocaine. The California samples also reported 'bad trips' and other unpleasant feelings associated with using various drugs. The San Antonio sample was the only one to report injection drug use, and, as such, these youth were potentially exposed to HIV or HCV via the sharing of needles or works, as well as other health risks related specifically to drug injection (e.g. abscesses).

6.3.3.2 Violent Victimization

Gang youth were victims of violence. For instance, in the Los Angeles sample, 90% reported being jumped, some more times than they could recall. Youth also reported scars from such incidents, such as various cut and stab wounds on their heads, faces, hands, and arms, as well as broken bones, missing teeth, concussions and periods of unconsciousness, at times requiring hospitalization. One youth talked about his girlfriend being shot by rival gang members:

> *Interviewer: What happened with your girlfriend?*
> Respondent: She got shot in the leg with a .22. They went looking for me but they could not find me. I got into a show with them down the street after they shot up her house. But she's doing alright right cuz she can walk still though.

Similar violent outcomes were reported by the San Antonio and San Francisco sample. Weapon use and victimization by weapons was also extensively reported between both Los Angeles and San Antonio. For instance, in Los Angeles, about eight in ten of the youth reported being shot at and 14% have been shot. Three-fourths of the sample felt 'likely' or 'very likely' that they will one day be killed violently. Violent death was also a reality for many of the fellow gang members or their acquaintances. For instances, youth interviewed in Los Angeles and San Antonio reported being in close proximity to incidents deadly violence, including witnessing: bullets rips through fellow homeboys who were standing next to them; a person smash someone the face with an axe; an individual get hit in the back of the head with a rock. For the Los Angeles sample, fear of violent death was the most commonly reported least favorite aspect about life in the gang. Many within that sample simply felt that their lives would be short.

Domestic violence was also reported among the San Antonio sample, with young females associated with gang members were more likely to report incidents of such abuse, as well as depression and childhood trauma symptomology, when compared to those with no such identification. Among the female gang members in San Francisco, domestic violence was pervasive. For instance, 60% were victims of domestic and/or household violence at least once a month. Over 40% reported that the police had been summoned to their homes, most commonly for family violence, domestic violence, or domestic disputes and 20% reported that they had been victims of domestic sexual abuse.

6.3.3.3 Risky Sexual Behavior

Pregnancy and childbirth reportage prior to adulthood was common among the gang youth. For instance, in San Francisco, 40% of the female gang members had children or were pregnant, and in Los Angeles, one third of the sample had either gotten someone pregnant or had become pregnant. In both sites, the mean age of each sample was 18 years or younger. In San Antonio, one in four of female gang members had given birth. Overall, many of the youth in all sites were still juveniles when they had children of their own. However, its linkage to positive development buffers the extent that teenage pregnancy among such youth is negative. For instance, in San Francisco, pregnancy among female gang members served as a respectful and safe way to exit gang life, and also contributed to such female's decreased involvement in crime, 'hard' substance use, and other risk behaviors. A similar sentiment was echoed by a gang interventionist in Los Angeles, who mentioned she does not discourage young women in gangs from becoming pregnant, as pregnancies among such women also served to provide a safe passage out of gang membership.

Regarding STIs, 17% of the Los Angeles sample reported previous or current infections, including one youth whose STI went untreated for 2 years. Another youth declared how 'thankful' he was that his Chlamydia infection was not HIV:

> Thank God it was Chlamydia, though, you know? That it was nothing else, and from there I had to get tested. And trust me, my boy, I have been way fuckin' careful because I have been in front of naked fuckin' booty, and I think about it twice, you know what I mean? It's crazy, 'specially now that I have my girl, you know? So I got tested and everything. I got HIV tested.

While none in any of the samples reported being HIV positive, one in ten in the Los Angeles sample reported having a friend or family member with HIV or AIDS. About half of the Los Angeles sample has been previously tested for HIV, usually during periods of incarceration.

San Antonio male gang members reported engaging in high risk sexual behaviors associated with negative health consequences. For instance, the average age of the first sexual experience was 13 years old, and 56% reported having had a sexual encounter where the female partner became pregnant. Also, approximately 82% reported having a steady girlfriend during the last 30 days of which 40% admitted to having a sexual encounter with someone else during this period. For instance, one youth described his feelings about being unfaithful to his previous partners:

> I've cheated on all of them. I really don't care about being faithful. If I see someone I want, I go for it. They find out sometimes, but they always get over it.

This is particularly important given that 47% reported having not used any form of contraceptive during their last sexual encounter Also, while the majority of the sample reported accurate HIV infection transmission knowledge, respondent's thought that not using condoms and having multiple sex partners did not put them at risk for becoming infected with HIV/AIDS.

6.4 Public Health Research on Gang Youth: Practical and Theoretical Implications

The data for this paper comes from three different research teams all of whom have emphasized the health consequences of gang members' high-risk behaviors. While recently there have been inroads in the field of gang research to include a more pronounced public-health focus, this has still largely been confined to a few studies. The overall goal of our research reported here is to more effectively bring together gang research in the field of criminal justice and criminology with that of public health.

Research often indicates that gang members are more involved in crime and delinquency than non-gang youth and the overwhelming majority of money and resources towards reducing ganging goes towards suppression efforts – police saturation techniques of gang communities and increased community penalties (e.g. arrest, incarceration, fines) associated with gang membership (Advancement Project 2007; Greene and Pranis 2007; Hall et al. 2006; Klein and Maxson 2006). As a result, the incarceration of youth has dramatically increased over the last two decades (Krisberg 2005). However, suppression-heavy approaches have done little to combat the origins of gangs, and national gang surveys have indicated significant increases in the overall number of gang members over the last 10 years (Egley et al. 2010; Egley and O'Donnell 2008). Moreover, the intent of gang suppression techniques is not to address the basic needs of gang-involved youth. Perhaps more of a public health-driven approach towards the study and solution of gang youth may offer more fruitful remedies.

A hallmark of the public health approach that has influenced the study of youth gangs is a preference for scientific evidence in the design, implementation, and evaluation of interventions. As well, attention to the relationships between individuals and community environments, the interplay of foreground and background factors, and the ecological model are also distinctive features of current approaches informed by the public health model (Valdez and Kaplan 2007; World Health Assembly 1996). The ecological model places importance on the social environment, the modification of group behavior, and individual change (Klein and Maxson 2006).

One of the most formidable challenges in designing interventions for youth gangs is the development of an appropriate definition of such groups. Youth is a stage in the life course of human development characterized by profound physical and psychosocial changes occurring from early adolescence to young adulthood (Elder 1998; Rindfuss et al. 1987). An awareness of this is needed when designing interventions for youth gangs, as are sufficiently nuanced definitions of the target groups. The Eurogang definition of youth street gangs is being durable over time, street-oriented, composed of youths, engaged in and oriented towards illegal or criminal behavior, and with an identity based on street codes and illegal acts (Klein and Maxson 2006). However, using a youth group continuum, delinquent youth may range from normal youth who engage in sporadic deviant behavior, troublesome youth, delinquent youth and street and drug gangs that are more organized (Klein and Maxson 2006).

Various community organizations need to work more closely to provide adequate prevention and intervention services for all youth along a continuum of gangs (Advancement Project 2007). Substance use, risky sexual behaviors, and, increasingly, violence, have become the domains of public health. Public health-driven interventions and efforts aimed at gang youth could complement current criminal justice ones with an overall idea of better alleviating the gang situation. For instance, substance use is pervasive among each sample, and substance use has been significantly linked to involvement in serious and violent crimes. By targeting substance use among gang members – a public health initiative – such an intervention could have a knock-on positive effect on reducing their participation in crime and delinquency. While the idea of integrating criminal justice and public health driven services is not new, how exactly this works is often unclear (Advancement Project 2007). Continued efforts at collaboration are likely to produce positive results.

'Prevention is the best cure' is a phrase touted within the public health community. Likewise, as it applies to gang involvement, preventing youth from joining in a powerful tool towards reducing gang involvement in communities. A nationally-based gang prevention educational package – Gang Resistance Through Education and Training – utilizes uniformed police officers to deliver multi-session educational curriculum, which, curiously, only mentions gangs in passing (Esbensen et al. 2001; Klein and Maxson 2006). The program, despite its multimillion-dollar price tag, has shown relatively limited positive results (Klein and Maxson 2006). If gangs pose such an incredible public safety threat, then surely better efforts can be designed. Moreover, by allowing trained, public health officials to deliver messages of prevention, safety and risk, police officers – who are not necessarily trained to be effective teachers – can resume their jobs as law enforcement. The investment in gang prevention has the potential to pay off the biggest dividends, and such prevention messages might be better designed and delivered by public health professionals with expertise in prevention techniques regarding substance use, violence and risky sexual behaviors.

References

Advancement Project. (2007). *A call to action: A case for a comprehensive solution to LA's gang violence epidemic*. Retrieved from www.advanceproj.com/doc/p3_report.pdf

Bendixen, M., Endresen, I. M., & Olweus, D. (2006). Joining and leaving gangs: Selection and facilitation effects on self-reported antisocial behaviour in early adolescence. *European Journal of Criminology, 3*, 85–114.

Brooks, R. A., Lee, S.-J., Stover, G. N., & Barkley, T. W., Jr. (2009). Condom attitudes, perceived vulnerability, and sexual risk behaviors of young Latino male urban street gang members: Implications for HIV prevention. *AIDS Education and Prevention, Supplement B, 21*(5), 80–87.

Cepeda, A., & Valdez, A. (2003). Risk behaviors among young Mexican American gang-associated females: Sexual relations, partying, substance use, and crime. *Journal of Adolescent Research, 18*, 90–107.

Durant, R. H., Altman, D., Wolfson, M., Barkin, S., Kreiter, S., & Krowchuk, D. (2000). Exposure to violence and victimization, depression, substance use, and the use of violence by young adolescents. *Journal of Pediatrics, 137*, 707–713.

Egley, A., Jr., & O'Donnell, C. E. (2008). *Highlights of the 2006 national youth gang survey*. Washington, DC: Office of Juvenile Justice and Delinquency Prevention.

Egley, A., Jr., Howell, J. C., & Moore, J. P. (2010). *Highlights of the 2008 national youth gang survey*. Washington, DC: Office of Juvenile Justice and Delinquency Prevention.

Elder, G. H. (1998). The life course and human development. In R. M. Lerner (Ed.), *Handbook of child psychology* (pp. 939–991). New York: Wiley.

Esbensen, F.-A., Osgood, D. W., Taylor, T. J., Peterson, D., & Freng, A. (2001). How great is G.R.E.A.T.? Results from a longitudinal quasi-experimental design. *Criminology & Public Policy, 1*, 87–118.

Gatti, U., Tremblay, R. E., Vitaro, F., & McDuff, P. (2005). Youth gangs, delinquency and drug use: A test of the selection, facilitation, and enhancement hypotheses. *Journal of Child Psychology and Psychiatry, 46*, 1178–1190.

Gordon, R. A., Lahey, B. B., Kawai, E., Loeber, R., Stouthamer-Loeber, M., & Farrington, D. P. (2004). Antisocial behaviors and youth gang membership: Selection and socialization. *Criminology, 42*, 55–87.

Greene, J., & Pranis, K. (2007). *Gang wars: The failure of enforcement tactics and the need for effective public safety strategies.* Justice Policy Institute Report, Justice Policy Institute.

Hall, G. P., Thornberry, T. P., & Lizotte, A. J. (2006). The gang facilitation effect and neighborhood risk: Do gangs have a stronger influence on delinquency in disadvantaged areas? In J. F. Short Jr. & L. A. Hughes (Eds.), *Studying youth gangs* (pp. 47–62). Lanham: Altamira Press.

Hamrin, V., Jonker, B., & Scahill, L. (2004). Acute stress disorder symptoms in gunshot-injured youth. *Journal of Child and Adolescent Psychiatric Nursing, 17*, 161–172.

Harper, G. W., Davidson, J., & Hosek, S. G. (2008). Influence of gang membership on negative affects, substance use, and antisocial behavior among homeless African American male youth. *American Journal of Men's Health, 2*, 229–243.

Howell, J. C. (1998). *Youth gangs: An overview.* Washington, DC: US Department of Justice, Office of Justice Programs, Office of Juvenile Justice and Delinquency Prevention.

Huebner, B. M., Varano, S. P., & Bynum, T. S. (2007). Gangs, guns and drugs: Recidivism among serious, young offenders. *Criminology & Public Policy, 6*, 187–222.

Hunt, G. P., Jo-Laidler, K., & Evans, K. (2002). The meaning and gendered culture of getting high: Gang girls and drug use issues. *Contemporary Drug Problems, 29*, 375–415.

Hunt, G., MacKenzie, K., & Joe-Laidler, K. (2005). Alcohol and masculinity: The case of ethnic youth gangs. In T. M. Wilson (Ed.), *Drinking cultures: Alcohol and identity* (pp. 225–254). Oxford: Berg.

Joe, K. A., & Hunt, G. (1997). Violence and social organization in female gangs. *Social Justice, 24*, 148–169.

Juarez, P. D. (1992). The public health model and violence prevention. In R. C. Cervantes (Ed.), *Substance abuse and gang violence* (pp. 43–59). London: Sage.

Klein, M. W., & Maxson, C. L. (2006). *Street gang patterns and policies.* New York: Oxford University Press.

Krisberg, B. (2005). *Juvenile justice: Redeeming our children.* Thousand Oaks: Sage.

Li, X., Stanton, B., Pack, R., Harris, C., Cottrell, L., & Burns, J. (2002). Risk and protective factors associated with gang involvement among urban African American adolescents. *Youth & Society, 34*, 172–194.

MacDonald, J., Ridgeway, G., Gover A. R., & Jennings, W. G. (2007). *Assessing the effects of gang membership on victimization using doubly robust propensity score modeling.* Retrieved from http://www.crim.upenn.edu/faculty/papers/macdonald/Gang%20Membership%20and%20Victimization.pdf

MacKenzie, K., Hunt, G., & Joe-Laidler, K. (2005). Youth gangs and drugs: The case of marijuana. *Journal of Ethnicity in Substance Abuse, 4*, 99–134.

Moloney, M., MacKenzie, K., Hunt, G., & Joe-Laidler, K. (2009). The path and promise of fatherhood for gang members. *British Journal of Criminology, 49*(305), 325.

Moloney, M., Hunt, G., & Joe-Laidler, K. (2010). Young mother (in the) hood: Gang girls' negotiation of new identities. *Journal of Youth Studies, 11*, 1–19.

Peterson, D., Taylor, T. J., & Esbensen, F. A. (2004). Gang membership and violent victimization. *Justice Quarterly, 21*, 793–815.

Rindfuss, R. R., Swicegood, C. G., & Rosenfeld, R. A. (1987). Disorder in the life course: How common and does it matter? *American Sociological Review, 52*, 785–801.

Salazar, L. F., Crosby, R. A., DiClemente, R. J., Wingood, G. M., Rose, E., Sales, J. M., & Caliendo, A. M. (2007). Personal, relational, and peer-level risk factors for laboratory confirmed STD prevalence among low-income African American adolescent families. *Sexually Transmitted Diseases, 334*, 761–766.

Sanders, B., & Lankenau, S. E. (2006). A public health model for studying youth gangs. In J. Short Jr. & L. A. Hughes (Eds.), *Studying youth gangs* (pp. 117–128). Lanham: Altamira Press.

Sanders, B., Lankenau, S. E., & Jackson Bloom, J. (2008). *A study of risk behaviors among gang youth in Los Angeles*. Retrieved from http://www.calstatela.edu/academic/hhs/crim_jus/PDF/A_Study_of_Risk_Behaviors_among_Gang_Youth_in_Los_Angeles.pdf

Sanders, B., Lankenau, S. E., & Jackson Bloom, J. (2009). Risky sexual behaviors among gang youth in Los Angeles. *Journal of Equity in Health, 2*, 61–71.

Sanders, B., Lankenau, S. E., & Jackson Bloom, J. (2010). Putting in work: Qualitative research on gang youth in Los Angeles. *Substance Use and Misuse, 45*, 736–753.

Schalet, A., Hunt, G., & Jo-Laidler, K. (2003). Respectability and autonomy: The articulation and meaning of sexuality among the girls in the gang. *Journal of Contemporary Ethnography, 32*, 108–143.

Sharp, C., Aldridge, J., & Medina, J. (2006). *Delinquent youth groups and offending behaviour: Findings from the 2004 Offending, Crime and Justice survey* (Home Office Online Report 12/6). London: Home Office.

Uman, G. C., Urman, H. N., Malloy, C. L., Martinez, B., & DeMorst, L. (2006). *Pilot study on HIV among gang members*. Los Angeles: City of Los Angeles AIDS Coordinator's Office.

Valdez, A., & Kaplan, C. D. (1999). Reducing selection bias in the use of focus groups to investigate hidden populations: The case of Mexican American gang members from South Texas. *Drugs and Society, 14*, 209–224.

Valdez, A., & Kaplan, C. (2007). Conditions that increase drug market involvement: The invitational edge and the case of Mexicans in South Texas. *Journal of Drug Issues, 37*, 893–917.

Valdez, A., Kaplan, C. D., & Codina, E. (2000). Psychopathy among Mexican American gang members: A comparative study. *International Journal of Offender Therapy and Comparative Criminology, 44*, 46–58.

Valdez, A., Kaplan, C. D., & Cepeda, A. (2006). The drugs-violence nexus among Mexican-American gang members. *Journal of Psychoactive Drugs, 38*, 109–121.

Valdez, A., Cepeda, A., & Kaplan, C. (2009). Homicidal events among Mexican American street gangs: A situational analysis. *Homicide Studies, 13*, 288–306.

Voisin, D. R., Salazar, L. F., Crosby, R., DiClemente, R. J., Yarber, W. L., & Staples-Horne, M. (2004). The association between gang involvement and sexual behaviours among detained adolescent males. *Sexually Transmitted Infections, 80*, 440–442.

Wingood, G. M., DiClemente, R. J., Crosby, R., Harrington, K., Davies, S. L., & Hook, E. W., III. (2002). Gang involvement and the health of African American female adolescents. *Pediatrics, 110*, 57–61.

World Health Assembly. (1996). *WHA49.25. Prevention of violence: A public health priority. Handbook resource, Vol. III* (3rd ed.). Geneva: World Health Organization.

Chapter 7
Towards an Explanation of the Recent Increase in Drug-Related Mortality

Richard Miech, Stephen Koester, and Brooke Dorsey Holliman

Abstract *The mortality rate due to illegal drug use has increased substantially in recent years, and the forces underlying this trend are unknown. In this paper, we conduct a mixed-method study to start an investigation into the underlying causes. In the quantitative analysis, we examine the trend in detail for people aged 25–64 years old using U.S. Vital Statistics and mortality information from Denver, Colorado. In the qualitative analysis, we generate hypotheses for the trend with interviews of first responders in Denver, including paramedics, police, emergency room physicians, and staff at the Medical Examiner's Office. The quantitative analysis: (a) confirms that the national drug-related mortality is increasing; (b) demonstrates that the trend is present across a wide range of drugs and is not specific to either cocaine, opioids, or stimulants; and (c) is concentrated among decedents with low education. This national pattern is mirrored in Denver. The qualitative interviews of first responders highlight four promising hypotheses to explain the quantitative pattern of results: (a) the increase in the number of released inmates in the general population; (b) the aging of the baby boom cohort; (c) the increase in polydrug use; and (d) an increase in the availability of prescription drugs. Future research is warranted to assess the relative plausibility of these four explanations, and develop information to inform policy and interventions to counteract the rise of drug-related mortality.*

R. Miech, Ph.D., M.P.H. (✉) • B.D. Holliman
Department of Health and Behavioral Sciences, University of Colorado Denver, Denver, CO, USA
e-mail: richard.miech@ucdenver.edu; brooke.dorsey@ucdenver.edu

S. Koester, Ph.D.
Department of Health and Behavioral Sciences, University of Colorado Denver, Denver, CO, USA

Department of Anthropology, University of Colorado Denver, Denver, CO, USA
e-mail: steve.koester@ucdenver.edu

B. Sanders et al. (eds.), *Crime, HIV and Health: Intersections of Criminal Justice and Public Health Concerns*, DOI 10.1007/978-90-481-8921-2_7,

Rates of death due to illegal drug use have increased substantially. Deaths that fall in the category of "unintentional poisoning" rose 62.5% from 1999 to 2004 (Paulozzi and Annest 2007), a trend that is a continuation of earlier increases during the 1980 and 1990s (Paulozzi et al. 2006a, b). Almost all deaths in this category are attributed to drug abuse. To our knowledge, Paulozzi and colleagues are among the few researchers to document this national trend, and no formal attempts to specify the underlying causes that drive it are known.

The purpose of this study is twofold. First, original analyses of the U.S. Vital Statistics are presented to disaggregate the overall trend in drug-related mortality by the specific drug classes of cocaine-related death, opioid-related death, and stimulant-related death. We examine if the trend is similar for all these types of drugs or driven by particular ones. The distribution of these trends by educational attainment is also investigated to see if these trends have magnified or created new disparities by socioeconomic status.

The second goal of this study is to begin to specify the underlying causes behind the trend by interviewing groups of first responders in Denver, Colorado – a city where drug-related mortality mirrors national patterns. The groups include police, paramedics, emergency room physicians, coroners, and the investigative staff of the Medical Examiner's Office, which were selected because they have direct experience with drug overdoses, and may have insights that are not found in the existing literature.

In this study we do not expect to arrive at the definitive reason for the increase rate of illegal drug use mortality. Instead, the aim of the chapter is to develop potential explanations for the trend and to then critically evaluate them. The end goal is to rank these explanations in terms of their plausibility as a guide for future research.

7.1 Methods

7.1.1 Quantitative Analyses of Secondary Data

Secondary data cover the period from the late 1980s to 2005 and draw on three data sources for respondents aged 25–64 years old: mortality information from the U.S. Vital Statistics; mortality information from Denver; and the U.S. Census.

The quantitative analyses focus on the drug-related mortality rate, utilizing the U.S. Vital Statistics to provide the number of deaths per year in the U.S. (the numerator) and also the U.S. Census to provide the population size (the denominator). All deaths that included any mention of cocaine, opioids, or stimulants as the underlying or contributing cause of death were coded as drug-related.[1] Physicians, coroners, and/or medical examiners provided information on the causes of death.

[1] Specifically, cocaine-related deaths included on the death certificate the ICD-9 (World Health Organization 1977) codes 305.5, 304.2, or 855.2 in the period from 1989 to 1998, and the ICD-10 (World Health Organization 1992) codes F14 or T40.5 in the year 1999 or later. Opioid-related deaths included on the death certificate the ICD-9 codes 304.7, 304.0, or 850.0 in the period from 1989 to 1998, and the ICD-10 codes F11 or T40.1 in the year 1999 or later. Finally, stimulant-related deaths included on the death certificate the ICD-9 codes 305.7, 304.4, or 854.20 in the period from 1989 to 1998, and ICD-10 codes F15 or T43.6 in the year 1999 or later.

A substantial revision took place in the classification system used by the U.S. Vital Statistics to record deaths in the year 1999, which is the midpoint of the study period for the analyses. From 1989 to 1998, all deaths were coded to the ICD version 9, and in 1999 and subsequently all deaths were coded to the ICD version 10. Consequently, any abrupt change in the mortality rate in the year 1999 may represent either a substantive change or a methodological artifact.

While the U.S. Census provides yearly information on the U.S. residential population, these estimates exclude people living in "group quarters," such as certain military lodgings or incarceration settings. Estimates for the total U.S. population that include those living in group quarters are only provided decennially. In these analyses, we assumed linear changes in the group quarters population between 1990 and 2000 and used a linear interpolation from 1989 to 2005 to add estimates of the group quarters population to the published residential population size.

The analyses also examined Denver's vital statistics in order to investigate if mortality trends in the city were similar to those observed nationally. Information on Denver deaths comes from death certificates as reported by the Colorado Department of Public Health and the Environment, and the estimated, total population size of Denver is based on data from the U.S. Census. These analyses use data from year 2000 and do not disaggregate trends by educational attainment because such data were not currently available.

This study uses data since 1989, the first year in which U.S. death certificates required information on the educational attainment of decedents. Funeral directors and/or informants report the educational information on death certificates. In the U.S. Vital Statistics, education is coded as "less than high school," "high school education," "some college," which indicates college attendance but no baccalaureate degree, and "college +". Because of smaller sample sizes in the Denver data, educational attainment is collapsed into the two categories of "high school or less" and "at least some college."

7.1.2 Qualitative Data Collection and Analysis

Semi-structured interviews were conducted in Denver with a purposive sample of three groups of first responders and the Medical Examiner's Office as a way to begin to identify and examine the forces behind trends in drug-related mortality. These participants were recruited because we wanted the insights of professionals with first-hand experience with drug-related mortality. The three groups of first responders included police officers, paramedics and emergency department physicians. A group interview was conducted with four police officers working on the narcotics squad of one of the city's two districts with the highest concentration of drug-related arrests. Two paramedics with approximately 10 years of experience in Denver were also interviewed. Both were employees of Denver Health, the city's publicly funded hospital, and both had been involved in a number of drug-related emergency calls. Three physicians currently working in the emergency department of Denver Health were also interviewed. Qualitative interviews were also conducted with staff of the Denver Medical Examiner's Office. Pathologists as well as two staff of the Chief

Investigator's Office were interviewed. The pathologists were medical doctors whose job duties included conducting autopsies. The staff were two ex-police officers who were members of the Investigator's Office and helped the Medical Examiner's Office arrive at a cause of death by investigating death scenes and interviewing friends and family of decedents.

All 13 participants were asked three questions about drug overdose. The first question was about their awareness of increases in drug-related mortality (i.e., Did the first responders note any overall trends in drug-related mortality?). The second question was about their perceptions regarding the causes for increases in drug-related mortality (i.e., What did they think was causing these increases in drug overdose?). The third question was about their perceptions of the overdose victim, including their background profiles (i.e., What characterized the typical overdose victim?). Responses to these questions invariably led to additional questions aimed at getting greater detail and explanation.

Interview data were recorded as notes and then summarized into field notes. Field notes were analyzed and coded by the research team. The most obvious codes were those that came directly from our questions and overdose hypotheses. Additional codes came from our participants, and finally, from our interpretation of the data. Codes were categorized into the themes and a matrix was used to compare themes across the four participant groups.

7.2 Analysis of U.S. and Denver Vital Statistics

7.2.1 U.S. Vital Statistics

Figure 7.1 indicates substantial increases in mortality for which illegal drug use was a contributing factor, as well as an increase in disparities across education. The first graph in Fig. 7.1 focuses on deaths in which cocaine is listed as a contributing cause of death, and for all education groups the rate increased from 1989 to 2005. Overall, for all education groups combined, the death rate for which cocaine played a role increased from 1.10 to 5.56 per 100,000. The second graph focuses on death in which opioids are listed as a contributing cause of death, and the rate increased for all educational groups from 1989 to 1998, and then the rate of increase remained positive but slowed somewhat afterwards. Overall, for all educational groups combined, the death rate for which opioids played a role increased from 0.86 to 1.94 per 100,000. Finally, the third graph focuses on stimulant-related death, which includes methamphetamine use, and for all educational groups the death rate increased, with a marked acceleration after the year 1998. Overall, for all educational groups combined, the death rate for which stimulants played a role increased from 0.09 to 1.39 per 100,000.

In addition to an overall increase in mortality due to illegal drug use, the graphs in Fig. 7.1 also show a growing disparity across education. For all three graphs, the increase in the disparities are indicated by a widening gap over historical time between the mortality rate of the lowest and highest educated groups, a gap that

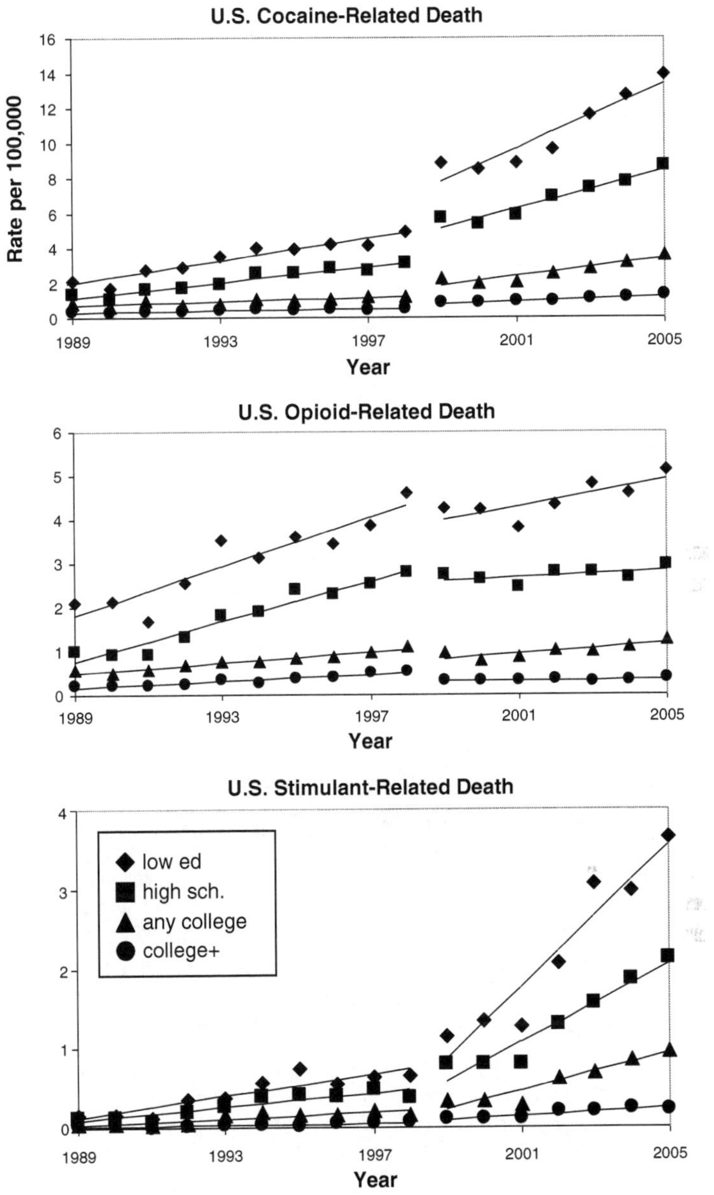

Fig. 7.1 Annual, national drug-related death rate by year and education ages 25–64 years old. Results were age-standardized to 2000 population. Note: Deaths are coded to the International Statistical Classification of Disease. From 1989 to 1998 deaths are coded to version 9 (ICD-9, World Health Organization 1977) and from 1998 to 2005 they are coded to version 10 (ICD 10, World Health Organization 1992). Deaths are classified as cocaine-related if a death certificate lists codes 305.6, 304.2, or 855.2 from 1989–1998, and if it lists codes F14 or T40.5 from 1999–2005. Codes for opioid-related deaths from 1989–1998 are 304.7, 304.0, and 850.0, and from 1999–2005 are F11 and T40.1. Codes for stimulant-related death from 1989–1998 are 405.7, 304.4, and 854.2, and from 1999–2005 are F15 and T43.6

increased dramatically. For example, for cocaine the difference in the mortality rate across educational groups in 1989 was 1.77 (2.13 in the lowest group versus .36 in the highest group), and in 2005 it was more than 700% greater at 12.61 (13.87 in the lowest group versus 1.26 in the highest group). For all drugs, both relative and absolute disparities increased over the time period from 1989 to 2005.

7.2.2 *Vital Statistics of Denver*

Figure 7.2 shows that the trends in drug-related death in Denver are consistent with the national picture. From the period 2000 to 2006, cocaine-related deaths more than doubled from 5.76 to 12.34 per 100,000. During this same period, opioid-related deaths increased from 1.44 to 4.52 per 100,000 and stimulant-related deaths increased from 0.72 to 1.74 per 100,000. For all drug-related death rates, the levels in Denver are similar to the national rates, and in both Denver and the U.S. the level of cocaine-related deaths are higher than opioid-related deaths, which are higher than stimulant-related deaths.

7.3 Qualitative Interviews: Searching for Reasons Behind the Trends

7.3.1 *First Responders' and the Medical Examiner's Staff's Awareness of Drug-Related Mortality*

Our expectation at the start of the project was that the four police officers interviewed would have considerable experience with drug-related emergencies and mortality, and would be aware that deaths from drug use were increasing. They worked in neighborhoods and commercial areas that have been known for drug copping (procurement) and using for decades. This police district includes a number of public and private drug treatment programs including methadone clinics, HIV prevention programs, a longstanding university-led intervention project, local community based organizations providing bleach kits and referrals, and two pharmacies that, in the absence of any needle exchange programs, have openly provided syringes to injection drug users at low cost.

In contrast to our expectations, the police officers interviewed had little knowledge of a substantial and on-going increase in drug-related deaths. Their experiences with drug-related deaths, a term they interpreted as heroin overdose, were limited to "a handful" of episodes a month, and one officer indicated that he had never been called to an opiate overdose. They did not define cocaine or methamphetamine related deaths as overdoses. As one police officer commented, "I've never heard of anybody dying from taking too much crack."

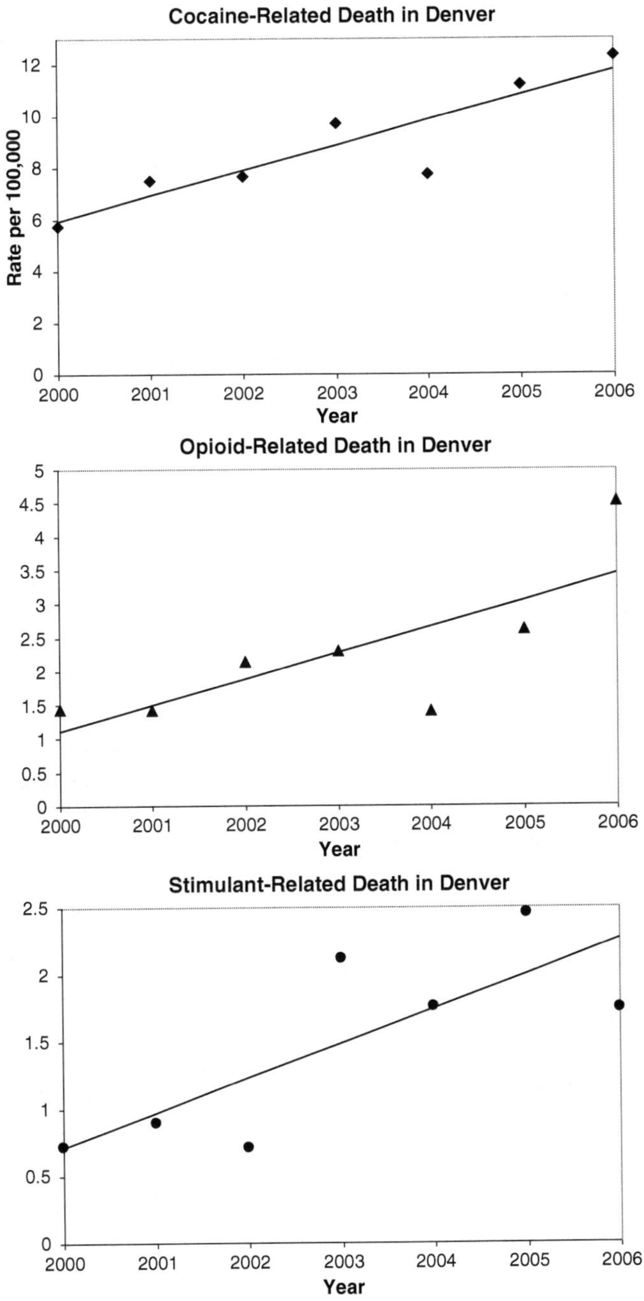

Fig. 7.2 Annual drug-related death rate in Denver by year (Source: Health Statistics Section, Colorado Department of Public Health and Environment. Note: Deaths are coded to the tenth version of the International Statistical Classification of Disease (World Health Organization 1992); Deaths are classified as cocaine-related if death certificate contains code T40.5, opioid-related if death certificate contains codes T40.1 or T40.2, and stimulant-related if death certificates contains code T43.6

The two paramedics interviewed were also unaware of an overall increase in drug-related deaths, but they did note increases in methadone overdose and overdoses among new drug users. They attributed the increase in methadone related overdoses to its diversion to the street, and they surmised the latter trend by the absence of older scar tissue and presence of "fresh tracks" or puncture wounds on the arms of users. Like the police, they distinguished an opiate overdose from a stimulant induced health crises. They pointed out the differences between "falling out" and the behavioral effects from taking too much cocaine or methamphetamine. They perceived a stimulant "overdose" as being determined by behavior, and explained that, in cases of extreme stimulant toxicity, their job is to manage a behavioral issue, not to respond to a drug-induced physical crisis like they would with heroin. They suggested that the medical or behavioral presentations of cocaine and methamphetamine toxicity are similar, and commented that they see about one case per month. Although they did not entirely discount a stimulant-induced overdose, the paramedics had never experienced such an event. They suggested that a stimulant-induced overdose might occur if someone "blew their heart out," an occurrence they described as hypothetical. As such, they were unclear why this might happen or how they would respond.

Emergency department physicians were also unaware of an overall increase in drug-related mortality. They explained that people often come to the emergency room septic and alone, and that in these cases, physicians have no way of knowing what drugs were involved. All three doctors expressed concern that they may not always recognize drug overdoses. When talking about drug-related deaths, these doctors emphasized opiate overdose, explaining that heroin was the drug involved in the cases they had witnessed and treated. They mentioned that they expected to see more methamphetamine-related health crises due to the toxicity of the chemicals used in manufacturing the drug.

Unlike the first responders, staff members at the Denver Medical Examiner's Office were aware of both an overall increase in drug-related mortality and changes in the types of drugs associated with these deaths. The staff, which included pathologists and investigators, based their hypotheses about the increase in drug-related deaths on their experiences processing death scenes and toxicology reports of autopsies. They were perhaps best positioned to know about these trends because they reported that they conduct standard toxicology tests on about 95% of decedents who die outside of the hospital, and such toxicology tests are the ultimate measure in drug-related deaths. Medical examiner staff commented that 5–10 years ago, heroin and cocaine were most often associated with drug-related deaths, but that the majority of drug-related deaths now are due to polydrug use, including mixtures of illicit and prescription drugs.

7.3.2 *Perceived Reasons for the Increase in Drug-Related Deaths*

Nine participant-generated contexts for the increase in drug-related deaths were identified. Members of all four groups noted the combined effects of aging and

Table 7.1 Hypotheses endorsed in qualitative interviews

Informant-generated hypotheses	Police	Paramedics	Emergency department doctors	Medical examiner staff
Long-term effects of chronic drug use (the "aging of the baby boom cohort")	x	x	x	x
Increased polydrug use	x	x	x	x
Increased adulterants in drugs	x	x		
Intentional overdose (suicide)	x	x		
Increased deaths due to violent conflict with first responders	x	x		
Inexperience of new users		x		
Increased methadone diversion		x		
Increase in released prisoners				x
Prescription drug use				x

long-term drug use and an increase in polydrug use as probable explanations for the increase in drug-related deaths. Police, paramedics and emergency department physicians mentioned suicides or intentional overdoses. Police and paramedics identified mortality due to violent encounters with first responders and an increase in adulterants in some street drugs as possible factors. Paramedics expressed the belief that an increase in inexperienced new users and an increase in methadone diversion might account for the increase in drug-related mortality, and staff at the medical examiner's office mentioned an increase in prison releases and an increase in the use of prescription drugs as possible contributing factors. Table 7.1 presents a summary overview of the reasons provided by each group interviewed.

7.3.2.1 Context 1: Long-Term Drug Use Among the 'Baby Boomers'

All four groups identified the effects of long-term drug use on an aging population as a reason for the increase in drug-related mortality. Police officers commented about the adverse consequences of long-term crack use and how, according to one officer, "a user's body just gives up." The paramedics agreed that chronic cocaine users may die as a consequence of their years of use, and attributed hypertension and heart attacks to long-term cocaine use. They expanded on the notion of cocaine-related deaths as well, explaining that a user could have cocaine in their system but not be acutely intoxicated and still have a heart attack. However, they said that such cases would *not* constitute an overdose. Emergency department doctors and staff at the Denver Medical Examiner's Office concurred with police and paramedics in speculating that chronic, cumulative drug use plays a role in the increase in drug-related deaths. Specifically, staff at the Medical Examiner's office pointed to Denver's aging heroin population and suggested that it may be at increased susceptibility of death due to the long-term effects of heroin use.

The "baby boom" cohort that came of age during the 1960s had much higher rates of illegal drug use than the cohorts that came before and after (Cross and Kleinhesselink 1985; Substance Abuse and Mental Health Services Administration [SAMHSA] 2008). This cohort also has a higher rate of people who developed long-term addictions to illegal drugs to the extent that a percentage of people who use illegal drugs eventually become addicted to them. According to this hypothesis, as this cohort enters into its 50s and 60s, rates of drug overdose should be expected to increase as the body eventually succumbs to the ravages of long-term illegal drug use and its associated lifestyle (Schlaerth 2007).

7.3.2.2 Context 2: Polydrug Use

Polydrug use is the simultaneous or sequential use of two or more substances over a short period of time. An increase in polydrug use was the only other context identified by all four groups as a possible factor for the increase in drug-related deaths. Police officers, paramedics and emergency department physicians all claimed that polydrug use was increasing and all felt that it might help to explain the increase in drug-related mortality. As one police officer commented, "[T]hey'll take whatever they can get their hands on." Consistent with these first responders, staff of the medical examiner's office partially attributed the increase in drug-related deaths to an increase in polydrug use. They reported that 5–10 years ago, drug-related deaths were due solely to cocaine or heroin. Now, however, they reported that toxicology reports often show mixtures of illicit drugs and/or prescription drugs. While they suspect a fair number of these deaths are actually intentional, they often lack sufficient information to make a conclusive determination.

7.3.2.3 Context 3: Suicide

Police and paramedics both believed that suicide was a factor in the increase in drug-related mortality. According to one police officer, "That stuff happens all the time." The officers were less certain about whether these deliberate overdoses involved illicit drugs. The paramedics said that prescription drugs were most often involved "when someone is deliberately trying to hurt themselves." Like the paramedics, the emergency department physicians associated intentional overdoses with prescription drugs. These responders therefore believed that at least part of the trend in increasing drug-related mortality was a methodological artifact and represented misclassified suicides.

7.3.2.4 Context 4: Violent Interactions with First Responders

Police officers also attributed an increase in drug-related deaths to an increase in drug-related violent conflict with first responders – a phenomenon they seemed to attribute primarily to stimulants. An officer explained how in stimulant cases, "a drug-related death" might be due to the person's drug-induced feelings of invincibility and the responding police officers' attempts to subdue the individual. An officer explained in those cases, "[Y]ou're lucky to come out not having been hit by another cop's nightstick." Another officer told a story about the death of a crack user who had just been released from prison. He locked himself in his mother's bathroom for several hours smoking crack. When he emerged, he was in a crack-induced psychosis. His mother called the police and, in their attempts to subdue him, he died. An officer described how the crack user picked him up by the collar and threw him (the 270 lb. officer) across the room "like a piece of paper." In the drug-related cases where the police do play a more active role, the perpetrator typically does not die. Such cases are usually stimulant-related, when police are called to respond to a situation where "someone is acting strange." In these cases, "[W]e're there to prevent them from hurting anyone. We're there to protect property, maintain the peace." Another officer added that usually a family member makes such calls. These situations rarely result in death unless, as in the story described earlier, the person is experiencing a drug-induced feeling of invincibility or rage, and dies in the course of being subdued.

The paramedics described similar situations in which two or more first responders had to "dogpile" or use more than one person to physically restrain an acutely intoxicated stimulant user in order to sedate them. They agreed with the police that in such a circumstance the drug user may die, perhaps from a pre-existing condition, overexertion or suffocation. They added that because of an increase in stimulant overdoses, police have received training in crisis intervention that aims to handle these incidents as a medical rather than a law enforcement issue and thus reducing the likelihood of a tragic outcome. As with the "suicide" context, this explanation for the increasing rate of drug overdose mortality posits that a substantial portion of deaths are misclassified and listed as the result of drug poisoning when the immediate cause of death is actually violence.

7.3.2.5 Context 5: Adulterants

Police officers and paramedics suggested that adulterants in illegal drugs were a possible contributing factor to the increase in drug-related deaths. They mentioned how methamphetamine users might be at risk of poisoning from the toxic chemicals used in the illegal manufacture of methamphetamine. These first responders identified changes in drug purity as contributing to drug-related mortality. They explained how heroin overdoses seem to occur in waves, a pattern they described as resulting from the introduction of a supply of heroin with a different level of purity than previous supplies.

7.3.2.6 Context 6 and 7: Methadone Diversion and Inexperienced Users

Paramedics mentioned two possible trends contributing to drug-related deaths that were not mentioned by any of our other respondents: an increase in methadone overdoses; and an increase in overdoses among new users. They suggested that many drug-related deaths may be the result of methadone use, and stated that methadone was easily accessible to those who were looking for it. They also speculated that some drug-related deaths were victims of inexperience, given that some had an absence of older scar tissue and presence of "fresh tracks" or puncture wounds.

7.3.2.7 Context 8: Recently Released Prisoners

Although the police officer's story about the recently paroled crack user dying while being subdued provides anecdotal support for the hypothesis linking recent prison release with drug-related mortality, only the medical examiner's staff made this connection explicit. The Chief Investigator explained that when investigative staff arrive at a death scene, they almost always ask the next-of-kin whether the deceased was recently released from prison, particularly in cases involving the death of someone 30 years of age or younger. He explained that his impression is that people recently released from jail comprise an increasing segment of drug overdose victims. In fact, when he arrives at the scene of a death that is potentially drug-related, the first question he asks is "Was this person just released from prison?" The frequency of these occurrences and the similarities between them has led investigators to conclude that inmates commonly engage in a "big hoorah" shortly upon release, which includes extensive drug use in a short period of time. Medical Examiner's staff added that these cases often occur within 24 hours of the individual's release from prison – a point that makes the association between prison release and drug-related mortality appear salient.

7.3.2.8 Context 9: Prescription Drug Use

Staff at the Denver Medical Examiner's Office mentioned an increase in prescription drug use as a possible reason for the increase in overdose mortality. They reported a shift toward prescription drug use among younger drug users. As one staff member commented, "In the past, young people died from abusing illegal drugs, but nowadays it's pharmaceuticals." Police, paramedics and emergency department doctors identified prescription drugs as a drug of choice in intentional overdoses, and all four groups associated it with polydrug use. However, none of them mentioned it as a separate contextual category that might account for the increase in drug-related mortality.

7.3.3 Perceived Characteristics of Drug-Overdose Victims

One theme that emerged from the interview data was that, with the exception of the Medical Examiner, each group interviewed were as cognizant that they were exposed to only a small, selected portion of drug-related deaths. This awareness emerged as each group were asked to describe what they viewed as the typical overdose victim, if such a category existed.

The police officers discussed only people in the lower social strata who were at a heightened risk for drug-related death, and acknowledged that they were unlikely to be aware of drug use or drug-related death among people in the higher social strata. Police officers seemed well aware of the skewed perspective their role provided on drug users and drug-related mortality, and they mentioned the role social class might play in their perceptions about drug-related deaths. They distinguished higher income, better-educated recreational users from the lower class habitual users they normally interacted with. An officer commented that they do not come into contact with the former category of drug users, and explained that it would be unlikely for these drug users to call the police in the event of an overdose: "We don't deal with the wealthy. If they've got money, they don't have the problems. They don't call us; we don't see those people." The police also pointed out that their perceptions of the 'typical' drug overdose victim were limited by the small role that they played at the scene of a drug-related death. Contrary to expectations that police would have an active role in cases of drug-related death, they explained that in the event of a heroin overdose they learn little information about the case. A policeman said that in the case of an opiate-related death, "We pretty much just hang back and let them (the paramedics) do their thing."

For emergency department physicians, the most salient characteristic of drug overdose victims was low socioeconomic status. Emergency department physicians said that the victims they saw in the hospital included a "lot of homeless" and that the typical overdose cases they treated involved the "downtrodden." While socioeconomic status was the main characteristic they mentioned, they also pointed to important nuances beyond this broad generalization. For instance, they observed that the age of patients admitted for drug overdose varied by drug, and that amphetamine cases were usually substantially younger than those admitted for overdoses of other illegal drugs. They also said that the age of patients admitted for severe cocaine abuse was wide-ranging and did not seem to be restricted to the young or old. They qualified all of these statements by noting that they often have only limited information from patients who arrive unconscious or disoriented, and that often they do not see the extensive toxicology tests that ultimately help determine the cause of death.

Paramedics distinguished between stimulant and opiate overdoses. Their comments indicate that stimulant overdose victims were often young and isolated from others, at least by the time the paramedics arrived. Such victims were alone because their behavior was often erratic and/or violent, and they have frightened others away or the police have isolated them. This description suggests that the typical stimulant overdose is younger and has sufficient strength that it requires several paramedics and police to subdue him or her. As for opiate-related overdoses, paramedics described two distinct categories of users susceptible to overdose. The first were chronic, long-term opiate users aged 30–40 years old with little income living in flophouses. The second were younger, recreational heroin users. They called this latter category a "typical Boulder heroin overdose" (referring to Boulder, CO, which has a reputation for high levels of drug use among college students) where they described "walking into a party and everyone is crying." The paramedics, like the emergency department physicians, noted that almost all stimulant and opiate overdose victims they encountered ultimately survived, and the paramedics were openly aware that they saw only a distinct subpopulation of all overdose cases.

The physicians and staff of the Denver Medical Examiner's Office were reluctant to paint a portrait of a typical overdose victim for three reasons. First, overdose deaths comprise a small portion of the approximately 4,000 yearly deaths in Denver, the vast majority of which are processed through the Medical Examiner's Office. The pathologists and staff of the Medical Examiner's Office have not been explicitly tracking overdose mortality, and they were cautious in describing trends they were not systematically assessing. A second, related reason is that statements from the Denver Medical Examiner's Office carry consequential legal implications, and such staff therefore offered general statements in a cautious manner. Third, the staff and pathologists at the Denver Medical Examiner's Office were more interested in relating quirky, interesting cases that defied easy categorization, such as senior citizens or professionals whose toxicology reports indicated illegal drugs as the cause of death to the complete surprise of family and friends.

With these caveats in mind, the Denver Medical Examiner's Office did eventually offer one characteristic of drug overdose victims that they found salient: often the victims were recently released inmates. Yet, at the same time, the Denver Medical Examiner's Office offered a further, unexpected insight. When the Chief Investigator was asked about the potential difficulties in tracking down the friends and families of drug overdose victims who were homeless, he replied that such cases would be exceedingly rare. Rather, in his opinion, the vast majority of drug overdose victims were not homeless, and many came from stable families. This comment contradicted the image of the typical drug overdose victim as a person who lived on the street. While overdoses among this population occurred and were salient to first responders interviewed, perhaps the majority of overdose cases took place outside this population and bypassed the first responder system – and the awareness of first responders – and went straight to the Denver Medical Examiner's Office.

7.4 Discussion

The aim of this study was to examine the recent increase in drug-related mortality in detail, and to begin preliminary investigation to specify the forces that are driving it. The study consisted of both a quantitative and qualitative component. In the quantitative analysis, U.S. Vital Statistics were examined to determine the trend in detail, with particular emphasis on whether overall increase in drug-related mortality was specific to one drug or present across a spectrum of drugs. Vital statistics in Denver were also examined, indicating that the city's trends in drug mortality were similar to the national picture, making the setting appropriate for an initial investigation into the underlying causes. We then interviewed first responders in Denver to generate potential hypotheses for the patterns of results we found. To our knowledge, this is one of the first in-depth projects to examine the recent increase in drug-related mortality.

The overall drug-mortality rate has increased considerably in recent years, both nationally and in Denver. This is somewhat surprising given that overall use of 'hard' drugs such as cocaine and heroin has been constant or even declining (SAMHSA 2010a). Moreover, the increase in drug-related mortality was not specific to any single drug, and substantial increases were readily apparent in every drug analyzed in the national data. From 1989 to 2005, for instance, drug-related deaths involving cocaine increased fivefold, for opioids it increased twofold, and for stimulants it increased more than 15-fold. Also, the increase in drug-related mortality is concentrated among people with low socioeconomic status, as measured by educational attainment. Quantitative analyses indicated that the increase was largest among those in the lowest educational category of "no high school education," a little smaller among those in the second-lowest educational category of "high school education," smaller still among those with "some college education," and least among those in the highest education category of "a college education or more."

In all, nine contexts emerged from the qualitative interviews with first responders about increases in drug-related mortality. Below, these nine potential explanations for the increasing drug-related mortality rate are critically reviewed. On the basis of the existing literature, two of them are ranked as highly plausible, two warrant more investigation, and five are less plausible.

7.4.1 *Most Plausible Explanations*

The "released inmates" hypothesis is one of the most promising to explain the drug-mortality trends and is worthy of future, detailed investigation for several reasons. First, if released inmates account for the recent, substantial increase in drug-related mortality, then a substantial increase in the number of released inmates in recent years would be expected. This is, in fact, the case. Between 1989 and 2003, the combined number of people released from state and federal prison increased by more than 50%. The number of released prisoners climbed steadily and monotonically from 400,000 per year in 1989 to more than 600,000 per year in 2003 (Pager 2007). Second, if released inmates are driving the trend, then the expectation would be that they have a high drug-related mortality rate driven by the desire to use of illicit drugs upon post-release in order to 'make up for lost time,' which often involves extreme substance use (Chap. 14 by O'Connell et al., this volume; Inciardi et al. 2007; Seal et al. 2003). This, in turn, heightens their risk for drug-related mortality due to heavy use compounded by low tolerance levels. For instance, recent research indicates that, in the first two weeks after release, the risk of death among former inmates from Washington State was 12.7 times that among the general population, and the leading cause of death among this population was drug overdose (Binswanger et al. 2007). These findings are consistent with studies based on other countries that show an elevated rate of drug-related mortality among recently released prisoners (Bird and Hutchinson 2003; Darke et al. 2000; Seaman et al. 1998; Seymour et al. 2000). Finally, a trend driven by released inmates would also explain why the drug-related mortality is concentrated in the lower educational strata. The educational attainment of adults who have been in prison rank among the lowest of all groups; 41% have not completed high school or its equivalent as compared to 18% of adults in the general population (Harlow 2003).

The other highly plausible explanation for the increase in drug-related mortality is the "chronic drug use among the baby boomers" hypothesis, which posits that long-term chronic drug users in the baby boom cohort drive the increase in drug-related mortality. This argument consists of two components. The first is that the baby boom cohort is likely to have disproportionately high levels of drug-related deaths because it has rates of illegal drug use substantially higher than the cohorts that came before and after it (SAMHSA 2008). Support for a unique effect of the baby boom cohort comes from a recent, age-period-cohort analysis that used U.S. Vital Statistics to show that baby boomers have odds of drug-related mortality that are twice as high as other birth cohorts, after controlling age and historical period influences (Miech et al. 2011).

A second component to this argument is that the risk of drug overdose mortality increases with prolonged use over time. As elaborated by our focus groups, the effects of illegal drug use on the human body appear to be cumulative so that the risk of death among chronic users increases every year. Medical complications associated directly with drug use that are more likely to be lethal with increasing age include arrhytmias, coronary vasospasm, myocardial ischemia, myocardial infarction, cardiomyopathy, hypertension, dyspnea, pulmonary hemorrhage, tracheobronchitis, pneumonias (lobar and nonlobar), pulmonary edema, chronic obstructive pulmonary disease (COPD), "crack lung," seizures, ischemic stroke, subarachnoid/intercerebral hemorrhage, optic neuropathy, methamphetamine-induced necrotizing vasculitis, balganglie/frontal cortex lesions resembling dementias, and Parkinsonian-like illness (Schlaerth 2007). Partial support for the aging hypothesis comes from the finding that the peak age for overdose mortality is not among the youngest (who have the highest rates of illegal drug use), but is instead among older adults between the ages of 35 and 54 (Paulozzi and Annest 2007). This finding suggests that the most common overdoses do not occur among new initiates, but rather among people who have extended histories of drug use.

The "chronic drug use among the baby boomers" hypothesis potentially explains all three of the key quantitative findings of this analysis. The entrance of a large number of chronic drug users into old age could potentially explain why the drug-related mortality rate has increased. The fact that chronic users of all drugs are potentially open to a wide spectrum of drug-related illness and conditions that are lethal could explain why drug-related mortality is found across a spectrum of drugs. And the finding that people in the baby boom cohort with higher education have been more successful in desisting from long-term illegal drug use could help explain why drug-related deaths have been concentrated in the lower educational strata (Miech 2008).

7.4.2 Explanations That Warrant Closer Consideration

A third hypothesis highlighted for future research is "polydrug use," which posits that drug users today are more likely to use multiple drugs within a short period of time. The Medical Examiners' endorsement of this hypothesis lends it special weight because they conduct and interpret toxicology tests on decedents, and are therefore in a unique position to have relevant, objective information. To the extent that polydrug use is on the rise, it would almost certainly lead to an increase in the drug-related mortality rate because polydrug use is particularly lethal. For example, among intravenous drug users in San Francisco, people who used heroin and cocaine simultaneously were 2.6 times more likely to report an overdose than drug users who had not used this drug combination (Ochoa et al. 2001). As another example, a toxicological analysis suggests that alcohol consumption lowers the level of heroin required to induce a fatal overdose (Darke et al. 2000). One indication of the lethality of polydrug use is that it accounted for approximately 55% of all drug-related deaths in New York from 1990 through 1998 (Coffin et al. 2003).

The polydrug hypothesis therefore readily explains two of the three key, quantitative findings of this study. If polydrug use is increasing, then the expectation is that the overall drug mortality rate would also increase. Trend data indicates that polydrug use has indeed increased in recent years (Green et al. 2011; Shah et al. 2007). Further, by definition, polydrug use would explain why overdose mortality is found across a wide range of drugs, and is not specific to a single one. However, the polydrug hypothesis requires further elaboration in at least two areas. Why polydrug use would be especially pronounced among drug users with low education is not immediately clear, although it seems plausible that it could be. Even more importantly, future research along these lines should explain why polydrug use has increased. It is unclear if the observed rise in polydrug use stems from greater availability of drugs (perhaps driven by diversification of drug cartels in the types of drugs they manufacture or distribute), a cultural shift among drug users, or some other reason. Specification of the reasons behind a rise in polydrug use would bolster the plausibility of this hypothesis and also guide future interventions.

A final explanation that we highlight for more research is the "prescription drug" hypothesis. While this potential explanation emerged from our focus groups only peripherally, we nevertheless believe it warrants considerable attention moving forward, given the evidence for it in the drug literature. The core of this explanation is that increasing availability of prescription drugs plays a major role in the increasing drug mortality rate. There can be little doubt that prescription drugs have indeed become increasingly prevalent; the director of the National Institute on Drug Abuse recently testified before congress that the number of scripts for opioids increased more than fourfold from 40 million in 1992 to 180 million in 2007 (Volkow 2010). Concomitant with this rise, prescription drugs have now surpassed heroin and cocaine in overdose deaths as the leading drugs involved (Paulozzi and Xi 2008).

At this stage, the "prescription drug" explanation leaves important questions unanswered. If prescription drugs are the driving force behind the increasing rate of drug-overdose mortality, why deaths due to cocaine, heroin, and stimulants have also increased in recent decades is not immediately clear. Further work is needed to determine if prescription drugs are being used in dangerous combinations with more traditional "harder" drugs, or if increases in deaths due to prescription drugs and "harder" drugs are independent of each other and indicate a broader social trend. Work along these lines should also explain the counterintuitive finding that increasing the availability of prescription drugs leads to more deaths in the lower social strata, which typically has less access to medical care and, consequently, less direct access to prescription medicines.

7.4.3 Explanations That Are Less Plausible

The remaining five hypotheses are less plausible explanations for the findings of this study. Paramedics mentioned an increase in methadone diversion, and it is possible both that methadone diversion has increased and that it has increased drug-related mortality. However, using this hypothesis to explain why the increase in drug-related mortality is general and found across a wide range of drugs, including cocaine and stimulants, is difficult. Paramedics also mentioned that recent years may have brought more cases of inexperienced new drug users who overdose and die. Working against this hypothesis is the national trend showing that, during the time period of this study, drug use prevalence has remained constant or actually declined (SAMHSA 2010b).

Both the police and paramedics suggested that increases in drug-related mortality might be the result of an increase in suicides, either covert or overt. While we acknowledge that a substantial portion of drug-related deaths are indeed suicides that are not recognized as such, we find little reason to believe that this portion of drug-related deaths has increased in recent years. Nationally, suicide deaths for the study period of this project among the age group analyzed have remained constant or declined (Centers for Disease Control and Prevention 2009). Police and paramedics also suggested that drug users' violent conflict with first responders may also contribute to the increasing drug-related mortality rate, but this factor, while potentially influential, seems unlikely to be large enough to account for the trends observed in this study. The drug-related mortality rate increased by about 5 per 100,000 over the study period, which would mean that first-responder deaths would need to account for about 8,000 deaths a year (given that that the U.S. population size of adults aged 25–64 years old is about160 million). This is an exceedingly high number that is more than five times the yearly total of homicides in New York and Los Angeles combined.

Finally, the police mentioned the potential influence of a greater concentration of adulterants in illegal drugs. Drug-related deaths may increase if illegal drugs are increasingly polluted or "cut" with lethal substances, or, the same effect may be achieved for the opposite reason and the purity of illegal drugs increases sharply and catches users by surprise. While either scenario is possible, it seems unlikely to account for the main empirical trends observed in this study. In our experience with drug users, they simply never know the purity or the content of the substances that they put into their bodies, given that the drug manufacture business is illegal and unregulated. Users have developed various ad hoc processes to test the purity of the drugs they use (such as first testing a small sample), which generally work well to help them achieve the dose they desire as the purity and quality of the drugs they procure ebbs and flows.

7.5 Limitations

This study has four limitations. First, in 1999 the U.S. Vital Statistics changed the coding system by which it classifies death, and updated to version 10 from version 9 of the International Classification of Death nosology. This update has the potential to lead to a disjuncture in the mortality rates in the year 1999, and, in fact, it did as Fig. 7.1 shows that the mortality rate for cocaine-related deaths jumped substantially in this year. However, the main focus of this project is on the trend in drug-related deaths over time – not mortality rates at particular years – and all quantitative analyses showed that: (a) the mortality rate continued to increase before and after the year 1999; and (b) the increase was concentrated among decedents with lower education. Consequently, the change in nosology in 1999 did not affect the main trends that are the focus of this project.

A second limitation is that the first responders were less aware of the trend in drug-related mortality than we had expected. Police, paramedics, and emergency room physicians all reported that they had little exposure to drug-related deaths and, therefore, were not in much of a position to offer insights into reasons behind any related trends. Further, all groups but the Denver Medical Examiner's Office were cognizant that in their work they witnessed only a small, select sample of all drug-related deaths. This finding highlights that the Medical Examiner's Office is best positioned to observe and analyze the trend – and has the best data on it – and points to the importance of collaboration with Medical Examiners' Offices for future researchers in this field.

A third limitation is that the insights and hypotheses generated from qualitative interviews in Denver do not necessarily extend to other regions of the country. Limited generalizability is an issue inherent in qualitative research. However, none of the first responders interviewed mentioned factors or issues that were inherently specific to the area, but instead focused on broader topics such as the national increase in the number of released prisoners or the aging of the baby boom cohort. We hope that future analyses will explicitly test the generalizability of the hypotheses this study has generated with analyses of nationally representative data.

A fourth limitation was ambiguity in the concept of a drug-related death. At the start of our project, we assumed that drug-related deaths were clear and that first responders would have a shared understanding of them. For example, people who die with syringes in their arms are most likely a clear case of a drug-related death.

However, in our interviews, we discovered cases that generated disagreement. For example, some first responders claimed that it was impossible to overdose on methamphetamine, an assertion contradicted by emergency room physicians. It was also unclear to many first responders if a death that resulted from an irrational act committed under the influence of drugs (e.g., charging a police officer with a car) should be attributed to the drug or instead attributed to behavior. This ambiguity is an important topic of research for future analyses, which ideally will put a handle on this ambiguity and assess the extent to which it influences the conclusions of professionals and researchers that deal with drug-related death.

7.6 Conclusion

The mortality rate due to illegal drug use has increased substantially in recent years, and the reasons for this increase are not well known. Further, to our knowledge, no one is actively working to specify the underlying causes. This initial investigation into the increase suggests four potential explanations that may work alone or in concert: the historical increase in released inmates; the aging of the baby boom generation; increases in polydrug use; and increases in non-medical use of prescription drugs. Future research is warranted to assess the relative plausibility of these four explanations, information that is needed to develop policy and interventions to counteract the rise of drug-related mortality and to save lives.

References

Binswanger, I. A., Stern, M. F., Deyo, R. A., Heagerty, P. J., Cheadle, A., Elmore, J. G., et al. (2007). Release from prison – A high risk of death for former inmates. *New England Journal of Medicine, 356*, 157–165.

Bird, S. M., & Hutchinson, S. J. (2003). Male drug-related deaths in the fortnight after release from prison: Scotland, 1996–99. *Addiction, 98*, 185–190.

Centers for Disease Control and Prevention. (2009). Web-based injury statics query and reporting system (WISQARS). *Fatal Injury Reports* [Data file]. Retrieved from www.cdc.gov/injury/wisqars/fatal.html

Coffin, P. O., Galea, S., Ahren, J., Leon, A. C., Vlahov, D., & Tardiff, K. (2003). Opiates, cocaine and alcohol combinations in accidental drug overdose deaths in New York city, 1990–98. *Addiction, 98*(6), 739–747.

Cross, H. J., & Kleinhesselink, R. R. (1985). The impact of the 1960s on adolescence. *Journal of Early Adolescence, 5*, 517–538.

Darke, S., Ross, J., Zador, D., & Sunjic, S. (2000). Heroin-related death in New South Wales, Australia: 1992–1996. *Drug and Alcohol Dependence, 60*, 141–150.

Green, T. C., Grau, L. E., Carver, H. W., Kinzly, M., & Heimer, R. (2011). Epidemiologic trends and geographic patterns of fatal opioid intoxication in Connecticut, USA: 1997–2007. *Drug and Alcohol Dependence, 115*, 221–228.

Harlow, C. W. (2003). *Education and correctional populations*. Washington, DC: Bureau of Justice Statistics.

Inciardi, J. A., Surratt, H. L., Martin, S. S., O'Connell, D. J., Salandy, A. D., & Beard, R. (2007). Developing a multimedia HIV and hepatitis intervention for drug-involved offenders reentering the community. *The Prison Journal, 87*(1), 111–142.

Miech, R. A. (2008). The formation of a socioeconomic health disparity: The case of cocaine use during the 1980s and 1990s. *Journal of Health and Social Behavior, 49*(3), 352–366.

Miech, R. A., Koester, S., & Dorsey-Holliman, B. (2011). Increasing U.S. mortality due to accidental poisoning: The role of the baby-boom cohort. *Addiction, 106*(4), 806–815.

Ochoa, K. C., Hahn, J. A., Seal, K. H., & Moss, A. R. (2001). Overdosing among young injection drug users in San Francisco. *Addictive Behaviors, 26*, 453–460.

Pager, D. (2007). *Marked: Race, crime, and finding work in an era of mass incarceration*. Chicago: University of Chicago Press.

Paulozzi, L. J., & Annest, J. (2007). Unintentional poisoning deaths – United States, 1999–2004. *Morbidity and Mortality Weekly Report, 56*(5), 93–96.

Paulozzi, L. J., & Xi, Y. (2008). Recent changes in drug poisoning mortality in the United States by urban–rural status and by drug type. *Pharmacoepidemiology and Drug Safety, 17*, 997–1005.

Paulozzi, L. J., Ballesteros, M. F., & Stevens, J. A. (2006a). Recent trends in mortality from unintentional injury in the United States. *Journal of Safety Research, 37*, 277–283.

Paulozzi, L. J., Budnitz, D. S., & Xi, Y. (2006b). Increasing deaths from opioid analgesics in the United States. *Pharmacoepidemiology and Drug Safety, 15*, 618–627.

Schlaerth, K. R. (2007). Older adults and illegal drugs. *Geriatrics and Aging, 10*(6), 361–364.

Seal, D. W., Margolis, A. D., Sosman, J., Kacanek, D., Binson, D., & The Project Study Start Group. (2003). HIV and STD risk behavior among 18- to 25-year-old men released from U.S. prisons: Provider perspectives. *AIDS and Behavior, 7*(2), 131–141.

Seaman, S. R., Brettle, R. P., & Gore, S. M. (1998). Mortality from overdose among injecting drug users recently released from prison: Database linkage study. *British Medical Journal, 316*, 426–428.

Seymour, A., Oliver, J. S., & Black, M. (2000). Drug-related deaths among recently released prisoners in the Strathclyde region of Scotland. *Journal of Forensic Sciences, 45*(3), 649–654.

Shah, N. G., Lathrop, S. L., Reichard, R. R., & Landen, M. G. (2007). Unintentional drug overdose death trends in New Mexico, USA, 1990–2005: Combinations of heroin, cocaine, prescription opioids and alcohol. *Addiction, 103*, 126–136.

Substance Abuse and Mental Health Services Administration. (2008). *Results from the 2007 national survey on drug use and health: National findings* (DHHS Publication No. SMA 08–4343). Rockville: Office of Applied Studies.

Substance Abuse and Mental Health Services Administration. (2010a). *Results from the 2009 national survey on drug use and health: Detailed tables* (NSDUH Series H-38A, HHS Publication No. SMA 10–4586). Rockville: Office of Applied Studies.

Substance Abuse and Mental Health Services Administration. (2010b). *Results from the 2009 national survey on drug use and health: Volume I. Summary of national findings* (NSDUH Series H-38A, HHS Publication No. SMA 10–4586). Rockville: Office of Applied Studies.

Volkow, N. D. (2010). *Report on Scientific Research on Prescription Drug Abuse*. Washington, DC: Congressional Caucus on Prescription Drug Abuse.

World Health Organization. (1977). *International statistical classification of diseases and related health problems (9th revision)*. Geneva: World Health Organization.

World Health Organization. (1992). *International statistical classification of diseases and related health problems (10th revision)*. Geneva: World Health Organization.

Chapter 8
Arrest Histories, Victimization, Substance Use, and Sexual Risk Behaviors Among Young Adults in Miami's Club Scene

Steven P. Kurtz

Abstract *This study examined the arrest histories and predictors of multiple arrests among 357 ethnically diverse polydrug users ages 18–25 years old who participate in the nightclub scene in Miami. The data were collected using structured assessments of respondents' substance use, as well as standardized measures of health, environmental, and social risks. Respondents were recruited using respondent-driven sampling. The sample reported high levels of childhood victimization, prior substance abuse treatment, and arrest. Powder cocaine, MDMA (ecstasy), marijuana, alcohol, and prescription benzodiazepines were used by large majorities of the sample. More than 75% met Diagnostic and Statistical Manual of Mental Disorders IV substance dependence criteria. History of three or more lifetime arrests (n = 110) was associated with male gender, low educational achievement, violent victimization, early sexual debut, and prior substance abuse treatment. Multiple arrestees reported higher levels of current use of powder cocaine, marijuana, and prescription benzodiazepines, as well as elevated levels of sexual risk behaviors, including anal intercourse, unprotected sex, and more sex partners. The high levels of interconnected health and social problems observed among this population appear to be underreported in the literature and require explanatory research designs to more fully understand. Implications for intervention approaches are also discussed.*

This research was supported by the National Institute on Drug Abuse (R01DA019048). The content is solely the responsibility of the authors and does not necessarily represent the official views of the National Institute on Drug Abuse or the National Institutes of Health. The author gratefully acknowledges the work of Dr. James A. Inciardi, Principal Investigator of the study from 2005 to 2008.

S.P. Kurtz, Ph.D. (✉)
Center for Applied Research on Substance Use and Health Disparities, Nova Southeastern University, 2121 Ponce de Leon Blvd., Suite 430, Coral Gables, FL 33134, USA
e-mail: steven.kurtz@nova.edu

B. Sanders et al. (eds.), *Crime, HIV and Health: Intersections of Criminal Justice and Public Health Concerns*, DOI 10.1007/978-90-481-8921-2_8,

The modern, all-night dance club culture has its most recent roots in the adolescent rave and gay male circuit party subcultures that emerged in the late 1980s, with more distant connections to the earlier New York nightclub scene epitomized by Studio 54 (Fritz 1999; Kurtz and Inciardi 2003; Silcott 1999; Thornton 1996). This type of nightlife is found in almost every large city, but is especially prevalent in major tourist destinations, including Miami, where people tend to look for an escape from their routines (Owen 2003; Shister 1999; Uriely and Belhassen 2006).

Except for MDMA (ecstasy), which has been a relative constant, the most common "club" or "dance drugs" have tended to vary over time and location, and have included such diverse substances as powder cocaine, methamphetamine, ketamine, rohypnol, gamma-hydroxybutyric acid (GHB), and LSD over the past two decades (Beck and Rosenbaum 1994; Measham et al. 2001; Reynolds 1998; Sanders 2006; Thornton 1996). More recently, prescription medications, primarily opioids and benzodiazepines, have become prevalent (Kelly and Parsons 2007; Kurtz et al. 2005). Alcohol use is also ubiquitous among club drug users (Kurtz et al. 2005; Mitcheson et al. 2008) but tends to supplement rather than substitute for club drug use (Hammersley et al. 1999; Kurtz 2004).

One of the attractions to these substances among the young adults who predominate in the club scene is the increased stamina that they engender, enabling participants to dance all night, as well as their intoxicating, euphoric, disinhibiting and sometimes hallucinogenic effects that are said to deepen the club or dance experience (Fritz 1999; Reynolds 1998; Silcott 1999). The drugs, like other aspects of the club culture, are usually portrayed as the height of fashion, exclusivity, and trendiness (Cooper 2007; Thornton 1996).

Because of the young age of the vast majority of club drug users and their tendency to mix numerous drugs during their typical drug binges, club drug users are at high risk for health problems (Boyd et al. 2003; Cottler et al. 2001; Freese et al. 2002). Many users experiment with a variety of club drugs and alcohol in combination, which can lead to unexpected adverse reactions (Measham et al. 2001; Pedersen and Skrondal 1999; von Sydow et al. 2002). Other studies have reported club drug use to be associated with high-risk sexual behaviors (Klitzman et al. 2002; Mattison et al. 2001; Semple et al. 2002), as well as depression, anxiety, and other mental health problems (McCardle et al. 2004; Measham et al. 2001; Parrott et al. 2001).

A large body of research has demonstrated a strong relationship between drug use and crime (Ball et al. 1982; Inciardi 2008). Offenders may become caught up in lifestyles that involve deviant activities on a daily or near-daily basis; drug dependency may lead to economic crimes; and the pharmacological effects of drug use may also lead to criminal activity due to increased aggressive tendencies, reduced inhibitions, and impaired judgment (Goldstein 1985). However, information about the criminal activity of participants in the club culture is scant within the scientific literature (Anderson et al. 2007; Krebs and Steffey 2005). Though nightclub owners and promoters have been implicated in organized crime and other forms of drug-related and violent crime (Cooper 2007; Owen 2003; St. James 2003), except for their use of illegal drugs, the young adult participants in the club scene are most often described as targets of police harassment or victims of predatory criminals in the street environments surrounding the clubs (Measham et al. 2001) rather than as perpetrators.

This study contributes to the understanding of criminal activity among participants in the club scene by examining the self-reported lifetime arrest histories of young adult polydrug users aged 18–25 years old in Miami's club culture. In addition, demographic characteristics, current drug use and sexual behaviors, and life historical social risk indices (e.g., victimization, age of sexual debut, and substance abuse treatment) are examined as predictors of multiple arrest in order to better understand the risk factors associated with recidivism among the youngest, legal cohort in the club scene. The goal of these analyses is to identify important avenues of inquiry in this rather new area of research, as well as to assess key targets for risk reduction intervention among this population.

8.1 Methods

Miami-Dade County, Florida, is a diverse community of 2.5 million people with large numbers of foreign-born (50.9%) residents (United States Census Bureau 2009). Hispanics (62.5%) are the largest ethnic group, with "Anglos" (the local term for non-Hispanic whites) representing 17.7%, and African-Americans/African-Caribbeans 16.6% of the county population. Miami is a national and international destination for partying, sexual tourism, and club drug use (Cooper 2007; Guzman 1999; Kilborn 2000; Marr 2004; Schwartz 2003). And to a great extent, South Beach has also become an East Coast center for the club culture – setting trends that are emulated and replicated elsewhere in the United States, Western Europe, and Latin America (Perrone 2009; Shister 1999).

Data were drawn from a natural history study of participants in Miami's club scene who use club drugs and also use prescription drugs for non-medical reasons. The major goals of the project were to examine the onset and progression of club and prescription drug abuse and to assess changes in health and social consequences of this abuse over time. Participants were interviewed at baseline and at three successive 6-month intervals. Data reported here are from the baseline interviews with 357 participants in the study who were between the ages of 18 and 25 years old. To be eligible, participants must have been willing to provide contact information, including a residential address and telephone number for scheduling follow-up appointments. Enrollment criteria included: (a) use of one or more club drugs at least three times during the past 90 days; (b) use of one or more psychoactive prescription medications three times or more in the past 90 days for non-prescribed reasons; and (c) attendance at recognized local nightclubs at least twice per month. Club drugs were defined to include powder cocaine, ecstasy, GHB, ketamine, and LSD.

Participants were recruited into the study between May 2006 and June 2008 through respondent-driven sampling (RDS; Heckathorn 1997), a form of chain referral sampling that aims to minimize sampling bias attributable to narrow social networks. In this study, initial respondents ("seeds") were recruited through outreach and existing contacts in the club culture. The seeds were chosen for their diversity in terms of gender, ethnicity, age, and sexual orientation. Each seed and subsequent study participant was provided with recruitment coupons to give to other club drug users in their social network, with the understanding that they would earn $50 for the recruitment of each additional eligible respondent. The coupons provided the recipient with information about the study and a telephone number to call for eligibility screening. Each respondent/recruiter was limited to five coupons in order to prevent a few recruiters with large social networks from biasing the overall sample toward those with similar demographic and drug using profiles (homophily) and in order to lengthen the recruitment chains (Heckathorn 1997). Theoretically, respondent-driven sampling has been shown to quickly reduce sources of respondent bias (such as ethnic and sexual identity, gender, and drug of choice) as successive branches or waves of respondent contacts are enrolled and then solicited for additional contacts (Heckathorn 1997, 2002). Although participants were not recruited at nightclubs, the clubs they reported patronizing most often were large dance clubs that are focused on the electronic music scene.

The project was housed in a field office strategically located to facilitate access to a diverse population of club and prescription drug users. This site was central to the hubs of nightclub activity, and easily reachable by public transportation from throughout the county. Private offices were used for all interviews. Data were collected using computer-assisted personal interviews. Clients received HIV education literature, condoms, and a $50 stipend upon completion of the baseline interview, which lasted about 2 h. The interviews assessed demographics, lifetime and current alcohol and drug abuse, *Diagnostic and Statistical Manual of Mental Disorders IV (DSM-IV)* substance and dependence criteria, sexual history and risk-taking, victimization, mental health problems, and drug treatment history, as well as criminal activity and arrest history. The University of Delaware's Institutional Review Board approved all human subject protocols.

The Global Appraisal of Individual Needs (GAIN, version 5.4; Dennis et al. 2002) was the primary component of the standardized baseline assessment. In addition to the collection of demographic, life history, and social and health risk data, the GAIN includes *DSM-IV-R* diagnostics for substance abuse and dependence, as well as clinical measures of depression and anxiety. Measures of mental health problems and drug abuse and dependence reflect symptoms experienced in the year prior to the baseline interview. Severe depression was defined as the endorsement of at least six of nine symptoms (e.g., feeling sad, lonely, or hopeless; being easily annoyed or irritated; feeling tired or having no energy), and severe anxiety as the endorsement of at least seven of 12 symptoms (e.g., feeling nervous, anxious, or tense; fear of open spaces or leaving home; unable to control worries).

The primary dependent variable was multiple lifetime arrest history, defined as three or more arrests, which was considered by the investigators to be a good measure of repeat offender status within this young adult age group. This item was assessed by the question, "How many times in your lifetime have you been arrested, charged with a crime, and booked?" The instrumentation also included an itemization of the charges for each reported arrest, which are listed in the tables under the general subcategories of property, violent, and alcohol/drug-related crimes. It should be noted that the instrumentation did not distinguish drug possession from drug distribution arrests. Parole violations and other offenses, such as criminal mischief, trespassing, and weapons possession charges were combined as "other" types of crime, but not separately identified.

To the extent possible, hypothesized predictors of multiple arrest history were assessed using lifetime historical measures, e.g., "How many times in your life have you received treatment for your use of alcohol or any drug?" or "Have you ever been sexually abused?" Substance use data were collected using 90-day measures of quantity and frequency. The quantity measure was assessed for each substance endorsed by a participant by the question, "How many ________ (e.g., drinks, joints, lines) did you use in a typical month in the past 90 days?" In the bivariate logistic regression models predicting multiple arrest history, these quantity measures were dichotomized into "high current use" and "not high current use" categories using the median as the cutoff point.

Data from the interview questionnaires were analyzed using Predictive Analytics Software (formerly SPSS) version 18. Descriptive statistics were calculated to describe the sample in terms of demographics, age of sexual debut, substance abuse treatment history, mental health, victimization, substance use, and sexual risk behaviors, as well as to investigate the nature and extent of the participants' arrest histories. Bivariate logistic regression models were developed to predict multiple (three or more times) arrest history by demographics and by hypothesized predictors, including substance use and treatment history, age of sexual debut, sexual risk behaviors, and victimization. A multivariate model was then constructed that included all of the significant demographic and lifetime historical bivariate predictors. Current substance use and sexual behaviors were not included in the multivariate model because of the lack of temporal congruence with lifetime arrest history.

8.2 Results and Analyses

8.2.1 Demographics, Social Stability, Mental Health and Victimization

Demographics, social stability, mental health, and victimization characteristics of the sample are shown in Table 8.1. The sample was predominately male (59.1%). The ethnic mix of Miami's population was fully represented in the sample. Few respondents (20.4%) had less than a high school or equivalent level of education. The mean age of the sample was 20.7 years. The majority (57.1%) of respondents was still living with their parents, which might be linked to their low median personal monthly income of $1,250.

Table 8.1 Demographic, health and social risk characteristics of young adult polydrug users in Miami's club scene (N=357)

	N	%
Demographics		
Age (mean, SD)	20.7 (2.44)	
Gender		
Male	211	59.1
Female	144	40.3
Transgender	2	0.6
Race/Ethnicity		
African American	61	17.1
Hispanic	222	62.1
White/Anglo	62	17.4
Other	12	3.4
Live with parents	204	57.1
Less than high school education	73	20.4
Monthly income (median)	$1,250	
Social stability (lifetime)		
First sex before age 14	111	31.1
Substance abuse treatment history	129	36.1
Illegal activity past 6 months (excl. drug use)	165	46.2
Arrest history	209	58.5
3 or more lifetime arrests	110	30.8
Mental health (past year)		
Severe clinical depression	83	23.2
Severe clinical anxiety	41	11.5
DSM-IV substance abuse	277	77.6
DSM-IV substance dependence	269	75.4
Victimization history (lifetime)		
Sexual abuse	54	15.1
Physical abuse	235	65.8
Emotional abuse	175	49.0
First abuse before age 18	244	68.3

Social risk indices were high, with 31.1% reporting first sex before age 14, 36.1% reporting prior substance abuse treatment, and 58.5% having been arrested; 30.8% had been arrested three or more times. Almost half (46.2%) reported illegal activity other than drug use in the past 6 months. In terms of mental health, severe depressive symptoms were reported by 23.2% and severe anxiety symptoms by 11.5% of respondents. Past year *DSM-IV-R* diagnostic criteria for substance dependence were met by 75.4% of participants. Lifetime rates of emotional, physical, and sexual victimization were very high as well, and 68.3% reported that the first episode of abuse occurred when they were minors. More than one-quarter (26.1%) of respondents were *currently* worried about being abused (data not shown).

Table 8.2 Past 90 day health risk behaviors of young adult polydrug users in Miami's club scene (N=357)

	N	%
Substance use[a]		
Powder cocaine	319	89.4
MDMA (Ecstasy)	313	87.7
LSD	84	23.5
Psilocybin (mushrooms)	57	16.0
Rx opioids (non-prescribed)	194	54.3
Rx benzodiazepines (non-prescribed)	325	91.0
$ drug/alcohol expense/mo (median)	$300	
Drug/alcohol expense/income ratio (%)	24.0%	
Sexual behaviors		
Anal intercourse	88	24.6
Unprotected anal/vaginal sex	227	63.6
Number of sex partners (mean, SD)	2.6 (2.83)	
Anal intercourse	88	24.6

[a]Over 90% report current tobacco, alcohol and marijuana use

8.2.2 *Substance Use and Sexual Risk Behaviors*

Table 8.2 shows current (past 90 day) substance use and sexual risk behaviors. In addition to almost universal use of alcohol, tobacco and marijuana, large majorities reported use of prescription benzodiazepines (91%), powder cocaine (89.4%) and MDMA (87.7%) A majority (54.3%) also reported non-prescribed use of prescription opioids, whereas recent LSD and psilocybin use was endorsed by fewer than one-quarter of the sample. Participants' median monthly expense for alcohol and drugs totaled 24% of their median monthly income.

Additional data not shown in the table indicate the striking extent, complexity, and multiplicity of substance use among the sample. Almost two-thirds (63.6%) of respondents reported current use of tobacco, alcohol, marijuana, powder cocaine, MDMA, *and* prescription sedatives within the past 90 days. Almost one-third (29.4%) reported current use of at least seven and as many as 13 different categories of substances, excluding tobacco. All respondents also reported recent polydrug use (co-ingesting, mixing, and/or sequencing substances during a single occasion). The sample reported being high or drunk all day on an average of 48 of the past 90 days

Participants also reported current high levels of sexual risk behaviors, including anal intercourse (24.6%), unprotected sex (63.6%), and multiple partners (50.4%). Only 4.8% of men, but 28.2% of women, reported same sex behaviors in the past year (data not shown).

Table 8.3 Lifetime arrest histories of young adult polydrug users in Miami's club scene by major crime category (N=209 arrestees)[a]

	N	%
Property crimes	*115*	*55.0*
Arson	6	2.9
Burglary	45	21.5
Larceny/theft/stolen goods	47	22.5
Motor vehicle theft	24	11.5
Shoplifting	23	11.0
Vandalism/criminal mischief	27	12.9
Passing checks/forgery	5	2.4
Violent crimes	*82*	*39.2*
Aggravated assault	19	9.1
Simple assault/battery	51	24.4
Robbery	28	13.4
Other violence (e.g., homicide, rape)	4	1.9
Drug/alcohol crimes	*135*	*64.6*
Possession/distribution of drugs	120	57.4
Driving under the influence	11	5.3
Drunkenness	19	9.1
Other crimes (e.g. weapons, parole)	*88*	*42.1*

[a]Respondents reporting arrests for different categories of crime and different crimes within categories do not add to 100% because many respondents reported arrests for multiple crimes

8.2.3 Arrest Histories

Arrest histories by type of crime are shown in Table 8.3. The distribution of crimes was widespread across all categories. Property crimes, reported by 55% of arrestees, were primarily related to theft rather than destruction. Violent crimes were reported by 39.2% and drug/alcohol-related crimes by 64.6% of arrestees. Of the 209 participants with arrest histories, 61 (29.2%) had been arrested only once, 38 (18.2%) two times, and a majority (52.6%) three or more times (data not shown).

8.2.4 Predictors of Arrest Histories

Results of bivariate logistic regression models predicting multiple arrest history are shown in Table 8.4, with the significance level set at $p<.05$. Multiple arrest histories were strongly predicted by being male and having less than a high school education, but not by race/ethnicity. Those who still lived with their parents were about half as likely as other participants to be multiple arrestees. Almost all of the hypothesized lifetime risk indices were significant in the models, with histories of substance abuse

Table 8.4 Predictors of multiple (three or more times) arrest history among young adult polydrug users in Miami's club scene (N=357)

	Triple arrestees (N=110)	
Bivariate models	Odds ratio (CI)	*p*
Demographics		
Male	9.528 (4.976, 18.242)	.000
Live with parents	0.531 (0.337, 0.836)	.006
Less than HS education	2.061 (1.212, 3.504)	.008
Black/African American		ns
White/Anglo		ns
Hispanic/Latino		ns
Social stability		
Sexual debut before age 14	3.411 (2.115, 5.500)	.000
Substance abuse tx history	4.130 (2.569, 6.640)	.000
Victimization		
Physical abuse history	5.328 (2.882, 9.850)	.000
Sexual abuse history		ns
Emotional abuse history		ns
First abuse before 18	2.333 (1.368, 3.980)	.002
High current substance use		
Alcohol[a]		ns
Marijuana[b]	2.144 (1.350, 3.404)	.001
Powder cocaine[c]	1.838 (1.164, 2901)	.009
MDMA (ecstasy)[d]		ns
Rx benzodiazepines[e]	1.830 (1.162, 2.881)	.009
Sexual behaviors (past 90 days)		
Unprotected anal/vaginal sex	1.932 (1.179, 3.167)	.009
Anal intercourse	1.708 (1.033, 2.825)	.037
2 plus partners	1.658 (1.052, 2.613)	.029

[a]more than 50 drinks per month (sample median)
[b]more than 50 joints per month (sample median)
[c]more than 40 lines per month (sample median)
[d]more than 5 pills per month (sample median)
[e]more than 8 pills per month (sample median)

treatment, early sexual debut, and childhood victimization demonstrating powerful predictive effects. In terms of current risk behaviors, high levels of marijuana, cocaine, and prescription benzodiazepine use predicted multiple arrest history, but high levels of alcohol and MDMA use did not. Higher levels of current sexual risk also characterized multiple arrestees.

In the multivariate model, which included the demographic and lifetime risk predictors that were significant in the bivariate models, six distinct characteristics were associated with multiple arrest history (see Table 8.5). Participants who lived with their parents were just 31% as likely to be multiple recidivists as those who lived on their own. Male participants were ten times more likely than females to be multiple arrestees. Those with histories of physical abuse and those with prior drug treatment experience were more than four times as likely to report three or more

Table 8.5 Predictors of multiple (three or more times) arrest history among young adult polydrug users in Miami's club scene (N=357)

Multivariate model[a]	Triple arrestees (N=110) Odds ratio (CI)	p
Demographics		
Male gender	10.006 (4.714, 21.238)	.000
Live with parents	0.312 (0.171, 0.567)	.000
Less than HS education	2.841 (1.418, 5.692)	.003
Social stability		
Sexual debut before age 14	2.700 (1.493, 4.884)	.001
Substance abuse tx history	4.400 (2.439, 7.940)	.000
Victimization		
Physical abuse history	4.013 (1.674, 9.618)	.002
First abuse before age 18	0.933 (0.421, 2.069)	.865

[a]Model includes all significant demographic and lifetime historical bivariate predictors from Table 8.4

lifetime arrests compared to those without those experiences. Early sexual debut and having less than a high school education also had significant, but somewhat less powerful, independent predictive relationships.

8.3 Discussion

The study has several important limitations. First, the results are likely not generalizable to the overall population of participants in the club culture in Miami because the eligibility requirements included current, frequent abuse of both club drugs and prescription medications. These requirements likely produced an especially high-risk sample. The instrumentation prevented the assessment of participants' participation in drug distribution crimes as distinct from drug possession and/or use. As a cross-sectional study with lifetime arrests as the main variable of interest, causal associations among, for example, childhood victimization, club scene involvement, substance use history, and criminal activity cannot be made. Finally, the data presented rely on self-report, and some respondents may have refrained from reporting the full extent of socially undesirable behaviors.

The literature on criminality among club drug users is inconsistent, with some researchers describing these young adults as generally conformist except for their drug use (Measham et al. 2001; Sanders 2006) and at least one study noting elevated rates of self-reported illegal behaviors compared to the general population (Hammersley et al. 1999). The high prevalence of more severe property and violent crimes perpetrated by club scene participants in the present study would appear to be previously unreported in the literature, however. Furthermore, it was quite common for respondents to have been arrested for *multiple types* of crime, and over 30% of them had been arrested three or more times. Although it is possible that many of the reported criminal arrests occurred during adolescence and were unrelated to participants' current involvement in the club scene, almost half of study respondents also reported *recent* illegal activity other than drug use.

The participants in this study mirrored the ethnic makeup of Miami-Dade County, reported stable housing (with many still living at home with their parents), and were well-educated relative to the 63.9% public school graduation rate for the county during the study recruitment period (Florida Department of Education 2008). Given these indices of social stability and educational attainment, the extent of the substance abuse and victimization histories reported by the study participants were unanticipated by the investigators. These risk factors – including high levels of cocaine, marijuana, and sedative use; substance abuse treatment history; and high levels of victimization that occurred during childhood or adolescence – were strong predictors of multiple criminal arrests as noted among other populations (Gendreau et al. 1996). Moreover, co-morbidities of childhood victimization, mental health problems, sexual risk behaviors, and criminal justice involvement have been described among several substance using populations (Morrill et al. 2001; Surratt et al. 2005; Widom et al. 1999) and have more recently been observed as syndemic (co-occurring, mutually reinforcing epidemics of health and social problems) among marginalized groups (Mustanski et al. 2007; Singer 1994; Stall et al. 2003).

Given that the absence of traditional developmental markers of syndemics on variables that we measured (e.g., poverty, ethnic marginalization, low education; Singer 1994), and our lack of measurement of others (e.g., physical health problems, stigma), the extent to which the term *syndemic* applies to this population remains an important and intriguing question for future research. Nevertheless, the demonstrated strong interrelationship among social and health risk factors does suggest that many club scene participants may be more similar to other marginalized drug-involved populations than previously considered. No matter the connecting routes, young club drug users with multiple arrest histories appear to be in great need of outreach for mental health and substance abuse treatment services. This population also exhibits high levels of sexual risk, and should be targeted with appropriate HIV and sexually transmitted disease prevention interventions. The primary risks among the sample in this study were unprotected vaginal and anal intercourse, partner concurrency, and rapid partner change in a heterosexual context.

There are, however, major stumbling blocks to developing substance use and sexual risk reduction interventions for this population, including: (1) how sexual freedom and drug use are considered fashionable in the club culture, not problematic; and (2) how these young men and women tend to be suspicious of and disinterested in anything health authorities say about the risks of sex and drug use (Marsden et al. 2006; Whittingham et al. 2009). Past intervention efforts specific to club drug users have been found to be largely unsuccessful, including motivational interviewing (Marsden et al. 2006) and the dissemination of educational materials (Whittingham et al. 2009). Given this, new approaches are needed, including, perhaps, web-based peer- and/or self-administered approaches that do not rely on academic, governmental, or other expert-delivered messages.

The criminality of young adult participants in the Miami's expensive nightclub scene also raises important questions about whether the vast majority of drug-related crime is in fact concentrated in stereotypical poor, ethnic, urban neighborhoods (Office of National Drug Control Policy 2000; Robinson and Rengert 2006). One interpretation of the results is that young adult polydrug abusers in the club culture remain under the radar of criminal justice surveillance systems and researchers because they are perceived to be less vulnerable – and perhaps less threatening to society – than street-based criminals. Siegal (2009) describes an adult drug-using "under the radar group" that he refers to as "winners;" these individuals use recreational drugs and commit hundreds of crimes a year, however, they are rarely arrested and are able to maintain normal lifestyles without the involvement of the criminal justice system. Another interpretation of our findings would be that cities that rely on nightclub activity to support tourism and other economic activity tend to look the other way when it comes to drug activity and other social problems associated with the scene (Uriely and Belhassen 2006). However, in relation to this point, the extent that or mechanisms by which the criminal activity of club attendees may be related to clubbing remains unclear. Structural-level research across a variety of urban environments with significant nightclub activities, and well as studies focusing on the motivations for and locations of offences committed by club attendees, would help to answer these questions.

References

Anderson, T. L., Kavanaugh, P. R., Bachman, R., & Harrison, L. (2007). *Exploring the drugs crime connection within the electronic dance music and hip hop night scene* (NIJ Publication No. 219381). Retrieved from http://www.ncjrs.gov/pdffiles1/nij/grants/219381.pdf

Ball, J. C., Rosen, L., Flueck, J. A., & Nurco, D. N. (1982). The lifetime criminality of heroin addicts in the United States. *Journal of Drug Issues, 12*, 225–239.

Beck, J., & Rosenbaum, M. (1994). *Pursuit of ecstasy: The MDMA experience*. Albany: State University of New York Press.

Boyd, C. J., McCabe, S. E., & d'Arcy, H. (2003). Ecstasy use among college undergraduates: Gender, race and sexual identity. *Journal of Substance Abuse Treatment, 24*(3), 209–215.

Cooper, G. (2007). *Diary of a South Beach party girl*. New York: Simon Spotlight Entertainment.

Cottler, L. B., Womack, S. B., Compton, W. M., & Ben Abdallah, A. (2001). Ecstasy abuse and dependence among adolescents and young adults: Applicability and reliability of DSM-IV criteria. *Human Psychopharmacology, 16*, 599–606.

Dennis, M. L., Titus, J. C., White, M. K., Unsicker, J. I., & Hodgkins, D. (2002). *Global appraisal of individual needs – Initial (GAIN-I)*. Bloomington: Chestnut Health Systems.

Florida Department of Education. (2008). *Statistical brief: Florida public high school graduation rates 2006–07*. Retrieved from http://www.fldoe.org/eias/eiaspubs/pdf/gradrate.pdf

Freese, T. E., Miotto, K., & Reback, C. J. (2002). The effects and consequences of selected club drugs. *Journal of Substance Abuse Treatment, 23*(2), 151–156.

Fritz, J. (1999). *Rave culture: An insider's overview*. Victoria: SmallFry Press.

Gendreau, P., Little, T., & Goggin, C. (1996). A meta-analysis of the predictors of adult offender recidivism: What works! *Criminology, 34*, 575–607.

Goldstein, P. J. (1985). The drugs/violence nexus: A tripartite conceptual framework. *Journal of Drug Issues, 39*, 493–506.

Guzman, R. (1999, September 8). Miami Beach scrambles to rein in its nightclubs. *The Wall Street Journal*, Sect. F1.

Hammersley, R., Ditton, J., Smith, E., & Short, I. (1999). Patterns of ecstasy use by drug users. *The British Journal of Criminology, 39*(4), 625–647.

Heckathorn, D. D. (1997). Respondent-driven sampling: A new approach to the study of hidden populations. *Social Problems, 44*(2), 174–199.

Heckathorn, D. D. (2002). Respondent-driven sampling II: Deriving valid population estimates from chain-referral samples of hidden populations. *Social Problems, 49*(1), 11–34.

Inciardi, J. A. (2008). *The war on drugs IV*. Boston: Pearson/Allyn and Bacon.

Kelly, B. C., & Parsons, J. T. (2007). Prescription drug misuse among club drug using young adults. *American Journal of Drug and Alcohol Abuse, 33*(6), 875–884.

Kilborn, P. T. (2000, February 27). Miami Beach clubgoers creating new, unwanted image. *New York Times,* Sect. 1.22.

Klitzman, R. L., Greenberg, J. D., Pollack, L. M., & Dolezal, C. (2002). MDMA ('Ecstasy') use, and its association with high risk behaviors, mental health, and other factors among gay/bisexual men in New York City. *Drug and Alcohol Dependence, 66*(2), 115–125.

Krebs, C., & Steffey, D. (2005). Club drug use among delinquent youth. *Substance Use & Misuse, 40*, 1363–1379.

Kurtz, S. P. (2004). Prescription drug abuse among ecstasy users in Miami. In *Epidemiologic trends in drug abuse advance report: Prescription drug abuse, community epidemiology work group: June 2004* (NIH Publication No. 04-5363A). Rockville: National Institute of Health.

Kurtz, S. P., & Inciardi, J. A. (2003). Crystal meth, gay men, and circuit parties. *Law Enforcement Executive Forum, 3*(4), 97–114.

Kurtz, S. P., Inciardi, J. A., Surratt, H. L., & Cottler, L. (2005). Prescription drug abuse among ecstasy users in Miami. *Journal of Addictive Diseases, 24*(4), 1–16.

Marr, M. (2004, October 8). Miami club mines glam from downtown's grit. *Miami Herald*, Sect. 27G.

Marsden, J., Stillwell, G., Barlow, H., Boys, A., Taylor, C., Hunt, N., & Farrell, M. (2006). An evaluation of a brief motivational intervention among young ecstasy and cocaine users: No effect on substance and alcohol use outcomes. *Addiction, 101*, 1014–1026.

Mattison, A. M., Ross, M. W., Wolfson, T., & Franklin, D. (2001). Circuit party attendance, club drug use, and unsafe sex in gay men. *Journal of Substance Abuse, 13*, 119–126.

McCardle, K., Luebbers, S., Carter, J. D., Croft, R. J., & Stough, C. (2004). Chronic MDMA (ecstasy) use, cognition and mood. *Psychopharmacology, 173*, 434–439.

Measham, F., Aldridge, J., & Parker, H. (2001). *Dancing on drugs: Risk, health and hedonism in the British club scene*. London: Free Association Books.

Mitcheson, L., McCambridge, J., Byrne, A., Hunt, N., & Winstock, A. (2008). Sexual health risk among dance drug users: Cross-sectional comparisons with nationally representative data. *International Journal of Drug Policy, 19*, 304–310.

Morrill, A. C., Kasten, L., Urato, M., & Larson, M. J. (2001). Abuse, addiction, and depression as pathways to sexual risk in women and men with a history of substance abuse. *Journal of Substance Abuse, 13*(1–2), 169–184.

Mustanski, B., Garofalo, R., Herrick, A., & Donenberg, G. (2007). Psychosocial health problems increase risk for HIV among urban young men who have sex with men: Preliminary evidence of a syndemic in need of attention. *Annals of Behavioral Medicine, 34*(1), 37–45.

Office of National Drug Control Policy. (2000). *Fact sheet: Drug related crime*. Washington, DC: Executive Office of the President.

Owen, F. (2003). *Clubland: The fabulous rise and murderous fall of club culture*. New York: St. Martin's Press.

Parrott, A. C., Milani, R. M., Parmar, R., & Turner, J. J. D. (2001). Recreational ecstasy/MDMA and other drug users from the UK and Italy: Psychiatric symptoms and psychobiological problems. *Psychopharmacology, 159*, 77–82.

Pedersen, W., & Skrondal, A. (1999). Ecstasy and new patterns of drug use: A normal population study. *Addiction, 94*(11), 1695–1706.

Perrone, D. (2009). *The high life: Club kids, harm and drug policy*. Monsey: Criminal Justice Press.
Reynolds, S. (1998). *Generation ecstasy: Into the world of techno and rave culture*. Boston: Little, Brown and Company.
Robinson, J. B., & Rengert, G. F. (2006). Illegal drug markets: The geographic perspective and crime propensity. *Western Criminology Review, 7*, 20–32.
Sanders, B. (2006). Young people, clubs and drugs. In B. Sanders (Ed.), *Drugs clubs and young people: Sociological and public health perspectives*. Aldershot: Ashgate.
Schwartz, N. (2003, November 6). Group warns of resurgence in drug use: Region's health, police officials form task force. *Sun-Sentinel*, Sect. 1B.
Semple, S. J., Patterson, T. L., & Grant, I. (2002). Motivations associated with methamphetamine use among HIV+men who have sex with men. *Journal of Substance Abuse Treatment, 22*(3), 149–156.
Shister, N. (1999, November 22). Club chaos: Understanding the South Beach effect. *Boston Review*. Retrieved from http://bostonreview.net/BR24.2/shister.html
Siegal, L. J. (2009). *Criminology*. Belmont: Thomson Higher Education.
Silcott, M. (1999). *Rave America: New school dancescapes*. Toronto: ECW Press.
Singer, M. (1994). AIDS and the health crisis of the U.S. urban poor: The perspective of critical medical anthropology. *Social Science and Medicine, 39*(7), 931–948.
St. James, J. (2003). *Party monster: A fabulous but true tale of murder in clubland*. New York: Simon & Schuster.
Stall, R., Mills, T. C., Williamson, J., Hart, T., Greenwood, G., Paul, J., Pollack, L., Binson, D., Osmond, D., & Catania, J. A. (2003). Association of co-occurring psychosocial health problems and increased vulnerability to HIV/AIDS among urban men who have sex with men. *American Journal of Public Health, 93*(6), 939–942.
Surratt, H. L., Kurtz, S. P., Weaver, J. C., & Inciardi, J. A. (2005). The connections of mental health problems, violent life experiences, and the social milieu of the "stroll" with the HIV risk behaviors of female street sex workers. *Journal of Psychology and Human Sexuality, 17*(1/2), 23–44.
Thornton, S. (1996). *Club cultures: Music, media and subcultural capital*. Hanover: University Press of New England.
United States Census Bureau. (2009). *Census state and county quickfacts, Miami-Dade County, FL*. Retrieved from http://quickfacts.census.gov/qfd/states/12/12086.html
Uriely, N., & Belhassen, Y. (2006). Drugs and risk-taking in tourism. *Annals of Tourism Research, 33*, 339–359.
von Sydow, K., Lieb, R., Pfister, H., Höfler, M., & Wittchen, H. U. (2002). Use, abuse and dependence of ecstasy and related drugs in adolescents and young adults – A transient phenomenon? Results from a longitudinal community study. *Drug and Alcohol Dependence, 66*(2), 147–159.
Whittingham, J. R. D., Ruiter, R. A. C., Bolier, L., Lemmers, L., Van Hasset, N., & Kok, G. (2009). Avoiding counterproductive results: An experimental pretest of a harm reduction intervention on attitude toward party drugs among users and nonusers. *Substance Use & Misuse, 44*, 532–547.
Widom, C. S., Weiler, B. L., & Cottler, L. B. (1999). Childhood victimization and drug abuse: A comparison of prospective and retrospective findings. *Journal of Consulting and Clinical Psychology, 67*(6), 867–880.

Part III
Crime, Space and Health

Chapter 9
Spatial Models of the Growth and Spread of Methamphetamine Abuse in California

Paul J. Gruenewald, William R. Ponicki, Lillian G. Remer, Fred W. Johnson, Lance A. Waller, Dennis M. Gorman, and Li Zhu

Abstract *This chapter examines the serious and growing public health problems related to methamphetamine abuse in the United States. It combines economic and mathematical epidemiological approaches to explaining the spread of drug abuse, treating methamphetamine use as a chronic relapsing disease that spreads through social contacts with the active facilitation of illegal drug markets. These models suggest that methamphetamine problems may exhibit typical disease characteristics such as spatial clustering and correlated growth, as would be consistent with the frequent references to methamphetamine as an epidemic. These models were tested using historical data on methamphetamine-related arrests and hospital discharges in California between 1980 and 2006. Statewide data suggest that both problem indicators grew exponentially during this period except for temporary supply reductions following the enactment of federal restrictions on the precursor chemicals used to*

Research for and preparation of this chapter was supported by National Institute on Drug Abuse Research Grant No. R21 DA024341 to Dr. Gruenewald and National Institute on Alcohol Abuse and Alcoholism Research Grant No. R21 AA016632 to Dr. Waller.

P.J. Gruenewald, Ph.D. (✉) • W.R. Ponicki, M.A.
• L.G. Remer, M.A., G.I.S.P. • F.W. Johnson, Ph.D.
Prevention Research Center, Pacific Institute for Research and Evaluation,
1995 University Ave., Suite 450, Berkeley, CA, USA
e-mail: paul@prev.org

L.A. Waller, Ph.D.
Department of Biostatistics and Bioinformatics, Rollins School of Public Health, Emory University, Atlanta, GA, USA

D.M. Gorman, Ph.D.
Department of Epidemiology & Biostatistics, Texas A&M Health Science Center School of Rural Public Health, College Station, TX, USA

L. Zhu, Ph.D.
Statistics Methodology and Applications Branch, Division of Cancer Control and Population Sciences, National Cancer Institute, National Institutes of Health, Bethesda, MD, USA

B. Sanders et al. (eds.), *Crime, HIV and Health: Intersections of Criminal Justice and Public Health Concerns*, DOI 10.1007/978-90-481-8921-2_9,

manufacture methamphetamine. The spatial spread of methamphetamine abuse was investigated using Bayesian space-time models of arrest counts in 330 California cities. These analyses found that cities varied considerably in both their underlying levels of amphetamine-related arrests and their growth rates over time. These growth rates were strongly correlated between nearby cities, as predicted by a disease approach in which a methamphetamine 'infection' spreads from person to person. These analyses suggested that methamphetamine growth was highest in rural northern and southern California between 1980 and 1989, then shifted to the central valley areas during the early 1990s before moving more into urban areas after 1997.

Methamphetamine abuse is a serious public health problem in the United States. The number of methamphetamine treatment episodes in the United States increased from 41,045 to 149,215 incidents per year from 1996 through 2006, a 364% increase during this time (Substance Abuse and Mental Health Services Administration [SAMHSA] 2008). Methamphetamine use among arrestees has been shown to be much greater in western cities (30–37% across Honolulu, San Jose, San Diego, and Sacramento) than eastern ones (1% or less across Washington, D.C., New York City, and Philadelphia; Yacoubian 2007). Moreover, one national study noted that methamphetamine use was 5.4 times higher in the west than in the northeast United States (Iritani et al. 2007). Law enforcement reporting to the National Drug Intelligence Center [NDIC] (2008) identifies methamphetamine production, availability, and use as the greatest drug threat throughout the western United States, with 87% of reports listing it as the top threat among five Pacific states (Washington, Oregon, Idaho, California, and Nevada). The typical methamphetamine user has been characterized as young, white, and male, often unemployed, impoverished, and living in his own residence (Iritani et al. 2007; Yacoubian 2007). Considering these patterns of growth, many researchers and public health advocates have concluded that the United States is in the early stages of a large-scale methamphetamine epidemic that is slowly spreading throughout the country (Iritani et al. 2007; Rawson et al. 2004).

Within California, incidence rates of hospital discharges for amphetamine or methamphetamine abuse increased 18-fold from 1983 to 2005 with a comparable 5-fold increase in rates of dependence (Gruenewald et al. 2010).[1] Figure 9.1 shows this dramatic increase and identifies the dates of four major federal laws restricting sales and distribution of bulk precursors (11/89), ephedrine products (8/95 and 10/96), and over the counter sales of pseudoephedrine products (10/97) used to prepare methamphetamine. Cunningham and Liu (2003) demonstrated that each of these restrictions significantly and substantively inhibited growth in the prevalence of methamphetamine abuse admissions per year. However, breaking the epidemic

[1] California hospital discharge data diagnostic codes for amphetamine and other psychostimulant dependence (ICD9-CM 304.4) or amphetamine and related acting sympathomimetic abuse (ICD9-CM 305.7).

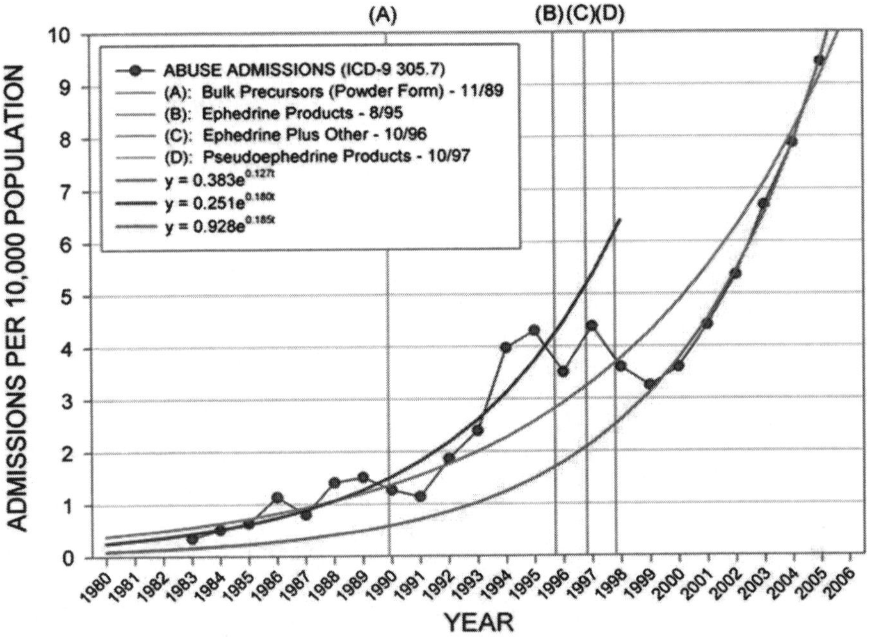

Fig. 9.1 Methamphetamine hospital discharges (methamphetamine, amphetamine and other psychostimulant abuse are inseparable in hospital discharge data, but, per TEDS data (see Table 2.1a of SAMHSA 2008), the proportion of cases which represent Methamphetamine abuse has increased from 77.5% in 1996 to 95.5% in 2006)

down into two basic phases, an early phase before 1997 and a late phase after 1998, early and late exponential growth of about 18% per year and overall growth of about 13% per year are apparent. Evidently, precursor laws have slowed but not stopped the growth of methamphetamine abuse in California.

Researchers have used two basic approaches to conceptualize the growth and spread of drug abuse. One is to examine the drug market in detail, considering the various ways in which production, distribution and sales meet demand and result in drug problems (Groff and Birks 2008). In this economic approach, the growth of a drug market is conceptualized in the same way as any emerging market for any commodity, but with the important caveat that market transactions are illegal (Caulkins 2007). The second approach is to conceptualize drug abuse as a social condition which spreads through populations like other socially transmitted problems through social contacts among users promoted by the activities of drug markets (Ditton and Frischer 2001). In this epidemiologic approach, the abuse of a particular drug may come to be labeled as 'epidemic,' connoting features associated with the dynamics of infectious disease: greater than desired prevalence, rapid (often exponential) growth, contagious spread through at risk populations, and facilitation by active disease agents.

This paper treats methamphetamine abuse as a chronic relapsing disease that spreads through social contacts with the active facilitation of illegal drug markets. It asks whether historical data on methamphetamine problems exhibit geographic signatures associated with disease spread like spatial clustering and correlated growth. It then asks how these approaches can produce better testable hypotheses about the future course of what is often considered to be a methamphetamine epidemic.

9.1 Methamphetamine Abuse in the United States

Much more powerful than its sister drug amphetamine, methamphetamine is a highly addictive stimulant that has similar but more profound effects on the user. Methamphetamine can be smoked, snorted, injected, or orally ingested. Use results in increased activity, talkativeness, decreased appetite, and an increased sense of well-being (Wyatt and Ziedonis 1998). When smoked, methamphetamine leads to a long lasting high, remains in the body for quite some time (more than 12 h), and dramatically affects the dopamine reward system (Sulzer et al. 2005; Urbina and Jones 2004). Use of methamphetamine can lead to cardiovascular problems, including rapid heart rate, irregular heartbeat, and increased blood pressure. Hyperthermia and convulsions are common consequences of an overdose as are cardiomyopathies among methamphetamine injectors (Kaye et al. 2008). Long-term abuse often leads to addiction (compulsive drug seeking), and chronic users experience anxiety, confusion, insomnia, mood disturbances, memory loss, and are prone to engage in violent behavior (National Institute on Drug Abuse [NIDA] 2006). Cognitive deficits in the areas of learning, executive function, memory, processing speed, visuoconstruction, and language are associated with continued use (Scott et al. 2007). Psychotic symptoms may include paranoia, visual and auditory hallucinations/delusions, and repetitive motor activity. Long-term use is associated with structural and functional changes in the brain related to emotion and memory (NIDA 2006). Substantial weight loss, malnutrition, and severe dental problems are characteristic of long-term use (NIDA 2006). Methamphetamine abuse is associated with other behavioral and psychological problems including risky sexual behavior, depression, child abuse and neglect (Cheng et al. 2010; Hohman et al. 2004; Sommers et al. 2006).

Methamphetamine is a synthetic drug that is relatively inexpensive and easy to produce, although the production process is somewhat dangerous (Lu and Burnum 2008). The primary precursor for methamphetamine is ephedrine, which can be extracted from legal medications containing ephedrine or pseudoephedrine. Chemical agents used in the production of methamphetamine include a number of flammable and potentially explosive ingredients (e.g., anhydrous ammonia from fertilizer, camp fuel, starting fluid, methanol, and red phosphorous). 'Cooking' large amounts of methamphetamine from these ingredients is a smelly and hazardous process and for these reasons methamphetamine labs are usually located in rural areas far from residential housing (Illinois Attorney General 2010). The primary limiting factor to production is the availability of ephedrine or pseudoephedrine, access to which is now curtailed by a number of 'precursor' laws. During the 1980s and into the 1990s, domestic methamphetamine labs produced large quantities for sale in the western United States. As demand for the drug grew and precursor laws were implemented, domestic production slumped and was largely taken over by Mexican drug cartels (NDIC 2009). While small-scale domestic production continues, Mexican drug cartels dominate the market, import large quantities of precursors from foreign sources through ports in the United States and Mexico, 'cook' the ingredients in 'super labs,' and distribute methamphetamine for sale (NDIC 2008). Recent restrictions on domestic sales of pseudoephedrine have led local producers to encourage 'smurfing', the purchase of many small amounts of pseudoephedrine products for use by domestic producers (NDIC 2009).

9.2 An Economic Approach to Understanding Drug Markets

Aside from the obvious difference in the legality of the drugs involved, legal alcohol markets and illegal drug markets are similar in many respects. Demand for a drug is met through the creation of a market: Market contracts must be maintained and enforced along the supply chain (i.e., among retailers, wholesalers, importers, and producers), retailers must market the drug to consumers, and sometimes use results in harmful outcomes. The primary difference is that most illegal drug market activities are hidden from view; production, importing, distribution, and sales tend to rely upon informal social networks and informal contracts sometimes enforced through violent means (Eck 1995; LaScala et al. 2005). As outlined in Fig. 9.2, the crucial differences between legal and illegal drug markets are related to the roles social networks and enforcement play in each. Alcohol markets are public, rely upon public contracts and legal agreements to make the market, and enforcement activities are

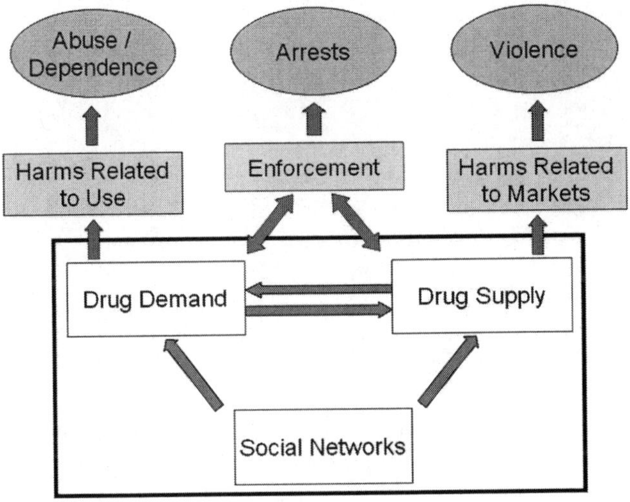

Fig. 9.2 Indicators of drug supply and demand

targeted at problems related to sales, distribution, and use. Illegal drug markets, on the other hand, are rarely public, rely upon social contacts and informal agreements to make the market, and enforcement is directed at both supply and demand since sales, distribution, use, and production are all illegal (Eck 1995). Consequently, harms related to drug use are distributed across these market activities (Holder and Treno 2005).

This description of the basic economics of illegal drug markets provides some valuable guidance to understanding outbreaks of drug abuse. Consider the emerging crack cocaine market of the 1980s in the United States. It can be argued that with continued growth in the number of users, the size of these markets eventually reached a critical level at which they tipped into more efficient and resilient forms. These larger markets achieved economies of scale denied to smaller markets, managed the costs and risks of production and distribution more efficiently, and led to lower prices and greater use. The result was a rapid expansion of the crack cocaine market that continued until demand was met, the negative consequences of competition among distributors and retailers limited sales, and enforcement activities hampered further growth (Caulkins 2007).

An economic approach to understanding drug markets can also provide guidance to the related roles of prevention, enforcement, and treatment efforts. In the early stages of a developing drug market, prevention and enforcement can constrain further growth (see Rigg et al. 2009). Prevention will be effective to the extent that it can limit market entry. Enforcement can be effective in removing retailers and distributors from the market or by generally increasing the costs of operation. But once a critical pool of users is established, treatment efforts alone lose effectiveness. Treatment entries often take place some 5–10 years later in the life cycle of addiction, long after the users have participated in the market and supported continued market growth for some time (Caulkins 2007). Data collected from outpatient treatment programs in the western United States and Hawaii suggest that the time between first methamphetamine use and appearance in treatment is about 7.5 years (Rawson et al. 2004).

Although this approach can provide a better understanding of the dynamics that underlie drug markets, it offers few new insights into what might work in prevention, enforcement, and treatment to deflect a growing wave of abuse. Prevention and enforcement in the early stages of market growth seem most valuable. Treatment may also be effective if early stage case finding were made very efficient. But, considering the growing drug market as an epidemic, perhaps the central questions that should be asked are: "Where will an illegal drug market emerge?"; and "How can prevention, enforcement, and treatment efforts be focused to best stave off its emergence?"

9.3 Mathematical Epidemiological Approaches

A complementary approach to understanding drug epidemics that provides a way to answer these questions treats emerging drug markets as epidemics that can be theoretically analyzed using classic disease models from mathematical epidemiology

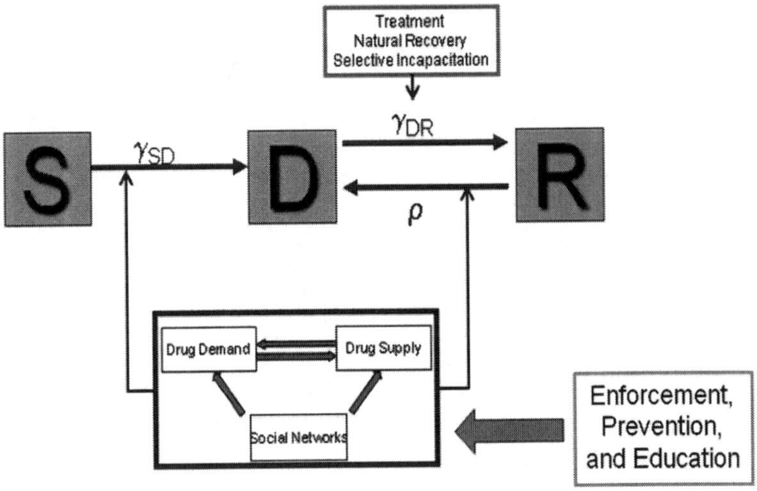

Fig. 9.3 Basic epidemiological model of a drug epidemic (*S* susceptible, *D* drug user, *R* recovered)

(Anderson and May 1991; Ditton and Frischer 2001; Hollingsworth 2009; Hunt and Chambers 1976; Rossi 2001). The core dynamics of these models are not supply–demand relationships in a marketplace, but rather contagious disease processes in social groups that convert susceptible individuals into drug users and help explain the growth of abuse over space and time. These models focus on the contagious spread of drug abuse, the recruitment of new users by current users, and rates of relapse and recovery as core features of drug epidemics. As shown in Fig. 9.3, the drug market continues to play an essential role in these models.

Common to all models of drug epidemics is some representation of the contagious dynamics of drug use, represented in the figure by the arrows linking populations of those persons liable to use drugs, that is, susceptibles (S), to drug users (D), and recovered users (R). Coefficients labeling the arrows identify parameters that must be estimated to get a basic idea of the disease dynamics involved. The arrow leading from S to D represents the rate at which susceptibles are converted to drug use over time. The arrow leading from D to R represents the rate at which drug users recover. The arrow leading back from R to D represents the rate of relapse. Influencing recovery, drug users may enter treatment, naturally recover, or be institutionalized under conditions in which use is not possible (i.e., selective incapacitation). Encouraging both the initiation of use and relapse among former users, illegal drug markets are able to maintain use despite legal sanctions. As Sanchez et al. (2007) found in relation to alcohol use, if relapse is substantial, as is often the case after drug treatment, it will be very difficult to extinguish an outbreak using treatment alone. Prevention, education, and enforcement efforts are essential to reduce initiation and relapse.

As Fig. 9.3 indicates, economic and epidemiologic approaches to understanding the population dynamics of drug abuse can be tightly integrated. However, the two approaches emphasize different aspects of this system and enable different questions about drug epidemics to be asked. Thus, epidemiologic approaches suggest that markets for illegal drugs are one component of several that affect abuse dynamics and, even in the absence of further knowledge about these markets, other aspects of the disease process may be profitably understood. Just as it has been possible to begin to understand other epidemics without a comprehensive understanding of the underlying biology (e.g. HIV; Anderson and May 1991), understanding drug epidemics without a comprehensive model of their market economics is also possible. Well-specified mathematical models of drug epidemics can provide analysts and statisticians with explicit guidance for seeking crucial parameters that affect epidemic growth, reproduction numbers, effective reproduction numbers, case fatality rates, and generation times (Hollingsworth 2009). A careful combination of data, methods, and mathematical models can lead to a much more detailed understanding of disease dynamics and the sources of disease outbreaks, whether HIV (Cassels et al. 2008), Severe Acute Respiratory Syndrome (Hsieh and Cheng 2006), Leishmaniasis (Mubayi et al. 2010), or influenza (Viboud et al. 2006). Well-specified models may also lead to simplified procedures that can be applied to establish model parameters using limited data (Wallinga and Teunis 2004) and inform back calculations that can be used to reconstruct the epidemic course (Rava et al. 2001).

Quantitative theoretical models of contagious processes can also provide guidance to statistical assessments of spatial data relevant to disease outbreaks. For example, Bjornstad et al. (2002), Grenfell et al. (2001, 2002) used estimates of the characteristic time scale of measles infections and population densities of at-risk populations to inform their analyses of the spatial etiology of these epidemics across British cities. Both spatial waves and hierarchical patterns of spread between cities were shown to characterize these epidemics and they were able to identify characteristic spatial scales and critical population sizes that enabled and sustained measles outbreaks (see also Viboud et al. 2006). Other examples include the use of disease models to study the spatial spread of rabies infections across topographically complex landscapes (Smith et al. 2002) and assess spatial barriers to disease spread (Wheeler and Waller 2008). Finally, epidemiologic models can suggest alternative conceptualizations of disease processes that may provide new insights into drug epidemics. Drug markets may be viewed as invasive parasites that harvest capital from drug users, reservoirs of potential abusers may be modeled as core groups observed in specific environments (e.g., ecstasy and raves, Song et al. 2006), and social networks may play heterogeneous roles in drug abuse dynamics (e.g., HIV, Curtis et al. 1995; binge drinking among youth, Cintron-Arias et al. 2009).

9.4 Spatial Epidemiology and Methamphetamine Abuse

Despite the theoretical possibilities that appear when contemplating these approaches, validation and testing of any proposed model will encounter the same empirical problem: How can the dynamics of a process whose components are largely hidden from view be studied? Detailed ethnographic surveys of drug markets and drug using groups as well as survey studies of general populations and clinical sub-populations of users would appear to satisfy much of this concern (e.g., Cheng et al. 2010; Curtis et al. 1995). Both data gathering strategies collect information directly from participants in the market and drug using communities, which will continue to provide much useful information about emerging drug problems in the future. But ethnographic studies are by their nature too limited in scope and survey studies too limited in depth to capture the spatial heterogeneity of changing patterns of drug abuse – a key feature to identify in the emergence of drug problems.

Alternatives to these empirical studies have emerged over the past two decades as researchers have turned to secondary data to understand the broad geographic outlines of public health problems, ascertaining where these problems emerge, how they spread, and where hot spots for problems might be found (Rengert et al. 2005; Weisburd and Mazerolle 2000). The growing availability of computerized databases housing extensive data on the time, locations, and types of problems related to illegal drugs provides a new opportunity for researchers to look into the growth of drug problems. The concurrent development of statistical techniques to analyze these data (Lipton et al. 2009) and computational engines for theoretically modeling these outcomes (Liu and Eck 2008) further advances interests in these approaches and highlights a new wave in drug research, spatial models of drug markets, drug crime, and drug problems. Thus, criminologists attempt to identify locations of drug markets in relation to other crime across community neighborhoods (Hunt et al. 2008; Rengert et al. 2005; Weisburd and Mazerolle 2000). Community epidemiologists attempt to understand relationships between environmental features of communities (e.g., alcohol outlets) and problem outcomes, such as drug crimes, accidents, and injuries (Banerjee et al. 2008). Although limited by the difficult issues involved in establishing the reliability and validity of specific indices of drug epidemics (Greene and McClintock 1985; Mounteney et al. 2010), results from studies of secondary data sources can be coordinated with other investigations to validate findings. And, with problems varying by more than an order of magnitude across the areas under investigation, the scale of the problems observed more than justifies the extensive work required to statistically analyze and model drug outcomes (see Fig. 9.5).

A good example is provided through an examination of the emergence of the methamphetamine epidemic over the past 30 years. As illustrated in Fig. 9.4, data available for California since 1980 indicate a dramatic increase in arrests for sales, possession and use of 'dangerous drugs' very similar to that shown for hospital discharges related to methamphetamine abuse and dependence shown in Fig. 9.1.[2] However, arrests for methamphetamine 'manufacturing' also rose quickly through the 1990s as domestic production increased, then leveled off, and declined thereafter (Cunningham and Liu 2005). This pattern reflects the impacts of methamphetamine

[2] The code for 'dangerous drugs' corresponds to felony possession, transport or selling of methamphetamine, amphetamine, hallucinogens, and related drugs, and specifically does not include narcotics, opiates, marijuana, and 'other drugs.' Estimated from recent city level data, more than 90% of 'dangerous drug' arrests are exclusively related to methamphetamine. These codes do not include manufacturing or possession of precursor chemicals, which are separately detailed under 'manufacturing' and again strongly dominated by arrests related to methamphetamine.

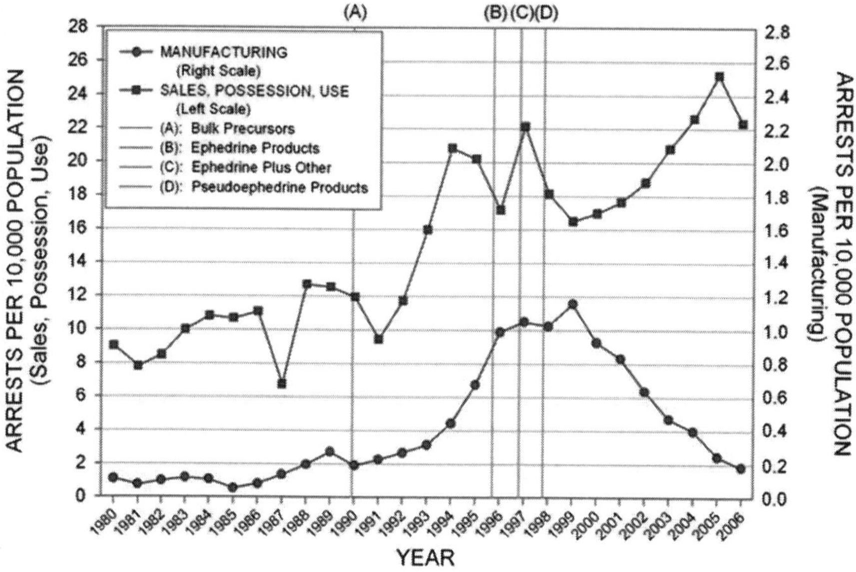

Fig. 9.4 Methamphetamine related arrests

precursor laws, especially those in the 1990s, as they reduced the availability of ephedrine and pseudoephedrine, severely limited domestic production, and led to a shift in production and distribution toward Mexican drug cartels. Importantly, looking at both Figs. 9.1 and 9.4, arrests *and* hospital discharges were responsive to these laws. But the global picture remained the same: Increasing problems temporarily delayed by restraints on production.

Figures 9.5 and 9.6 provide yet more detail about the methamphetamine epidemic in California during this time. Figure 9.5 presents rates of methamphetamine hospital discharges for abuse and dependence per 10,000 people between 1995 and 2005 for zip code areas of the state. The figure shows both the dramatic increases seen in admissions and the spatially heterogeneous patterns of these changes, with rates of admissions growing very rapidly in some areas and slowly or not at all in others. Figure 9.6 presents rates of arrest from 1980 to 2006 for 330 cities in California. Again, dramatic increases are seen across the state with rates in some cities growing much more rapidly than others.

9.5 Bayesian Spatial Disease Models

Although these data provide valuable resources for describing the growth of methamphetamine abuse in California, without further analysis they reveal nothing about the underlying population dynamics of these problems. The growth rates of methamphetamine problems appear to be exponential (Fig. 9.1), but other classic features of

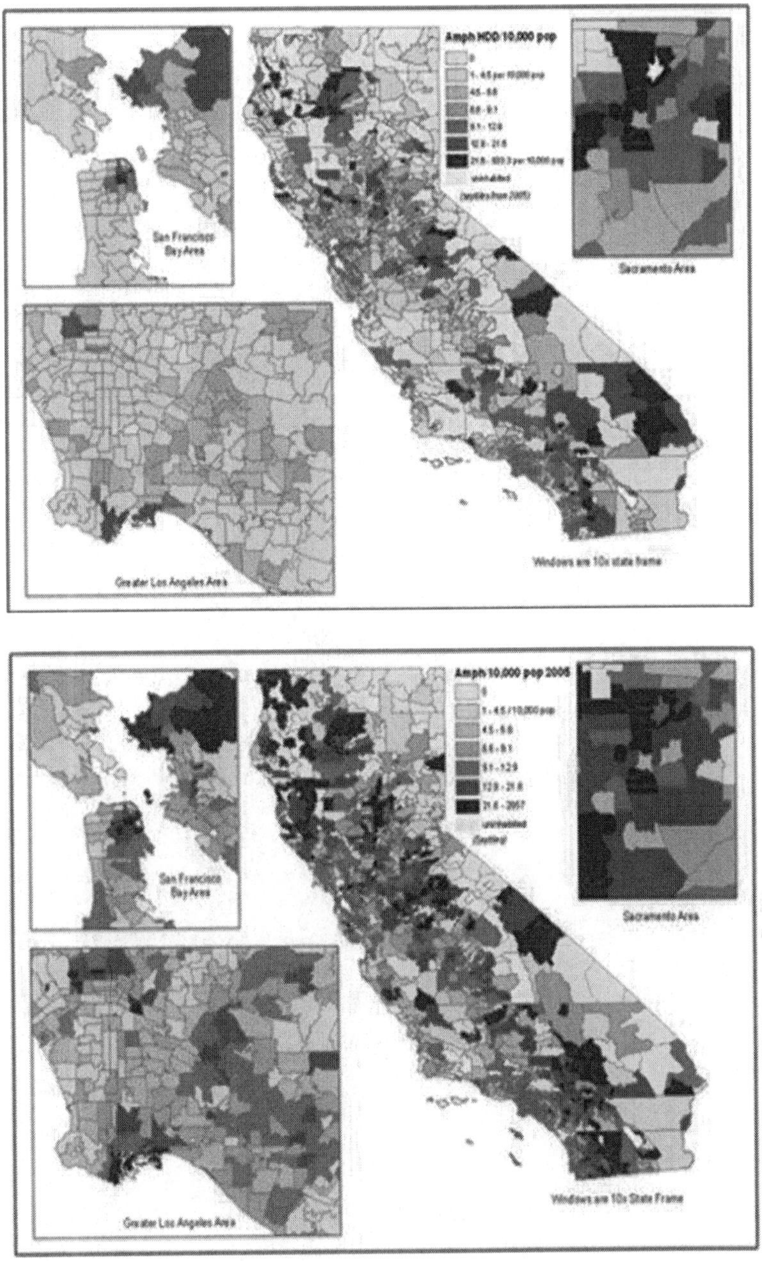

Fig. 9.5 Growth of methamphetamine hospital discharges in California 1995–2005

epidemics may not apply, such as contagious spread through contacts among infected hosts and heterogeneities in population risks for 'infection'. At a population level, epidemic characteristics can be identified in the growth of methamphetamine problems

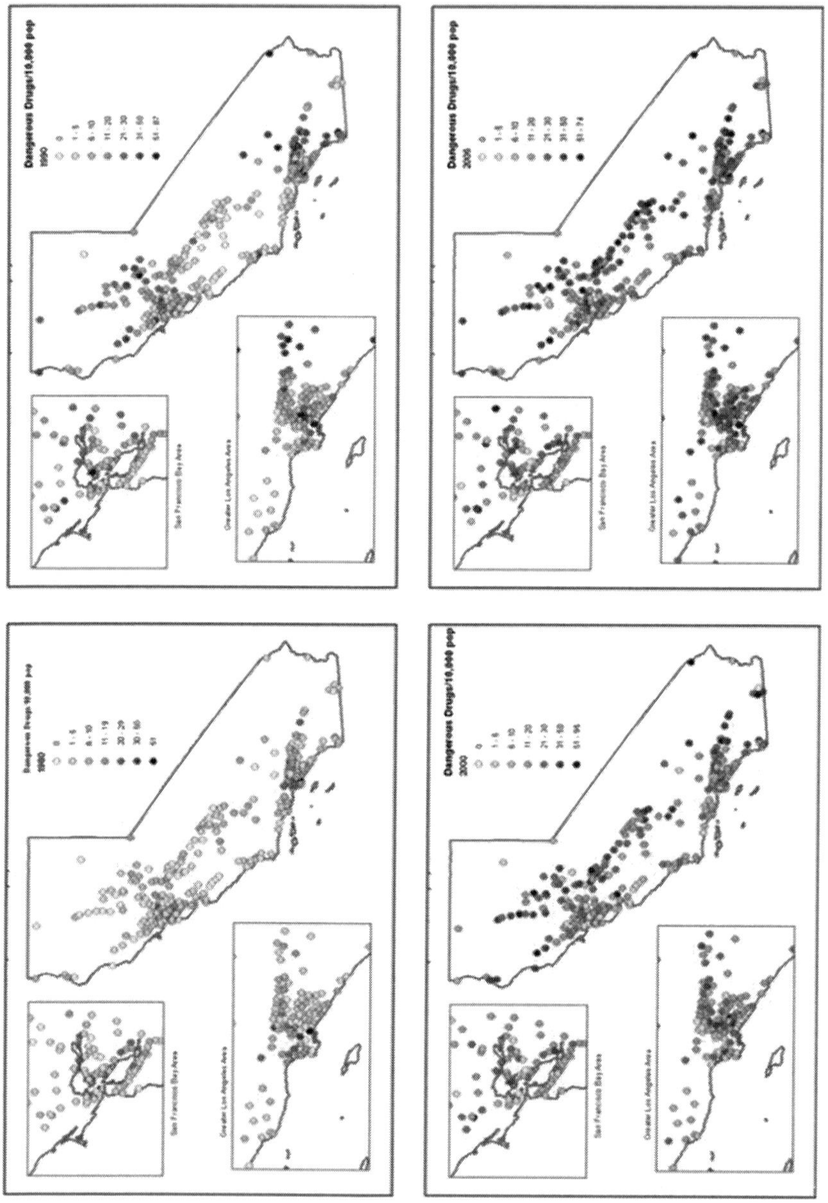

Fig. 9.6 Growth of amphetamine related arrests in 330 California cities, 1980–2006

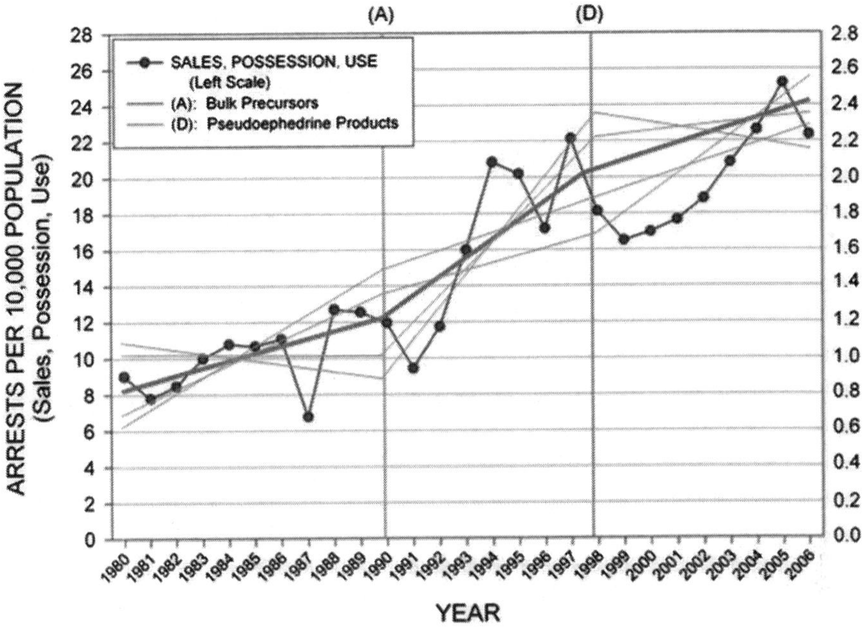

Fig. 9.7 A simplified model of epidemic growth (Piecewise Bayesian nonlinear varying parameter model)

through the application of spatial statistical models that: (1) Measure the correlated growth in problems between areas (i.e., spatial waves of 'infection') that suggests contagion; and (2) assess rates of problem growth in response to population 'frailties' (those conditions that place populations at risk for greater problems).

As a demonstration of how one statistical approach can inform understanding of the growth of methamphetamine problems in the state, Figs. 9.7, 9.8, and 9.9 present the results of a Bayesian spatial disease model of methamphetamine ('dangerous drug') arrests across 330 cities from 1980 to 2006, the raw rates for which are presented in Fig. 9.6. This was a spatial Poisson model in which the expected number of arrests in each city was assumed to be a function of population size. Different rates of growth in arrests over years, and in relation to other variables in the model, were then assessed relative to these expectations. The analysis divided the full time period into three phases: An early phase of relatively slow growth (1980–1989); a middle phase during which growth appeared to continue more rapidly (1989–1997); and a late phase during which rates of growth appeared to decrease once again (see Fig. 9.7; the specific breaks were defined by precursor laws that took effect in the middle of years 1989 and 1997). The model assumed linear growth within each of these periods (the dark lines in the figure), but included random effects for each city (spatial heterogeneity), and assumed that growth in each period would be correlated between cities (spatial correlation). Thus, each city could exhibit a unique rate of growth in each time period (the light lines in Fig. 9.7), but each rate could also be correlated among nearby cities.

(330 cities x 27 years = 8,910)

	Variable:	Coefficient:	95% Credible Interval:
	Constant (α)	-1.6090	-1.6410 to -1.5740
	Precursor Laws		
Law Effects	Law 1 (1990)	-0.3682	-0.3932 to -0.3409
Law Effects	Law 2 (1995)	-0.5584	-0.5807 to -0.5361
Law Effects	Law 3 (1997)	-0.3295	-0.3418 to -0.3172
	Time Trends:		
	Time (1980-89, β_1)	0.0683	0.0638 to 0.0721
	Time (1990-97, β_2)	0.1805	0.1741 to 0.1870
	Time (1998-06, β_3)	-0.1991	-0.2043 to -0.1942
	Spatial Random Effects:		
Random Effects	Units, $\sigma^2(v)$	2.1110	1.9400 to 2.3000
Random Effects	Time (1980-89), $\sigma^2(u)$	0.2450	0.2256 to 0.2663
Random Effects	Time (1990-97), $\sigma^2(\delta_1)$	0.3718	0.3424 to 0.4040
Random Effects	Time (1998-06), $\sigma^2(\delta_2)$	0.3225	0.2967 to 0.3510

Fig. 9.8 Piecewise Bayesian varying parameter model

An assumption was made that contagion would appear as spatial correlations in rates of growth between adjacent places. Spatial correlations between units were assessed using a Gaussian conditional autoregressive (CAR) model with a binary connection matrix representing links between nearby cities (determined by tessellations constructed around city centroids).[3] The model included effects related to precursor laws in 1989, 1995, and 1997 (the 1996 law was nearly contemporaneous with those in the previous and following years and so dropped). Uninformative low precision priors were assumed for all parameters of the model.

The results of this analysis, presented along with 95% credible intervals for the parameters, are presented in Fig. 9.8. As indicated, the effects of each precursor law were uniformly negative with tight credible intervals. The precursor laws were on average potent in reducing arrests, with each reducing relative risks of arrest by factors of 0.692, 0.572, and 0.719 respectively. The linear time trends were also very efficiently estimated and reflect particularly rapid growth in arrests in the second period. The coefficients for the time trends were cumulative, so the effect in the first phase was $b=0.0683$, the cumulative effect in the second phase was $b=0.0683+0.1805=0.2488$, and the cumulative effect in the third phase was $b=0.0683+0.1805–0.1991=0.0497$. The coefficients themselves refer to the log relative risks of arrest per year, so corresponding increases in relative risks were 1.071, 1.282 and 1.051. Of greatest interest

[3] Specifically, the centroid of each city was located within California and tessellations constructed around each centroid. Cities that shared a common tessellated boundary were considered as connected one to the other.

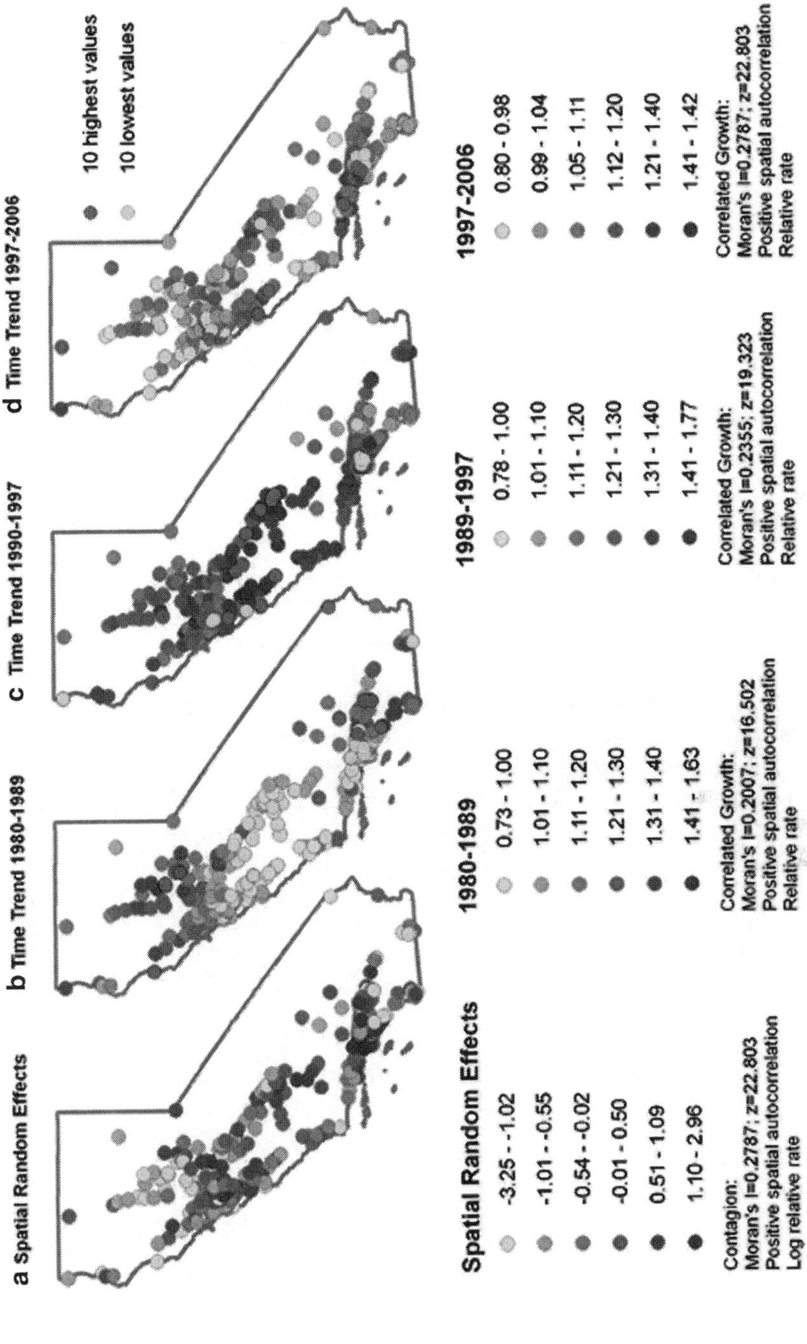

Fig. 9.9 Methamphetamine arrests in 330 CA cities

in the current analyses are effects related to the CAR effect between cities and spatial correlated growth, represented by the last four parameters in the table. The first of these represents the standard deviation of the variance component explained by aggregate CAR among units. The last three lines represent the standard deviations of variance components explaining spatial correlated growth in rates of arrests between cities. Note that all four variance components were substantial.

Variance components related to the conditional autoregressive terms in the model cannot be interpreted other than graphically. For this purpose, Fig. 9.9 presents posterior log relative rates centered on the average rate of arrest across all time periods (the first CAR term, Fig. 9.9a), and relative rates of growth for the different periods of time for all cities (the next three CAR terms, Fig. 9.9b, c, d) centered on the average growth rates in each phase of the epidemic. In each figure, large positive rates are in dark blue and low negative rates are in light blue. Concentrations of dark or light blue reflect spatial autocorrelations among nearby units. At the bottom of each figure the Moran's I coefficient is presented, which measures the extent of spatial autocorrelation among the posterior estimates presented in each figure. In all cases, the spatial autocorrelations were positive and significant suggest contagion among adjacent units overall across time (the first CAR term) and correlated growth of adjacent units within each phase of the epidemic (the next three CAR terms). This last observation is particularly important as it demonstrates that strong upward pressure on the increase of methamphetamine arrests in an area would be reflected in correlated change in nearby areas, a possible sign of contagious spread.

Some cities in Fig. 9.9b, c, d are colored either red or yellow. These represent the ten most rapidly growing and the ten least rapidly growing cities in the set, respectively. Notably, these all appear near to one another (reflecting positive spatial autocorrelation and correlated growth). But more importantly, they reflect a pattern of growth and spread of methamphetamine market activities through the state noted by law enforcement agencies during this time. In the early phase, most growth was observed in rural northern and southern areas of the state (red circles in Fig. 9.9b), places where domestic methamphetamine production was taking place. During the middle phase, as the Mexican drug cartels became more active, the fastest growth took place in the central valley areas (Fig. 9.9c), and in the late phase these activities began to move into urban areas (Fig. 9.9d).

9.6 Current Problems and Future Directions for Research

This chapter has briefly summarized two theoretical approaches that can be used to explain the growth and spread of illegal drug use: Economic models of drug markets and mathematical epidemiological models of drug abuse. Economic models emphasize market factors and exchanges as crucial elements of an epidemic, arguing that as drug markets grow, economies of scale lead to lower drug prices and hence greater sales. Epidemiological models emphasize contagious processes in which current users influence others to initiate and use drugs. Unlike many disease models where exposure, contagion, and host susceptibility are the sole cause of disease, drug addiction is a chronic relapsing disease and many former users will relapse back to use over time. Epidemic outbreaks arise as drug availability and social influence processes reach a tipping point leading to rapid expansion of use. Neither model is exclusive of the other. The primary issue of concern is not which is right but what emphasis is most appropriate for formulating a practical model that can be used to predict the evolution of an epidemic. This is a difficult question, but these models can help to formulate quantitative bases that will lead researchers in the right direction.

As a didactic device, this chapter posed the question: "Is the methamphetamine epidemic really an epidemic?" The purpose of this question was to emphasize that answers to it are not evident or necessarily simple. As minimal criteria, an epidemic may be identified as such because case rates are high, case rates grow exponentially, or growth exhibits contagious dynamics. Whether a particular outbreak of drug abuse, such as the methamphetamine epidemic, exhibits some or all of these features is a matter of empirical inquiry. More importantly, as researchers attempt to formulate population models of drug abuse epidemics, identification of the core dynamics of these epidemics will be the central concern. Whether driven by market dynamics or contagious processes of social influence, or both, identification of these key dynamics will indicate where prevention efforts will be more profitably allocated (Caulkins 2005).

Finally, statistical approaches to modeling changing patterns of drug use over time are only as good as the underlying theory and methods on which they are based. While viewing illegal drug use as reflecting supply and demand in an economic market has its benefits, when viewed as an epidemic, other interesting theoretical and empirical questions become evident. This chapter has provided an example of one such application showing how space-time data on rates of arrest for methamphetamine possession and use can be used to assess contagion in a Bayesian spatial model. As observed, the rates of methamphetamine arrests were similar between nearby cities and, more importantly, growth and decline in these rates were also correlated between these areas. These observations reinforce a much more dynamic view of this emerging drug problem that may also lead to both more formal and specific theoretical and empirical inquiries.

References

Anderson, R. M., & May, R. M. (1991). *Infectious diseases of humans: Dynamics and control*. London: Oxford University Press.

Banerjee, A., LaScala, E. A., Gruenewald, P. J., Freisthler, B., Treno, A., & Remer, L. (2008). Social disorganization, alcohol and other drug markets, and violence: A space-time model of community structure. In Y. F. Thomas, D. Richardson, & I. Cheung (Eds.), *Geography and drug addiction* (pp. 117–130). New York: Springer.

Bjornstad, O. N., Finkenstadt, B. F., & Grenfell, B. T. (2002). Dynamics of measles epidemics: Estimating scaling of transmission rates using a time series SIR model. *Ecological Monographs, 72*, 169–184.

Cassels, S., Clark, S. J., & Morris, M. (2008). Mathematical models for HIV transmission dynamics: Tools for social and behavioral science research. *Journal of Acquired Immune Deficiency Syndrome, 47*, S34–S39.

Caulkins, J. (2005). Investing for cost-effectiveness in the face of uncertainty: Applying financial portfolio optimization to prevention programming. In T. Stockwell, P. J. Gruenewald, J. W. Toumbourou, & W. Loxley (Eds.), *Preventing harmful substance use: The evidence base for policy and practice* (pp. 401–414). New York: Wiley.

Caulkins, J. (2007). The need for dynamic drug policy. *Addiction, 102*, 4–7.

Cheng, W. S., Garfein, R. S., Semple, S. J., Strathdee, S. A., Zians, J. K., & Patterson, T. L. (2010). Binge use and sex and drug use behaviors among HIV(−), heterosexual methamphetamine users in San Diego. *Substance Use and Misuse, 45*, 115–133.

Cintron-Arias, A., Sanchez, F., Wang, X., Castillo-Chavez, C., Gorman, D. M., & Gruenewald, P. J. (2009). The role of nonlinear relapse on contagion amongst drinking communities. In G. Chowell, J. M. Hyman, L. M. A. Bettencourt, & C. Castillo-Chavez (Eds.), *Mathematical and statistical estimation approaches in epidemiology* (pp. 343–360). New York: Springer.

Cunningham, J. K., & Liu, L. M. (2003). Impacts of federal ephedrine and pseudoephedrine regulations on methamphetamine-related hospital admissions. *Addiction, 98*, 1229–1237.

Cunningham, J. K., & Liu, L. M. (2005). Impacts of federal precursor chemical regulations on methamphetamine arrests. *Addiction, 100*, 479–488.

Curtis, R., Friedman, S. R., Neaigus, A., Jose, B., Goldstein, M., & Ildefonso, G. (1995). Street-level drug markets: Network structure and HIV risk. *Social Networks, 17*, 229–249.

Ditton, J., & Frischer, M. (2001). Computerized projection of future heroin epidemics: A necessity for the 21st century? *Substance Use and Misuse, 36*, 151–166.

Eck, J. E. (1995). A general model of the geography of illicit retail market places. In J. E. Eck & D. Weisburd (Eds.), *Crime and place: Crime prevention studies* (Vol. 4, pp. 67–94). Monsey: Criminal Justice Press.

Greene, J., & McClintock, C. (1985). Triangulation in evaluation: Design and analysis issues. *Evaluation Review, 9*, 523–545.

Grenfell, B. T., Bjornstad, O. N., & Kappey, J. (2001). Travelling waves and spatial hierarchies in measles epidemics. *Nature, 414*, 716–723.

Grenfell, B. T., Bjornstad, O. N., & Finkenstadt, B. F. (2002). Dynamics of measles epidemics: Scaling noise, determinism and predictability with the TSIR model. *Ecological Monographs, 72*, 185–202.

Groff, E., & Birks, D. (2008). Simulating crime prevention strategies: A look at possibilities. *Policing, 2*, 175–184.

Gruenewald, P. J., Johnson, F. W., Ponicki, W. R., Remer, L. G., & LaScala, E. A. (2010). Assessing correlates of the growth and extent of methamphetamine abuse and dependence in California. *Substance Use and Misuse, 45*(12), 1948–1970.

Hohman, M., Oliver, R., & Wright, W. (2004). Methamphetamine abuse and manufacture: The child welfare response. *Social Work, 49*, 373–381.

Holder, H. D., & Treno, A. J. (2005). Moving toward a common evidence base for alcohol and other drug prevention policy. In T. Stockwell, P. J. Gruenewald, J. W. Toumbourou, & W. Loxley (Eds.), *Preventing harmful substance use: The evidence base for policy and practice* (pp. 351–366). Chichester: Wiley.

Hollingsworth, T. D. (2009). Controlling infectious disease outbreaks: Lessons from mathematical modeling. *Journal of Public Health Policy, 30*, 328–341.

Hsieh, Y. H., & Cheng, Y. S. (2006). Real-time forecast of multiphase outbreak. *Emerging Infectious Diseases, 12*, 122–127.

Hunt, L., & Chambers, C. (1976). *The heroin epidemics: A study of heroin use in the United States, 1965–1975*. New York: Spectrum.

Hunt, E. D., Sumner, M., Scholten, T. J., & Frabutt, J. M. (2008). A data-driven strategy to implement a focused deterrence model and understand the elements of drug markets. In Y. F. Thomas, D. Richardson, & I. Cheung (Eds.), *Geography and drug addiction* (pp. 117–130). New York: Springer.

Illinois Attorney General. (2010). *Recognizing a structure containing a meth lab*. Retrieved from http://www.illinoisattorneygeneral.gov/methnet/recognizingmeth/outside.html

Iritani, B. J., Halfors, D. D., & Bauer, D. J. (2007). Crystal methamphetamine use among young adults in the USA. *Addiction, 102*, 1102–1113.

Kaye, S., Darke, S., Duflou, J., & McKetin, R. (2008). Methamphetamine-related fatalities in Australia: Demographics, circumstances, toxicology and major organ pathology. *Addiction, 103*, 1353–1360.

LaScala, E. A., Freisthler, B., & Gruenewald, P. J. (2005). Population ecologies of drug use, drinking and related problems. In T. Stockwell, P. J. Gruenewald, J. W. Toumbourou, & W. Loxley (Eds.), *Preventing harmful substance use: The evidence base for policy and practice* (pp. 67–78). West Sussex: Wiley.

Lipton, R., Gorman, D., Wieczorek, W., Gruenewald, P. J., & Bannerjee, A. (2009). Geography and public health: Putting people in places. In M. Khosrow-Pour (Ed.), *Encyclopedia of information science and technology* (2nd ed., pp. 1634–1645). Hershey: Information Science Reference, IGI Global Inc.

Liu, L., & Eck, J. (2008). *Artificial crime analysis: Using computer simulations and geographic information systems*. Hershey: Information Science Reference, IGI Global Inc.

Lu, M., & Burnum, J. (2008). Spatial patterns of clandestine methamphetamine labs in Colorado Springs, Colorado. In Y. F. Thomas, D. Richardson, & I. Cheung (Eds.), *Geography and drug addiction* (pp. 193–207). New York: Springer.

Mounteney, J., Fry, C., McKeganey, N., & Haugland, S. (2010). Challenges of reliability and validity in the identification and emerging of drug trends. *Substance Use and Misuse, 45*, 266–287.

Mubayi, A., Castillo-Chavez, C., Chowell, G., Kribs-Zaleta, C., Siddiqui, N. A., Kumar, N., & Das, P. (2010). Transmission dynamics and underreporting of Kala-azar in the Indian state of Bihar. *Journal of Theoretical Biology, 262*, 177–185.

National Drug Intelligence Center. (2008). *National methamphetamine threat assessment* (Publication No. 2008-Q0317-006). Washington, DC: US Department of Justice.

National Drug Intelligence Center. (2009). *Situation report: Pseudoephedrine smurfing fuels surge in large-scale methamphetamine production in California* (Publication No. 2009-S0787-007). Washington, DC: US Department of Justice.

National Institute on Drug Abuse. (2006). *Methamphetamine abuse and addiction* (NIH Publication No. 06–4210). Bethesda: National Institutes of Health, DHHS.

Rava, L., Calvani, M. G., Heisterkamp, S., Wiessing, L., & Rossi, C. (2001). Incidence indicators for policy-making: Models, estimation and implications. In United Nations Office on Drugs and Crime (Ed.), *Bulletin on narcotics, volume LIII – Dynamic drug policy: Understanding and controlling drug epidemics* (pp. 135–155). New York: United Nations.

Rawson, R. A., Marinelli-Casey, P., Anglin, M. D., Dickow, A., Frazier, Y., Gallagher, C., Galloway, G. P., Herrell, J., Huber, A., McCann, M. J., Obert, J., Pennell, S., Reiber, C., Vandersloot, D., & Zweben, J. (2004). A multi-site comparison of psychosocial approaches for the treatment of methamphetamine dependence. *Addiction, 99*, 708–717.

Rengert, G., Ratcliffe, J. H., & Chakravorty, S. (2005). *Policing illegal drug markets: Geographic approaches to crime reduction*. Monsey: Criminal Justice Press.

Rigg, N. R., Chou, C. P., & Pentz, M. A. (2009). Preventing growth in amphetamine use: Long-term effects of the Midwestern Prevention Project (MPP) from early adolescence to early adulthood. *Addiction, 104*, 1691–1699.

Rossi, C. (2001). A mover-stayer type model for epidemics of problematic drug use. In United Nations Office on Drugs and Crime (Ed.), *Bulletin on narcotics, volume LIII: Dynamic drug policy – Understanding and controlling drug epidemics* (pp. 39–64). New York: United Nations.

Sanchez, F., Castillo-Chavez, C., Gorman, D., & Gruenewald, P. (2007). Drinking as an epidemic – A simple mathematical model with recovery and relapse. In K. Witkiewitz & G. A. Marlatt (Eds.), *Therapist's guide to evidence-based relapse prevention* (pp. 354–368). New York: Elsevier.

Scott, J. C., Woods, S. P., Matt, G. E., Meyer, R. A., Heaton, R. K., Atkinson, J. H., & Grant, I. (2007). Neurocognitive effects of methamphetamine: A critical review and meta-analysis. *Neuropsychological Review, 17*, 275–297.

Smith, D. L., Lucey, B., Waller, L. A., Childs, J. E., & Real, L. A. (2002). Predicting the spatial dynamics of rabies epidemics on heterogeneous landscapes. *Proceedings of the National Academy of Sciences, 99*, 3668–3672.

Sommers, I., Baskin, D., & Baskin-Sommers, A. (2006). Methamphetamine use among young adults: Health and social consequences. *Addictive Behaviors, 311*, 1469–1476.

Song, B., Castillo-Garsow, M., Rios-Soto, K. R., Mejran, M., Henso, L., & Castillo-Chavez, C. (2006). Raves, clubs and ecstasy: The impact of peer pressure. *Mathematical Biosciences and Engineering, 3*(1), 1–18.

Substance Abuse and Mental Health Services Administration, Office of Applied Studies. (2008). *Treatment episode data set (TEDS): 1996–2006* (DHHS Publication No. (SMA) 08–4347). Rockville: National Admissions to Substance Abuse Treatment Service.

Sulzer, D., Sonders, M. S., Poulsen, N. W., & Galli, A. (2005). Mechanisms of neurotransmitter release by amphetamines: A review. *Progress Neurobiology, 75*, 406–433.

Urbina, A., & Jones, K. (2004). Crystal methamphetamine, its analogues, and HIV infection: Medical and psychiatric aspects of a new epidemic. *Clinical Infectious Diseases, 38*, 890–894.

Viboud, C., Bjornstad, O. N., Smith, D. L., Simonsen, L., Miller, M. A., & Grenfell, B. T. (2006). Synchrony, waves, and spatial hierarchies in the spread of influenza. *Science, 312*, 447–451.

Wallinga, J., & Teunis, P. (2004). Different epidemic curves for severe acute respiratory syndrome reveal similar impacts of control measures. *American Journal of Epidemiology, 160*, 509–516.

Weisburd, D., & Mazerolle, L. G. (2000). Crime and disorder in drug hot spots: Implications for theory and practice in policing. *Police Quarterly, 3*(3), 331–349.

Wheeler, D. C., & Waller, L. A. (2008). Mountains, valleys, and rivers: The transmission of raccoon rabies over a heterogeneous landscape. *Journal of Agricultural, Biological and Environmental Statistics, 13*, 1–19.

Wyatt, S. A., & Ziedonis, D. (1998). Psychological and psychiatric consequences of amphetamines. In R. E. Tarter, R. T. Ammerman, & P. J. Ott (Eds.), *Handbook of substance abuse: Neurobehavioral pharmacology* (pp. 529–544). New York: Plenum Press.

Yacoubian, G. S. (2007). Assessing environmental prevention strategies for reducing the prevalence of associated harms of methamphetamine use. *Journal of Drug Education, 37*, 31–53.

Chapter 10
Crime Rates, Crime Spikes and Cardiovascular Health in an Urban Population

Christopher R. Browning, Kathleen A. Cagney, and James Iveniuk

Abstract *We draw on theories of neighborhood social organization and environmental stress in an effort to explain variation in cardiovascular risk in a large urban population. We focus on the role of rapid increases in the crime rate ("crime spikes") in influencing an indicator of inflammatory processes related to cardiovascular health – C-reactive protein (CRP). Employing data from the Dallas Heart Study (2000–2002), a large-scale probability study of adults aged 18–65 years old, we examine the association between measures of census tract level burglary rates and CRP. Neighborhood fixed effects models reveal that both changes in the overall prior-year burglary rate and short-term change in the burglary rate between the first and last 6 months of the prior year are positively associated with CRP. Above a threshold of four burglaries per 1,000 population, a one burglary increase in the short-term burglary rate change measure is associated with a 9% increase in CRP, net of individual controls, time-invariant neighborhood characteristics, and calendar month. These findings offer additional evidence supporting the hypothesis that contextual stressors have implications for cardiovascular health and suggest that short-term changes in environmental stressors may independently shape health risk outcomes.*

We thank Helen Hobbs and James De Lemos of the University of Texas Southwestern Medical Center at Dallas for generously providing access to the Dallas Heart Study data. We also gratefully acknowledge seed grant support from the Ohio State University Initiative on Population Research.

C.R. Browning, Ph.D. (✉)
Department of Sociology, The Ohio State University, 238 Townshend Hall,
1885 Neil Ave Mall, Columbus, OH 43210, USA
e-mail: browning.90@sociology.osu.edu

K.A. Cagney, Ph.D.
Departments of Sociology, Health Studies, and Comparative Human Development,
University of Chicago, Chicago, IL, USA

J. Iveniuk
Department of Sociology, University of Chicago, Chicago, IL, USA

B. Sanders et al. (eds.), *Crime, HIV and Health: Intersections of Criminal Justice and Public Health Concerns*, DOI 10.1007/978-90-481-8921-2_10,

Inequalities in cardiovascular health risks across demographic and socioeconomic characteristics have become a focus of increasing attention among researchers and policy makers. Recent research has emphasized the potential role of geographic and social context in attempting to explain ongoing disparities in cardiovascular health (Diez Roux 2005). Drawing on an extensive literature in sociology documenting persistent segregation by socioeconomic status and race/ethnicity (Massey and Denton 1993; Wilson 1996), contextual research on cardiovascular health has generated a provocative set of findings demonstrating the potential for neighborhood environments to independently contribute to cardiovascular risk (Cubbin et al. 2006; Diez Roux et al. 2001).

Empirical research on the neighborhood context of cardiovascular health, however, has largely focused on the effects of between-neighborhood differences in social structural characteristics in predicting health outcomes. For instance, studies have observed associations between cardiovascular risk and characteristics of urban neighborhoods, such as poverty (Boardman et al. 2005), racial segregation (Chang and Hillier 2009), and the built environment (Sallis and King 2007; Zick and Smith 2009). However, theories linking neighborhood structural characteristics with cardiovascular health emphasize potential sources of environmentally-based stress, such as crime and disorder, that tend to accompany social structural disadvantage (Augustin et al. 2008). In contrast to relatively stable forms of structural disadvantage (e.g. poverty, residential instability, racial segregation), cues of potential threat in the local environment may be subject to short-term change. Indeed, rapid increases in the crime rate ("crime spikes") may be independently associated with stress-related health outcomes, above and beyond average differences in crime rates across neighborhoods.

In this chapter, we draw on theories of neighborhood social organization, fear of crime, and the individual-level stress process to develop hypotheses regarding the association between short-term changes in crime and variation in C-reactive protein (CRP) – a widely acknowledged indicator of cardiovascular risk-related inflammatory processes. We employ data from the 2000–2002 Dallas Heart Study, which captures extensive survey-based indicators of socio-demographic characteristics and carefully measured biomarker data related to cardiovascular health. These data are combined with incident-based, geo-coded information on index crimes in the City of Dallas from the National Neighborhood Crime Study (Peterson and Krivo 2010), offering a unique opportunity to explore the link between environmental stress and cardiovascular health.

10.1 Theoretical Background

Research on neighborhood environments suggest that structural disadvantages such as poverty, residential instability, and ethnic heterogeneity limit the organizational capacity of neighborhood residents, compromising their collective ability to sustain local health and well-being (Sampson 2003). This research has been largely rooted in social disorganization theory (Shaw and McKay 1969), which was originally developed to explain inter-neighborhood variability in crime rates. Decades of empirical research have provided strong support for the basic claims of the model with respect to the criminogenic role of disadvantaged community structure (Bursik 1988).

A recent advance on the social disorganization approach – collective efficacy– points to the combination of neighborhood-level mutual trust and local attachments (social cohesion) and shared normative orientations regarding beneficial action on behalf of the local community (informal social control) as a key mechanism linking structural disadvantage to compromised community health (e.g., Browning and Cagney 2002; Sampson et al. 1997; Sampson and Wilson 1995). Research on collective efficacy has offered evidence that the combination of low levels of social cohesion and weak informal social control norms tends to be found in communities with high concentrations of poverty, residential instability, and racial and ethnic heterogeneity (Sampson et al. 1997). Collective efficacy mediates a substantial proportion of the link between structural disadvantage and measures of property and violent crime (Browning 2009; Sampson et al. 1997).

Beyond the well-established literature linking neighborhood factors to crime, a growing body of research demonstrates significant associations between contextual disadvantage – including collective efficacy – and a variety of health-related outcomes (Browning and Cagney 2002, 2003; Cagney and Browning 2004; MacIntyre and Ellaway 2003; Sampson 2003). Collective efficacy has been linked with compromised health through a number of mechanisms including lower quality or unavailable health services, less effective management of local physical hazards, the psychosocial consequences of limited social cohesion, and weak social control of health-compromising behavior (Browning and Cagney 2003; Kawachi and Berkman 2000). However, the established associations between collective efficacy and both crime and health suggest that crime itself may play an important role in shaping the health of local residents.

10.1.1 Neighborhood Stressors and Health: Crime Rates, Crime Spikes, and Cardiovascular Risk

High rates of crime are likely to be a significant source of stress within neighborhood environments with consequences for the mental and physical health of urban residents (Gehlert and Sohmer 2008). Victimization itself has obvious and often profound consequences for health. Yet, crime may also operate indirectly to influence health outcomes through health-consequential stress processes. Higher crime rates may influence health through both the direct effects of stress on pathophysiological processes and the consequences of increased fear for health behaviors (Crimmins and Seeman 2004). First, fear associated with exposure to threatening environments may be accompanied by a physiological stress response, with implications for processes such as glucocorticoid hormone production and inflammation. Second, high levels of neighborhood crime are likely to increase security-related anxiety and decrease use of public space for exercise, recreation, or instrumental walking (e.g., errand running). Indeed, neighborhoods characterized by high rates of criminal activity and disorder have been positively linked with high blood pressure (Glass and Rasmussen 2006), mortality (Wen and Christakis 2005), cardiovascular disease (Sundquist and Theobald 2006), and obesity (Augustin et al. 2008).

Research investigating the influence of crime on health has assumed that chronic exposure to high levels of crime, as captured by between-neighborhood differences in crime rates, are likely to have the most significant consequences for health (Browning and Cagney 2003). However, relatively rapid increases in the crime rate, or crime "spikes," may also lead to significant stress responses. A short-term increase in crime may present residents with an immediate and unpredictable threat that amplifies feelings of vulnerability (Robinson et al. 2003). While neighborhood residents may find ways to adapt to relatively stable neighborhood conditions, short-term increases in crime may be perceived to signal the breakdown or collapse of the existing community's capacity to control crime. Beyond the increased threat of victimization that may result from crime spikes, anxiety and withdrawal responses to crime spikes may occur as residents contemplate the uncertain longer-term implications of changes in criminal activity.

10.1.2 Neighborhood Crime and CRP

Our analysis considers the link between stress and CRP – a biomeasure of inflammation hypothesized to be responsive to environmental stress. Elevated CRP captures inflammatory processes relevant to the development of cardiovascular disease (Danesh et al. 2000), type II diabetes (Pradhan et al. 2001), and mortality (Jenny et al. 2007).

Psychosocial stress is a well-known predictor of cardiovascular risk (Everson-Rose and Lewis 2005) and has been linked with the production of pro-inflammatory cytokines (Lutgendorf et al. 1999; Owen et al. 2003) and elevated CRP levels. Elevated CRP is usually understood as the consequence of years of stressful experience, or negative health behaviors. However, CRP may reach clinically significant levels following short periods of acute stress (Abramson and Vaccarino 2002; Kasapis and Thompson 2005; McDade et al. 2006; Mattusch et al. 1999; McDade et al. 2006). Elevated CRP production may be triggered by sudden increases in vascular shear stress, brought on by intense physical or mental exhaustion, even if this exhaustion lasts just a few days; sleep deprivation or emotional conflicts with friends and family are two such examples (Fuligni et al. 2009; Meier-Ewert et al. 2004). These increases in CRP are usually accompanied by reports of depression and rises in blood pressure over the observation period, implying that CRP levels are closely connected to other physiological and mental states, and, moreover, that CRP is highly responsive to environmental changes (Ma et al. 2011).

Crime spikes may influence stress through perceptions of safety and victimization potential. We hypothesize that relatively shorter-term (i.e. over the course of a year) changes in the crime rate will influence CRP levels. Although crime-related stress is likely to be associated with reduced exercise, possible weight gain, and, potentially, other coping mechanisms such as smoking and drinking, we hypothesize a direct effect of stress on CRP levels independent of these potentially mediating mechanisms.

Research on environmental stressors has typically neglected the role of environmental volatility, precluding assessment of the extent to which changes in environmental stressors independently influence health. With respect to CRP, few studies, cross-sectional or longitudinal, have examined the effects of neighborhood environments on CRP. Examining data from the Multi-Ethnic Study of Atherosclerosis, Nazmi and colleagues (2010) found that measures of neighborhood deprivation, problems, safety, and cohesion were cross-sectionally associated with levels of CRP. However, neighborhood associations were no longer significant with adjustment for race. Pollitt et al. (2007) reported evidence of a positive association between neighborhood SES and CRP for whites, but not African Americans (see also Petersen et al. 2008). No studies, however, have examined the link between crime rates and CRP.

10.2 Data

The analyses employ data from an unprecedented study of the social determinants of cardiovascular health – the 2000–2002 Dallas Heart Study (DHS) – a probability-based sample of Dallas County adults (Victor et al. 2004). In combination with data from the National Neighborhood Crime Study (Peterson and Krivo 2010), these data offer a unique opportunity to examine the impact of short-term changes in the crime rate on an important but understudied outcome relevant to cardiovascular risk.

The DHS data collection effort involved three stages. First, a sample of non-institutionalized, English- or Spanish-speaking Dallas County residents aged 18–65 years old was administered a household health interview (N=6,101). The interview protocol incorporated a number of modules including demographic background, socioeconomic status, health history, neighborhood conditions, social support, and health behavior. A subsample of participants provided in-home fasting blood and urine samples (phlebotomy: visit 2) and were assessed using a variety of imaging technologies (clinic: visit 3). The participation rate for the initial survey round was 80.4%. Of those respondents eligible for follow-up assessments (N=4,525), 75.1% and 65.7% participated in the phlebotomy and clinic visits, respectively. CRP was measured from blood samples drawn at visit 2; accordingly, our analyses are based on data from visits 1 and 2. Data from the 2000 Census and the 1999–2001 National Neighborhood Crime Study (Peterson and Krivo 2010) on census tract-level crime rates in the City of Dallas were merged with the DHS in order to investigate the effects of crime on CRP.

The final analytic sample from the DHS included respondents who resided in the City of Dallas and began the study between July 1, 2000 (the DHS start date) and December 31, 2001 (to align with available crime data from NNCS). The sample was also limited to respondents who completed visit 2 (phlebotomy) within 30 days of the initial visit in order to avoid the potential for significant change in health-related controls between visits.[1] Our main analytic sample included 1,449 cases in 324 census tracts after additional exclusions based on CRP levels indicative of acute events and outlier crime rates (see measures section below). Missing data on income (13%) and our measure of physical activity (10%) led us to employ multiple imputation methods[2] for the final models. The study design oversampled African American respondents, and the racial composition of the sample was 30% white, 15% Latino, 53.5% African American, and 1.5% other race/ethnicity. Our analytic strategy employs neighborhood fixed effects regression, which allows us to adjust the results for oversampling within certain geographic areas of the city by census tract.

10.3 Measures

10.3.1 Dependent Measure

The dependent variable, high sensitivity CRP, was measured at visit 2. Blood samples were obtained after an overnight fast and stored in EDTA tubes for 4 h or less at 4 °C before processing. Plasma aliquots were frozen at −80 °C until assays were performed. High-sensitivity CRP measurements were performed on thawed samples using the Roche/Hitachi 912 System, Tina-quant assay, a latex-enhanced immunoturbidimetric method (Khera et al. 2005). The minimal detectable range of this assay is 0.1 mg/l, and the upper limit is 20 mg/l. The median CRP of the sample was 3.2. Because CRP levels above 10 mg/l may be indicative of an acute phase response to infection, we excluded cases with CRP >10 mg/l from our principal analyses (McDade et al. 2006). However, this exclusion led to a loss of 18.6% of the sample, indicating that the sample exhibited elevated CRP levels by comparison with (typically smaller scale) prior studies. Accordingly, we also fit final models including cases up to 20 mg/l in order to consider the robustness of our findings to incorporation of cases exhibiting higher levels of CRP (Khera et al. 2005).

10.3.2 Independent Measures

Crime measures are constructed for the year prior to each respondent's first DHS visit date. Because burglary involves home invasion, evidence suggests that it provokes comparatively high levels of fear (Skogan 1986; Sprott and Doob 1997).[3] Accordingly, we constructed person-specific overall average burglary rates (capturing

[1] Comparison of means indicates that minimal differences exist between the samples of respondents who completed visit 2 before and after 30 days had elapsed from visit 1.

[2] We used Stata's ICE command (Imputation with Chained Equations).

[3] For women, an obvious crime to consider would be sexual assault. However, evidence suggests that administrative data on sexual assault are difficult to collect with accuracy.

somewhat longer-term trends in the burglary rate) and measures of short-term change in the burglary rate in the year prior to the second DHS (phlebotomy) visit. The median person-specific total burglary rate was 15 per 1,000 population. The burglary rate change score is a simple measure subtracting the burglary rate for the most recent 6 months before the second DHS interview from that of the 6 months just prior. The median person-specific burglary rate change score is 0. Respondents are coded as residing in a crime spike neighborhood if the absolute value of the change in crime rate over the previous year is in the top 10%. This cut point corresponds to an increase of four burglaries per 1,000 population or an average total increase of 16 burglaries (assuming an average population of 4,000 residents per tract). We incorporate the effects of increases in the crime rate change beyond 4 per 1,000 population by fitting a linear spline for the effect of burglary rate change for the top 10% of respondents.[4] We also fit splines for the effects of changes in rates below 0 and between 0 and 4 burglaries.

We included a number of control variables drawn from the DHS survey data including age, gender, race/ethnicity (African American, Latino, and other race/ethnicity vs. white), marital status (currently married = 1), education in six categories (8th grade or less, some high school, high school graduation, some college, college graduation, and more than college education), total combined family income in the last 12 months (in 13 categories, from less than $5,000–100,000 or more), immigrant status, visit 1 body mass index (BMI), physical activity level (exercise dose per week in metabolic equivalents), frequency of alcohol consumption in the last 12 months (a nine category measure – never to every day), smoking status (never smoked vs. ever smoked), and cholesterol level (physician-indicated high cholesterol with and without treatment vs. never told by a doctor that the respondent had high cholesterol). Finally, because crime rates tend to fluctuate seasonally, we included fixed effects for calendar month of DHS survey interview.

10.4 Analytic Strategy

The neighborhood fixed effects approach capitalizes on within-neighborhood change in burglary rates occurring over the July, 1999 to December, 2001 period to estimate burglary rate effects on CRP that are unconfounded with time-invariant neighborhood characteristics. The model can be stated as follows:

$$Y_{ij} = \alpha_j + \sum_{p=1}^{P} \beta_p X_{ij} + \gamma_1 (BR_{ij}) + \sum_{h=1}^{3} \delta_h (Z_{ijh}) + e_{ij}$$

[4] We capped the burglary rate change score variable at less than 22 burglaries per 1,000 population, dropping seven cases from the analysis that had rates exceeding 22. Among these cases were four instances in which the burglary rate was 0 in the first 6 months with an implausibly high burglary rate in the last 6 months, calling into question the accuracy of the data. Analyses including these cases revealed comparable results.

where Y_{ij} is the outcome, log CRP for person i in neighborhood j; α_j are the fixed neighborhood effects; β_p are the effects of P covariates X; γ_1 is the effect of change in the person-specific prior-year residential tract overall burglary rate (BR_{ij}); δ_h are the effects of person-specific short-term change in the residential tract burglary rate (ΔBR_{ij}) in the prior year where h indexes the piecewise slope coefficients capturing the effects of burglary rate change and the covariates Z_{ijh} are defined as follows:

$$Z_{ij1} = \begin{cases} \Delta BR_{ij} \ if \ \Delta BR_{ij} < 0 \\ 0 \ otherwise \end{cases}$$

$$Z_{ij2} = \begin{cases} 0 \ if \ \Delta BR_{ij} < 0 \\ \Delta BR_{ij} \ if \ 0 \le \Delta BR_{ij} < 4 \\ 4 \ if \ \Delta BR_{ij} \ge 4 \end{cases}$$

$$Z_{ij3} = \begin{cases} 0 \ if \ \Delta BR_{ij} < 4 \\ \Delta BR_{ij} - 4 \ if \ \Delta BR_{ij} \ge 4 \end{cases}$$

The coefficient of interest for the hypothesis of a crime spike effect is δ_3, the estimate of the effect of burglary rate change at above four burglaries per 1,000 population. Finally, e_{ij} is an independently and identically distributed error term with mean 0 and constant variance.

10.5 Results

Table 10.1 reports descriptive statistics for variables in the analysis. The sample is 46% male, 29% white, 53% African American, 15% Latino, and 2% other race/ethnicity. The average age of the sample is 43.9 years.

Table 10.2 reports models of log CRP for values less than 10 mg/l. Model 1 includes demographic background factors and socioeconomic status. Consistent with prior research, women and older adults had higher levels of CRP. African American race and Latino ethnicity also were positively associated with log CRP, although the latter coefficient did not achieve significance at the conventional level. Income was negatively and significantly associated with log CRP, but the models offered no evidence of an association between education and log CRP.

Model 2 adds health status and behavior variables. With the exception of visit 1 BMI, none of the other health controls achieved significance (elevated cholesterol was marginally positively associated with log CRP ($p<.10$)). Visit 1 BMI, however, exerted a powerful positive association with log CRP ($p<.001$) and, in combination with the (largely insignificant) effects of other health variables, accounted for nontrivial proportions of the effects of sex (25%), African American race (50%), Latino ethnicity (30%), and income (25%).

Table 10.1 Descriptive statistics for variables in the analysis

Variables	Mean	Std dev.
Log CRP	.666	1.064
Male	.461	–
Age	43.949	8.822
Race/ethnicity		
White	.294	–
African American	.532	–
Latino	.153	–
Other	.021	–
Married	.444	–
Education (vs. HS grad)		
8th grade	.088	–
Some high school	.128	–
High school degree	.301	–
Some college	.270	–
College grad	.118	–
More than college	.095	–
Income	7.066	3.808
Foreign born	.148	–
Health behaviors		
Visit 1 BMI	28.458	6.343
Physical activity	463.028	769.230
Alcohol consumption	5.615	2.635
Never smoked	.527	–
Cholesterol		
Doctor never told R of cholesterol elevation	.764	–
Doctor indicated elevation	.167	–
Doctor indicated elevation (on medication)	.069	–
Crime rates		
Overall burglary rate	15.456	11.496
Burglary rate change-piecewise linear effects		
below 0	-.997	1.988
0 to 4	.927	1.366
4 and above	.232	1.290

Model 3 adds the person-specific overall prior year burglary rate measure. The coefficient for the overall burglary rate is positive and significant ($p < .01$), indicating that increases in the burglary rate are associated with elevated log CRP, net of all time-invariant neighborhood characteristics. Specifically, a one burglary per 1,000 population increase in the overall rate within neighborhood is associated with a 4.2% increase in CRP.

Finally, Model 4 adds the piecewise linear slopes for the effect of short-term burglary rate change in the last year below 0, between 0 and 4, and above 4. The coefficients indicate that, although short-term burglary rate change slopes below 4

Table 10.2 Neighborhood fixed effects models : C-reactive protein regressed on overall burglary rates last year, linear splines for burglary rate change last year, month fixed effects, and controls (N = 1,462)[a]

Independent variables	C-reactive protein (<=10 mg/l) 1		2		3		4	
Individual								
Sex	–.271	(.065)***	–.205	(.063)**	–.205	(.063)**	–.202	(.062)**
Age	.013	(.004)**	.012	(.003)***	.013	(.003)***	.013	(.003)***
Race/ethnicity								
African American	.244	(.112)*	.123	(.102)	.120	(.102)	.118	(.102)
Latino	.308	(.158)	.213	(.143)	.201	(.142)	.196	(.142)
Other	–.126	(.274)	–.049	(.243)	–.045	(.242)	–.054	(.242)
Married	.035	(.072)	.000	(.066)	.009	(.066)	.003	(.066)
Education (vs. HS grad)								
8th grade	–.038	(.145)	–.120	(.135)	–.105	(.135)	–.112	(.134)
Some high school	.060	(.107)	–.013	(.098)	–.008	(.098)	–.001	(.098)
Some college	.137	(.083)	.059	(.077)	.068	(.076)	.063	(.076)
College grad	–.056	(.118)	–.109	(.109)	–.112	(.109)	–.107	(.108)
More than college	.179	(.136)	.146	(.125)	.157	(.125)	.157	(.125)
Income	–.029	(.011)**	–.022	(.010)*	–.023	(.010)*	–.024	(.010)*
Foreign born	.084	(.149)	.167	(.134)	.174	(.134)	.178	(.134)
Health behaviors								
Visit 1 BMI	–		.058	(.005)***	.058	(.005)***	.059	(.005)***
Physical activity	–		.000	(.000)	.000	(.000)	.000	(.000)
Alcohol consumption	–		–.021	(.012)	–.020	(.012)	–.021	(.012)
Never smoked	–		–.011	(.060)	–.004	(.060)	.000	(.060)
Cholesterol								
Doctor indicated elevation	–		.144	(.081)	.135	(.081)	.144	(.081)
Doctor indicated elevation (on medication)	–		.228	(.127)	.221	(.126)	.205	(.126)

Crime rates								
Overall burglary rate	–		–		.042	(.014)**	.035	(.014)*
Burglary rate change-piecewise linear effects								
Below 0	–		–		–		.006	(.021)
0 to 4	–		–		–		–.028	(.030)
4 and above	–		–		–		.093	(.034)**
Intercept	.517	(.196)**	–1.087	(.224)*	–1.739	(.311)***	–1.637	(.312)

Note: All models include dummy variables for calendar month of first interview
*p<.05; ** p<.01; *** p<.001 (two–tailed)
[a]All models were fit using multiple imputation

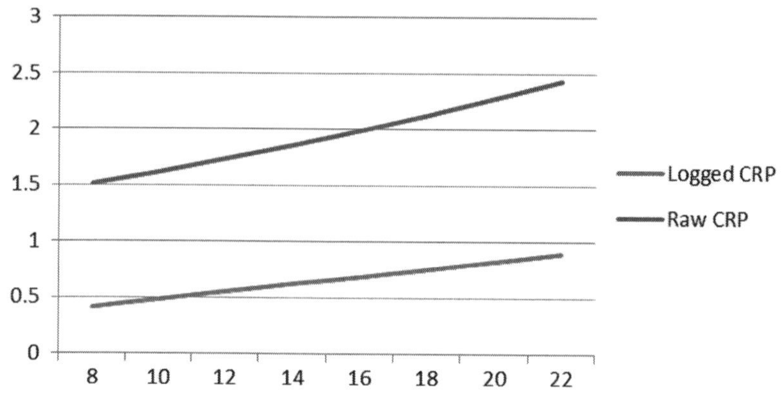

Fig. 10.1 Predicted C-reactive protein level by overall burglary rate in the prior year (Models excluding CRP > 10 mg/l)

are not significant, the effect of the variable at an increase of more than four burglaries is positive and significant ($p < .01$). The slope indicates that a one burglary per 1,000 population short-term increase in the burglary rate over the last year is associated with a 9% increase in CRP, net of individual controls and both calendar month and neighborhood fixed effects. The effect of change in the overall prior-year burglary rate remains positive and significant ($p < .05$) in Model 4, but decreases in magnitude by some 17%. After adjustment for the effect of short-term burglary rate change, a one burglary increase in the overall prior-year rate is associated with a 3.5% increase in CRP. This finding indicates that the effect of the overall burglary rate is confounded with short-term change in the burglary rate, which exerts an independent effect on log CRP.

Figures 10.1 and 10.2 plot the predicted CRP level at selected values of overall prior-year burglary rate and short-term burglary rate change (above 4). Focusing on the overall burglary rate in Fig. 10.1, log CRP ranges from .41 to .89 as the burglary rate increases from 8 to 22 (roughly corresponding to the 25th and 75th percentiles of the overall burglary rate distribution). These values of log CRP correspond to a raw CRP score range from 1.51 to 2.44. With respect to the burglary rate change effect, we plot the predicted log and raw CRP levels from a 4 burglary increase to a 12 burglary increase (roughly corresponding to the 90th and 99th percentiles on the distribution of the burglary rate change score). The log CRP score ranges from .67 to 1.40, corresponding to CRP raw scores of 1.95 to 4.07. The predicted scores reveal non-trivial changes in CRP levels with increases in the overall prior-year burglary rate and short-term burglary rate change measures.

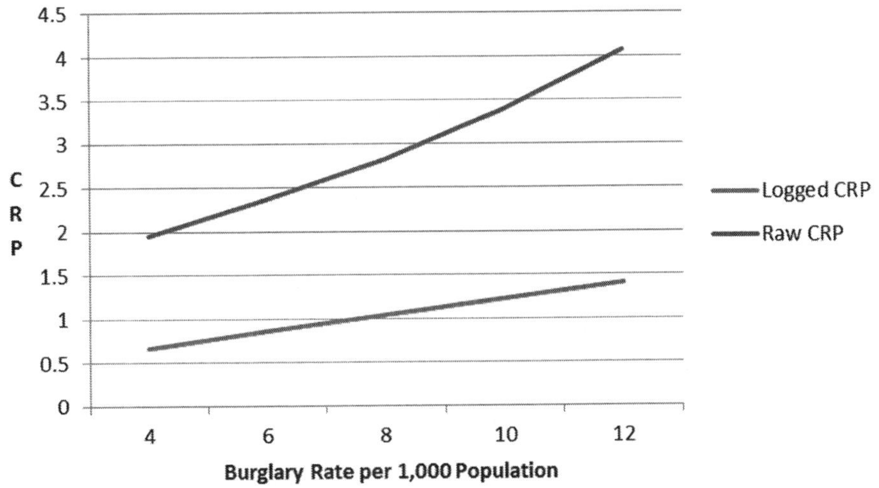

Fig. 10.2 Predicted C-reactive protein level by change in burglary rate in the prior year (Models excluding CRP>10 mg/l)

10.5.1 Additional Analyses

We conducted a number of additional analyses to determine the robustness of the findings to various alternative model specifications. First, the analyses presented in Table 10.2 cap the short-term burglary rate change score at 22 (see footnote 4). In order to determine whether the slope for the effect of burglary rate change at more than four burglaries was sensitive to the inclusion of large values of burglary rate change, we re-estimated the models capping the change score at a 10 burglary increase in the rate (dropping approximately 1.3% of the sample). The effects of the slope for burglary rate change at 4 burglaries and above actually increased somewhat in magnitude and remained statistically significant ($p<.05$).

We also examined the extent to which capping CRP at 10 mg/l affected the results of the analyses. As noted, some analyses of CRP effects have excluded those with CRP greater than 10 mg/l under the assumption that these respondents are experiencing acute events that may obscure the stress-related elevation of CRP (McDade et al. 2006). In the context of the DHS, this results in a substantial loss of cases (18.6%), reflecting the overall elevation of CRP levels in this sample. Accordingly, we estimated models including respondents with CRP levels under 20 in order to determine the extent to which burglary rate effects are robust to the inclusion of respondents who exhibit elevated CRP and who may be experiencing acute events. Results of neighborhood fixed effects models with multiple imputation indicated that the overall prior burglary rate measure was no longer significant ($\gamma 1 = .014$). However, the coefficient for the piecewise linear slope of short-term burglary rate change at more than four burglaries remained significant and at a comparable magnitude ($\delta 3 = .09$; $p < .01$), indicating that the short-term burglary rate change effect is robust to the inclusion of respondents with CRP levels between 10 and 20 mg/l.

Finally, we estimated an interaction term between short-term burglary rate change above 4 and the overall prior-year burglary rate measure in order to assess whether the effect of increases in the burglary rate was dependent on the overall crime rate of the neighborhood. Substantial increases in the burglary rate may induce higher levels of stress if the crime rate is already high in the neighborhood. On the other hand, individuals who experience lower overall crime rates may experience greater levels of stress when faced with crime rate increases due to the relative uncertainty associated with higher crime rates. These additional models revealed no evidence of an interaction between burglary rate change above 4 and the overall burglary rate measure, suggesting that increases in the short-term burglary rate exert similar influence on CRP levels across overall burglary rate levels.

10.6 Discussion

Over the last few decades, research on urban neighborhoods has yielded robust evidence of both variability in levels of structural advantage characterizing small urban areas, as well as nontrivial consequences of this variability for the health and well-being of residents. Building on the social disorganization framework developed in the early twentieth century Chicago School of sociology, this literature has primarily emphasized the role of economic disadvantage in shaping neighborhood- and individual-level outcomes. More recently, the literature has moved beyond a focus on economic status to encompass a wide variety of potentially consequential dimensions along which neighborhoods vary. Research emphasizing collective efficacy – or the combination of social cohesion and informal social control – and its consequences for levels of crime within urban neighborhoods has offered an important extension of the disorganization model for understanding contextual influences on health.

In the current analysis, we consider the association between crime rates and cardiovascular health – an outcome of increasing concern to health researchers and policy makers (Victor et al. 2004). The geographic clustering of cardiovascular risk (Diez Roux 2005) highlights the need to isolate factors that may play a role in this clustering. Our analyses draw on theories linking neighborhood structural disadvantage and compromised social organization to higher crime rates and the associated potential for chronic exposure to this potentially significant stressor. A key extension of our model, however, is an emphasis on the potential for rapid increases in the crime rate, or crime "spikes" to exert independent effects on cardiovascular health.

We consider the association between measures of crime and CRP, a biomarker of inflammatory processes hypothesized to be responsive to stress. Employing neighborhood fixed effects models to investigate the links between crime spike measures in the year prior to the respondents' DHS phlebotomy visit, and CRP levels measured at the second interview, we find evidence that crime has short-term effects on CRP. Specifically, our models indicate that change in the overall prior-year burglary rate is positively associated with CRP, net of individual-level controls, calendar month of DHS survey interview, and all time-invariant neighborhood characteristics. Our models offer evidence for the effect of change in the overall burglary rate on CRP for respondents with CRP levels below 10 mg/l, but not when respondents with CRP levels between 10 and 20 mg/l were included in the analysis. These findings provide evidence demonstrating that change in the overall burglary rate exerts independent effects on CRP, but suggest that the exclusion criteria applied to the dependent variable have substantial effects on the magnitude and significance of crime rate coefficients. The short-term elevation in CRP levels typically accompanying acute health events may obscure the effects of environmental stressors. However, omitting respondents with high levels of CRP also may bias estimates of CRP predictors. Future research should be sensitive to the treatment of the dependent variable in evaluating the robustness of contextual stress effects.

The effects of short-term burglary rate change on CRP – the principal focus of our analyses – were consistently positive and significant. Burglary rate change effects on CRP levels were non-trivial, indicating that stressful changes in the neighborhood context have consequences for cardiovascular health in the short-term. Including the measure of short-term change in the burglary rate explained a portion of the overall prior-year burglary rate change coefficient, indicating that between-neighborhood analyses of crime rate effects on cardiovascular health may be partially capturing the effects of crime spikes rather than longer term trends in exposure to burglary.

These findings have implications for public policy oriented toward reducing the stress consequences of neighborhood crime. For instance, law enforcement strategies involving targeted crackdowns on high crime areas may simply shift criminal activity to another area (Barr and Pease 1990; Braga 2001; Eck 1993; Hesseling 1994). This may result in little net reduction in crime, but the potential introduction of a crime spike to a new neighborhood. Our results suggest that policies resulting in the mobility of crime, rather than the reduction of it, may actually lead to overall increases in negative health reactions to crime. Consequently, law enforcement approaches to addressing "hot spots" of criminal activity should be highly sensitive to the potential for crime displacement rather than crime reduction. In addition, future research should explore how informal social processes within communities help to manage not only the prevalence of crime but its consequences. For instance, communities with high levels of collective efficacy with respect to the control of crime may help allay individual concerns about short-term changes in the crime rate. High collective efficacy neighborhoods may foster a sense of confidence that increases in crime can be effectively countered by joint action. This then may reduce the stress-producing potential of crime rate change.

Our analyses are not without limitations. Ideally, the analyses would have investigated the effects of short-term change in burglary rates on changes in CRP levels. Such a design would provide more rigorous evidence of a causal neighborhood effect on health. Unfortunately, the data provided only one measure of CRP, precluding investigation of longitudinal changes in this outcome. Nevertheless, the unique data source we employed provided an opportunity to examine person-specific measures of neighborhood crime based on the dates of DHS visits.

We also lacked data on changes in health behaviors in response to crime rates, leading us to focus on the crime effects above and beyond the influence of health behaviors measured at the first DHS visit. This relatively conservative approach, however, may underestimate the total impact of crime rates on CRP to the extent that health behavior changes, such as avoidance of outdoor activity or changes in caloric intake, may also impact short-term changes in CRP. Longitudinal data collection efforts capturing changes in contextual stressors, health behaviors, and stress responses will more effectively identify the pathways through which local stressors impact cardiovascular health.

Our analyses add to the mounting evidence that the effects of crime go far beyond the immediate and often tragic impacts for victims and their families. As our findings attest, both concentrations of crime and volatility in the potential for victimization represent sources of stress for neighborhood residents. Although research is only beginning to isolate the impact of crime and other contextual stressors for a variety of health outcomes, the evidence of environmental stress effects on health is increasingly apparent. Identifying the mechanisms through which crime and other sources of environmental stress influence health outcomes will be a critical step in addressing pervasive geographic inequities in health. Policies aimed not only at assisting individuals to change behavior, but also at shoring up the ability of communities to respond to crises, may very well have a greater and more long-lasting impact on the health of residents.

References

Abramson, J. L., & Vaccarino, V. (2002). Relationship between physical activity and inflammation among apparently healthy middle-aged and older US adults. *Archives of Internal Medicine, 162*, 1286–1292.

Augustin, T., Glass, T. A., James, B. D., & Schwartz, B. S. (2008). Neighborhood psychosocial hazards and cardiovascular disease: The Baltimore Memory Study. *American Journal of Public Health, 98*, 1664–1670.

Barr, R., & Pease, K. (1990). Crime placement, displacement, and deflection. *Crime and Justice, 12*, 277–318.

Boardman, J. D., Saint Onge, J. M., Rogers, R. G., & Denney, J. (2005). Race differentials in obesity: The impact of place. *Journal of Health and Social Behavior, 46*, 229–243.

Braga, A. (2001). The effects of 'hot spots' policing on crime. *Annals of the American Academy of Political and Social Science, 578*, 104–125.

Browning, C. R. (2009). Illuminating the downside of social capital: Negotiated coexistence, property crime, and disorder in urban neighborhoods. *American Behavioral Scientist, 52*, 1556–1578.

Browning, C. R., & Cagney, K. A. (2002). Neighborhood structural disadvantage, collective efficacy, and self-rated physical health in an urban setting. *Journal of Health and Social Behavior, 43*, 383–399.

Browning, C. R., & Cagney, K. A. (2003). Moving beyond poverty: Neighborhood structure, social processes, and health. *Journal of Health and Social Behavior, 44*, 552–571.

Bursik, R. J. (1988). Social disorganization and theories of crime and delinquency: Problems and prospects. *Criminology, 26*, 519–551.

Cagney, K. A., & Browning, C. R. (2004). Exploring neighborhood-level variation in asthma and other respiratory diseases: The contribution of neighborhood social context. *Journal of General Internal Medicine, 19*, 229–236.

Chang, V. W., & Hillier, A. E. (2009). Neighborhood racial isolation, disorder and obesity. *Social Forces, 87*, 2063–2092.

Crimmins, E. M., & Seeman, T. E. (2004). Integrating biology into the study of health disparities. *Population and Development Review, 30*, 89–107.

Cubbin, C., Sundquist, K., Ahlen, H., Johansson, S., Winkleby, M. A., & Sundquist, J. (2006). Neighborhood deprivation and cardiovascular disease risk factors: Protective and harmful effects. *Scandinavian Journal of Public Health, 34*, 228–237.

Danesh, J., Whincup, P., Walker, M., Lennon, L., Thomson, A., Appleby, P., Gallimore, J. R., & Pepys, M. B. (2000). Low grade inflammation and coronary heart disease: prospective study and updated meta-analyses. *British Medical Journal, 321*, 199–204.

Diez Roux, A. V. (2005). Persistent social patterning of cardiovascular risk: Rethinking the familiar. *Circulation, 111*, 3020–3021.

Diez Roux, A. V., Merkin, S. S., Arnett, D., Chambless, L., Massing, M., Javier Nieto, F., Sorlie, P., Szklo, M., Tyroler, H., & Watson, R. L. (2001). Neighborhood of residence and incidence of coronary heart disease. *New England Journal of Medicine, 345*, 99–106.

Eck, J. (1993). The threat of crime displacement. *Problem Solving Quarterly, 6*, 1–7.

Everson-Rose, S. A., & Lewis, T. T. (2005). Psychosocial factors and cardiovascularv disease. *Annual Review of Public Health, 25*, 469–500.

Fuligni, A. J., Telzer, E. H., Bower, J., Cole, S., Kiang, L., & Irwin, M. (2009). A preliminary study of daily interpersonal stress and C-reactive protein levels among adolescents from Latin American and European backgrounds. *Psychosomatic Medicine, 71*(3), 329–333.

Gehlert, S., & Sohmer, D. (2008). Targeting health disparities: A model linking upstream determinants to downstream interventions. *Health Affairs, 27*, 339–349.

Glass, T. A., & Rasmussen, M. D. (2006). Neighborhoods and obesity in older adults: The Baltimore Memory Study. *American Journal of Preventive Medicine, 31*, 455–463.

Hesseling, R. (1994). Displacement: A review of the empirical literature. In R. Clarke (Ed.), *Crime prevention studies* (Vol. 3). Monsey: Criminal Justice Press.

Jenny, N. S., Yanez, N. D., Psaty, B. M., Kuller, L. H., Hirsch, C. H., & Tracy, R. P. (2007). Inflammation biomarkers and near-term death in older men. *American Journal of Epidemiology, 165*, 684–695.

Kasapis, C., & Thompson, P. D. (2005). The effects of physical activity on serum C-reactive protein and inflammatory markers. *Journal of the American College of Cardiology, 45*, 1563–1569.

Kawachi, I., & Berkman, L. F. (2000). Social cohesion, social capital, and health. In L. F. Berkman & I. Kawachi (Eds.), *Social epidemiology* (pp. 174–190). Oxford: Oxford University Press.

Khera, A., McGuire, D. K., Murphy, S. A., Stanek, H. G., Das, S. R., Vongpatanasin, W., Wians, F. H., Jr., Grundy, S. M., & de Lemos, J. A. (2005). Race and gender differences in C-reactive protein levels. *Journal of the American College of Cardiology, 46*, 464–469.

Lutgendorf, S. K., Garand, L., Buckwalter, K. C., Reimer, T. T., Hong, S., & Lubaroff, D. M. (1999). Life stress, mood disturbance, and elevated interleukin-6 in healthy older women. *Journal of Gerontology, 54A*, M434–9.

Ma, Y., Chiriboga, D. E., Pagoto, S., Rosal, M., Li, W., Merriam, P., Hebert, J., Whited, M., & Ockene, I. (2011). Association between depression and C-reactive protein. *Cardiology Research and Practice, 2011*, 1–8.

Macintyre, S., & Ellaway, A. (2003). Neighborhoods and health: An overview. In I. Kawachi & L. Berkman (Eds.), *Neighborhoods and health* (pp. 20–44). New York: Oxford University Press.

Massey, D., & Denton, N. A. (1993). *American apartheid: Segregation and the making of the underclass*. Cambridge, MA: Harvard University Press.

Mattusch, F., Dufaux, B., Heine, O., Mertens, I., & Rost, R. (1999). Reduction of the plasma concentration of c-reactive protein following nine months of endurance training. *International Journal of Sports Medicine, 21*, 21–24.

McDade, T. W., Hawkley, L. C., & Cacioppo, J. T. (2006). Psychosocial and behavioral predictors of inflammation in middle-aged and older adults: The Chicago health, aging, and social relations study. *Psychosomatic Medicine, 68*, 376–381.

Meier-Ewert, H. K., Ridker, P. M., Rifai, N., Regan, M. M., Price, N. J., Dinges, D. F., & Mullington, J. M. (2004). Effect of sleep loss on C-reactive protein, an inflammatory marker of cardiovascular risk. *Journal of the American College of Cardiology, 43*, 678–683.

Nazmi, A., Diez Roux, A. V., Ranjit, N., Seeman, T. E., & Jenny, N. S. (2010). Cross-sectional and longitudinal associations of neighborhood characteristics with inflammatory markers: Findings from the multi-ethnic study of atherosclerosis. *Health & Place, 16*, 1104–1112.

Owen, N., Poulton, T., Hay, F. C., Mohamed-Ali, V., & Steptoe, A. (2003). Socioeconomic status, C-reactive protein, immune factors, and responses to acute mental stress. *Brain Behavior and Immunity, 17*, 286–295.

Petersen, K. L., Marsland, A. L., Flory, F., Votruba-Drzal, E., Muldoon, M. F., & Manuck, S. B. (2008). Community socioeconomic status is associated with circulating interleukein-6 and c-reactive protein. *Psychosomatic Medicine, 70*, 646–652.

Peterson, R. D., & Krivo, L. J. (2010). *Divergent social worlds: Neighborhood crime and the racial-spatial divide*. New York: Russell Sage.

Pollitt, R. A., Kaufmann, J. S., Rose, K. M., Diez-Roux, A. V., Zeng, D., & Heiss, G. (2007). Early-life and adult socioeconomic status and inflammatory risk factors in adulthood. *European Journal of Epidemiology, 22*, 55–66.

Pradhan, A. D., Manson, J. E., Rifai, N., Buring, J. E., & Ridker, P. M. (2001). C-reactive protein, interleukin 6, and risk of developing type 2 diabetes mellitus. *Journal of the American Medical Association, 286*, 327–334.

Robinson, J. B., Lawton, B. A., Taylor, R. B., & Perkins, D. D. (2003). Multilevel longitudinal impacts of incivilities: Fear of crime, expected safety, and block satisfaction. *Journal of Quantitative Criminology, 19*, 237–272.

Sallis, J. F., & King, A. C. (2007). Perceived environmental predictors of physical activity over 6 months in adults: Activity counseling trial. *Health Psychology, 26*, 701–709.

Sampson, R. J. (2003). Neighborhood-level context and health: Lessons from sociology. In I. Kawachi & L. Berkman (Eds.), *Neighborhoods and health* (pp. 132–146). New York: Oxford University Press.

Sampson, R. J., & Wilson, W. J. (1995). Toward a theory of race, crime, and urban inequality. In J. Hagan & R. Peterson (Eds.), *Crime and inequality* (pp. 37–56). Stanford: Stanford University Press.

Sampson, R. J., Raudenbush, S. W., & Earls, F. (1997). Neighborhoods and violent crime: A multilevel study of collective efficacy. *Science, 227*, 918–923.

Shaw, C. R., & McKay, H. D. (1969). *Juvenile delinquency and urban areas: A study of rates of delinquents in relation to differential characteristics of local communities in American cities*. Chicago: University of Chicago Press.

Skogan, W. (1986). Fear of crime and its behavioral implications. In E. A. Fattah (Ed.), *From crime policy to victim policy: Reorienting the justice system* (pp. 167–188). London: Macmillan.

Sprott, J. B., & Doob, A. (1997). Fear, victimization and attitudes to sentencing, the courts, and the police. *Canadian Journal of Criminology, 39*, 275–291.

Sundquist, K., & Theobald, H. (2006). Neighborhood violent crime and unemployment increase the risk of coronary heart disease: A multilevel study in an urban setting. *Social Science & Medicine, 62*, 2061–2071.

Victor, R. G., Haley, R. W., Willett, D. L., Peshock, R. M., Vaeth, P. C., Leonard, D., & Hobbs, H. H. (2004). The Dallas Heart Study: A population-based probability sample for the multidisciplinary study of ethnic differences in cardiovascular health. *The American Journal of Cardiology, 93*, 1473–1480.

Wen, M., Christakis, N. A. (2005). Neighborhood effects on posthospitalization mortality: A population-based cohort study of the elderly in Chicago. *Health Services Research, 40*, 1108–1127.

Wilson, W. J. (1996). *When work disappears: The world of the new urban poor*. New York: Knopf.

Zick, C. D., & Smith, K. R. (2009). Running to the store? The relationship between neighborhood environments and the risk of obesity. *Social Science & Medicine, 69*, 1493–1500.

Chapter 11
Between Spaces: Understanding Movement to and from Prison as an HIV Risk Factor

Kim M. Blankenship and Amy B. Smoyer

Abstract *In the United States, the prevalence of HIV among people who are incarcerated, or have a history of incarceration, is higher than among the general public. Similarly, HIV rates are highest in United States neighborhoods that are disproportionately impacted by incarceration, parole and probation. The association between incarceration and HIV has been partially attributed to high-risk sex and drug use behavior inside correctional facilities. The lack of access to condoms or clean syringes in United States prisons and most jails makes sexual intercourse and injection drug use in these places risky. Research has also found that the disruption of primary sexual relationships resulting from incarceration is associated with an increase in sexual risk in the community, including multiple partners and concurrency. Here, we explore numerous disruptions created by incarceration, including sexual partnerships, to better understand the community-based HIV risk that is produced by the movement to and from prison. Building on Clear et al.'s (Justice Quarterly 20:33–64, 2003) research about the impact of coercive mobility on neighborhood crime rates, we use theories of social disorganization to suggest how criminal justice-induced movement creates HIV risk for both individuals who are incarcerated and members of their social networks by undermining relationship, housing, and economic stability. Preliminary findings from a mixed methods study of parolees and probationers illustrate these arguments and suggest further avenues for HIV prevention research.*

Funding for this study was provided by NIH/NIDA R21 DA019186, PI Blankenship. We also wish to thank Katina Gionteris, Elizabeth Puloka, and Alana Rosenberg for research assistance.

K.M. Blankenship, Ph.D. (✉)
Department of Sociology, American University,
Washington, DC, USA

Center on Health, Risk and Society, American University,
Washington, DC, USA
e-mail: Kim.blankenship@american.edu

A.B. Smoyer, Ph.D., M.S.W.
Silberman School of Social Work, Hunter College, City University of New York,
New York, NY, USA

B. Sanders et al. (eds.), *Crime, HIV and Health: Intersections of Criminal Justice and Public Health Concerns*, DOI 10.1007/978-90-481-8921-2_11,

One of the most pronounced characteristics of the HIV/AIDS epidemic within the United States is that it disproportionately affects African-Americans. While African Americans comprise only 13% of the population, they represent 46% of all people living with HIV in the United States (Center for Disease Control and Prevention [CDC] 2010). In 2008,African-American women had an HIV diagnosis rate 19 times greater than white women, and African- American men had a rate eight times greater that of white men (CDC 2011). African Americans are disproportionately represented among IDU-related HIV cases: African American women represent 60% of all IDU-related HIV cases among women, while among men, African Americans represent 55% of all IDU-related cases (CDC 2005). These trends are likely to continue, or even worsen. African Americans accounted for 50% of the new HIV diagnoses reported in the United States between 2005–2008 (CDC 2011). During the same period, African Americans comprised 62% of all new HIV diagnoses among 13–19 years olds (CDC 2011).

The over representation of African Americans has also been a defining characteristic of United States criminal justice systems almost since their inception (Oshinsky 1997). In 2008, 38% of the 1.6 million sentenced prisoners in the United States were African American (Sabol et al. 2009). African American men are 6.5 times more likely to be incarcerated than White men and African American women are three times more likely than White women to be in prison or jail (Sabol et al. 2009). As of 2001, an African American male had a 1 in 3 chance of going to prison in his lifetime, as compared to a chance of 1 in 17 for a White male (Bonczar 2003). In addition, African-Americans are disproportionately represented among those under community supervision: 39% of the people on parole and 30% of the people on probation are African American (Glaze and Bonczar 2010).

The last 40 years has seen a growth in this racial disparity, in addition to an overall increase in the size of the incarcerated population. These trends are largely a product of United States drug policy (Clear 2007; Fagan and Meares 2008; Moore and Elkavich 2008; Western 2006). Drug offenders accounted for 74% of the growth in state prison populations from 1985 to 1995 (Mumola and Beck 1997). The number of state inmates serving time for a drug offense increased from 1 out every 16, in 1980, to 1 out of every 5 in 2006 (Mauer 1999; Sabol et al. 2009). Similarly, in 2009, 26% of probationers and 36% of parolees were under community supervision for a drug offense (Glaze and Bonczar 2010). African Americans have been disproportionately represented in this increased incarceration of drug offenders. While the number of Whites serving time for drug offenses tripled between 1985 and 1995, this number increased seven-fold for African Americans (Mumola and Beck 1997). Among African American women, the rise in drug related incarceration has been particularly acute. Between 1986 and 1991, the number of African American women incarcerated for drug offenses rose by 828% while incarceration rates for drug offenses among White women increased by 241% (Frost et al. 2006).

A small body of literature has demonstrated an association between incarceration and sexually transmitted infections (STIs), including HIV. For example, using data from North Carolina counties, Thomas and Torrone (2006, 2008) and Thomas and Sampson (2005) found significant correlations between incarceration and rates of teen pregnancy, Chlamydia and gonorrhea, as well as modest correlations with HIV. Using time-lagged analyses, Johnson and Raphael (2006) have demonstrated a significant association between incarceration rates and AIDS infection rates across states. However, limits to such quantitative analyses exist, and according to Thomas et al. (2007), "County-level correlations…do not elucidate the mechanisms by which incarceration leads to individual behaviors and community dynamics favoring STI transmission" (pp. 90–91).

This chapter seeks to expand understanding of the relationships between HIV risk and criminal justice systems. It considers the risk associated with prison life itself, as well as the HIV risk associated with incarceration that is produced in the community. But we also suggest that the *movement* between prison/jail and the community impacts on HIV risk, and that the level of disorder within the neighborhood to which formerly incarcerated people return, fueled in part by this movement, and the degree to which individuals are monitored by community supervision systems (parole and probation), may have an impact on their HIV risk as well. Building on Clear et al.'s (2003) research about the impact of coercive mobility on neighborhood crime rates, we use theories of social disorganization to suggest how criminal justice-induced movement creates HIV risk for both individuals who are incarcerated and members of their social networks by undermining relationship, housing, and economic stability.

11.1 Connecting the Dots Between HIV Risk and Incarceration

There is research to suggest that prisons and jails comprise an HIV/AIDS risk environment, both as the location of a disproportionately high number of HIV-infected individuals and as a high risk setting for the transmission of HIV/AIDS. Researchers estimate that the rate of HIV among federal and state prisoners is about 1.5%, or four times the rate in the general community (Gough et al. 2010). However, while the presence of people with HIV in prison has been documented, the rates of intraprison HIV transmission have not been clearly established. Prisons do not routinely test inmates for HIV at entry and release so data on this issue is not systematically available. In one study, Krebs and Simmons (2002) found that among a sample of 5,265 inmates, the intraprison HIV transmission rate was 0.63%, largely due to having sex among inmates.

There is certainly evidence of both consensual and non-consensual sex in prison between inmates and between inmates and correctional staff (Abiona et al. 2009; Arp 2009; Harawa et al. 2010; Hensley and Tewksbury 2002; Jenness et al. 2007; Seal et al. 2008). Estimates about what percent of inmates are sexually active, the frequency of this behavior and the HIV risk associated with these acts vary depending on the demographics of the population studied, how sexual behavior is defined (anal, vaginal, oral) and whether consensual and/or forced sex is measured. For example, Abiona et al.'s (2009) survey of 1,819 Illinois prisoners found that 19% of the men and 5% of the women had sex while incarcerated. Among the men who reported having sex, 61% reported oral sex, which carries little to no risk of HIV transmission, 34% reported vaginal sex, presumably with correctional staff and again with small risk to the male prisoner, and only 5% reported anal sex. In contrast, 55% of the women who reported sex in prison had vaginal sex and 30% reported anal sex, both of which carry considerable HIV risk for the female inmate. In another study, Fleisher and Krienert (2006) interviewed 564 inmates in 10 states about the behavior of *other* inmates: women reported that 70% of female inmates, and men reported that 42% of male inmates "engaged in homosexual conduct" (p. 11).

Whatever the prevalence, the vaginal and anal intercourse that takes place in prison almost always carries some degree of HIV risk because condoms are largely unavailable in US correctional facilities. Injection drug use and tattooing in prison are two other dimensions of prison life that carry considerable HIV risk as clean injection and tattooing equipment is not available (Abiona et al. 2009; Bonnycastle 2011). These activities, and correctional policy that prohibits the distribution of condoms and clean syringes, contribute to HIV risk in prison.

While research demonstrates that prison life includes some degree of HIV risk, other work suggests that the HIV risk associated with incarceration is primarily produced in the community. Qualitative studies conducted with formerly incarcerated people and their sex partners does document the perception that men who identify as heterosexual may have sex with men while incarcerated, but the data focus more on the financial and emotional insecurity that requires individuals who are *not* incarcerated to establish new relationships when their partners are incarcerated and may necessitate concurrent partnerships for ex-offenders upon release (Adimora et al. 2001; Adimora and Schoenbach 2005; Khan et al. 2011b; Thomas et al. 2007). Research has found that primary partnerships prior to incarceration are associated with fewer sexual partners and that 30–40% of these relationships end when one of the partners becomes incarcerated (Khan et al. 2011a, b). Whether and for how long the disrupted primary relationships would have continued in the community had a partner *not* been incarcerated and if the relationship may be reestablished upon the prisoners' release is not known. Longitudinal research is needed to better understand the "life course" of relationships interrupted by incarceration. However, it is reasonable to suggest that separation due to incarceration may facilitate and/or accelerate relationship dissolution that, in turn, increases the number of lifetime partners for ex-offenders and their partners.

11.2 Social Disorganization, Coercive Mobility and HIV Risk

Social disorganization theory is a well-developed sociological theory aimed at identifying neighborhood factors associated with crime (Shaw and McKay 1942; Travis and Wall 2003). Specifically, it holds that high rates of crime result from social factors that produce social disorganization, in the form of poverty, and population transiency and heterogeneity. In the face of social disorganization collective efficacy is undermined. Neighborhoods with collective efficacy display a high degree of residential stability in which residents are typically involved in complex and sustained social networks, have a high level of commitment to the community, and work together to maintain social control (Sampson 2002; Sampson et al. 1997). Residential mobility is a critical social factor in this model, with high mobility representing a source of low collective efficacy (Golembeski and Fullilove 2008).

Coercive mobility builds on social disorganization theory by highlighting a new form of residential mobility associated with high rates of incarceration (Clear 2007; Rose and Clear 1998). Typically, mobility is viewed as voluntary, but criminal justice policies have produced high rates of involuntary mobility (*coercive mobility*) that is both outward (to prison/jail) and inward (re-entry). Specifically, Clear et al. (2003) operationalized coercive mobility at the neighborhood level in two ways: number of prison admissions and number of prison releases, and analyzed the effects on crime of each separately. Using the work of Morenoff et al. (2001), they measured social disorganization with a Concentrated Disadvantage Index that combined the *z*-scores of the percentage of families receiving public assistance, percentage of individuals who are unemployed, percentage of female-headed households with children, and percentage of residents who are African American in the neighborhood. Somewhat counter intuitively, Rose and Clear (1998) suggest that "the side effects of policies intended to fight crime by controlling individual criminals may exacerbate problems that lead to crime in the first place" (p. 441). By weakening family and community structures, heavy reliance on incarceration and the coercive mobility it produces has actually furthered social disorganization (see also DeFina and Hannon 2010).

Coercive mobility produces social disorganization in at least two ways. First, by removing residents from communities, it represents a significant source of residential mobility that has been associated with social disorganization. On the one hand, it may seem that removing individuals who commit crimes will make neighborhoods safer and foster stronger community structures. But many of those removed are non-violent drug offenders who have complex relationships to the networks in which they are embedded—contributing to them in both positive (e.g. financial resources, supervision of children) and negative (e.g. substance use, violence) ways—and their removal has both positive and negative consequences for those networks and the larger community. Second, by returning a group of 'high-needs' residents from the prisons/jails back into these communities, coercive mobility contributes to economic and family stress and diverts neighborhood resources from the building of collective efficacy.

The coercive mobility theory further suggests that there will be a tipping point to this process, with the most deleterious effects occurring in communities where a large number of people have been caught up in the removal and return cycle (Clear et al. 2003). It also argues that these consequences will be felt not only by those who are incarcerated, but also by their friends and family. Finally, in assigning a causal role for incarceration in relation to crime, the theory of coercive mobility expands on social disorganization theory by offering a non-recursive model in which policy (a criminal justice approach focused on incarceration) represents not just a response to crime (as social disorganization theory holds) but also contributes to the social factors (coercive mobility) that produce crime (Clear 2007).

11.3 Modeling Pathways to HIV Risk

Although social disorganization and coercive mobility were developed to explain persistent or growing crime rates, they also have important implications for HIV risk. Early work by Wallace (1990) examining patterns of rising homicide, suicide, substance use, and AIDS deaths in the Bronx indicates that both the overburdening of the criminal justice system in New York and the city's inability to meet demands for medical services are expressions of a process of social disorganization caused by government policy and resulting in increased rates of HIV/AIDS. More specifically, some of the very same mechanisms through which coercive mobility is hypothesized to produce crime may also be associated with HIV risk, namely, residential, economic, and relationship instability. Nevertheless, very little research has systematically examined the mechanisms through which coercive mobility produces instability in the lives of individuals or their partners, and in turn, makes them vulnerable to HIV. Furthermore, while social disorganization and coercive mobility theory view the incarceration-re-entry cycle as a product of a criminal justice policy focused on incarceration, they do not systematically explore how alternatives to incarceration and other policy factors contribute to or ameliorate coercive mobility. Of particular relevance to coercive mobility are, on the one hand, policies that determine how much time a drug offender spends incarcerated and, on the other hand, policies that pose barriers to the re-entry process.

Using the theories of social disorganization and coercive mobility, we propose a model that is depicted in Fig. 11.1 linking incarceration with race disparities in HIV/AIDS. The incarceration/re-entry cycle represents a form of coercive mobility that creates instability in the lives of individual drug offenders (Path A)—including housing and economic instability, and instability of sexual partnerships—that in turn, promotes vulnerability to HIV/AIDS (Path B). These impacts will be exacerbated for individuals who return to communities that have been hard hit by patterns of coercive mobility and the community-wide social disorganization that it produces (Path C). Further, alternatives to incarceration programs, as well as sentencing policies and welfare policies that dictate access to social services for drug offenders, will affect this process through their impact on coercive mobility (Path D). Coercive

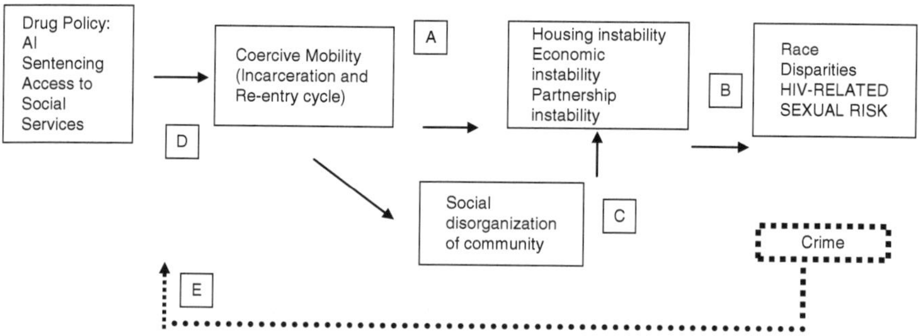

Fig. 11.1 Social disorganization and coercive mobility theory and HIV-related sexual risk

mobility theory also suggests that these same forces will impact on crime, sending some individuals back into the criminal justice system to perpetuate the incarceration/re-entry cycle (Path E), which ultimately, has implications for HIV/AIDS. This model suggests that drug offenders who have been incarcerated will have greater residential, economic, and relationship instability and therefore, will engage in more HIV-related sexual risk behaviors than those who have been placed on probation with no prison/jail time.

These processes may contribute to greater race disparities in HIV/AIDS in a number of ways. To the extent that African Americans are more likely than whites to be incarcerated, they will face any associated HIV related risks to a greater degree than Whites. This could happen, for example, if African Americans are more likely than Whites to be incarcerated rather than placed on probation for drug related offenses and to the extent that incarceration produces greater HIV related risks than alternative forms of community supervision. It may also happen if African Americans are more likely to face drug policy-related penalty enhancements such as greater prison time for being arrested in a drug free zone. Further, if the hypothesized impacts of incarceration—for example economic instability, relationship breakdown—are greater for African Americans than they are for whites, the model may also help account for race disparities. And, if African Americans and their sexual partners are more likely than Whites, as they likely are, to live in neighborhoods characterized by social disorganization, then any related impacts on HIV risk will affect them to a greater degree than Whites.

11.4 Building Knowledge About Risk Between Spaces: The SHARPP Study

Between, 2005 and 2007, we conducted a pilot study in New Haven, CT, called Structures, Health and Risk among Probationers and Parolees (SHARPP), which explored how involvement in the criminal justice system shapes the HIV related risks and behaviors of formerly incarcerated people on parole and probation with a history of drug use, and how this risk varies by race and gender.

In total, 178 participants were enrolled in this mixed methods study: 48 participated in a series of three longitudinal interviews (at baseline, 6 months, 1 year) and 130 participated in a cross-sectional survey (17 participated in both the survey and the qualitative interviews, so there were 161 unique participants). At the time of enrollment, all participants were over 18 years old and being supervised by either parole or probation after having spent at least 3 months in prison in the past year for a non-violent offense related to drugs. Retention rates in the longitudinal interviews were high, with 46 of the 48 participants interviewed at the 6-month follow up, and 37 of these interviewed at the 1 year follow up. Participants were interviewed about their drug use behavior, sexual partnerships, social networks (including family), criminal justice history, housing, physical and mental health, health care utilization, and education. They were also asked their opinions about the criminal justice system and details about their experiences with parole and probation. Participants were paid for their participation and the protocol was reviewed by the Institutional Review Board at the Yale School of Medicine.

The study sample was approximately 80% male, 63% African American, 15% Latino/a and 25% White. The Latino/a participants were primarily Puerto Rican (75%). About 12% of the sample identified as gay, lesbian, bisexual or transgendered. On average, the length of the most recent incarceration was longer for the survey sample (27 months) than the interview sample (18 months). Similarly, the participants in the survey reported a greater number of lifetime incarcerations (6.8 incarcerations), when compared to the interview participants (3.9 incarcerations). Findings from this pilot research shed light on how coercive mobility may impact HIV risk.

11.4.1 Relationship Stability

As described earlier, one of the ways that incarceration may produce risk for STIs and HIV outside the prison walls is by increasing concurrency, or the likelihood that people will be involved in more than one sexual relationship at the same time. Not only is there considerable literature suggesting that concurrency increases HIV risk and transmission (e.g. Aral 2004; Morris and Kretzschmar 1997), but research by Adimora and colleagues have identified incarceration as one of the factors consistently and significantly associated with concurrency. For example, an analysis of data from the 2002 National Survey of Family Growth by Adimora et al. (2007), indicates that concurrency among men is associated with being incarcerated in the past year. Similarly, among African Americans reported to the North Carolina health department as having been HIV infected in the past 6 months through heterosexual sex, concurrency rates were high, and in multivariate analyses, they were associated with incarceration (Adimora et al. 2003). Incarceration of a sex partner was also associated with concurrency in a random sample of North Carolinians selected from the driver's license rolls (Adimora et al. 2004). In a recent review article, Harawa and Adimora (2008) outline a research agenda for understanding the relationship among incarceration, African Americans and HIV, concluding: "Research is needed to determine how both incarceration itself and the high rates of incarceration within African-American communities affect HIV risk behaviors and HIV incidence among: (1) those incarcerated, (2) the sexual partners and personal networks of those left behind, and (3) the community at large" (p. 59).

Our study findings begin to address some of these issues by unpacking the ways in which incarceration impacts relationship stability. The disruption of relationships that participants reported was extensive and stable relationships were not immune. Among survey participants, only 37% have ever been married, with over a fourth of those reporting being married more than once. Almost 40% (39.5%) of the people who reported being married at either their first or most recent incarceration stated that the incarceration led to their divorce. Similarly, at the time of their most recent incarceration, 58% of respondents reported being in a committed relationship, and of those, 48% indicated that the incarceration led to the breakup of the relationship.

Although the numbers were too small to draw statistical inferences, Whites reported slightly lower rates of breakup (43%) as compared to African Americans (50%), and women reported lower rates (33%) than men (54%).

Qualitative interviews further elucidate the challenges of maintaining marriages and long term, stable relationships through periods of incarceration. Consider Curtis, a 42-year-old married African American man, whose wife had regularly visited him while he was serving time in jail. Upon release, he hoped to move back in with his wife and son and resume a monogamous relationship with his wife. Instead, however, at all three interviews he was living with another woman, who he referred to as his girlfriend, because his wife and son lived in public housing and, as an ex-felon he was prohibited from living there. According to Curtis: "Yes...I have intentions on getting back with her [my wife]...And this right here, with this girlfriend, it's like a thing where I'm just...I just came out and I needed a residence and residence with my wife is public housing and it doesn't allow convicted felons to be in there..." He indicated that he is sexually active with both women, and does not use condoms with or disclose his concurrency to either of them.

The relationship instability produced by incarceration in the lives of respondents was not restricted to sexual partners. Fully 66% of survey respondents report that incarceration has caused estrangement from family members. Qualitative interviews provide further insight into this process. Most notably, they suggest that it is the relationships with the greatest potential to ease the burden of re-entry, by providing needed resources and support to ex-offenders that are the ones most harmed by incarceration. While a frequent condition of community supervision programs is to cease interacting with former drug using friends, the majority of participants in our in-depth interviews (n=29) returned to the same low-income, low-resourced, drug using networks that they were in when they were incarcerated. On the other hand, incarceration does seem to have a detrimental effect on more supportive relationships. Eleven participants returned to the same supportive networks (employed, non-drug users with access to housing and other resources) that they had been a part of prior to incarceration, but in each of these cases those relationships had been weakened. In only a minority of situations (n=7), did the lives of the participants improve post-incarceration as compared to pre-incarceration. For three, systemic support—disability and/or supportive subsidized housing—accounted for the improvement; for the other four, success was related to individual efforts (i.e. personal dedication to work, religion) and/or new sex partners without criminal justice or drug using histories. For most of the study participants, each incarceration further distanced them from supportive social relationships and exacerbated economic vulnerability associated with HIV risk.

11.4.2 *Residential Stability*

For SHARPP respondents in both the survey and the in-depth interviews, housing instability appears to be associated with movement in and out of prison/jail. Nearly one fifth of survey respondents indicated that since turning 18, they have lived in more than ten different houses. Seventy percent report ever being homeless—spending at least one night in a shelter or public place—and 35.9% reported being homeless in the past year. Forty three percent of respondents indicated that their name had been on a lease or they had owned a home, but more than half of these (53%) lost the lease or home because of incarceration. Homelessness also appears to be associated with number of times incarcerated. While about 60% of respondents with three or fewer incarcerations reported ever being homeless, 79% of those with more than three reported a history of homelessness as did fully 91% of those who have been incarcerated more than ten times. Participants in the qualitative interviews experienced high levels of housing insecurity, as well, with most living in two (48%) or three (29%) different places during the one-year study time period. Only 11 (23%) participants lived in the same place for the entire year of the study. Levels of homelessness and housing instability are exacerbated for women. Female relatives and sex partners were a primary source of housing for male participants coming out of prison. Women, however, were often unable to access the housing resources of their female relatives because those family members were caring for the women's minor child(ren) and were unable or unwilling to house the women as well. This may help explain why only 14% of the women participating in qualitative interviews were living with female relatives at baseline. Meanwhile, that only 7% of the women lived with male sex partners indicates that housing resources in low-income communities are often controlled by women. Unable to access female controlled resources, women in the study were more likely than men to be living in institutional housing (halfway house, sober house) or to be homeless at all three study time points.

SHARPP interviews also highlight the housing stressors experienced in the community by the non-incarcerated sexual partners of people who are incarcerated. Among survey respondents, 33% reported that someone they were living with became homeless as a result of their incarceration. Six of 48 participants in qualitative interviews reported that the sexual partners, parents, and/or children with whom they were living were displaced at the time of their incarceration. While only one of these transitions resulted in homelessness, their stories indicate that the movement was disruptive for all who experienced it. For example, one 34-year-old White man, who bonded out for a brief time period between his arrest and incarceration, found his long-term sexual and drug-using partner, with whom he had been living at arrest, at her father's home injecting heroin, something she had never done before. This indicates how quickly a situation can deteriorate and elevate HIV risk once a partner is removed by the criminal justice system. It is noteworthy that this often happens to partners who themselves, have no history of drug use or criminal justice involvement.

11.5 Structural Interventions to Address HIV Risk Related to Coercive Mobility

Structural interventions (SIs) are public health interventions that alter the structural context within which health is produced and reproduced (Blankenship et al. 2000, 2006). They differ from individual focused interventions in that they locate the source of public health problems in structural, contextual or environmental factors that influence risk behavior or disease transmission, rather than in the characteristics of individuals who engage in risk behaviors. It is likely that to be most effective SIs should reflect sound theory and a complete understanding of the risk environment that produces HIV (Blankenship et al. 2006).

Coercive mobility and the social disorganization that it produces are structural sources of HIV risk, as are the policies that contribute to coercive mobility. Structural interventions are likely necessary to address their impacts. But effective structural interventions require an in-depth understanding of how these processes and policies operate to produce HIV risk. At the most general level, these interventions may be focused either on reducing the number of individuals moving through the criminal justice system to begin with, or simplifying or enhancing the re-entry process for those who have come under its jurisdiction. Both are likely to involve policy reforms. Further, to the extent that research can enhance our conceptual understanding of the association among incarceration and HIV risk, it can expand both social disorganization and coercive mobility theories and the theoretical foundations on which SIs are developed. Finally, because these theories developed to explain crime but can be applied to health, they have the potential to suggest interventions that meet both public health and criminal justice priorities. It is reasonable to suggest that this will increase the chances for their implementation.

More extensive use of alternative to incarceration programs that reduce or eliminate prison or jail time and provide for some form of community supervision is an example of an SI that has the potential to modify the HIV/AIDS risks associated with coercive mobility by reducing the movement between spaces. Research is needed to determine if this SI would be effective. For example, parole and probation may moderate the impact of confinement by reducing the time an individual spends incarcerated. However, when released to these programs, most individuals are subject to active and continued supervision by the criminal justice system, reporting to a probation authority (70% of probationers) or a paroling agency (83% of parolees) (Glaze and Bonczar 2007). In addition, most inmates are required to meet certain conditions while on probation or parole, and violations of these conditions can send them back to prison, even when no new crime has been committed. Nationally, of those parolees discharged from supervision in 2005, fully 38% had been returned to incarceration, three-fourths of whom had committed rule violations rather than new offenses; 16% of probationers were returned to incarceration (Glaze and Bonczar 2007). According to another study, two-thirds of those released on parole are back in prison within 3 years (Petersilia 2001). For many, then, early release through probation or parole does not, in the long term, reduce the time incarcerated or even the incarceration/re-entry cycle. Some research indicates that our current parole supervision system actually increases, rather than reduces recidivism (Austin and Hardyman 2004). Based on this it is not clear whether probation or parole serve as alternatives to incarceration that reduce or exacerbate coercive mobility (Clear 2008).

Changes to sentencing guidelines and to policies that create 'collateral consequences' of incarceration, namely access to income support, food stamps and housing upon release, are examples of other SIs that could reduce coercive mobility and/or moderate the impacts of criminal justice involvement (see also Adimora and Auerbach 2010). For example, consider mandatory minimums sentences that specify by statute the sentence that must be applied to all those convicted of particular crimes. These policies all have implications for coercive mobility insofar as they relate to whether drug offenders will be incarcerated and for how long, and whether they may be at increased risk for returning to prison/jail.

A number of other policies targeted to drug users have implications for coercive mobility through their impact on the ability of drug offenders to access social services and in turn, their potential impact on the re-entry process. These include policies that permit public housing authorities to deny admission to those convicted of a felony drug offense and prohibit anyone with a drug conviction from receiving federal financial aid for post-secondary education.

11.6 Conclusion

Ample evidence confirms that African Americans are disproportionately impacted by HIV/AIDS and disproportionately likely to be incarcerated. Also, a clear association exists between incarceration and drug policies on the one hand, and incarceration and HIV, on the other, but there is a dearth of research on the mechanisms that link them or that explain how these links produce race disparities in HIV/AIDS. Theories of social disorganization and coercive mobility offer a promising approach to understanding these connections, though to date they have not been systematically used for these purposes. Incarceration produces race disparities in HIV/AIDS. SIs can break these linkages, and reduce what is a major health crisis in the African American community and the United States.

References

Abiona, T. C., Adefuye, A. S., Balogun, J. A., & Sloan, P. E. (2009). Gender differences in HIV risk behaviors of inmates. *Journal of Women's Health, 18*(1), 65–71.

Adimora, A. A., & Auerbach, J. D. (2010). Structural interventions for HIV prevention in the United States. *Journal of Acquired Immune Deficiency Syndrome, 55*(Suppl. 2), S132–S135.

Adimora, A. A., & Schoenbach, V. J. (2005). Social context, sexual networks, and racial disparities in rates of sexually transmitted infections. *Journal of Infectious Diseases, 191*, S115–S122.

Adimora, A. A., Schoenbach, V. J., Martinson, F. E. A., Donaldson, K. H., Fullilove, R. E., & Aral, S. O. (2001). Social context of sexual relationships among rural African Americans. *Sexually Transmitted Diseases, 28*(2), 69–76.

Adimora, A. A., Schoenbach, V. J., Martinson, F. E. A., Donaldson, K. H., Stancil, T. R., & Fullilove, R. E. (2003). Concurrent partnerships among rural African Americans with recently reported heterosexually transmitted HIV infection. *Journal of Acquired Immune Deficiency Syndromes, 34*(4), 423–429.

Adimora, A. A., Schoenbach, V. J., Martinson, F., Donaldson, K. H., Stancil, T. R., & Fullilove, R. E. (2004). Concurrent sexual partnerships among African Americans in the rural South. *Annals of Epidemiology, 14*(3), 155–160.

Adimora, A. A., Schoenbach, V. J., & Doherty, I. A. (2007). Concurrent sexual partnerships among men in the United States. *American Journal of Public Health, 97*(12), 2230–2237.

Aral, S. O. (2004). Sexual risk behavior and infection: Epidemiological considerations. *Sexually Transmitted Infections, 80*(Suppl. 2), 8–12.

Arp, W. (2009). Race, incarceration and HIV/AIDS in Louisiana: Risky sexual behavior demands mandatory testing. *Race, Gender and Class, 16*(1/2), 228–237.

Austin, J., & Hardyman, P. L. (2004). The risks and needs of the returning prisoner population. *Review of Policy Research, 21*, 13–29.

Blankenship, K. M., Bray, S. J., & Merson, M. H. (2000). Structural interventions in public health. *AIDS, 14*(Suppl. 1), S1–S11.

Blankenship, K. M., Friedman, S. R., Dworkin, S., & Mantell, J. E. (2006). Structural interventions: Concepts, challenges, and opportunities for research. *Journal of Urban Health, 83*, 59–72.

Bonczar, T. P. (2003). *Prevalence of imprisonment in the U.S. population, 1974-2001*. Bureau of Justice Statistics Special Report (Publication No. NCJ 197976). Washington, DC: Bureau of Justice Statistics.

Bonnycastle, K. D. (2011). The social organization of penal tattooing in two Canadian federal male prisons: Locating sites of risk for empirically-based health care interventions. *Howard Journal of Criminal Justice, 50*(1), 17–33.

Center for Disease Control and Prevention. (2005). Trends in HIV/AIDS diagnoses—33 states, 2001–2004. *MMWR Weekly, 54*, 1149–1153.

Center for Disease Control and Prevention. (2010). *HIV among African Americans*. Retrieved from http://www.cdc.gov/hiv/topics/aa/resources/factsheets/pdf/aa.pdf

Center for Disease Control and Prevention. (2011). Disparities in diagnoses of HIV infection between Black/African Americans and other racial/ethnic populations—37 States, 2005-2008. *MMWR Weekly, 60*(4), 93–98.

Clear, T. R. (2007). *Imprisoning communities: How mass incarceration makes disadvantaged neighborhoods worse*. New York: Oxford University Press.

Clear, T. R. (2008). The effects of high imprisonment rates on communities. In M. Tonry (Ed.), *Crime and justice: A review of research* (Vol. 37, pp. 97–132). Chicago: University of Chicago Press.

Clear, T. R., Rose, D. R., Waring, E., & Scully, K. (2003). Coercive mobility and crime: A preliminary examination of concentrated incarceration and social disorganization. *Justice Quarterly, 20*, 33–64.

DeFina, R., & Hannon, L. (2010). For incarceration, there is no time like the present: The lagged effects of prisoner reentry on property and violent crime rates. *Social Science Research, 39*, 1004–1014.

Fagan, J., & Meares, T. L. (2008). Punishment, deterrence and social control: The paradox of punishment in minority communities. *Ohio State Journal of Criminal Law, 6*, 173–228.

Fleisher, M. S., & Krienert, J. L. (2006). *The culture of prison sexual violence* (Document No. 216515). Washington, DC: National Institute of Justice.

Frost, N. A., Greene, J., & Pranis, K. (2006). *Hard hit: The growth in the imprisonment of women, 1977–2004*. Boston: Institute on Women in Criminal Justice.

Glaze, L. E., & Bonczar, T. P. (2007). *Probation and parole in the United States, 2006*. Bureau of Justice Statistics Bulletin (Publication No. NCJ 220218). Washington, DC: Bureau of Justice Statistics.

Glaze, L. E., & Bonczar, T. P. (2010). *Probation and parole in the United States, 2009*. Bureau of Justice Statistics Bulletin (Publication No. NCJ 231674). Washington, DC: Bureau of Justice Statistics.

Golembeski, C., & Fullilove, R. (2008). Criminal (in)justice in the city and its associated health consequences. *American Journal of Public Health, 98*(1), S185–S190.

Gough, E., Kempf, M. C., Graham, L., Manzanero, M., Hook, E. W., Bartolucci, A., & Chamot, E. (2010). HIV and Hepatitis B and C incidence rates in US correctional populations and high risk groups: A systematic review and meta-analysis. *BMC Public Health, 10*, 777–790.

Harawa, N., & Adimora, A. (2008). Incarceration, African Americans and HIV: Advancing a research agenda. *Journal of the National Medical Association, 100*, 57–62.

Harawa, N. T., Sweat, J., George, S., & Sylla, M. (2010). Sex and condom use in a large jail unit for men who have sex with men (MSM) and male-to-female transgenders. *Journal of Health Care for the Poor and Underserved, 21*, 1071–1087.

Hensley, C., & Tewksbury, R. (2002). Inmate-to-inmate prison sexuality: A review of empirical studies. *Trauma Violence Abuse, 3*(3), 226–243.

Jenness, V., Maxon, C. L., Matsuda, K. N., & Sumner, J. M. (2007). *Violence in California correctional facilities: An empirical examination of sexual assault*. Irvine: University of California, Center for Evidence-Based Corrections.

Johnson, R. C., & Raphael, S. (2006). The effects of male incarceration dynamics on AIDS infection rates among African-American women and men (unpublished paper), Goldman School of Public Policy, UC Berkeley. The Johnson and Raphael paper appears to be 2006, http://ist-socrates.berkeley.edu/~ruckerj/johnson_raphael_prison-AIDSpaper6-06.pdf.

Khan, M. R., Behrend, L., Adimora, A. A., Weir, S. S., Tisdale, C., & Wohl, D. A. (2011a). Dissolution of primary intimate relationships during incarceration and associations with post-release STI/HIV risk behavior in a Southeastern city. *Sexually Transmitted Diseases, 38*(1), 43–47.

Khan, M. R., Behrend, L., Adimora, A. A., Weir, S. S., White, B. L., & Wohl, D. A. (2011b). Dissolution of primary intimate relationships during incarceration and implications for post-release HIV transmission. *Journal of Urban Health, 88*(2), 365–375.

Krebs, C. P., & Simmons, M. (2002). Intraprison HIV transmission: An assessment of whether it occurs, how it occurs, and who is at risk. *AIDS Education and Prevention, 14*, 53–64.

Mauer, M. (1999). *Race to incarcerate*. New York: The New Press.

Moore, L. D., & Elkavich, A. (2008). Who's using and who's doing time: Incarceration, the war on drugs, and public health. *American Journal of Public Health, 8*(5), 782–786.

Morenoff, J. D., Sampson, R. J., & Raudenbush, S. W. (2001). Neighborhood inequality, collective efficacy, and the spatial dynamics of urban violence. *Criminology, 39*, 517–559.

Morris, M., & Kretzschmar, M. (1997). Concurrent partnerships and the spread of HIV. *AIDS, 11*(5), 641–648.

Mumola, C. J., & Beck, A. J. (1997). *Prisoners in 1996*. Bureau of Justice Statistics Bulletin (Publication No. NCJ 164619). Washington, DC: Bureau of Justice Statistics.

Oshinsky, D. M. (1997). *Worse than slavery: Parchman farm and the ordeal of Jim Crow justice*. New York: Simon & Schuster.

Petersilia, J. (2001). When prisoners return to communities: Political, economic and social consequences. *Federal Probation, 65*, 3–6.

Rose, D. R., & Clear, T. R. (1998). Incarceration, social capital, and crime: Implications for social disorganization theory. *Criminology, 36*, 441–479.

Sabol, W. J., West, H. C., & Cooper, M. (2009). *Prisoners in 2008*. Bureau of Justice Statistics Bulletin (Publication No. NCJ 228417). Washington, DC: Bureau of Justice Statistics.

Sampson, R. J. (2002). Transcending tradition: New directions in community research, Chicago style. *Criminology, 40*(2), 213–230.

Sampson, R. J., Raudenbush, S. W., & Earls, F. (1997). Neighborhoods and violent crime: A multilevel study of collective efficacy. *Science, 277*, 918–924.

Seal, D. W., Margolis, A. D., Morrow, K. M., Belcher, L., Sosman, J., Askew, J., & Project START Substudy Group. (2008). Substance use and sexual behavior during incarceration among 18- to 29-year old men: Prevalence and correlates. *AIDS and Behavior, 12*(1), 27–40.

Shaw, C. R., & McKay, H. D. (1942). *Juvenile delinquency and urban areas*. Chicago: University of Chicago Press.

Thomas, J. C., & Sampson, L. A. (2005). High rates of incarceration as a social force associated with community rates of sexually transmitted infection. *Journal of Infectious Diseases, 191*(Suppl. 1), 55–60.

Thomas, J. C., & Torrone, E. (2006). Incarceration as forced migration: Effects on selected community health outcomes. *American Journal of Public Health, 96*, 1762–1765.

Thomas, J. C., & Torrone, E. (2008). Incarceration as forced migration: Effects on selected community health outcomes. *American Journal of Public Health, 98*(Suppl. 1), S181–S184.

Thomas, J. C., Lavandowski, B. A., Isler, M. R., Torrone, E., & Wilson, G. (2007). Incarceration and sexually transmitted infections: A neighborhood perspective. *Journal of Urban Health, 85*(1), 90–98.

Travis, J., & Wall, M. (Eds.). (2003). *Prisoners once removed: The impact of incarceration and reentry on children, families, and communities*. Washington, DC: The Urban Institute Press.

Wallace, R. (1990). Urban desertification, public health, and public order: Planned shrinkage, violent death, substance abuse and AIDS in the Bronx. *Social Science and Medicine, 31*, 801–813.

Western, B. (2006). *Punishment and inequality in America*. New York: Russell Sage.

Part IV
Public Health Interventions with Criminal Justice Populations

Chapter 12
Youth Violence Prevention: Public Health Intervention and High Risk Populations

Tanya Nieri, Jennifer L. Matjasko, Kirk R. Williams, and Nancy G. Guerra

Abstract *This chapter describes a public health approach to preventing youth violence in high-risk populations. The discussion uses two case studies to illustrate the potential impact of public health interventions on reducing delinquency among a population of youth in Southern California. It reviews evaluation data from two community-based studies conducted by the Southern California Academic Center of Excellence on Youth Violence Prevention at the University of California at Riverside, funded by the Centers for Disease Control and Prevention. The first study is an implementation of the Families and Schools Together intervention in Santa Ana, California, and the second is the Arlanza Neighborhood Initiative in Riverside, California. In addition to highlighting evaluation results, the chapter reviews the need for public health intervention across the life course, including long term assessment, the importance of family, school, and community outcomes, tailoring interventions to specific individuals and communities, and assessing effectiveness among subgroups.*

The findings and conclusions of this report are those of the authors and do not necessarily represent the official position of the Centers for Disease Control and Prevention. Support for this chapter was provided by the Southern California Academic Center of Excellence on Youth Violence Prevention at the University of California, Riverside and funded by a cooperative agreement with the Centers for Disease Control and Prevention (#5U49CE00073). Please send all inquires to: Tanya Nieri, Ph.D., Sociology, University of California, Riverside, 1216 Watkins Hall, Riverside, CA 92521, (951) 827-5854 (office) (951) 827-3330 (fax) tanyan@ucr.edu

T. Nieri, Ph.D. (✉)
Department of Sociology, University of California at Riverside (UCR), Riverside, CA, USA
e-mail: tanyan@ucr.edu.

J.L. Matjasko, Ph.D.
Division of Violence Prevention, Centers for Disease Control and Prevention, Atlanta, GA, USA

K.R. Williams
Department of Sociology, University of Arizona, Tucson, AZ, USA

N.G. Guerra, Ph.D.
Department of Psychology, University of California, Riverside, CA, USA

B. Sanders et al. (eds.), *Crime, HIV and Health: Intersections of Criminal Justice and Public Health Concerns*, DOI 10.1007/978-90-481-8921-2_12,

Youth homicide is the second leading cause of death for young people between the ages of 10 and 24 years old (Centers for Disease Control and Prevention [CDC] 2009a). The CDC has funded several Academic Centers of Excellence (ACE) across the country to address this important public health problem. The ACEs are engaged in the surveillance of youth violence and implementing behavioral interventions. Each ACE works within the community to encourage participation and partnership, and to mobilize residents and researchers to craft effective solutions for violence prevention tailored to the community. This chapter reviews the public health approach and presents two case studies of public health interventions implemented with high risk populations in Southern California by the CDC-funded Academic Center of Excellence in Youth Violence Prevention at the University of California at Riverside (ACE-UCR). Finally, the chapter proposes future research questions about public health intervention with high-risk populations.

12.1 An Overview of Public Health Interventions

The term 'intervention' as used in this chapter refers to any strategy, program, policy, or practice that aims to address a public health problem. Public health interventions focus on population health to prevent morbidity and mortality related to disease, illness, and injury. A main feature of this approach is a focus on primary prevention – that is, intervening prior to the onset of problems. This approach is distinct from the medical model in which interventions occur only after problem onset (Weitz 2006). That said, public health interventions might also aim to prevent either the onset of problems among high-risk groups (secondary prevention) or the continuation or escalation of problems (tertiary prevention). While primary prevention is sometimes referred to as 'prevention' and secondary and tertiary prevention are referred to as 'intervention,' this chapter addresses all three forms as interventions, each of which has prevention as its aim (United States Department of Health and Human Services [USDHHS] 2001).

The social ecological model, which is used by some in public health in order to understand where risk factors are situated, is a model wherein the individual level is nested within relationships, the community and the larger society (Stokols 1996; see Fig. 12.1.) These four interconnected levels reinforce each other, while representing separate, but complementary avenues for intervention. The social ecological model highlights that it might be advantageous to modify individual behavior directly while also modifying individual behavior by changing the environment and systems that also influence the behaviors.

Implementation of the public health approach and application of the social ecological model involve a series of specific steps, illustrated in Fig. 12.2. The first step, describing the problem, is systematically uncovering as much basic knowledge as possible about the problem, including the size, location, and whom it affects. It also involves tracking the problem to detect changes and assess trends. The second step entails identifying the risk and protective factors associated with the problem. A third step involves developing and testing prevention strategies – i.e., interventions. Finally, the fourth step is promoting the widespread adoption of effective interventions.

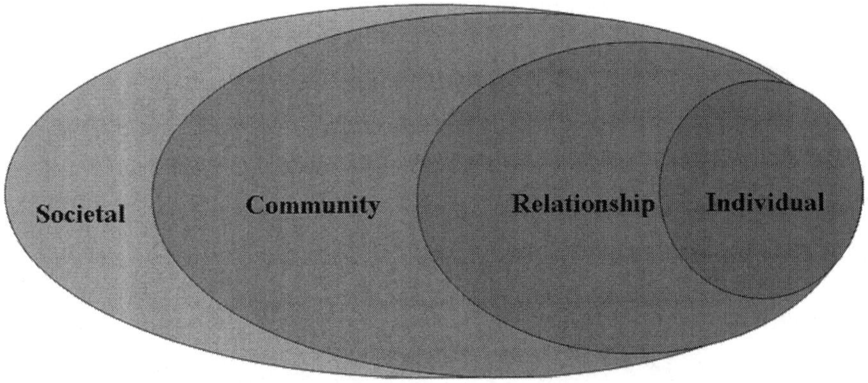

Fig. 12.1 Public health and the social ecological model (Adapted from National Center for Injury Prevention and Control (2009))

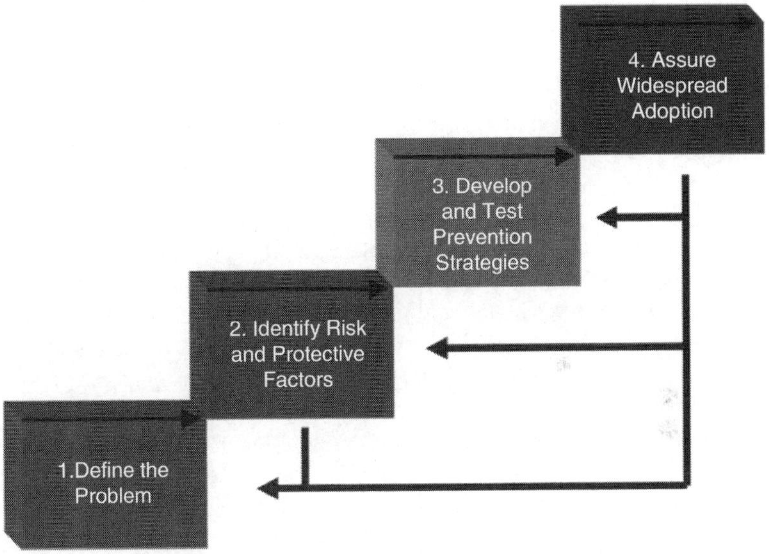

Fig. 12.2 Public health approach to prevention (Adapted from Mercy et al. (1993))

12.1.1 Step 1: Describing the Problem

The first step in preventing violence is to get a sense of the problem – knowing the magnitude and scope of the problem, those experiencing the problem, where it occurs, and other characteristics. Systematically gathering this information, as well as analyzing, interpreting, and tracking it over time, is important in order to determine whether rates are increasing or decreasing, and to compare data across communities and time (McMahon 2000). Table 12.1 illustrates data from a community in Santa Ana, CA, targeted for intervention by the ACE-UCR. The table provides details on the target area – the 92701 zip code – and the city of Santa Ana. These data indicate

Table 12.1 Population data for Santa Ana, CA: demographic characteristics

	92701	Citywide
Total population	61,363	337,977
African American	<1%	1.7%
Latino	92%	76.1%
Asian	1%	8.8%
White Non Latino	5.3%	12.4%
Native American	<1%	1.2%
Other Pacific Islander	<1%	<1%
Youth under 18	75.3%	34.2%
Median household income	$33,728	$43,412
Level of education (for residents aged 25 years and over)		
Less than 9th grade	48.1%	36.3%
9th to 12th grade	21.7%	20.5%
High school graduate	12.6%	16.0%
Some college	9.3%	13.9%
Associates degree	2.8%	4.1%
Bachelors degree	3.6%	6.4%
Graduate or professional degree	2.0%	2.8%

that large Latino and youth populations characterize the area. Additionally, people with lower levels of education are overrepresented, and the area has a lower median household income than the citywide median.

Table 12.2 provides data on economic and other population characteristics as well as information on youth crime. These data specify that the distribution of youth crime-by-crime type within the target area is comparable to that citywide. However, as indicated in the bottom panel's rightmost column, the target area has a disproportionate amount of youth crime in the city. Over half (56%) of all the youth crime in the city occurred in this area. The disparity in violent crime is even greater; two-thirds of homicides citywide occurred in this area, suggesting it would be a promising place to intervene to prevent further violent crime.

12.1.2 Step 2: Identifying Risk and Protective Factors

The next step is identifying risk and protective factors, and answers to the following questions are sought: What protects youth? What increases their risk? What prevents youth from perpetrating violence? What increases their risk of perpetrating violence? Which factors (i.e., attitudes, behaviors, policies) could be successfully targeted by an intervention? Which groups (i.e., age, gender, ethnicity, income, location) are most at risk for violence?

Numerous risk factors for violence have been identified (CDC 2010; Guerra and Williams 2002; USDHHS 2009). Risk factors at the individual level include substance use, attention deficits, hyperactivity, learning disorders, poor behavior regulation, antisocial beliefs and attitudes, low IQ, high emotional distress, social cognitive or

Table 12.2 Santa Ana, CA: indicators of risk and youth crime

	92701	Citywide	% of Citywide
Risk factors			
Female-headed household with children	10.4%	7.6%	na[a]
Foreign born	59.5%	53.3%	na
Unemployed	5.6%	4.7%	na
Families in poverty	26.4%	16.1%	na
Youth crime in 2003			
All crime	574	1,028	55.8%
Homicide	<1%	<1%	66.7%
Rape	1.6%	1.6%	56.3%
Robbery	4.5%	3.4%	74.3%
Assault	7.3%	6.1%	66.7%
Drug crimes	17.1%	19.2%	49.7%
Misdemeanors	69.2%	69.5%	55.6%
Child abuse reports from child protective services	1,455	3,957	36.8%

[a]*na* not available. City reported only percentages

information processing deficits, family violence exposure, a history of violent victimization, early aggressive behavior, or treatment for emotional problems. Family risk factors include authoritarian parenting attitudes, harsh, lax, or inconsistent disciplinary practices, low parental involvement, parental substance abuse or criminality, low emotional attachment to parents/caregivers, low parental education or income, poor family functioning, and poor monitoring and supervision of children. Peer and social risk factors include association with delinquent peers, lack of involvement in pro-social activities, low commitment to school, involvement in gangs, social rejection by peers, poor academic performance and school failure. Community risk factors include diminished economic opportunities, high concentrations of poor residents, high level of transiency, high level of family disruption, low levels of community participation, and socially disorganized neighborhoods.

Research has also begun to identify protective factors for violence, though results are preliminary (CDC 2010; Guerra and Williams 2002). Protective factors are those variables that have a moderating effect on risk factors. Individual-level protective factors may include intolerance of deviance, high IQ, high grade point average, positive social orientation, religiosity, involvement in social activities, and connectedness to adults outside the family (CDC 2010). Recent research has also shown that strength-based factors, such as core competencies formed in adolescence, can foster resilience in youth, protecting them from violence, other problem behaviors, and negative health outcomes (e.g., Guerra and Bradshaw 2008; Kim et al. 2008). Family protective factors may include connectedness to family, ability to discuss problems with parents, perceived high parental expectations about school performance, frequent shared activities with parents, and consistent presence of parent during key daily events. Peer and social protective factors may include commitment to school and involvement in social activities (CDC 2010). Aggregate (neighborhoods and schools) level research has also shown that youth can be protected from violence and other aggressive behaviors by building collective efficacy, meaning fostering cohesion and trust among community members and their willingness to intervene for the common good (e.g., Sampson et al. 1997; Williams and Guerra in press).

12.1.3 Step 3: Developing and Testing Prevention Strategies

Step 3 involves developing and implementing prevention strategies to address risk and protective factors, often using data collected through steps 1 and 2. Those data inform the content, scope, and audience of prevention strategies. Efforts at this step address such questions as, "What works?", "For whom?", and "Under what conditions?" These three critical questions are key in generating research findings that can lead to actionable public health interventions.

Prevention strategies may target specific ecological levels (i.e., individual, family, or community), or they may target multiple levels simultaneously. An example of an individual-level intervention is Positive Life Changes, developed by Nancy Guerra (2009). A cognitive-behavioral mindfulness intervention for adolescents aged 14–21 years old in schools or alternative education settings, Positive Life Changes, promotes the core competencies of youth development for the prevention of violence and other problem behaviors: Positive sense of self, self-control, a moral system of belief, pro-social connectedness, and decision-making skills. The intervention has three components with ten lessons each that can be delivered separately or together.

An example of a family-level intervention is the Triple P: Positive Parenting Program (http://www1.triplep.net/), developed by Matt Sanders (Sanders et al. 2002). Triple P focuses on social, emotional, and behavioral problems in childhood, child maltreatment, and attempts to strengthen parenting skills and parent-child relationships. The intervention draws on social learning, cognitive-behavioral and developmental theory, as well as research into risk and protective factors associated with the development of children's social and behavioral problems. Triple P is multi-level, organized for population dissemination, and can be tailored to family needs through flexible formats and delivery.

Youth Empowerment Solutions for Peaceful Communities (YES) is an example of a community-level intervention. YES is an interdisciplinary project developed by The Flint Youth Violence Prevention academic-community partnership (http://www.sph.umich.edu/yvpc/projects/yes/index.shtml). Empowerment theory, positive youth development, and ecological theory guided the development and evaluation of the intervention. YES provides youth with meaningful opportunities for youth violence prevention and community change by enhancing neighborhood organizations' engagement of youth, and changing the community's social and physical environment to prevent violence.

As illustrated by these examples, effective public health interventions tend to be grounded in a theory of change that explicitly outlines the mechanisms through which an intervention has effects and targets risk and protective factors, mediating mechanisms, and behavioral outcomes. They are also adaptable to meet the needs of individuals, families, schools, and/or communities, matched to the target population, and implemented in communities that have the necessary capacity for implementation.

12.1.4 Step 4: Promoting Widespread Use

Once an intervention has empirical support, developers make it available for widespread use by disseminating information about its availability and effectiveness. Communities must assess whether it constitutes a good match with their needs. Technical assistance may be provided to enable communities to implement the intervention effectively, maintaining fidelity to the intervention design. Multi-site implementation of an intervention allows for the understanding of ways to build the individual, organizational, and community capacities to effectively use and deliver empirically supported interventions in different settings with various populations.

12.2 Two Case Studies of Public Health Intervention

In this section, two case studies of public health intervention with a special emphasis on developing and testing prevention strategies are presented. These case studies are efforts of the ACE-UCR (http://www.stopyouthviolence.ucr.edu). The first is an implementation of Families and Schools Together (FAST), a multi-level intervention targeting individual outcomes, and the second is the Arlanza Neighborhood Initiative, a community-level intervention.

12.2.1 Families and Schools Together in Santa Ana, California

Consistent with the public health model, a specific area within Santa Ana, California was targeted based on data showing a high-prevalence of low-income undocumented immigrants and families without many resources. The intervention chosen was FAST, a Substance Abuse and Mental Health Services Administration (SAMHSA) model intervention (National Registry of Evidence-Based Programs and Practices 2010). FAST had been tested previously with low income and ethnic minority populations, providing a good match to the target population, and it incorporated the family, a highly salient institution for Latino youth (Cauce and Domenech-Rodríguez 2000). Implementation of FAST in Santa Ana took into consideration the needs of the local community and its infrastructure; for example, the intervention was implemented in a community center rather than schools because the center had better access to families. Rigorous efforts were made to maintain the fidelity of implementation of FAST.

FAST promotes healthy youth development by jointly engaging students, families, and schools (http://www.wcer.wisc.edu/fast). The theory of change for this intervention is that when parents have social resources via connections to schools, neighbors, and other parents, they can better preserve relationships with their children and effectively help their children address challenges they face, thereby preventing youth problem behavior. Families participate in two initial home visits and then meet in 10 weekly 2–3 hour sessions with other families.

The ACE-UCR conducted a quasi-experimental evaluation of the intervention (see Knox et al. 2011). Two treatment and two control communities in the 92701 zip code of Santa Ana participated. In 3 years, 282 parents and 282 9–12 year old children (one from each family) participated in the intervention. Parents and children were surveyed at baseline and 3–9 months post-intervention. Focus groups with parents were also conducted.

Preliminary quantitative results from the evaluation are promising. They suggest that among parents, the intervention had statistically significant effects on perceptions of community-level collective efficacy and social support at 3 months post-intervention and on support from neighbors and social support at 9 months post-intervention. The results also suggest that among children, the intervention had statistically significant effects on problem solving skills at 9 months post-intervention. Focus group data provided information about participants' experiences with the intervention and their perceptions of the effectiveness of FAST. Parents reported the intervention increased their level of social support. One parent responded to the question: *How did the FAST program benefit you?*

> Social capital. It is very important because here, you feel alone, don't have your extended family to rely on, that you could leave your kids with or things like that. So if you have a group of friends that you can trust…. If you would see the stories that the moms tell us…, as A. told me the other day, one of the moms lose her kid (kid got lost) and all of the mothers that lived there and that had attended FAST helped her find her kid. So imagine, you don't feel you are alone anymore.

Focus group participants cited specific examples of ways in which they applied the strategies they learned in FAST in their day-to-day interactions with their children. A participant described how a fellow participant benefitted from the intervention by using a strategy called 15 minutes, which encourages parents to take time, at least 15 minutes, each day to focus on their children and cultivates closeness and improved communication between parents and children:

> She got into a fight with her daughter …and it was a big one. So she started shouting at her daughter, and her daughter calmed down and said to her, 'Mami, so soon did you forgot to give me my 15 minutes?' So the mom said that when her daughter told her that, everything inside her got removed. Everything that she was told in the program. 'So I stopped what I was doing, left my other kid with someone, and gave to my daughter her 15 minutes.' They were talking, and the daughter said, 'You have to continue in the program even if it's over.

You have to continue doing what you learned in FAST.' So that daughter had seen that those 15 minutes that she shared with her mother made a huge difference.

While the preliminary quantitative data did not demonstrate statistically significant differences between the FAST and comparison groups on children's aggression, this result may be due to the low baseline rates of aggression in the sample for the children. Nonetheless, both the quantitative and the qualitative data clearly suggest that a positive intervention effect emerged on key family processes that are related to youth aggression and violence. Positive impacts on aggression and violence may be seen as the children age.

12.2.2 *Arlanza Neighborhood Initiative in Riverside, CA*

The second case study reports on a neighborhood-level intervention, the Arlanza Neighborhood Initiative (see Payne 2006; Payne and Williams 2008), to promote the well being of children up to 5 years old and their families and reduce youth violence through neighborhood mobilization. The Arlanza neighborhood experienced significant stressors in the 1990s because of the replacement of residential areas with industrial areas, neighborhood turnover due to the departure of a major employer, a consequent reduction in social connections among residents, and a rise in crime and violence. The Initiative followed a public health model in which surveillance data, along with community-participatory processes, informed intervention efforts. The theory of change was that mobilizing and enhancing the neighborhood's resources would improve the surveillance of and response to youth violence on several ecological levels. For example, individual youth were targeted with gang prevention programming, families were targeted with family counseling and other services, and the neighborhood was targeted through coordinated efforts to engage residents and build social capital. Since the youth in the community participated in each of these levels, the intervention had a strong potential to boost their support and prevent delinquent behavior.

The intervention involved asset mapping and service delivery. Asset mapping not only identified institutions and organizations that could build social connections and provide services, but also engaged residents and promoted social relationships, thereby cultivating social capital and strengthening the neighborhood social fabric. Fifteen agencies in the neighborhood, including schools, health care providers, law enforcement, community service organizations, foundations, and county agencies, were identified and helped with the service delivery and the formation of a community center.

Service delivery entailed several community organizations: The Riverside Youth Violence Prevention Policy Board; the English Learning Advisory Committee (whose goal was to assist monolingual Spanish parents to engage in their children's schools); and the Arlanza Area Clergy Team (whose focus was neighborhood engagement and beautification). The Eric M. Solander Arlanza Youth and Family Resource Center was also established. The Center provided an array of services, such as childcare, gang prevention, Women, Infants, and Children (WIC) nutritional and health services, counseling services, and parenting classes, and was a community meeting space. Childcare services were provided to 300 of the 352 eligible families in the neighborhood. WIC services were provided to 3,883 neighborhood women, infants, and children.

The final outcome evaluation results are not yet available, but preliminary results are promising. Evaluators found evidence of collective and collaborative actions by neighborhood members, improvements in the services infrastructure, and increases in social capital (Payne and Williams 2008) – that is, reductions in community-level risk factors for violence and other delinquency (CDC 2010; Sampson et al. 1997, 1999). In terms of delinquency, juvenile arrests in the neighborhood dropped by 41% post intervention. However, in the absence of a randomized trial, this decline cannot be definitively attributed to the intervention (Payne and Williams 2008).

The two case studies presented illustrate the application of the public health approach to the development, testing, implementation, and replication of interventions for violence prevention. They have demonstrated that behavioral interventions targeting youth within the community have promise for preventing youth violence, as well as reducing levels of youth violence in the community.

12.3 The Future of Public Health Approaches to Violence Prevention

Years of developing a base of evidence to prevent and interrupt youth violence has led researchers, policy makers, and practitioners to ask complicated questions. An increasing interest persists in the effects of interventions across time, across ecological levels, across outcomes, and across subgroups.

First, an examination of intervention effects across the life course is critical. Many points in the life course can be identified for beneficial intervention, and interventions must be adapted to fit participants' developmental needs. For instance, numerous age-specific versions of the FAST intervention are available: Baby FAST, pre-K FAST, Middle school FAST, Teen FAST, etc. (http://familiesandschools.org/). Assessments should also occur across the life course. Collecting multiple waves of data are important to help answer the "what works" question at any one time point and specifies when an intervention works and for how long. Such information indicates the best time to intervene, when intervention effects take hold, and how long they will last. An excellent example of research on these issues is found in recent studies of the Good Behavior Game, an intervention implemented by teachers in schools and directed at first and second graders (Kellam et al. 2008). The intervention socializes children into the student role, and reduces aggressive, disruptive classroom behavior – an early risk factor for adolescent and adult problem behavior (Kellam et al. 2008). Although the intervention is implemented in early life, the researchers assessed intervention effects through the age of 21 years old.

Second, intervention effects can be examined at multiple ecological levels, not just the individual level. Effects at the relationship or community levels may be more than simply the sum of individual effects. Therefore, measuring things such as relational constructs (e.g., mutuality, closeness among friends and family) and neighborhood-level processes (e.g., social capital among community members) that are more than just a sum of individual-level assessments are important (Jordon 1986; Portes 2003). Some recent advances have been made to capture processes at various levels of the social ecology (e.g., systematic social observations) that could be employed when examining intervention effects on youth violence prevention (Raudenbush and Sampson 1999).

Third, intervention effects can be assessed on a broad range of outcomes because many risk and protective factors addressed by interventions operate similarly for a range of youth risk behaviors (Biglan and Cody 2003). For example, although Life Skills Training (Botvin and Kantor 2000) targets substance use among youths, this intervention has been shown to have effects on youth violence (Botvin et al. 2002) and risky sexual behavior (Griffin et al. 2006). Likewise, Project AIM (Adult Identity Mentoring) was developed to target risky sexual behaviors, but also had an effect on youth violence (Chap. 12 by Clark and Humphries, this volume). Interventions may positively affect a range of behaviors.

Fourth, it is vital to identify the subgroups that benefit most from an intervention and to understand why. Variations in intervention effects may depend on risk status, culture, and responsiveness, and variations in participants' risk for the targeted behavior may condition their response (Wright and Zimmerman 2006; USDHHS 2001). For instance, do some participants benefit more or less than others? If so, which participants demonstrate the best response and why? Are there differences in patterns of response among different groups of participants? An example of research in this vein is that of Holsen and colleagues (2009), who assessed differences in the effectiveness of the Second Step violence prevention intervention by the socioeconomic status of youth participants. Another way to answer the question, "What works for whom?" is to examine variations in effectiveness by intervention responsiveness. Responsiveness could mean the characteristics of individuals other than their risk and protective factors for the specific target behavior (to the extent that these can be separated), such as cognitive ability, or it could mean the set of characteristics more generally, including risk and protective factors, that influence an individual's responsiveness to an intervention. Analyses could assess, for example, the participant profile that is associated with the highest responsiveness to an intervention. As adaptation and tailoring of interventions become more common, such information will prove vitally important (Collins et al. 2004).

12.4 Conclusion

Research on public health interventions related to youth violence has generated information about efficacy and effectiveness and produced many evidence-based interventions that are now widely used. Contemporary emphasis on evidence-based practice (Flay et al. 2005) and translational research (CDC 2009b) has recognized the importance of linking research, policy, and practice. Broad public health approaches to violence prevention should support interventions that research shows are successful, and practice should reflect the state of the art as identified through research. Although progress has been made, many ineffective or not-yet-proven interventions are in use, and sometimes evidence-based interventions are not widely used or do not work as anticipated. Even when the four steps of the public health approach are followed, challenges remain. This chapter has reviewed the public health approach, provided examples of its application to youth violence, and described questions to be addressed in future research. While new interventions may be needed, researchers can help to maximize the benefits of existing public health interventions by examining how they perform across time, on what ecological levels they are implemented, the outcomes they address, and the subgroups they affect the most.

References

Biglan, A., & Cody, C. (2003). Preventing multiple problem behaviors in adolescence. In D. Romer (Ed.), *Reducing adolescent risk: Toward and integrated approach* (pp. 125–131). Thousand Oaks: Sage Publications.

Botvin, G. J., & Kantor, L. W. (2000). Preventing alcohol and tobacco use through life skills training. *Alcohol Research & Health, 24*(4), 250–257.

Botvin, G. J., Mihalic, S. F., & Grotpeter, J. K. (2002). *Life skills training*. Boulder: Center for the Study and Prevention of Violence, Institute of Behavioral Science, University of Colorado.

Cauce, A. M., & Domenech-Rodríguez, M. (2000). Latino families: Myths and realities. In J. M. Contreras, K. A. Kerns, & A. M. Neal-Barnett (Eds.), *Latino children and families in the United States: Current research and future directions* (pp. 3–25). Westport: Praeger.

Centers for Disease Control and Prevention. (2009a). *Violence prevention: The public health approach to violence prevention*. Retrieved from http://www.cdc.gov/ViolencePrevention/overview/publichealthapproach.html

Centers for Disease Control and Prevention. (2009b). *Youth violence: Translation*. Retrieved from http://www.cdc.gov/ViolencePrevention/youthviolence/translation.html

Centers for Disease Control and Prevention. (2009c). *Understanding youth violence fact sheet 2010*. Retrieved from http://www.cdc.gov/ViolencePrevention/pdf/YV-FactSheet-a.pdf

Centers for Disease Control and Prevention. (2010). *Youth violence: Risk and protective factors*. Retrieved from http://cdc.gov/ViolencePrevention/youthviolence/riskprotectivefactors.html

Collins, L. M., Murphy, S. A., & Bierman, K. L. (2004). A conceptual framework for adaptive preventive interventions. *Prevention Science, 5*(3), 185–196.

Flay, B. R., Biglan, A., Boruch, R. F., Castro, F. G., Gottfredson, D., Kellam, S., Moscicki, E. K., Schinke, S., Valentine, J. C., & Ji, P. (2005). Standards of evidence: Criteria for efficacy, effectiveness and dissemination. *Prevention Science, 6*(3), 151–175.

Griffin, K. W., Botvin, G. J., & Nichols, T. R. (2006). Effects of a school-based drug abuse prevention program for adolescents on HIV risk behaviors in young adulthood. *Prevention Science, 7*, 103–112.

Guerra, N. G. (2009). *Positive life changes: A cognitive-behavioral intervention for adolescents and young adults*. Champaign: Research Press Publishers.

Guerra, N. G., & Bradshaw, C. P. (2008). Linking the prevention of problem behaviors and positive youth development: Core competencies for positive youth development and risk prevention. *New Directions for Child and Adolescent Development, 122*, 1–17.

Guerra, N. G., & Williams, K. R. (2002). *Fact sheet: Youth development and violence prevention: Core competencies*. Retrieved from http://stopyouthviolence.ucr.edu/factsheets/violenceprevention.pdf

Holsen, I., Iversen, A. C., & Smith, B. (2009). Universal social competence programme in school: Does it work for children with low socio-economic background? *Advances in School Mental Health Promotion, 2*(2), 51–60.

Jordon, J. V. (1986). *The meaning of mutuality*. Wellesley: Stone Center for Developmental Services and Studies.

Kellam, S. G., Reid, J., & Balster, R. L. (2008). Effects of a universal classroom behavior program in first and second grades on young adult problem outcomes. *Drug and Alcohol Dependence, 95*(Supplement 1), S1–S4.

Kim, T., Guerra, N. G., & Williams, K. R. (2008). Preventing youth problem behaviors and enhancing physical health by promoting core competencies. *Journal of Adolescent Health, 43*, 401–407.

Knox, L., Guerra, N. G., Williams, K. R., & Toro, R. (2011). Preventing children's aggression in immigrant Latino families: A mixed methods evaluation of the Families and Schools Together (FAST) program. *American Journal of Community Psychology, 48*(1/2), 65–76.

McMahon, P. M. (2000). The public health approach to the prevention of sexual violence. *Sexual Abuse: Journal of Research and Treatment, 12*, 27–36.

Mercy, J. A., Rosenberg, M. L., Powell, K. E., Broome, C. V., & Roper, W. L. (1993). Public health policy for preventing violence. *Health Affairs, 12*, 7–29.

National Center for Injury Prevention and Control. (2009). *CDC Injury Research Agenda, 2009–2018*. Atlanta: United States Department of Health and Human Services, Centers for Disease Control and Prevention.

National Registry of Evidence-Based Programs and Practices. (2010). *Families and Schools Together*. Retrieved from http://www.nrepp.samhsa.gov/ViewIntervention.aspx?id=30

Payne, P. R. (2006). *Youth violence prevention through asset-based community development*. El Paso: LFB Scholarly Publishing.

Payne, P. R., & Williams, K. R. (2008). Building social capital through neighborhood mobilization: Challenges and lessons learned. *American Journal of Preventive Medicine, 34*(3S), S42–S47.

Portes, A. (2003). Social capital: Its origins and applications in modern sociology. *Annual Review of Sociology, 24*, 1–24.

Raudenbush, S. W., & Sampson, R. J. (1999). Ecometrics: Toward a science of assessing ecological settings, with application to the systematic social observation of neighborhoods. *Sociological Methodology, 29*(1), 1–41.

Sampson, R. J., Raudenbush, S. W., & Earls, F. (1997). Neighborhoods and violent crime: A multilevel study of collective efficacy. *Science, 277*, 918–924.

Sampson, R. J., Morenoff, J. D., & Earls, F. (1999). Beyond social capital: Spatial dynamics of collective efficacy for children. *American Sociological Review, 64*, 633–660.

Sanders, M. R., Turner, K. M. T., & Markie-Dadds, C. (2002). The development and dissemination of the Triple P-Positive Parenting Program: A multi-level, evidence-based system of parenting and family support. *Prevention Science, 3*(3), 173–198.

Stokols, D. (1996). Translating social ecological theory into guidelines for community health promotion. *American Journal of Public Health, 10*(4), 282–298.

United States Department of Health and Human Services. (2001). *Youth violence: A report from the Surgeon General*. Rockville: U.S. Department of Health and Human Services, Public Health Service, Office of the Surgeon General.

United States Department of Health and Human Services. (2009). *Understanding youth violence: Fact sheet*. Atlanta: U.S. Department of Health and Human Services, Centers for Disease Control and Prevention.

Weitz, R. (2006). *The sociology of health, illness, and health care: A critical approach*. Belmont: Wadsworth Publishing Company.

Williams, K. R., & Guerra, N. G. (in press). Perceptions of collective efficacy and bullying perpetration in schools. *Social Problems*.

Wright, J. C., & Zimmerman, M. A. (2006). Culturally sensitive interventions to prevent youth violence. In N. G. Guerra & E. Phillips Smith (Eds.), *Preventing youth violence in a multicultural society* (pp. 221–247). Washington, DC: American Psychological Association.

Chapter 13
Project AIM: Bringing Evidence-Based Programs into Community-Based Services

Leslie F. Clark and Mia D. Humphreys

Abstract *Project Adult Identity Mentoring (AIM) is a positive youth development program targeting HIV risk prevention in middle school students that is currently designated as an Effective Behavioral Intervention by the Centers for Disease Control and Prevention. Project AIM has been piloted among diffuse populations of youth. This chapter discusses the implementation of Project AIM among youth at risk for joining gangs in Los Angeles and examines the appropriateness, acceptability, feasibility and accuracy of Project AIM's delivery within community services. Specifically, evaluations are provided on the responses of relevant stakeholders, including those of case managers, parents of youth, and the youth themselves. Program staff had the capacity to deliver Project AIM with accuracy, and the responses from the youth were uniformly favorable. Results suggest that Project AIM is an excellent fit to the service setting and program mission of city-initiated*

Data presented in this chapter were gathered during a study funded by the Clinical and Translational Science Institute Pilot and Feasibility Grant Program at the University of Southern California. The pilot project entitled "Translating Science-based Intervention into Practice: Project AIM and High-risk Adolescents," was integrated into two violence prevention programs at the Division of Adolescent Medicine at Children's Hospital Los Angeles (CHLA): the Hollywood Bridges Youth Violence Prevention Program (July – December 2008), and the Cypress Park/Northeast Gang Reduction Youth Development Program (January 2009 – July 2010). The original study "Adult Identity mentoring" was supported by cooperative agreement #U64/CCU41327 from the Centers of Disease and Prevention. Dr. Clark, is the author of Project AIM and CHLA holds the copyrights and, as a result, may gain financially from future commercialization of Project AIM. If you have any questions regarding this disclosure, please contact the Office of Research Compliance at CHLA (323) 361-5760.

L.F. Clark, Ph.D., M.P.H. (✉)
Division of Adolescent Medicine, University of Southern California,
Los Angeles, CA, USA
e-mail: lclark@chla.usc.edu

M.D. Humphreys, M.S.W.
Adolescent Medicine Children's Hospital, Los Angeles, CA, USA

B. Sanders et al. (eds.), *Crime, HIV and Health: Intersections of Criminal Justice and Public Health Concerns*, DOI 10.1007/978-90-481-8921-2_13,

gang-prevention and reduction services. A discussion provides an overview of the challenges and successes of integrating sustainable evidence-based prevention programs into existing practices.

Positive youth development refers to an ongoing process in which youth attempt to meet their basic personal and social needs and to build the skills needed to function and contribute in their daily lives (Pittman et al. 2000). Participation in positive youth development programs are associated with both increased social competence and decreased externalizing behaviors among youth (cf. Finkelhor et al. 2009; Youngblade et al. 2007). Such programs support basic developmental goals of competence (e.g. academic, social), self-confidence, and establishing pro-social connections, as well as help youth to successfully confront the pressures of growing up in communities of risk (Catalano 2003; House et al. 2010; Nicholson et al. 2004). For example, a study of 80 neighborhoods found that the adverse effects of pre-existing negative familial and peer influences on youth were ameliorated by greater concentrations of community organizations/services targeting the prevention of youth violence (Molnar et al. 2008). Programs that take a developmentally informed approach to both reducing risk and promoting protective factors are especially promising for preventing future problem behaviors in young adolescents (Catalano et al. 2003; Dodge and Petit 2003).

Project AIM (Adult Identity Mentoring) is an evidence-based positive youth development program to prevent HIV and reduce sexual behaviors among middle school youth in communities of poverty (Clark et al. 2005). This chapter discusses the experiences of integrating Project AIM into the existing services of agencies that work with gang youth and delinquent youth at-risk for joining gangs. First, some of the challenges associated with implementing science-based prevention programs in everyday practice are discussed. Second, the Integrated Systems Framework approach for program implementation is introduced. Third, an overview of Project AIM is provided. Lastly, examples from two Los Angeles neighborhoods where Project AIM was implemented as part the city's recent initiative to reduce gang involvement and promote positive youth development are discussed.

13.1 Putting Evidence-Based Prevention Programs into Practice

While the use of evidence-based prevention programs in community practice settings is recommended to improve outcomes, details about the adoption process (also referred to as prevention technology transfer), how to ensure quality program delivery, and the types of needed environmental support are still limited (Thornton et al. 2002). Implementation of an evidence-based prevention program requires consideration of agencies' capacity to appropriately fund and train staff, recruit and retain participants, and deliver the program in accordance with the program curriculum. A prevention program's effectiveness depends as much on the environmental support (e.g. agency commitment) and quality of implementation (e.g. fidelity to the curriculum) as it does on the specific prevention program content (Office of the Surgeon General 2001). For example, Promoting Alternative Thinking Strategies (PATHS), is an evidence-based violence prevention program, that was effective in schools only where both the principal supported the program and a high quality of implementation fidelity to the original evidence-based program was present (Chi-Ming et al. 2003; see Ozer 2006 for a review of delivery fidelity in school based violence prevention programs). Similar general challenges, such as program training to accommodate agency staff turnover, as well as challenges unique to each program, such as service learning requirements and the use of specific therapeutic techniques, exist across other arenas of evidence-based program adoption (see Kalichman 1998 for discussion of HIV prevention programs; see Lessene et al. (2010) for a discussion of pregnancy prevention programs).

Many barriers hamper the transference of science-based prevention programs to frontline practice, including the 'cultural divide' between behavioral scientists and practitioners (Beutler et al. 1995; Brown 1995). This cultural divide refers to the tension between the promise of replicating effective outcomes predicated on the rigor of an implementation's faithfulness to the original effective program (scientists) and the need for tailoring and ownership, as well as practical constraints on delivery experienced in a given community context (practitioners). For these reasons, practitioners should be a part of the 'packaging process' of evidence based interventions, such as training and guidance materials, in order to ensure that intervention packages are accessible and relevant to end users (i.e. practitioners) (Saul et al. 2008).

A similar divide appears in the ways in which adopted programs are evaluated. Program evaluation generally takes a social science approach, which employs traditional experimental research methods, including randomized control trials (Brown 1995). Stakeholder approaches, on the other hand, are often valued for their responsiveness, relevancy and inclusiveness; however, when conducted appropriately, they can also meet expectations of scientific rigor (Chen 1990, 2005). Community-based evaluation is a stakeholder approach that emphasizes equity among research evaluators and stakeholders in the evaluation process, uses a community's existing strengths and resources, and works for the mutual benefit of all partners (Israel et al. 1998; Telfair 1999).

The fidelity with which an empirically tested original intervention is implemented in the field is an additional concern of technology transfer experts (Flaspohler et al. 2008). However, these challenges, often a function of how well an intervention 'fits' the community and the agency's willingness to faithfully implement the intervention, become much less difficult when service providers collaborate in program development, implementation and evaluation processes (Brown 1995). Issues around translating programs into community agency practice include staff resistance to change, executive level support of facilitators, setting characteristics (e.g. facilities), existence of supportive services (e.g. transportation, health), and administrative practices. For example, the fit of the prevention program with the agency's mission and priorities, organizational will (or buy-in), parental acceptance of programs, competition with other activities for youth, and staff burden and turnover will determine the likelihood that the agency can successfully adopt and maintain a particular science-based program (Wandersman et al. 2008). In addition, the quality of program training, supervision, and technical support all affect the accuracy with which facilitators can reproduce the program implementation experience that yielded the original risk reduction outcomes in youth (Julian et al. 2008).

13.2 The Integrated Systems Framework Approach

An Integrated Systems Framework (ISF) approach for dissemination and implementation offers a useful guide to examine processes related to the functions and structures needed to move evidence-based interventions from research to practice and support successful implementation in community settings (Wandersman et al. 2008). The ISF characterizes the capacity needed to adopt and implement evidence-based interventions, and has been used to identify deficits in agency capacity to implement interventions, specifically the under-funding of training and technical assistance support (Julian et al. 2008). The ISF has been used in the Centers for Disease Control and Prevention's (CDC) efforts to disseminate evidence-based programs and build community capacity to prevent teen pregnancy (Lesesne et al. 2008). Evaluation of the CDC's efforts have indicated that training and technical assistance played a critical role in bridging the gap between research and practice, which could be addressed by conducting more research evaluating the types and forms of capacity building supports (i.e. training and technical assistance) most useful for adoption, dissemination, and outcome evaluation (Julian et al. 2008; Lesesne et al. 2008).

The ISF defines three systems necessary for successful implementation of evidenced-based programming: *Prevention Synthesis and Translation; Prevention Support;* and *Prevention Delivery*. The *Prevention Synthesis and Translation* system addresses the need for agencies to review and identify packaged interventions appropriate to their needs (Guerra and Knox 2008). The *Prevention Support* system ensures that capacity-building activities occur so that those who implement the intervention have the necessary skills and support. *Prevention Support* involves determining the appropriate levels of: (1) direct service and supervisory staff needed; (2) buy-in from agency's executive staff; (3) intervention-specific training required; (4) resources needed within the agency to support effective intervention; and (5) skills needed to ensure quality delivery. The *Prevention Delivery* system includes: (1) providers' experience using evidence-based interventions; (2) providers' understanding of the selected intervention; and (3) access to training and technical assistance needed to ensure effective and sustained implementation. It includes the amount of time agencies provide for their staff to deliver interventions, facilities, incentives and supplies, transportation provided to clients, translation services, and specific outreach and recruitment.

Table 13.1 Overview of Integrated Systems framework and components

ISF systems	Community capacity	Organization (agency) capacity	Facilitator capacity
Prevention Delivery system – functions to carry out activities related to program implementation	**General**		
	Agency partnerships county-wide funding	Fit with agency priorities	Services for at-risk youth
		Ability to retain staff	Ability to lead youth groups
	Project AIM Specific		
	Fully packaged curricula	Technical assistance	Facilitator supervision
		Facilitation as staff duties	Case manager toolkit
Prevention Support system – functions to support the efforts of those implementing an intervention	**General**		
	Grant writing expertise Evidenced-based program required for funding	Agency buy-in for EBP Agency experience in communities of poverty	Openness to new programs
			Job pressures/demands
	Project AIM Specific		
	Presence of Project AIM developer at home agency	Recruitment and retention trained supervisors	Facilitator training
			Facilitator handbook

The ISF addresses issues of both general (e.g. staff supervision) and program specific (e.g. training) capacities needed for successful adaptation of evidence-based prevention programs. Three levels of capacity to consider are: the community, the organization, and the facilitator in each of the three ISF systems. The community level refers to connections among organizations, community involvement, and the degree of understanding and commitment among major public systems, schools, agencies, civic leaders, and elected officials about the targeted issue and the need for evidence-based interventions. The organizational level refers to the agency structure, resources, and staff capacity to implement the specific intervention – the fit of program objectives with the organization's mission ensuring buy-in and support, and training and technical assistance. The facilitator level addresses the general capacity of staff, including their openness, flexibility, and capabilities, and their intervention-specific capacity, such as their understanding of the intervention, their self-efficacy for facilitation, and their commitment to and beliefs about the intervention. Organizational capacity at the *Prevention Delivery* system, and training and technical assistance that are available at the *Prevention Support* system have been shown to be particularly critical keys to successful implementation and institutionalization of well-packaged evidence-based interventions in community settings (Durlak and DuPre 2008). Table 13.1 presents a grid of types (general and program-specific), and the three levels of capacity for the *Prevention Support* and *Program Delivery* systems separately.

13.3 Overview of Project AIM

Project AIM is a theory-based intervention program designed to reduce HIV risk behaviors, as well as promote positive youth development, among adolescents in resource-poor, high-crime communities (Clark et al. 2005; Miller et al. 2009a, b). Project AIM's primary goal is to steer adolescents away from risky behavioral choices by offering alternative avenues to define themselves as adults. The intervention is a 6-week, 12-session, strengths-based program that helps youth to envision and articulate both positive and negative possible future selves. The program promotes youth capacity to create constructive adult identities and perseverance to attain their chosen positive adult identities and avoid risk behaviors that might adversely impact them. Project AIM encourages youth to consider their responsibility for their own future and how their behaviors may promote or impede the attainment of desired future self-identities. Specifically, it encourages youth to think about their desired future as adults and how their current risky behavioral choices could adversely affect this future. Project AIM is considered an Effective Behavioral Intervention by the CDC (www.effectiveinterventions.org/en/Interventions/AIM.aspx).

Project AIM is based on the Theory of Possible Selves, which maintains that individuals are presently motivated by mental images of our potential (or 'possible') future selves (Markus and Nurius 1986). The theory states that a balance is needed between both these positive and negative images of an individual's possible future. In the event that only positive future selves are envisioned, chances at success may not accurately gauged, and no preparation is made to successfully navigate obstacles, setbacks or short-term disappointments. Alternatively, with only negative future selves in mind, no belief that a positive future is possible exists, plans for the future are not made, and motivation to pursue long-term goals is absent. In addition, the better positive possible future selves are envisioned and articulated, the more attainable that future seems, and the more motivated an individual becomes to achieve it.

The Theory of Possible Selves has been used to successfully predict delinquency, such as smoking and drinking among adolescents living in high crime inner city environments (Stein et al. 1998). The balance of positive and negative possible future selves has predicted recidivism among African-American male juvenile offenders within 18 months of release (Oyserman et al. 1995; Oyserman and Saltz 1993). The balance between negative and positive possible future selves has also predicted which African-American male adolescents graduated from versus dropped out of high school (Oyserman and Markus 1990). In addition, the theory was used to create "School to Jobs," an intervention program for inner city 8th grade students to improve their academic performance and commitment to school (Oyserman et al. 2001).

The original setting for testing Project AIM was a city in the Birmingham, Alabama area that had high rates of unemployment, crime and drug use. The school was on academic probation and drew students from a distressed community where the median home income in 1996 was significantly below Federal poverty levels. A total of 20 seventh grade health education classes ($n=211$) were randomly assigned to receive either Project AIM (twice a week, 6 week curriculum) intervention or a standard health education curriculum (i.e. comparison). Surveys about sexual activity were conducted before the intervention, 12 weeks post-intervention (19 weeks past baseline), and again at 1 year after the intervention ended. Hierarchical logistic regression analyses, taking into account both semester level and class groupings, were performed on sexual risk outcomes. Participants were analyzed as originally assigned, regardless of intervention exposure, using appropriate cluster (i.e. group level) analysis, which took into account the classroom level. Results showed a significant reduction in sexual intentions across 3 month follow up and increases in sexual abstinence, both 3 months 12 weeks after the end of the intervention (Clark et al. 2005).

13.4 Examples of Project AIM with Gang and Delinquent Youth in Los Angeles

The implementation of Project AIM was examined within two community settings to determine the required processes for achieving adoption, facilitating fidelity of implementation, and securing sustainability of evidence-based interventions in practice settings. These settings were the Bridges Youth Violence Prevention Program (henceforth 'Bridges') and The Gang Reduction Youth Development (GRYD) Program. Each of these programs was funded by The City of Los Angeles. Project AIM was integrated into these two service settings in efforts to prevent youths' involvement in gangs, violence and delinquency through intensive case management of identified high-risk youth and ancillary services (e.g. safety programs, tutoring, parenting programs).

Documented considerations reported on here include the feasibility, acceptability, and sustainability of Project AIM within each of these service settings. For instance, the *Prevention Support* and *Prevention Delivery* systems of the ISF guided our adoption activities for placing Project AIM into these settings, and some findings are organized around issues that arose with these two systems. In addition, evidence of delivery fidelity and youth response to the program are provided. Examples are also added of parents' perceptions and agency staff's experiences with infusing Project AIM concepts in to their existing case management services.

13.4.1 Example 1: The Los Angeles Bridges Youth Violence Prevention Program

Bridges was an inter-agency collaborative funded by the Community Development Department of the City of Los Angeles to target high-risk youth 10-to-14-years old for prevention case management services. Each Bridges program provided intensive case management services in order to increase academic performance, and connectedness to school, family and their community with the goal of preventing low school functioning, delinquent behavior, and gang involvement. The Division of Adolescent Medicine (DAM) at Childrens Hospital Los Angeles served as the Bridges Hollywood site, which worked closely with two middles schools in the area: Bancroft and LeConte. Project AIM was incorporated into the Bridges program during its last few months of funding with case managers playing a significant role in the adaptation of Project AIM.

13.4.2 Example 2: The Gang Reduction and Youth Development Program

The GRYD program, funded out of the Office of the Mayor of Los Angeles, designated 12 communities, or 'zones' of high gang activity to receive program funding to reduce violence, avert gang involvement, promote positive youth integration into existing community services, and identify best practices for targeting youth aged 10-to-15-year olds who were at risk of joining gangs. This age range was set by the Los Angeles Mayor's office. The programs offered through Cypress Park/Northeast GRYD site were coordinated to provide accessible, comprehensive services that included parent education and support, individual intensive case management, recreation/cultural activities, counseling, adult-youth mentoring, and sport activities and leagues (i.e. the Anahuak Youth Sports Association). DAM staff in the Cypress Park/Northeast GRYD program site worked closely and with two middle schools in the zone: Irving and Nightingale.

13.4.3 Differences Between Service Settings

While the goal of prevention through case management and community service integration were similar in the Bridges and GRYD programs, they differed in their referral process, their use of prescreening assessment tools, and the mix of services used. In general, the role of case manager was similar in both programs, though the case managers served as Project AIM facilitators for GRYD groups, while specific coordinator staff filled this role in the Bridges program. Youth from Bridges were older and already integrated into the Bridges programs, with Project AIM acting as an exit activity to an ending program. For GRYD sites, Project AIM provided an introduction to program services. Case managers were more closely involved with Project AIM as facilitators, but were also involved with start-up activities with the GRYD program, including an intensive outreach process. While the Bridges staff played a large part in the adaptation process of integrating Project AIM into case management styles, the GRYD program provided the opportunity for initially establishing and sustaining Project AIM as an integral part of the GRYD's overall prevention strategy and framework. The challenges and successes of these adoption efforts are described in Table 13.2.

Table 13.2 Challenges and successes within the Integrated Systems Framework

ISF aystem	Community capacity	Organizational/agency capacity	Facilitator/Case Manager (CM) capacity
Prevention Delivery system – functions to carry out activities related to implementation	**Challenges**		
	Connections among organizations	Recruiting youth through new service site (GRYD)	Youth consistent attendance
	Community Participation		Staff burden of EBP tasks Staff burden to evaluate
	Successes		
	Fit with GRYD agency partners priorities i.e. Positive Parenting; Youth Mentoring Connections	Staff meetings and case conferences "normalized" Project AIM activities	CM aided retention to groups
	Project AIM graduation invited agency partners	Project AIM as a framework for unifying services Project AIM as an entrée into or exit from services	AIM toolkit enhanced CM services to: Reinforce EBP impact Advocate on youth's behalf Incorporate a positive focus on client youth's future
Prevention Support system - functions to support the efforts of those implementing an intervention.	**Challenges**		
	Lack of research funding	Complex service settings	Burden of high fidelity implementation
	Requirements of service funders	Start up of GRYD services	External pressures/demands
	Successes		
	Project AIM Package did not require adaptation for this setting or target population	Project AIM specific parent orientation	Focus groups as a way to achieve staff buy-in
	Project AIM included in partner agency updates	Project AIM specific Coordinator/Supervision	Development of a CM Project AIM toolkit facilitated the use of AIM concepts in regular practice

13.4.4 Prevention Support System: Project AIM's Fit with Service Priorities

Prior to the introduction of Project AIM, qualitative information was collected from mothers or guardians of the youth receiving Bridges services to ascertain their perceptions of these services, their child's risk, and the potential of their child's future. Their concerns included fears such as "He has bad friends" and "He's going to end up in a gang." As clients of Bridges, mothers/guardians could point to specific outcomes they attributed to the case management services. Examples included, "[My son] wasn't going to graduate [middle school], but [Case Manager] was able to go talk to the counselor and he was able to graduate in the end", and "Since they started to help in LA Bridges I realized that I needed to change and that LA Bridges was going to help me." However, when asked whether they felt positive about their child's future, they expressed pessimism. For instance, one mother said, "I want to be honest, and no, I don't feel positive about his future." Project AIM's fit with the mission of both service settings in terms of: the client population of youth aged 10–15 years old in low income and high violence

Communities; the positive youth development approach to preventing high-risk behavior among clients; and the feasibility of its twice weekly small group delivery format, which greatly enhanced adoption efforts.

13.4.5 Prevention Support System: Engagement of Program Staff in Adoption of Project AIM

Focus groups with Bridges and GRYD staff, including supervisors and case managers, were used to discuss the role of case managers in their programs and the feasibility of incorporating Project AIM as 6 week (twice a week) groups reinforced by the practice of case management. Case managers spoke of their need for youth-sensitive, evidence-based programs, techniques to reinforce good client behavior, and ways to engage parents in their child's progress. They also expressed the difficulty of addressing anything other than current family crises or consequences related to child's adverse behavior (e.g. school suspensions; aggression; probation).

Basic details of Project AIM were presented through a 15-min presentation, a brochure and examples of youth worksheets created by previous Project AIM youth participants. Case managers responded positively to Project AIM's focus on motivating youth to think about their future, as well as the potential for engaging parents around positive communication with youth clients. Their dedication to their client families and openness to consider ways to expand their case management techniques was a strong resource for the adoption of Project AIM.

13.4.6 *Prevention Support System: Development of Agency Protocol and Staff "Toolkit"*

During the focus groups and subsequent staff meetings (using Bridges case management staff), case managers suggested ways in which concepts could be integrated into existing case management services. These included the creation of parent/teacher brochure describing Project AIM, the development of a parental orientation meeting prior to starting a Project AIM group, the provision of social marketing items (e.g. pens, mugs and cubicle posters to remind case managers of Project AIM concepts), their invitation to Project AIM graduation ceremonies, and requesting youth to share their Project AIM portfolios with case managers at completion of group participation. As a result, a specific case management service protocol and 'tool kit', for reinforcing Project AIM concepts were created, which included information about key concepts, a case manager log for conversations with youth clients, parents and other adults using Project AIM concepts, and a youth agenda that case managers could provide to teach time management and planning with their youth clients.

13.4.7 *Prevention Delivery System: Training and Technical Assistance*

Project AIM training was specifically shortened from 3 to 2 days in order to reduce staff burden. For each setting, all case managers and other staff who might be facilitating Project AIM groups along with their direct supervisors attended a 2-day formal training designed to familiarize them with the goals, theoretical basis, and curriculum activities. This training provided an opportunity for trainees to practice the delivery of sessions with trainer feedback. Training also covered important aspects of pre-session preparation and out-of-session tasks to be completed by facilitators. In addition, the specialized Project AIM case management protocol and tool kit provided assessment instruments to document case managers' reinforcement of Project AIM concepts. Project AIM supervision was provided through regular case conference meetings and specific weekly Project AIM supervision/debriefing sessions, both of which became agenda items on regular program staff meetings. This allowed for discussion of program technical assistance materials (e.g. use of instructional guidance), and individual client issues (e.g. attendance) that supported the delivery of Project AIM. Debriefing also allowed for weekly feedback on questions of delivery and evaluation (e.g. youth satisfaction surveys) and recruitment of new Project AIM groups.

13.4.8 *Prevention Delivery System: Recruitment and Retention*

For each program, youth were referred primarily through their schools, but also through the probation department, police department and other community-based

Table 13.3 School profiles (LAUSD 2008–2009; CADOE 2008–2009)

School profile 2008–2009

	Hollywood		Cypress Park/Northeast	
	Bancroft MS	LeConte MS	Irving MS	Nightingale MS
Enrollment	1,270	1,701	1,318	1,859
Economic disadvantaged	79%	80%	85%	91%
% Latino	81%	79%	86%	70%
Suspension rate	11.3% (149)	7.3% (134)	7.1% (103)	8.6% (163)
CST ELA proficient	40.7%	61.2%	35.1%	33.0%
CST Math proficient	31.8%	59.3%	26.9%	32.4%
# Violence/Drug suspensions	94	111	56	88

organizations (e.g. churches, YMCA, or Boys and Girls clubs). Table 13.3 provides an overall description of the four middle schools used for referrals. Youth were referred due to their behaviors or family circumstances that placed them at elevated levels of risk within high-risk communities. Challenges facilitators experienced were in the realm of initial recruitment, especially given the need for formal consent processes, ongoing retention of youth returning to sessions across the 6 weeks, and out-of-session facilitator tasks that added a burden to the already overloaded service staff. A total of 11 case-managed youth from Bridges participated in Project AIM. Of these youth, nine graduated from the program. All youth were Latino and lived or went to school in the Hollywood area. A total of nine case-managed youth in the GRYD program participated, with eight graduating the program. Most youth were Latino and lived or went to school in the Cypress Park/Northeast zone.

13.4.9 Fidelity in Implementation Delivery of Project AIM and Client Responses

The fidelity of Project AIM delivery was assessed through: (a) direct observations of group sessions; (b) a facilitator fidelity checklist; and (c) youth opinion data. The facilitator fidelity checklist documented what activities in each session were delivered, challenges facilitators encountered delivering the program, and whether materials specified for each session were utilized. In each setting, process evaluation data indicated that facilitators were able to deliver the program activities (two facilitators for each session) with high fidelity (over 90%) and few difficulties within the 1.5 hours allotted for the sessions.

Youth opinion surveys indicated that 91% of youth completing Project AIM across both settings reported that "Project AIM helped me to think about my future" and all graduating youth agreed or strongly agreed that, "Project AIM facilitators were a positive influence on me." When asked about how Project AIM can help them succeed, youth commented on both the future oriented nature (e.g. "It made me realize how much my future really matters.") and motivational aspects of Project AIM (e.g. "It'll make me focus more, it's really a motivation."). The comments of parents/guardians also acknowledged the future oriented nature of Project AIM. Examples included, "[My daughter] said that she wanted to be a chef. She got excited by it. It made her excited to think about what she wanted to be", and "He became more open-minded to other possibilities of a career." Parent/guardians also perceived that Project AIM impacted current behavioral issues as depicted in one parent's comment: "It [Project AIM] helped him with his behavior. I am very thankful for all the help that you have given us."

13.4.10 Reinforcement and Diffusion of Project AIM Concepts Through Existing Service Practices

At the community level, Project AIM graduations and orientations were used as a point of contact with partner agencies. These contracted service providers requested more information about Project AIM and the ways in which concepts could be integrated into their positive parenting practices and adult-youth mentoring programs. At the agency level, it became clear that the groups served an important function in exiting clients (Bridges) from or introducing clients (GRYD) to agency services. Agency involvement in building the capacity of case managers to incorporate Project AIM concepts into existing practice, and case managers' assistance in the development of the case management toolkit demonstrated how the buy-in and ownership were also important factors required for successful evidence-based program adoption in community settings.

Case managers used forms or checklists to record their use of Project AIM concepts in their case management practice. Analysis of these forms revealed that case managers spent between 5 and 25 min in interactions with youth and adults around Project AIM concepts related to all three core elements (e.g. youth's future, present skills, and risk reduction). Across a 2–3 month period, these types of conversations ranged from 3 to 16 per youth. Conversations directly with youth addressed: (1) problems with consistent group attendance; (2) sharing youth's Project AIM work; and (3) the use of Project AIM skills in current life situations. Surprisingly, case managers were just as likely (and more likely in GRYD setting) to use Project AIM concepts in speaking with parents and other adults (e.g. school personnel, probation) about their client youth. These conversations consisted of telling adults about youth's personal strengths and aspirations, advocating for future-oriented views on addressing youth difficulties, and encouraging positive recognition and future-oriented discussions with youth. These experiences led case managers to report that they found their work more hopeful and were more able to advocate for youth when confronted with problem behavior trajectories, academic failure and juvenile justice involvement.

13.5 Conclusion

The importance of city-level funding tied to requirements of evidence-based programming cannot be underestimated in the current efforts we have described. The agency support of staff training for Project AIM indicated their prevention support, while dedicating time to Project AIM issues in staff meetings and client conferences are examples of prevention delivery support that built facilitator capacity critical to successful adoption experiences at each site. Supervisory debriefing and staff meetings ensured faithful implementation, and also elicited innovative strategies to disseminate Project AIM concepts through existing services. This funding approach provided an opportunity to examine what is needed by community-based agencies to adopt an evidence-based program as part of their routine practice, in order to improve outcomes for local children, youth and families.

We strongly recommend the use of structured activities (e.g. staff focus groups or observations) and client views to determine the current climate, existing services, and unmet needs in bringing evidence-based programs to practice. Securing "buy-in" at all levels of agency staff (e.g. executive, supervisory, facilitator and case manager) is also critical. We directly engaged 'frontline' agency staff (e.g. case managers) to develop materials (e.g. brochures) and procedures (e.g. parent orientations) for program adoption. The role of 'champions' of the program within the agency setting cannot be understated.

The use of a national program package we developed (i.e. training, youth curricula, technical assistance and evaluation guidance) did not require adaptation for these youth and settings. Case managers as 'frontline' staff and their supervisors became channels for the recruitment, retention, and reinforcement of Project AIM concepts. We believe that in this instance infusion of Project AIM concepts into case management practice positively impacted on the adoption and maintenance (sustainability) of Project AIM as an evidence-based program within these gang prevention and delinquency program service settings. Finally, in order for an evidence-based prevention intervention to be functional and longstanding, it must be consistent with the mission, priorities, and resources of the organization, and reflect the cultural realities of both the service environment and the community it serves.

Acknowledgement We are indebted to Ms. Audruin Pittman, whose creativity and dedication ensured the success of this project. We also acknowledge the selfless support of Aida Cerda, MPH, the program manager, the clinical supervisors, Irene Lim, LCSW, Maria Solano, LCSW, and Krysia Dankowski, LCSW for their willingness to allow us into their programs and staff meetings.

We are profoundly grateful to the following case managers: Jennifer Alfaro, Claudia Flores, Sergio Gonzalez, Sandra Lopez, Ron Portillo for embracing Project AIM within their practice. Finally, we wish acknowledge with great appreciation, the families of youth for their efforts to address their concerns for their children, as well as the youth themselves for sharing their dreams.

References

Beutler, L., Williams, R., Wakefield, P., & Entwistle, S. (1995). Bridging scientist and practitioner perspectives in clinical psychology. *American Psychologist, 50*, 984–994.

Brown, B. S. (1995). Reducing impediments to technology transfer in drug abuse programming. In T. E. Backer, S. L. David, & G. Soucy (Eds.), *Reviewing the behavioral science knowledge base on technology transfer* (pp. 169–185). Rockville: National Institute on Drug Abuse.

Catalano, R. F., Mazza, J. J., Harachi, T. W., Abbott, R. D., Haggerty, K. P., & Fleming, C. B. (2003). Raising healthy children through enhancing social development in elementary school: results after 105 years. *Journal of School Psychology, 41*, 143–164.

Chen, H. T. (1990). *Theory-driven evaluations*. Newberry Park: Sage.

Chen, H. T. (2005). *Practical program evaluation: Assessing and improving planning, implementation, and effectiveness*. Thousand Oaks: Sage.

Chi-Ming, K., Greenberg, M. T., & Walls, C. T. (2003). Examining the role of implementation quality in school-based prevention using the PATHS curriculum. *Prevention Science, 4*(1), 55–63.

Clark, L. F., Miller, K. S., Nagy, S. S., Avery, J., Roth, D. L., Liddon, N., & Mukherjee, S. (2005). Adult identity mentoring: Reducing sexual risk in African American seventh grade students. *Journal of Adolescent Health, 37*, el1–el10.

Dodge, K. A., & Petit, G. S. (2003). A biopsychsosocial model of development of chronic conduct problems in adolescence. *Development Psychology, 39*(2), 349–371.

Durlak, J. A., & DuPre, E. P. (2008). Implementation matters: A review of research on the influence of implementation on program outcomes and the factors affecting implementation. *American Journal of Community Psychology, 41*(3–4), 327–350.

Finkelhor, D., Turner, H., Ormrod, R., & Hamby, S. L. (2009). Youth, violence, abuse, and crime exposure in a national sample of children and youth. *Pediatrics, 124*(5), 1411–1423.

Flaspohler, P., Duffy, J., Wandersman, A., Stillman, L., & Maras, M. A. (2008). Unpacking prevention capacity: An intersection of research-to-practice models and community- centered models. *American Journal of Community Psychology, 41*(3–4), 182–196.

Guerra, N. G., & Knox, L. (2008). How culture impacts the dissemination and implementation of innovation: A case study of the families and schools together program (FAST) for preventing violence with immigrant Latino youth. *American Journal of Community Psychology, 41*(3–4), 304–313.

House, L. D., Bates, J., Markem, C. M., & Lessene, C. (2010). Competence as a predictor of sexual and reproductive health outcomes: A systematic review. *Journal of Adolescent Health, 46*, S7–S22.

Israel, B. A., Schultz, A. J., Parker, E. A., & Becker, A. B. (1998). Review of community-based research: Assessing partnership approaches to improve public health. *Annual Review of Public Health, 19*, 173–202.

Julian, D. A., Ross, M., & Partridge, C. (2008). Challenges in supporting community implementation of science-based programs: A critical review of local partnership for success plans. *American Journal of Community Psychology, 41*(3–4), 351–360.

Kalichman, S. C. (1998). *Preventing AIDS: A sourcebook for behavioral interventions*. Mahwah: Lawrence Erlbaum Associates.

Lesesne C. A., Lewis K. M., White C. P., Green D. C., Duffy J. L., & Wandersman A. (2008). Promoting science-based approaches to teen pregnancy prevention: Proactively engaging the three systems of the interactive systems framework. *American Journal of Community Psychology, 41*(3–4): 379–392.

Markus, H., & Nurius, P. (1986). Possible selves. *American Psychologist, 41*, 954–969.

Miller, K. S., Fasula, A. M., Poulsen, M. N., Parker, J. T., Zackery, S., Wyckoff, S. C., & Clark, L. F. (2009a). Sexual health disparities among African American youth and the need for early prevention approaches: Parenting and youth development programs as strategies for pre-risk prevention. *The Journal of Health and Equity, 2*(1), 19–28.

Miller, K. S., Clark, L. F., Fasula, A. M., Parker, T., Zackery, S., Wyckoff, S. C., & Poulsen, M. N. (2009b). Two pre-risk prevention programs to address sexual health disparities among African American youth. *The Journal of Health and Equity, 2*, 42–49.

Molnar, B. E., Cerda, M., Roberts, A. L., & Buka, S. L. (2008). Effects of neighborhood resources on aggressive and delinquent behaviors among urban youth. *American Journal of Public Health, 98*, 1086–1093.

Nicholson, H. J., Collins, C., & Holmer, H. (2004). Youth as people: The protective aspects of youth development in after-school settings. *The Annals of the American Academy of Political and Social Science, 591*, 55–71.

Office of the Surgeon General. (2001). *Youth violence: A report of the Surgeon General.* Rockville: Office of the Surgeon General.

Oyserman, D., & Markus, H. (1990). Possible selves and delinquency. *Journal of Personality and Social Psychology, 59*, 112–125.

Oyserman, D., & Saltz, E. (1993). Competence, delinquency, and attempts to attain possible selves. *Journal of Personality and Social Psychology, 65*(2), 360–374.

Oyserman, D., Gant, L., & Ager, J. (1995). A socially contextualized model of African American identity and possible selves. *Journal of Personality and Social Psychology, 69*, 1216–1232.

Oyserman, D., Terry, K., & Bysbee, M. (2001). A possible selves intervention to enhance school involvement. *Journal of Adolescence, 25*, 313–326.

Ozer, E. J. (2006). Contextual effects in school-based violence prevention programs: A conceptual framework and empirical review. *Journal of Primary Prevention, 27*(3), 315–340.

Pittman, K., Irby, M., & Ferber, T. (2000). *Unfinished business: Further reflections on a decade of promoting youth development.* Washington, DC: The Forum for Youth Investment.

Saul, J., Duffy, J., Noonan, R., Lubell, K., Wandersman, A., Flaspohler, P., Stillman, L., Blachman, M., & Dunville, R. (2008). Bridging science and practice in violence prevention: Addressing ten key challenges. *American Journal of Community Psychology, 41*(3–4), 197–2005.

Stein, K. F., Roeser, R., & Markus, H. R. (1998). Self-schemas and possible selves as predictors and outcomes of risky in adolescents. *Nursing Research, 47*(2), 96–106.

Telfair, J. (1999). Improving the prospects for a successful relationship between community and evaluator. *New Directions for Evaluation, 83*, 55–65.

Thornton, T. N., Craft, C. A., Dahlberg, L. L., Lynch, B. S., & Baer, K. (2002). *Best practices of youth violence prevention: A sourcebook for community action (Rev.).* Atlanta: Centers for Disease Control and Prevention, National Center for Injury Prevention and Control.

Wandersman, A., Duffy, J., Flaspohler, P., Noonan, R., Lubell, K., Stillman, L., & Saul, J. (2008). Bridging the gap between prevention research and practice: The interactive systems framework for dissemination and implementation. *American Journal of Community Psychology, 41*(3–4), 171–181.

Youngblade, L. M., Theokas, C., Schulenberg, J., Curry, L., Huang, I., & Noval, M. (2007). Risk and promotive factors in families, schools, and communities: A contextual model of positive youth development in adolescence. *Pediatrics, 119*, 47–53.

Chapter 14
A Continuum of Care Model for HIV in Correctional Settings

Daniel J. O'Connell, Holly Swan, Steven S. Martin, Hilary L. Surratt, Christy A. Visher, Carl Leukefeld, Faye S. Taxman, and Anne Rhodes

Abstract *The rates of HIV and Hepatitis C (HCV) in prisons in the United States exceed those among the general population. Prisoners represent some of the highest risk groups for HIV and HCV, notably injection drug users, sex workers, and substance-addicted persons. The high risk for disease transmission among prison inmates prior to their incarceration, as well as the relative ease in accessing these populations, underscores the importance of implementing HIV/HCV prevention/intervention services in incarcerated settings. An HIV/HCV Continuum of Care that includes testing, linkage to care for those who test positive, and prevention efforts prior to inmate release, provides a useful model. This chapter presents an overview of this model, as well as an example of a research project focused on one of its*

The findings and conclusions of this chapter are those of the authors and do not necessarily represent the official position of the National Institute on Drug Abuse (NIDA). The Criminal Justice Drug Abuse Treatment Studies, a cooperative agreement with NIDA (grant U01 DA16230), funded this research. Please send all inquiries to: Daniel J. O'Connell, Ph.D., Center for Drug and Alcohol Studies, 257 E. Main Street, Newark, DE 19716 (302) 831-6107 (office) (302) 831-3307 (fax) oconnell@udel.edu.

D.J. O'Connell, Ph.D. (✉) • S.S. Martin, • C.A. Visher, Ph.D.
Center for Drug and Alcohol Studies, University of Delaware, Newark, DE, USA
e-mail: oconnell@udel.edu

H. Swan
Sociology and Criminal Justice Department, University of Delaware Newark, DE, USA

C. Leukefeld, Ph.D.
Department of Behavioral Science, University of Kentucky, Lexington, KY, USA

H.L. Surratt, Ph.D.
Center for Research on Substance Use and Health Disparities, Nova Southeastern University, Coral Gables, FL, USA

F.S. Taxman, Ph.D. • A. Rhodes, M.S.
Criminology, Law and Society Department, George Mason University, Fairfax, VA, USA

B. Sanders et al. (eds.), *Crime, HIV and Health: Intersections of Criminal Justice and Public Health Concerns*, DOI 10.1007/978-90-481-8921-2_14,

components: prevention among inmates just prior to their release. First, HIV/HCV in prisons is discussed. Second, existing HIV/HCV intervention and prevention packages geared towards inmates are reviewed. Next, an HIV Continuum of Care model is presented, which includes various recommendations based on the immediate needs of the inmates, as well as evidence from a case study from the prevention aspect of the model. A discussion on the implications of the HIV Continuum and other similar programs concludes the chapter.

Human Immunodeficiency Virus (HIV) is a well documented problem in prisons in the United States (Center for Disease Control [CDC] 2009), while a growing, but less well documented problem is that of Hepatitis C (HCV) infections (Martin et al. 2008). Prisoners also represent some of the highest risk groups for HIV and HCV, notably injection drug users (IDUs), sex workers, and substance-addicted persons in general. While most agree that these conditions pose problems and opportunities for prison officials, how to develop proper responses to them is less clear (CDC 2009).

An examination of the literature and policies suggest the need for prison based HIV and HCV prevention, intervention and care models that: (1) screen all persons coming into prisons for HIV/HCV infection; (2) provide appropriate care to HIV/HCV positive persons in custody and link them to appropriate care upon release; and (3) provide HIV/HCV prevention programming for those about to be released. Such an approach would take advantage of one benefit high incarceration rates provide: access to HIV/HCV infected and populations at increased risk for exposure to these viruses. A program that tests as many people as possible, provides care through the reentry period for the infected, and informs those about to reenter the community of behaviors that increase risk for HIV/HCV *and* how to avoid them, as well as promotes overall public health and public safety, capitalizes on this accessibility.

This chapter first provides an overview of HIV/HCV in prisons in the United States. Then, recommendations from the CDC and the National Institutes of Health (NIH) are used to outline an HIV Continuum of Care model for correctional settings. Federal guidelines related to HCV prevention in correctional settings are less established than those for HIV for a number of reasons, including relatively sparse empirical examination of HCV services in correctional settings, as well as greater levels of limited correctional resources for HCV care than is available for HIV care (e.g., funding, facilities, and staff for HCV testing and treatment). As such, an HCV Continuum of Care for correctional settings has fewer grounds to be modeled on than HIV. An exception to this limitation is with respect to the prevention component of the continuum. In fact, the CDC has called for HCV prevention to be incorporated into existing and newly developed HIV interventions because the risk factors for these diseases are very similar (Weinbaum et al. 2003). To be sure, the CDC recommends testing and treatment for HCV in all high-risk settings, including corrections (Weinbaum et al. 2003), but how to implement these in an efficient and effective manner has yet to be determined. Based on this, we provide a detailed review of recommendations for each Continuum component for HIV, as well as evidence from a case study supporting the HIV/HCV prevention component of the model. A discussion of the implications of an HIV model, a call for the development of a complementary HCV model, and similar programs concludes the chapter.

14.1 HIV and HCV in Prisons in the United States

The rate of HIV infection among prisoners is estimated at 2.5 times that of the general population: 0.43% for prisoners and 0.17% for the general population (Maruschak and Beavers 2009). Rates of HCV infection are also much higher among prisoners compared to the general population and are estimated to be between 20 and 40% of all inmates (Weinbaum et al. 2003). Moreover, both infections might co-occur. For instance, a sample of jails found that 38% of HIV positive inmates were also HCV positive (Hennessey et al. 2008). Studies have shown that not only are there higher rates of infectious diseases in the criminal justice population than in the general population, but also higher rates of IDUs, a particularly high-risk population for the contraction and spread of infectious diseases. Further, incarcerated IDUs have higher rates of infectious diseases than non-incarcerated IDUs (Andia et al. 2005; McBride and Inciardi 1990). The prevalence of infectious diseases such as HIV and HCV as well as intravenous drug use among incarcerated populations has led practitioners and researchers to view the criminal justice system as a key place to intervene with disease prevention and treatment programs (CDC 2009).

Many correctional systems implement some HIV/HCV prevention and care services, but few approach them in an organized fashion to ensure that inmates are receiving the appropriate elements at the appropriate times. According to a research report submitted to the U.S. Department of Justice, the majority of systems at all levels make anti-retroviral treatment available to inmates who test positive for HIV; however, additional research has shown that the treatment regimens are less than what is recommended (Hammett et al. 2007). The regimens also tend to be narrower in city and county jail systems than state and federal systems (Hammett et al. 2007). With respect to medication administration, this report showed that HIV medications are typically administered through a pill line, but state and federal systems tend to also utilize keep-on-person methods of administration. Though city and county level systems tend to only use pill line methods of administration, they also tend to employ direct observation of administration, such as inspection of the mouth (Hammett et al. 2007). Very few sites employed pill counts as a method of monitoring treatment adherence, and the majority utilized pharmacy records and self-report. Finally, this report revealed that the majority of state and federal systems pay for HIV treatment out of their own budgets (81%) and less than half of the examined city/county systems pay out of their own budgets (42%; Hammett et al. 2007). Most states supply a minimal amount of medications and some provide a referral to service, but few follow up to ensure the people are linked into appropriate care. Some released persons relapse or drop out of sight of correctional agencies shortly after release, and many of those fail to link into proper care.

Although the implementation of prevention and intervention programs in prison systems is challenging for a number of reasons (i.e., lack of time and resources, contradictory missions between public health and corrections), the prevalence of infectious disease and the pivotal period of re-entry make it an important task (Hammett 1991, 2006). Despite higher rates of HCV than HIV among drug-using offenders, evidence-based interventions specifically designed for HCV prevention among the criminal justice population are even more lacking than HIV interventions. The risks involved in contracting and spreading HIV (e.g., unprotected sex, sharing needles) are quite similar to the risks for contracting and spreading HCV. Not surprisingly then, most HCV prevention interventions are incorporated into HIV prevention protocols (e.g., Grinstead et al. 2008). However, less is known about correctional protocols for testing inmates for HCV and care for those who test positive, but evidence suggests that these protocols are less established and even less complete than those for HIV (Weinbaum et al. 2003).

14.2 The HIV Continuum of Care Models for Correctional Populations

As part of the Criminal Justice Drug Abuse Treatment Studies (CJ-DATS), the HIV prevention research group worked to develop and implement a model program designed to deliver an HIV/HCV prevention intervention to prisoners about to reenter the community, as well as encourage them to be tested for HIV/HCV. A Continuum of Care model was used as the framework to develop this intervention. Although a Continuum of Care model for HCV might look similar to the model for HIV, this has been less established with the exception of the prevention component. As such, the model described here will only focus on HIV. The structure of a Continuum of Care model takes as its starting point the flow of persons through the correctional system, and can be conceptualized as a systems process that involves input (e.g., infected or at-risk persons), throughput (e.g., what happens in the system), and output (e.g. the released individual). For infected persons, this entails knowing their status, being on a health regimen, and being linked into a health care system upon release. For non-infected persons, throughput consists of prevention interventions to make them aware of health risks and provides strategies to avoid these risks.

Figure 14.1 diagrams the full HIV Continuum of Care model that is based on recommendations from the CDC and the NIH. As shown in Fig. 14.1, the starting point is intake. Ideally, all persons should be tested upon entry into the correctional system. Many systems currently test at some level, and 16 states claim to test all inmates (Maruschak and Beavers 2009). According to the CDC, 69% of state prison inmates, 77% of federal prison inmates, and 18.5% of jail inmates reported being tested for HIV since admission to the facility (CDC 2009). A census of state and federal prisons found that 79% of facilities offered some kind of HCV testing and 94% of all inmates were housed in facilities that offer HCV testing (Beck and Maruschak, 2004). Testing only those who report risk factors for HIV/HCV exposure,

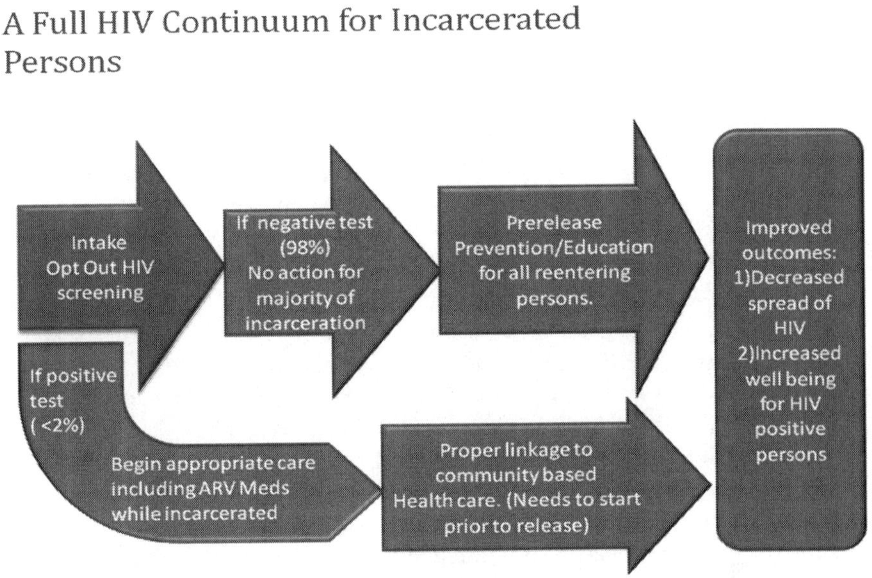

Fig. 14.1 A model HIV continuum of care for incarcerated persons

however, has been demonstrated to miss a large proportion of cases. For instance, a recent study in New York City jails found that testing only those who report risk factors missed 28% of HIV infections (Begier et al. 2009). Thus, a full Continuum of Care focuses on testing *all* persons at intake.

The Continuum of Care track splits depending on the intake test result. Based on this model, those found to be HIV-positive should begin appropriate care while incarcerated. This includes not only providing Antiretroviral Medication (ARV), but also educational programming to prepare infected persons for an ARV regimen. During our research, some physicians said they were hesitant to begin ARV regimens with inmates they felt were not prepared to maintain the program because starting and stopping an ARV regimen would lead to a resistance to certain strains of HIV medications. Regardless, at minimum, HIV-positive persons should have their viral loads and white blood cell counts monitored, and those who show signs of deteriorating conditions should be encouraged to begin an ARV regimen. HIV-positive persons should also be linked to appropriate care upon release. Two of the main types of risk behaviors for both HIV and HCV are intravenous drug use and unprotected sex. The extent to which prisoners engage in these risk behaviors before, during, and after confinement varies across jurisdictions. However, realizing that opportunities to engage in risky behavior are present at each stage (i.e., before, during, and after confinement) and need to be considered in a full Continuum of Care model is important (Arriola 2006; Beckwith et al. 2006; Chandler et al. 2009; Inciardi et al. 2007).

Although participation in risky behaviors tends to decline once an individual is incarcerated due to the reduction in access to the risky situations they encountered prior to incarceration, some evidence suggests that participation in risky behavior can continue during incarceration (Arriola 2006; Beckwith et al. 2006). Engaging in risk behaviors during incarceration appears to be associated with prison policies. For example, one pattern that emerges from the literature is that, once sentenced to prison, IDUs tend to reduce their frequency of injecting. However, when they can inject, they increase the rate of lending and borrowing needles/syringes due to the limited access to injection equipment in correctional institutions (Shewan et al. 1994; Mahon 1996). Only a few prisons in selected countries (e.g., Switzerland) offer sterile injection equipment to prisoners, and needles/syringes are not distributed to inmates in prisons in the U.S. The availability of bleach for cleaning needles is restricted in all but 10 prison systems and eight jail systems in the U.S. Unclean needles are a leading agent for spreading both HIV and HCV, heightening the potential for infection among incarcerated populations (CDC 2009; Weinbaum et al. 2003).

In addition, men having sex with men may occur in correctional institutions (Brewer and Derrickson 1992; Lichtenstein 2000; Saum et al. 1995). Condoms, however, are available (at least officially, but not necessarily in practice) in only two prison systems in the U.S. (Vermont and Mississippi – and Mississippi, at least, restricts use to those in their conjugal visit program). Additionally, five jail systems reportedly supply condoms only to certain inmates (Los Angeles County, New York City, Philadelphia, San Francisco, and Washington, DC; Nerenberg 2002). Although the risk of HCV transmission through sexual contact is low, the same cannot be said for exposure to HIV. As such, the HIV infection potential through sexual transmission among incarcerated populations is considerable. To address heightened risks for infection during incarceration, the CDC recommends that correctional facilities with inmates from high prevalence communities routinely offer testing prior to release in addition to admission screening (Saum et al. 1995; see Sect. 14.2.1 below).

Critically important is the fact that HIV/HCV risk behaviors engaged in prior to incarceration typically resume and/or increase after release from the institution (Braithwaite and Arriola 2003). Especially troubling is that many offenders attempt to "make up for lost time," which often involves seeking and engaging in risky sexual behavior and drug use (Inciardi et al. 2007; Chap. 7 by Miech et al., this volume; Seal et al. 2003). Findings from the CDC sponsored Project START indicate that 13% of parolees engaged in risky sex within one week of reentry into the community, and that 36% reported engaging in risky sex within six months of release (MacGowan et al. 2003). The reentry period is thus a pivotal one in which prevention efforts have the potential for significant impact. By engaging in safe sex and drug use practices upon release, non-infected individuals can reduce their exposure to HIV/HCV, and infected individuals can reduce the risk of spreading HIV/HCV to their sex and/or drug using partners (Grinstead et al. 2005; Kim et al. 2002; McBride and Inciardi 1990).

HIV/HCV prevention just prior to release can include a wide range of approaches, such as education, drug treatment, the provision of sterile needles and other injection equipment, as well as the distribution of bleach and condoms. In 2011, the National Institutes of Health (NIH) has again made the development, evaluation, and dissemination of HIV interventions for at-risk populations a priority (Whitescarver 2011). Although most HIV prevention programming for inmates are available immediately following upon entry into prison, considerably fewer seem to be offered as part of pre-release, transitional, or post release programs. This is perhaps the most important time for risk reduction interventions to occur, since HIV/HCV risks likely increase as offenders return to the community (see Sect. 14.2.4 below).

Because of the described factors related to the heightened risks for HIV/HCV among incarcerated populations, the CDC and the NIH have developed recommendations for each of the four parts of the HIV Continuum of Care Model for correctional populations: testing; care during incarceration for those who test positive; linkage to care in the community after release for people who test positive; and prevention interventions at entry and release from custody. These recommendations are outlined below. The testing and linkage to care after release components of the Continuum of Care model have recommendations that are somewhat more feasible for HIV care in correctional settings than for HCV care. Regardless, the CDC and NIH recommendations for preventing and caring for both HIV *and* HCV are included below for consideration.

14.2.1 Recommendation 1: Screening for HIV and HCV in Correctional Settings

In 2009, the CDC published guidelines for the implementation of HIV testing in correctional settings (CDC 2009). The literature on HIV testing in correctional settings has indicated that greater numbers of individuals are reached and tested when opt-*out* rather than opt-*in* HIV testing is routinely offered during the intake medical examination (CDC 2009; Desai et al. 2002). Though still voluntary, the opt-out option means that inmates will be tested with informed consent and without coercion unless they expressly choose not to be tested. Because of the benefits of opt-out testing, the CDC recommends this procedure, but also acknowledges that limitations of resources and security may require alternative testing procedures (CDC 2009). The alternative testing procedures that the CDC recommends when opt-out testing is not feasible are risk-based screening (i.e. when screening is routinely offered to high risk populations, but see Begier et al. 2009), clinical screening (i.e. screening based on clinical indication, such as pregnancy or tuberculosis), demographic screening (i.e. screening based on high risk demographics), custody-based screening (i.e. screening based on multiple incarcerations or specific high risk crimes such as drug offenses), and/or a combination of multiple testing and screening approaches (CDC 2009).

With respect to the actual testing procedures, the CDC (2009) has different recommendations based on the type of correctional facility. For prisons, where people are in one facility for extended periods, the CDC recommends conventional blood testing, which is considered the "gold standard" in HIV testing, but has a lengthy turnaround time for results; oral testing, which is quicker and not as invasive as blood testing, but more expensive; or rapid testing with blood/oral fluid confirmation. For jails, where turnover is rapid and people may only be confined for a short period of time, the CDC recommends rapid testing with blood/oral fluid confirmation. For correctional facilities with limited laboratory capacity (e.g., halfway houses, drug treatment facilities), the CDC recommends rapid testing with oral fluid alone or with confirmation. Regardless of the setting, the CDC recommends a confirmatory test whenever rapid tests are used for screening.

As alarming as rates of HIV in corrections may be, rates of HCV are exponentially higher. In response, the CDC has recommended that inmates be screened upon entry into correctional facilities and that high-risk inmates are tested for HCV (Weinbaum et al. 2003). Similar to their recommendations for HIV screening, the CDC recommends that HCV testing should include both an antibody screening assay and supplemental or confirmatory assay testing in order to avoid false-negative results (Weinbaum et al. 2003). In recognizing variability in specific laboratory testing capabilities, the CDC concludes that supplemental testing should be performed on at least those inmates whose signal-to-cutoff ratio is low (Weinbaum et al. 2003).

Unfortunately, enzyme immunoassay tests are unable to differentiate between acute, chronic, and resolved HCV infection; moreover, HCV infection is often asymptomatic, making screening based on symptomatology problematic (Weinbaum et al. 2003). The CDC guidelines maintain that when symptoms *are* present, acute HCV should be included in diagnosis, but confirmation is needed. Confirmation of acute HCV infection can be achieved through (1) a negative test result for hepatitis A and hepatitis B (suggesting the need to test for these as well), and (2) a positive test result for the HCV antibody through supplemental testing or a high signal-to-cutoff ratio (Weinbaum et al. 2003). The CDC guidelines also note that, on occasion, symptomatology may be present prior to seroconversion and, as such, follow-up antibody testing may be necessary in order to confirm HCV infection (Weinbaum et al. 2003). Again, the presence of the HCV antibody alone cannot distinguish between acute and chronic HCV infection. CDC guidelines state that individuals testing positive for the HCV antibody for over six months can be diagnosed as having chronic HCV infection (Weinbaum et al. 2003). Finally, when an inmate is identified as being HCV positive, particularly if they have been incarcerated for more than six months, the CDC maintains that correctional officials and health authorities need to investigate the source of infection and depending on what they find, may need to test other inmates who were in contact with the infected inmate and/or the source of infection (Weinbaum et al. 2003).

Despite these recommendations, little is systematically known about testing protocols and practices that are actually being implemented in correctional settings, though our understanding is that not much testing for HCV is taking place for a number of reasons that have been mentioned. Increased efforts to address these shortcomings are sorely needed.

14.2.2 Recommendation 2: Care during Incarceration for People who Test Positive for HIV/HCV

Federal guidelines state that health care, including access to ARV medication, should be made available to all inmates who test positive for HIV (CDC 2009). As soon as possible after infection is detected, the inmate should be referred to an HIV specialist;

if this is not feasible, they should at least be referred to a health care provider with enough HIV expertise to offer an initial assessment, routine follow-up, and to determine appropriateness for ARV therapy (CDC 2009). Some physicians in correctional settings may be hesitant to begin ARV regimens with inmates they feel are not prepared to maintain the program or who will not be in custody long enough for them to monitor (Weinbaum et al. 2003). At minimum, though, positive persons should have their viral loads and white blood cell counts monitored, and those who show signs of deteriorating conditions should be encouraged to begin an ARV regimen.

In addition to basic clinical HIV care and providing ARV medication when appropriate to people who are HIV positive, the CDC (2009) also recommends that care include counseling, co-morbidity referrals and treatments (e.g., mental health support), and supplemental care specific to HIV medical issues, particularly for pregnant women. Pregnant women are a unique population with respect to HIV issues as they have the potential of passing the virus to their child. The CDC recommends that females who test positive for HIV should be immediately tested for pregnancy as well (CDC 2009). For those who are pregnant, CDC guidelines indicate that they should be referred to an HIV specialist and started on ARV as quickly as possible to reduce the likelihood for mother-to-child transmission (CDC 2009). Like all inmates who test positive for HIV, pregnant women should receive prevention counseling and be linked to care either in the facility or in the community depending on their length of stay (CDC 2009).

Guidelines for caring for individuals who test positive for HCV are less explicit than those for HIV, particularly with respect to correctional populations. However, the basic premises of prevention counseling and access to antiviral medications outlined for HIV hold for HCV guidelines as well. Federal and CDC guidelines for caring for inmates who test positive for acute HCV indicate that antiviral treatment should begin immediately (Bureau of Prisons 2009; Weinbaum et al. 2003). For chronic HCV individuals, pre-treatment counseling and screening to discuss potential benefits and side effects of treatment, and to determine the presence of mental illness, substance use or alcohol use, and pregnancy are recommended by clinical guidelines (Bureau of Prisons 2009).

Treating an individual infected with both HCV and HIV with antiviral medications is even more complicated due to interactions between medications for each virus. The CDC contends that appropriate antiviral care for HIV/HCV comorbidity should be determined by health care professionals on a case by case basis (Weinbaum et al. 2003).

14.2.3 Recommendation 3: Linkage to Care for Inmates upon Release

In an effort to keep HIV/HCV positive inmates engaged in treatment and maintain health improvements that have occurred based on care received, linking these individuals to services in the community upon reentry is essential. However, explicit recommendations for linking HCV positive inmates to care in the community have yet to be developed. As such, the following recommendations are specific to linking HIV positive inmates to HIV care in the community.

The CDC recommends a number of actions to assist the HIV positive inmate upon reentry to the community, including providing a list of treatment providers in the inmate's community, assisting them with scheduling, remembering their first appointment, filling out forms, and the utilization of case management services in order to assist in accessing HIV-related services (CDC 2009). One such service that inmates need to access is their ARV medication; regulations for providing HIV medications to former inmates vary by state. Upon release, individuals need to be informed of when and how to administer their ARV medications and when and how supplies can be obtained, especially in order to prevent resistance to their medications (Baillargeon et al. 2009; CDC 2009). The CDC also recommends that HIV positive inmates engage in Partner Services, a venue for assisting former inmates in the disclosure of their positive status to past and present sexual and needle-sharing partners. Each state has their own policies for referring inmates to Partner Services (CDC 2009).

Other efforts have also been put forth in designing case management interventions for former inmates who are HIV positive, such as the federally funded Project Bridge. Project Bridge is a demonstration project that was designed to intensively case manage HIV positive inmates being released to the community in Rhode Island (Rich et al. 2001; Zaller et al. 2008). Inmates who are HIV positive tend to have co-occurring issues, such as mental illness, substance abuse/addiction, and homelessness, thus creating a number of challenges regarding health services upon release into the community (Zaller et al. 2008). To address these challenges, Project Bridge was designed to provide intensive case management through a team consisting of a professional social worker and an outreach worker (Zaller et al. 2008). The intent of the case management was to promote continuity of medical care through a wrap-around approach designed to assist inmates in obtaining care in each area of need, thus producing a level of social stabilization on the part of the ex-offender (Rich et al. 2001). Indeed, this study showed that HIV positive former inmates, despite their heightened health and service needs, were able to achieve and maintain continuity of care when the resources and support needed were provided through ongoing case management following release from custody (Rich et al. 2001; Zaller et al. 2008). Such approaches may be expensive, but the savings in terms of preventing new infections and sustaining increased health for those infected are potentially substantial.

14.2.4 Recommendation 4: Offering HIV/HCV Prevention for Reentering Persons

Approximately 700,000 state and federal prisoners are released into the community each year (Guerino, Harrison, and Sabol 2011), and roughly 12 million individuals are released from local jails (Solomon et al. 2008). The period of reentry to the community from secure custody is of particular importance for disease prevention efforts because offenders often return to previous patterns of high-risk behavior, or engage in even higher levels of risky behaviors (Inciardi et al. 2007; Chap. 7 by Miech et al., this volume). Re-entering persons are preparing to make a major life transition, patterns of old behavior have been interrupted by a period of incarceration, and many individuals may be amenable to considering behavioral change (Inciardi et al. 2007). Therefore, intervening just prior to release into the community has great potential for preventing or reducing risky sex and substance use. Several programs have been designed in an effort to prevent the contraction and spread of infectious diseases amongst former inmates upon release, and among their sex and drug partners (Barry 1999; Bauserman et al. 2003; Braithwaite et al. 2005; el-Bassel et al. 1995; Grinstead et al. 1999, 2001, 2008; Magura et al. 1994; Sifunda et al. 2008; Wexler et al. 1994; Wolitski and the Project START Writing Group 2006). However, many of these interventions require extensive time and resources on behalf of the criminal justice system and, as such, tend to reach fewer individuals than desired. The need for effective and brief prevention interventions is paramount considering that roughly 700,000 persons are released from prisons and 12 million are released from jails every year.

Research in a variety of health-related fields indicates that to reach the largest number of individuals receiving an evidence-based intervention, a focused intervention requiring no more than one or two sessions is ideal (Barry 1999). Yet, most of the programs that have established effectiveness in reducing HIV/HCV- related risk behavior post-release (e.g., increased condom use, reduction in needle sharing) require extensive time and resources for implementation in a criminal justice setting (Bauserman et al. 2003; Braithwaite et al. 2005; Grinstead et al. 2001; Magura et al. 1994; Sifunda et al. 2008; Wolitski and the Project START Writing Group 2006). For instance, one protocol involved 24 small group sessions over eight weeks and 48 h of staff time (Wexler et al. 1994) and another required 16 two-hour sessions (el-Bassel et al. 1995). The least involved protocol consisted of two sessions inside the institution and four sessions post release (Wolitski and the Project START Writing Group 2006). While many of these interventions have shown signs of efficacy, few were in widespread use due to constraints of the correctional environment.

One protocol, designed by Grinstead and colleagues (1999), has met the brief intervention standard (it included only a single 30 min session) and provided some evidence that a brief intervention can be effective on post-release risk behaviors related to HIV/HCV amongst inmates (see Martin et al. 2008 for a review). However, findings from a study published later that showed greater effectiveness of six group sessions, plus an additional 60–90 min personalized session, and four post-release sessions compared to a single 60–90 min session (Grinstead et al. 2008). While this finding is not surprising, it poses the same problem as the previously mentioned protocols in that it requires time and resources that correctional systems often lack.

A recent study by Copenhaver et al. (2009) sought feedback from prisoners and providers to adapt HIV interventions to correctional population. Table 14.1 summarizes the needed elements for an HIV intervention as reported by prisoners and providers in this study. As illustrated, implementing a full HIV or HCV Continuum of

Table 14.1 Prisoner and provider reports of needed elements in brief interventions[a]

Prisoners	Providers
Intervention needs to cover safe sex and drug behaviors, specifically condom use and needle cleaning, and needs to enhance motivation to practice safe behavior	Intervention should include information about safe sex and drug use
Intervention needs to help with overcoming stigma attached to HIV + status	Sessions should be 35–45 min
Group settings are preferred over individualized settings, but privacy about status needs to be ensured and maintained; also, having an option for group or individual (flexible intervention) is optimal for reaching the greatest number	Prefer group settings, but also believe applicability to group or individual setting is ideal
They are more likely to opt-in to coping rather than prevention – prevention needs to be motivating	Intervention material should be at the 8-10th grade education level
Videos and PowerPoint are preferred because they're engaging and active – handouts are discouraged, tend to be thrown away and not read	PowerPoint and video are preferred
	Basically, the intervention should be brief, engaging, and tailored to the population

[a]Source: Copenhaver et al. (2009)

Care model that addresses prevention, testing and care requires time, resources, and commitment by corrections agencies that may not consider HIV/HCV a priority. Accordingly, health practitioners in this environment need to accommodate the constraints of working in correctional settings.

14.3 The CJ-DATS DVD Based Intervention for Reentering Persons: A Case Example

14.3.1 Background

The research study presented next was conducted as part of the first phase of the CJ-DATS Cooperative (CJDATS1).[1] NIDA provided funding for CJ-DATS1, which included the participation of nine research centers and a coordinating center located in different cities across the nation. The stated vision was to conduct studies in multiple sites with the goal of improving substance abuse-related outcomes for incarcerated persons. The first phase was conducted over ten multi-site research projects and focused on the assessment and treatment of adult and juvenile incarcerated drug users. A key focus of CJ-DATS1 was the improvement of HIV/HCV care in corrections.

[1] The Cooperative has continued into a second phase, CJ-DATS2, focusing exclusively on implementation science related to drug abuse issues in criminal justice See http://www.cjdats.org for more information.

The goal of the CJ-DATS HIV/HCV study was to develop a prevention program that had the potential to be delivered in correctional settings with high fidelity and low cost to a wide audience.

For broad adoption, programs that have a high level of practical generalizability are logically more likely to be implemented. The program cannot be too intensive or it will become cost prohibitive, nor can it be so time consuming that it will not fit seamlessly into the reentry process. Thus, many correctional systems are unlikely to implement multi-session prevention programs for those leaving their institutions. Therefore, single or two session interventions are simpler to implement, more cost effective, and have greater capacity to reach larger audiences. The tradeoff is the strength of effect, but on balance, a brief intervention for reentering persons possesses great potential. Manualized interventions designed for widespread use often suffer from fidelity issues; the developer conceives how an intervention should be implemented, but counselors in the field adapt it to their own techniques (Angotti 2010; Chap. 4 by Clark and Humphries, this volume). Interventions are tools used by counselors, but whether the adaptations are effective is often unclear, even though the tested intervention may possess significant demonstrated efficacy (Angotti 2010).

In addition to the intensiveness of the prevention program, the approach used in delivering the program is also relevant for a program's success or failure in reducing risk behaviors. Existing data from the Delaware Department of Correction's KEY and CREST Outreach Center therapeutic community programs suggest that HIV prevention programs that are typically provided to clients in treatment had little or no lasting effects on sexual risk behaviors. These data demonstrate that only small proportions of the sample reported always using condoms at 18 and 42 months; multiple sex partners appeared to be the norm at each contact; and significant proportions reported trading sex for money (Martin et al. 1999). However, because these individuals were in structured therapeutic community treatment programs, drug-related risk behaviors were significantly reduced (Martin et al. 1999). These findings suggest that the conventional educational HIV prevention initiatives used in the KEY and CREST programs - professionally-led or peer-led, non-interactive, didactic seminars in a group format using readily available HIV prevention materials - are generally ineffective in reducing sexual risk behaviors. Unfortunately, the prevention approach used in the KEY and CREST programs is similar to that used in many correctional institutions and drug treatment programs.

14.3.2 Intervention Development

Development of the HIV Continuum of Care intervention proceeded in phases. First, the design of the intervention was modeled after the NIDA Standard Intervention for HIV and modified for a criminal justice population. Early work on the original (Version 1) NIDA Standard Intervention found that intervention and post-test counseling produced reductions in drug-using behaviors for at-risk clients in a variety of community settings (Coyle 1993). However, few significant changes in sexual risk behaviors were evident (Broadhead et al. 1998; Cottler et al. 1997). The NIDA Standard Intervention was subsequently expanded and revised (Version 2) by investigators under the auspices of NIDA's AIDS Cooperative Agreement to include more information on sexual risks (Wechsberg et al. 1997), and again in 2000 to include information on HBV and HCV infection (Version 3; NIDA 2000). In a recent study of probationers in Delaware, Martin and colleagues (1999) further refined the NIDA Standard Intervention Version 3 to make the material more relevant to correctional clients. This Version 3 was contrasted with a "Probationer Focused Intervention," that incorporated personalized strategies for protecting the individual and their partners from HIV infection, using a technique known as "thought mapping" (Knight et al. 1994; Leukefeld et al. 2001). This was one of the first trials to comply with federal guidelines that require a "meaningful" intervention to *all* subjects in an experimental trial. Significantly, both interventions also included a booster session 3 months after the post-test counseling session.

The results were encouraging in terms of improvements in both drug use and sexual risk behaviors, but no significant benefits were observed for the "Probationer Focused" intervention compared to the NIDA Version 3. Both interventions led to reductions in the percentage of probationers using heroin or cocaine, injecting drugs, engaging in transactional sex, or having multiple sex partners; the mean number of unprotected sex acts also decreased for both groups during the follow-up period (Knight et al. 1994; Leukefeld et al. 2001). Although the probation focused additions to the intervention did not produce significant improvements over the NIDA Version 3 intervention, both interventions produced positive outcomes. They demonstrated that one-on-one interventions that are designed specifically with the target population in mind and implemented by someone trained in the intervention *and* accustomed to working with this population can be effective in reducing high risk behaviors in criminal justice clients.

For CJDATS1, in late 2003 and early 2004, the Delaware CJ-DATS1 investigators conducted focus groups and in-depth interviews with 110 correctional clients in Delaware and Florida for the purpose of amplifying the NIDA Version 3 intervention to address risk reduction issues and barriers of concern specific to community corrections populations. The intervention was then augmented by video components designed to create buy-in, make the message relevant, and engage the client. The result was a DVD-based, peer delivered protocol to be conducted immediately prior to an inmate's return to the community (Inciardi et al. 2007; Martin et al. 2008). The focus of the intervention was the reentry period, and clients were provided the opportunity to consider the issues they would likely face upon release. The intervention included education on facts about HIV/HCV, as well as strategies to avoid exposure to these infections. The intervention was also tailored to the unique culture of the target population and encouraged testing in compliance with CDC recommendations (CDC 2009). While not designed to eliminate counselor input altogether by essentially locking the key intervention content into the DVD, counselors are less able to skip elements of the intervention. This helps ensure that everyone receives the full "dose", and reduces a potential fidelity issue. Moreover, while some efforts have shown promise for reducing risk behaviors after release from custody (e.g. Project START), the CJDATS1 DVD intervention was designed as a more limited intervention that would hopefully, if shown to be effective, lend itself to more widespread implementation in community supervision settings.

In order to address situations that persons reentering the community may encounter that put them at-risk for HIV/HCV and substance abuse, the team needed a sense of what individuals experience when they are about to be released from incarceration and the challenges they face once released. Therefore, in the second phase of development, focus groups with formerly incarcerated substance abusers in residential community treatment facilities were conducted to ascertain a descriptive account of the experiences before and during the reentry process. The results pointed to specific situations that reentering individuals found challenging upon their release from incarceration. Meeting old friends who still used drugs and/or had unprotected sex were the most difficult situations faced by reentering offenders who were trying to limit their at-risk behaviors. These situations became the two at-risk scenarios in the intervention. Focus groups members also indicated that they would like to see individuals who they could relate to talk about HIV and HCV. As a result, individuals who had a history of being incarcerated and were substance abusers were identified and recruited to be actors in the DVD components of the intervention, and asked to provide commentaries and offer testimonials about their experiences. In addition, people who were HIV and HCV positive (race and gender specific) were recruited to tell their stories in the HIV and HCV video components.

Based on race and sex profiles of the participants in the focus groups, four DVD tracks were created: African American male, White male, African American female, and White female.[2] Each race/sex track of the intervention contained five types of video components: (1) an introduction video delivered by a former substance abuser/offender; (2) demonstration of the needle cleaning process; (3) testimonials from HIV and HCV positive persons; (4) vignettes that demonstrated condom negotiation and confronting a friend who possess drugs; and (5) positive and negative commentaries that showcase what other substance abusers/offenders have done in situations that may have exposed them to HIV/HCV.

The third phase of development was filming the video segments. The material was only minimally scripted, and selected participants were asked to speak freely about their experiences in the commentaries and testimonials. These dialogues were edited later. With respect to the acted out scenarios, participants were told what the scene was and directed as to the action that was to take place. They were free to use their own language throughout in an attempt to maintain a sense of genuineness in the scenario. The end result was a series of race and sex tracked, DVD based interventions that speak to the target population from the perspective of the target population (see Inciardi et al. 2007 for a complete review of the development of the DVD intervention).

[2] Versions for other race/ethnicities were not created because the study population did not include many other than White and African American to test hypotheses.

Table 14.2 Proportion of unprotected sex acts in the 90 days post-release by Race and Sex

Proportion of sex acts w/o Condom 90 days	DVD group mean	Comparison mean	Std. dev.	Cohen's D
Full Sample				
DVD vs. NIDA standard	.31	.40	.46	−.20
DVD vs. conventional video	.31	.43	.46	−.26
African American				
DVD vs. NIDA standard	.30	.42	.44	−.27
DVD vs. conventional video	.30	.40	.44	−.23
White				
DVD vs. NIDA standard	.32	.36	.46	−.09
DVD vs. conventional video	.32	.48	.46	−.35
Female				
DVD vs. NIDA standard	.36	.32	.45	.09
DVD vs. Conventional video	.36	.46	.45	−.22
Male				
DVD vs. NIDA standard	.31	.43	.44	−.27
DVD vs. conventional video	.31	.41	.44	−.23

14.3.3 *Outcome Analysis*

The HIV/HCV DVD was tested in a three-site (Delaware, Kentucky, and Virginia) clinical trial framework as part of CJ-DATS. Just prior to release from prison, inmates were randomized to one of three conditions where they received either: a conventional video that follows CDC "standard" protocols intervention; the NIDA Standard intervention in cue card format delivered one-on-one by a health professional; or the DVD based intervention delivered one-on-one by a peer interventionist. All subjects were provided with HIV and HCV testing and post test counseling. Institutional Review Board approval was granted prior to the start of the study.[3]

For the study, inmates were interviewed prior to randomization and 30 and 90 days after release from incarceration. From December, 2006 through June, 2008, 685 persons were randomly selected: 97 did not receive the intervention due to release or transfer, and 54 were lost to follow up, leaving a sample of 534 (Inciardi et al. 2007). To measure the main effect outcome – proportion of protected sex acts – subjects were asked how many sex acts they had engaged in and on how many of those occasions they used a condom. This was used to form the proportion of unprotected sex acts in the 90 days just after release from prison. Table 14.2 reports the results of this variable and the corresponding effect size. As shown, the DVD intervention provided a modest effect size when compared to both the NIDA Standard condition and the conventional video group. In the full sample, the DVD

[3] For a complete and detailed review of the three conditions, see Inciardi et al. 2007.

group reports 31% of sex acts were unprotected at 90 days post release, while 40% of the NIDA Standard group and 43% of the conventional video group's acts were unprotected. Utilizing Cohen's D effect sizes, this translated into a −.20 comparing the DVD to the NIDA Standard and −.26 comparing the DVD to the conventional video.

The differences between groups were similar across race and sex when comparing the DVD intervention to the conventional video. Comparisons between the DVD and the NIDA Standard were modest in the African American and male sample, but very small in White and female samples. Thus, the DVD intervention's effects were consistent across race and sex groups compared to a conventional video. The NIDA Standard intervention performed almost as well as the DVD for the White sample and actually performed marginally better among females.

In all, the project demonstrated that delivering a low cost client centered intervention that is race and sex specific in a way that retains fidelity and possesses the capacity of large-scale distribution is possible.

14.4 Discussion

The HIV Continuum of Care model is an example of how an intervention can be developed at a moderately low cost, potentially reach a large number of inmates, and fit within the framework of the reentry process. Such interventions are best if kept brief, conducted in the language of the target audience, and culturally competent in terms of race and sex, but also in recognizing the prison/jail culture and reentry process. The brief nature of this type of intervention has resulted in modest effects, but such programs that are designed to reach large audiences can have a truly high impact through the size of the audience reached. Thus, such an approach should be considered modest effect-high impact.

The nature of HIV/HCV in prisons continues to pose both problems and opportunities. The problems stem from treating people with infections and the challenges of linking them to appropriate care upon release. Access to this afflicted population through their incarceration presents an important public health opportunity. A truly functioning HIV Continuum of Care approach could potentially test all persons entering the correctional system. Proper care for those found to be positive coupled with programs to link and retain them in care upon release can reduce the likelihood of further transmission, as well as improve the health of those currently afflicted. Providing intervention programs as part of reentry services can prepare those who have been out of their community to be ready for the risk situations they are likely to encounter upon release from incarceration. While much of this is being done in a largely ad-hoc basis in many correctional systems, combining all three elements - testing, linkage to care, and prevention - into one unified Continuum of Care model has the potential to significantly impact the spread of HIV and HCV among incarcerated populations.

References

Andia, J. F., Sherry, D., Robles, R. R., Kang, S., Colón, H. M., Oliver-Velez, D., & Finlinson, A. (2005). Factors associated with injection and noninjection drug use during incarceration among Puerto Rican drug injectors in New York and Puerto Rico. *The Prison Journal, 85*(3), 329–342.

Angotti, N. (2010). Working outside of the box: How HIV counselors in Sub-Saharan Africa adapt Western HIV testing norms. *Social Science & Medicine, 71*(5), 986–993.

Arriola, K. R. J. (2006). Debunking the myth of the safe haven: Toward a better understanding of intraprison HIV transmission. *Criminology & Public Policy, 5*(1), 137–148.

Baillargeon, J., Giordano, T. P., Rich, J. D., Wu, Z. H., Wells, K., Pollock, B. H., & Paar, D. P. (2009). Accessing antiretroviral therapy following release from prison. *Journal of the American Medical Association, 301*(8), 848–857.

Bauserman, R. L., Richardson, D., Ward, M., Shea, M., Bowlin, C., Tomoyasu, N., & Solomon, L. (2003). HIV prevention with jail and prison inmates: Maryland's prevention case management program. *AIDS Education and Prevention, 15*(5), 465–480.

Barry, K. L. (Consensus Panel Chair). (1999). *Brief interventions and brief therapies for substance abuse, Treatment Improvement Protocol (TIP) Series 34* (DHS Publication No. (SMA) 99-3353). Rockville: U.S. Department of Health and Human Services, Public Health Service, Substance Abuse and Mental Health Services Administration, Center for Substance Abuse Treatment..

Beck, A. J., & Maruschak, L. M. (2004). *Hepatitis testing and treatment in State Prisons* (Bureau of Justice Statistics, NCJ199173). Washington, DC: US Department of Justice. Office of Justice Programs..

Beckwith, C. G., Zaller, N., & Rich, J. D. (2006). Addressing the HIV epidemic through quality correctional healthcare. *Criminology & Public Policy, 5*(1), 149–156.

Begier, E. M., Bennani, Y., Forgione, L., Punsalang, A., Hanna, D. B., Herrera, J., & Parvez, F. (2009). Undiagnosed HIV infection among New York City jail entrants, 2006: Results of a blinded serosurvey. *Journal of Acquired Immune Deficiency Syndromes, 54*(1), 93–101.

Braithwaite, R. L., & Arriola, K. R. J. (2003). Male prisoners and HIV prevention: A call for action ignored. *American Journal of Public Health, 93*(5), 759–763.

Braithwaite, R., Stephens, T. T., Treadwell, H., Braithwaite, K., & Conerly, R. (2005). Short-term impact of an HIV risk reduction intervention for soon-to-be-released inmates in Georgia. *Journal of Health Care for the Poor and Underserved, 16*, 130–139.

Brewer, T. F., & Derrickson, J. (1992). AIDS in prison: A review of epidemiology and preventive policy. *AIDS, 6*(7), 623–628.

Broadhead, R. S., Heckathorn, D. D., Weakliem, D. L., Anthony, D. L., Madray, H., Mills, R. J., & Hughes, J. (1998). Harnessing peer networks as an instrument for AIDS prevention: Results from a peer-driven intervention. *Public Health Report, 113*(Suppl. 1), 42–57.

Bureau of Prisons. (2009). *Guidelines for the prevention and treatment of hepatitis C and cirrhosis: Federal Bureau of Prisons clinical practice guidelines.* Retrieved from www.bop.gov/news/PDFs/hepatitis_c.pdf

Centers for Disease Control and Prevention. (2009). *HIV testing implementation Guidance for correctional settings.* Retrieved from www.cdc.gov/hiv/topics/testing/resources/guidelines/correctional-settings

Chandler, R. K., Fletcher, B. W., & Volkow, N. D. (2009). Treating drug abuse and addiction in the criminal justice system: Improving public health and safety. *Journal of the American Medical Association, 301*(2), 183–90.

Copenhaver, M., Chowdhury, S., & Altice, F. L. (2009). Adaptation of an evidence-based intervention targeting HIV-infected prisoners transitioning to the community: The process and outcome of formative research for the Positive Living Using Safety (PLUS) intervention. *AIDS Patient Care and STDs, 23*(4), 1–11.

Cottler, L., Compton, W., Hoffman, J., Klein, H., Desmond, D., & Zule, B. (1997). *The NIDA cooperative agreement standard intervention: Protocol changes suggested by the continuing HIV/AIDS epidemic*. Bloomington: Chestnut Health Systems Lighthouse Institute..

Coyle, S. (1993). *The NIDA HIV counseling and education intervention model* (NIH Pub. No. 93-3508). Rockville: National Institute on Drug Abuse..

Desai, A. A., Latta, E. T., Spaulding, A., Rich, J. D., & Flanigan, T. P. (2002). The importance of routine HIV testing in the incarcerated population: The Rhode Island experience. *AIDS Education and Prevention, 14*(SuppB), 45–52.

el-Bassel, N., Ivanoff, A., Schilling, R. F., Gilbert, L., Borne, D., & Chen, D. L. (1995). Preventing HIV/AIDS in drug-abusing incarcerated women through skills building and social support enhancement: Preliminary outcomes. *Social Work Research, 19*, 131–141.

Grinstead, O. A., Zack, B., Faigles, B., Grossman, N., & Blea, L. (1999). Reducing postrelease HIV risk among male prison inmates: A peer-led intervention. *Criminal Justice and Behavior, 26*(4), 453–465.

Grinstead, O. A., Zack, B., & Faigles, B. (2001). Reducing postrelease risk behavior among seropositive prison inmates: The health promotion program. *AIDS Education and Prevention, 13*, 109–119.

Grinstead, O. A., Faigeles, B., Comfort, M., Seal, D., Nealey-Moore, J., Belcher, L., & Morrow, K. (2005). HIV, STD, and hepatitis risk to primary female partners of men being released from prison. *Women & Health, 41*(2), 63–80.

Grinstead, O., Eldridge, G., Macgowan, R., Morrow, K. M., Seal, D. W., Sosman, J. M., Zack, B., & the Project START study group. (2008). An HIV, STD, and hepatitis prevention program for young men leaving prison: Project START. *Journal of Correctional Health Care, 14*(3), 183–196.

Guerino, P., Harrison, P. M., & Sabol, W. J. (2011). *Prisoners in 2010*. (NCJ Publication No. 236096). Washington, DC: US Department of Justice, Office of Justice Programs, Bureau of Justice Statistics.

Hammett, T. (1991). Stemming the spread of HIV among IV drug users, their sexual partners, and children: Issues and opportunities for criminal justice agencies. *Crime & Delinquency, 37*(1), 101–124.

Hammett, T. (2006). HIV in prisons. *Criminology & Public Policy, 5*(1), 109–112.

Hammett, T. M., S. Kennedy, & Kuck, S. (2007). *National survey of infectious diseases in correctional facilities: HIV and sexually transmitted diseases*. Electronically available through the NCJRS..

Hennessey, K. A., Kim, A. A., Griffin, V., Collins, N. T., Weinbaum, C. M., & Sabin, K. (2008). Prevalence of infection of hepatitis B and C viruses and co-infection with HIV in three jails: A case for viral hepatitis prevention in jails in the United States. *Journal of Urban Health, 86*(1), 93–105.

Inciardi, J. A., Surratt, H. L., Martin, S. S., O'Connell, D. J., Salandy, A. D., & Beard, R. (2007). Developing a multimedia HIV and hepatitis intervention for drug-involved offenders reentering the community. *The Prison Journal, 87*(1), 111–142.

Kim, A., Page-Shafer, K., Ruiz, J., Reyes, L., Delgado, V., Klausner, J., Molitor, F., Katz, M., & McFarland, W. (2002). Vulnerability to HIV among women formerly incarcerated and women with incarcerated sexual partners. *AIDS and Behavior, 6*(4), 331–338.

Knight, K., Simpson, D. D., & Dansereau, D. F. (1994). Knowledge mapping: A psychoeducational tool in drug abuse relapse prevention training. *Journal of Offender Rehabilitation, 20*, 187–205.

Leukefeld, C. G., Godlaski, T., & Logan, T. K. (2001). Thought mapping: An HIV prevention approach for drug abusers. *Health & Addiction, 1*(1), 71–93.

Lichtenstein, B. (2000). Secret encounters: Black men, bisexuality, and AIDS in Alabama. *Medical Anthropology Quarterly, 14*, 374–393.

MacGowan, R. J., Margolis, A., Gaiter, J., Morrow, K., Zack, B., Askew, J., McAuliffe, T., Sosman, J. M., Eldridge, G., & the Project START study group. (2003). Predictors of risky sex of young men after release from prison. *International Journal of STD and AIDS, 14*, 519–523..

Magura, S., Kang, S. Y., & Shapiro, J. L. (1994). Outcomes of intensive AIDS education for male adolescent drug users in jail. *Journal of Adolescent Health, 15*, 457–463.

Mahon, N. (1996). New York inmates' HIV risk behaviors: The implications for prevention policy and programs. *American Journal of Public Health, 86*, 1211–1215.

Martin, S. S., Butzin, C. A., Saum, C. A., & Inciardi, J. A. (1999). Three-year outcomes of therapeutic community treatment for drug-involved offenders in Delaware: From prison to work release to aftercare. *The Prison Journal, 79*, 294–320.

Martin, S. S., O'Connell, D. J., Inciardi, J. A., Surratt, H. L., & Maiden, K. M. (2008). Integrating an HIV/HCV brief intervention in prisoner reentry: Results of a multisite prospective study. *Journal of Psychoactive Drugs, 40*(4), 427–436.

Maruschak, L. M., & Beavers, R. (2009). *HIV in prisons, 2007–08* (NCJ Publication No. 228307). Washington, DC: US Department of Justice, Office of Justice Programs, Bureau of Justice Statistics.

McBride, D. C., & Inciardi, J. A. (1990). AIDS and the IV drug user in the criminal justice system. *Journal of Drug Issues, 20*(2), 267–280.

National Institute on Drug Abuse. (2000). *The NIDA community-based outreach model: A manual to reduce the risk of HIV and other blood-borne infections in drug users.* (NIH Publication No. 00-4812). Rockville: National Institute on Drug Abuse.

Nerenberg, R. (2002). *Spotlight: Condoms in correctional settings.* Retrieved from www.thebody.com/content/esp/art13017.html

Rich, J. D., Holmes, L., Salas, C., Macalino, G., Davis, D., Ryczek, J., & Flanigan, T. (2001). Successful linkage of medical care and community services for HIV-positive offenders being released from prison. *Journal of Urban Health, 78*(2), 279–289.

Saum, C. A., Surratt, H. A., Inciardi, J. A., & Bennett, R. E. (1995). Sex in prison: Exploring the myths and realities. *The Prison Journal, 75*(4), 413–430.

Seal, D. W., Margolis, A. D., Sosman, J., Kacanek, D., Binson, D., & the Project START Study Group. (2003). HIV and STD risk behavior among 18- to 25-year-old men released from U.S. prisons: Provider perspectives. *AIDS and Behavior, 7*(2), 131–141.

Shewan, D., Gemmell, M., & Davies, J. B. (1994). Prison as a modifier of drug using behavior. *Addiction Research, 2*, 203–215.

Sifunda, S., Reddy, P. S., Braithwaite, R., Stephens, T., Bhengu, S., Ruiter, R. A. C., & van den Borne, B. (2008). The effectiveness of a peer-led HIV/AIDS and STI health education intervention for prison inmates in South Africa. *Health Education & Behavior, 35*(4), 494–508.

Solomon, A. L., Osborne, J. W. L., LoBuglio, S. F., Mellow, J., & Mukamal, D. A. (2008). *Life After Lockup: Improving Reentry from Jail to the Community*. Washington DC: Urban Institute, Justice Policy Center.

Wechsberg, W. M., MacDonald, B., Dennis, M. L., Inciardi, J. A., Surratt, H., Leukefeld, C., Farabee, D., Cottler, L., Compton, W., Hoffman, J., Klein, H., Desmond, D., & Zule, B. (1997). *The NIDA cooperative agreement standard intervention: Protocol changes suggested by the continuing HIV/AIDS epidemic. Bloomington: Chestnut Health Systems Lighthouse Institute.*

Weinbaum, C., Lyerla, R., & Margolis, H. S. (2003). Prevention and control of infections with hepatitis viruses in correctional settings. *Morbidity and Mortality Weekly Report. Recommendations and Reports, 52*(RR-1), 1–33.

Wexler, H. K., Magura, S., Beardsley, M. M., & Howard, J. (1994). ARRIVE: An AIDS education/relapse prevention model for high-risk parolees. *International Journal of the Addictions, 29*, 361–386.

Whitescarver, J. (2011). *National Institutes of Health: Trans-NIH AIDS Research By-Pass Budget Estimate Trans-NIH plan for HIV-related research.* Bethesda: Office of AIDS Research.

Wolitski, R., & the Project START Writing Group. (2006). Relative efficacy of a multisession sexual risk-reduction intervention for young men released from prison in 4 states. *American Journal of Public Health, 96*, 1854–1861.

Zaller, N. D., Holmes, L., Dyl, A. C., Mitty, J. A., Beckwith, C. G., Flanigan, T. P., & Rich, J. D. (2008). Linkage to treatment and supportive services among HIV-positive ex-offenders in Project Bridge. *Journal of Health Care for the Poor and Underserved, 19*, 522–531.

Author Index

B. Sanders et al. (eds.), *Crime, HIV and Health: Intersections of Criminal Justice and Public Health Concerns*, DOI 10.1007/978-90-481-8921-2,

D

E

F

H

S

Subject Index

B. Sanders et al. (eds.), *Crime, HIV and Health: Intersections of Criminal Justice and Public Health Concerns*, DOI 10.1007/978-90-481-8921-2,

Printed by Publishers' Graphics LLC